A MIRROR TO DEVOUT PEOPLE
(SPECULUM DEVOTORUM)

EARLY ENGLISH TEXT SOCIETY
O.S. 346
2016 for 2015

Here be gynnyth a prefacyon to the boke folowynge ~

Goostly syster in Ihu cryste I trowe hyt be not
hyt fro zoure mynde that whene we shol
be laste to gydder I be hette zow a medytacyon
of the passyon of our lorde the whyche a mysse
I haue not ~ putte fro mynde but be dyuers
tymys be the grace of god I haue pyfurnyyd hyt
as I myytfte. our lorde ymutte hyt be to hym
plescable ʒ to zow pfytable or to eny othyr be
not squut of god But I do zow to wyte that
be conseyle I put to myche mor thane I hette
zow to mor enecfynge of zoure loue to god ʒ
uertuys or eny othyr that myyth be grace of god
pfyte be the same. as ʒe maye see schortly in the
tabyl folowynge thys prefacyon. ffor I haue dy
uydyd the boke folowynge in thys ʒ thyrty cha
petehys to the westhype of the thys ʒ thyrty ʒer
that our saupour knyde in erthe. ʒ I haue sette ʃ
tytyllhys of hem alle in a tabyl aftyr thys pfa
cyon a fore the boke that he so euer hykyth to
zede hyt maye see ther schortly thes all the
mautey of the boke folowynge ʒ zede whef thys
hykyth best ʒ that he myythte y somyr fyn
ʒe that he deskryth moste. ʒ the bettyr kepe hyt
m mynde. ʒ also zedelokyr fynde hyt yf thy
lyste to see hyt a zen · not wythstondynge hyt

A MIRROR TO DEVOUT PEOPLE (SPECULUM DEVOTORUM)

EDITED BY

PAUL J. PATTERSON

Published for
THE EARLY ENGLISH TEXT SOCIETY
by the
OXFORD UNIVERSITY PRESS
2016 for 2015

OXFORD
UNIVERSITY PRESS

Great Clarendon Street, Oxford, OX2 6DP,
United Kingdom

Oxford University Press is a department of the University of Oxford.
It furthers the University's objective of excellence in research, scholarship,
and education by publishing worldwide. Oxford is a registered trade mark of
Oxford University Press in the UK and in certain other countries

© Early English Text Society 2016

The moral rights of the author have been asserted

First edition published in 2016
Impression: 1

British Library Cataloguing in Publication Data

Data available

ISBN 978-0-19-874497-9

Typeset by Anne Joshua, Oxford
Printed in Great Britain
on acid-free paper by
TJ International Ltd, Padstow, Cornwall

Links to third party websites are provided by Oxford in good faith and
for information only. Oxford disclaims any responsibility for the materials
contained in any third party website referenced in this work.

TO MY MOTHER
for her strength, love, and joy of learning

PREFACE

This book began as a dissertation under the direction of Professor Jill Mann at the University of Notre Dame. Without Jill's patient guidance and direction, this project would not have been possible. Dr Jesse Lander, Dr Maura B. Nolan, Dr Graham Hamill, and Professor Vincent Gillespie read many drafts of the edition in its earliest stages. It was Professor Gillespie who encouraged me to submit it to the Early English Text Society, and for that I am most grateful.

Numerous colleagues and scholars have contributed to this project over the years. I am grateful to the National Endowment for the Humanities for a Summer Stipend that allowed me to bring the edition near to completion. The British Academy awarded me two travel grants, one in conjunction with the Newberry Library and one with the Huntington Library. Both awards allowed me to complete work on the Cambridge University copy of the *Mirror to Devout People*. My home institution, Saint Joseph's University, awarded me two Faculty Development Summer Grants, which gave me time to complete large portions of the project. My participation in the Mellon Foundation Penn Humanities Forum as a Regional Scholar at the University of Pennsylvania gave me the opportunity to rethink aspects of my project through the lens of adaption. The interdisciplinary seminar, led by the indefatigable Dr Jim English, was invaluable. I am especially grateful to the Department of Special Collections at the University of Notre Dame and the Department of Manuscripts and University Archives at the University of Cambridge for giving me access to their collections. Dr David Gura, Curator of Ancient and Medieval Manuscripts, Early Imprints, and History of the Book at the University of Notre Dame, was especially helpful during the course of this project. The work of Dr Ian Johnson, Dr Stephen Kelly, Dr Ryan Perry, Dr Allen Westphall, and Professor John Thompson on the *Geographies of Orthodoxy* project is an important contribution to tracking lives of Christ, such as the *Mirror*, in late medieval England. The 'Mapping Late Medieval Lives of Christ' conference they organized at Queens University Belfast on 10–13 June 2010 and the ensuing publications it inspired continue to deepen our understanding of these important religious works. For information on the dialect of the Notre Dame copy of the *Mirror*, I am indebted to Professor Jeremy Smith. Professor A. S. G. Edwards and Professor Michael Sargent deserve a special thank you for encouraging me early in the project. I am also grateful to Dr Shannon Gayk, Dr Peter Norberg, Dr Jason Powell, and Dr Richard Fusco for feedback on the introduction and edition and my colleagues at Saint Joseph's University for their support. Professor Daniel Wakelin provided invaluable feedback in the final stages of the project, for which I am most grateful.

Finally, I wish to thank Professor David Wallace for supporting my work and inviting me to present my research at the University of Pennsylvania's Medieval/Renaissance Reading Group; Dr Helen Spencer, who has patiently guided me through the process of publishing with EETS; Bonnie Blackburn and Anne Joshua for bringing many improvements to the edition; the EETS anonymous readers, whose insight made this a much-improved text; and my children, Cassandra and Caedmon, who were born during the early years of this project and will be most thankful for its completion.

P.J.P.

CONTENTS

LIST OF PLATES

ABBREVIATIONS

Briquet	C.-M. Briquet, *Les Filigranes: Dictionnaire historique des marques du papier dès leur apparition vers 1282 jusqu'en 1600*, 4 vols. (Geneva, 1907)
Catalogue	Charles Hardwick and Henry Richards Luard, *Catalogue of the Manuscripts Preserved in the Library of the University of Cambridge*, 5 vols. (Cambridge, 1856)
CCCM	Corpus Christianorum, Continuatio Mediaeualis
CCSA	Corpus Christianorum, Series Apocryphorum
CCSL	Corpus Christianorum, Series Latina
CSEL	Corpus Scriptorum Ecclesiasticorum Latinorum
LALME	*A Linguistic Atlas of Late Mediaeval England*
MED	*Middle English Dictionary*
MVC	*Meditationes Vitae Christi* of Iohannis de Caulibus
ODNB	*Oxford Dictionary of National Biography*, ed. H. C. G. Matthew and Brian Harrison (Oxford, 2004); www.oxforddnb.com
PG	*Patrologia Graeca*, ed. J. P. Migne (Paris, 1857–92)
PL	*Patrologia Latina*, ed. J. P. Migne (Paris, 1844–64)
Postilla	*Postilla super totam bibliam* of Nicholas of Lyre
RB	*Revue bénédictine*

INTRODUCTION

I. *MIRROR TO DEVOUT PEOPLE*

A Mirror to Devout People, also known as the *Speculum devotorum*, is a fifteenth-century Middle English life of Christ in the tradition of lives of Christ that were based on or similar to the pseudo-Bonaventuran *Meditationes Vitae Christi* (*MVC*). In the opening lines of the Preface of the *Mirror*, the author says that he promised to write 'a medytacyon of the Passyon of oure Lorde' for the 'gostly syster' to whom he addresses the work (ll. 2–4). A Latin colophon in both extant copies of the *Mirror*—Notre Dame, University of Notre Dame, Hesburgh Library, cod. Eng. d. 1 (*olim* MS 67) (N) and Cambridge, University Library, MS Gg.1.6 (Gg)—places the origin of the text at the House of Jesus of Bethlehem at Sheen. This suggests that an anonymous Carthusian monk of the Sheen Charterhouse wrote it for a nun at the neighbouring Birgittine Syon Abbey.

By the early fifteenth century, a number of Middle English texts that were adaptations of or commentaries on the *MVC* were in circulation. While the *Mirror to Devout People* follows in the tradition of the *MVC* through its structure and tone, it also adapts material from numerous sources to address the specific audience at the Birgittine Syon Abbey. The *Mirror* primarily relies on a harmonization of the four gospels to recount the details of Christ's life from the Nativity to the Crucifixion along with some post-Resurrection appearances. It is organized into thirty-three chapters, one for each year of Christ's life, and it divides the Passion narrative into the canonical hours of the Divine Office. The *Mirror* opens with a sophisticated prologue in a scholastic style that draws on traditional rhetorical discourse often found in medieval academic prologues. In the opening lines the author establishes his pure intentions to translate a life of Christ and establishes his authority by describing how he received the permission of his Prior. His *utilitas* and *intentio* are to edify the simple souls who will read his text by providing what he refers to as the most 'edyfycatyf' genre, the life of Christ.[1] In the

---

[1] See Ian Johnson, 'Prologue and Practice: Middle English Lives of Christ', in Roger Ellis et al. (eds.), *The Medieval Translator: The Theory and Practice of Translation in the Middle Ages* (Cambridge, 1989), 69–85.

first two chapters of the *Mirror*, the stories of the Creation and Fall are recounted, which is unusual for late medieval English lives of Christ. Throughout the text, the reader is encouraged to meditate on the events taking place, particularly the Passion. In the final chapter, the reader is repeatedly told to focus on miracles associated with Mary and St John that result from the reciting the *O intemerata*, a prayer in honour of the two figures. The *O intemerata* follows the final chapter of the *Mirror*.

Two editions of the *Mirror* were completed as dissertations in the 1950s and an incomplete version was published in 1973. Bridget Ann Wilsher completed an unpublished M.Phil. dissertation in 1956 at the University of London and John Patrick Banks completed an unpublished doctoral dissertation in 1959 at Fordham University. Wilshire used Gg as her base text and noted a number of, though not all, variations in N. Banks, on the other hand, used N as his base text; however, he relied on microfilm to consult both N and Gg and, like Wilshire, only noted some of the variations. In 1973, James Hogg produced a partial edition of the *Mirror* for the Analecta Cartusiana series; however, his edition omits the introduction and the final third of the text.[2] This present edition offers for the first time a complete edition of the *Mirror to Devout People* that notes all substantive variations.

2. MANUSCRIPTS AND EARLY PROVENANCE

Although the *Mirror* originated at the Sheen Charterhouse, the origins of the two manuscripts indicate a broader awareness of the *Mirror* by readers outside the monastic setting. While Gg appears to have originated at the Sheen Charterhouse, the Scropes, an influential aristocratic family, owned N. On the opening folio of N is an armorial initial that features the impaled arms of the Scrope and Chaworth familes, which suggests John Scrope, 4th Baron Masham, and his wife Elizabeth (née Chaworth) owned the manuscript. The secular ownership of the *Mirror* is an important indication of the continued interest in religious writings by the laity. The early fifteenth century

---

[2] See John Patrick Banks, '*Speculum Devotorum*: An Edition with Commentary' (Ph.D. diss., Fordham University, 1959); Bridget Ann Wilsher, 'An Edition of "Speculum Devotorum," a Fifteenth Century English Meditation on the Life and Passion of Christ, with an Introduction and Notes' (M.Phil. thesis, University of London, 1956); and *The 'Speculum Devotorum' of an Anonymous Carthusian of Sheen, Edited from the Manuscripts Cambridge University Library Gg. 1.6 and Foyle, with an Introduction and a Glossary*', ed. James Hogg, Analecta Cartusiana, 12–13 (Salzburg, 1973–4).

saw an unprecedented rise in devotional writing for and by women. This rise was paralleled by the English Church's efforts to limit secular access to vernacular writing. Archbishop Thomas Arundel's *Constitutions* of 1409 attempted to restrict vernacular preaching, teaching, and writing in response to Wycliffite controversies.[3] Even as attempts at censorship persisted, the post-1409 production of texts for women did not seem to change, and if anything it increased.[4] New and often freshly translated works of writing for and by women arrived in England from the Continent at an unparalleled rate, often through abbeys, especially the newly established Birgittine Syon Abbey, and Carthusian monasteries. But it also arrived through commissions from aristocratic laywomen who desired theological and mystical writings for their own personal devotion.[5] Access to devotional works was often limited to select and well-connected members of the aristocratic and merchant classes who used their connections to gain access to texts. The instructional role of the *Mirror* as a guide to affective meditation on the life of Christ places it within the genre of texts sought after by members of the laity with access to devotional writings. Religious guidebooks, which instructed the reader in devotional and mystical practices, continued to grow in popularity amongst the laity throughout the fifteenth century.[6]

---

[3] For the role of the *Constitutions* in limiting access to and production of vernacular religious texts, see Nicholas Watson, 'Censorship and Culture Change in Late Medieval England: Vernacular Theology, the Oxford Translation Debate, and Arundel's Constitutions of 1409', *Speculum*, 70 (1995), 822–64. For more on the complex role of censorship and its effects on vernacular writing see Kathryn Kerby-Fulton, *Books under Suspicion: Censorship and Tolerance of Revelatory Writing in Late Medieval England* (Notre Dame, Ind.: University of Notre Dame Press, 2006); Ian Forrest, *The Detection of Heresy in Late Medieval England* (Oxford, 2005); Fiona Somerset, 'Censorship', in Alexandra Gillespie and Daniel Wakelin (eds.), *The Production of Books in England 1350–1500* (Cambridge, 2011), 239–58.

[4] Kerby-Fulton, *Books under Suspicion*, Appendix A.

[5] For a detailed chronological chart of the commissions, translations, and authors of vernacular theology by and for women, see Carol M. Meale (ed.), *Women and Literature in Britain, 1150–1500*, 2nd edn. (Cambridge, 1996), pp. xi ff.

[6] For more on the growing popularity of devotional guides, see Jocelyn Wogan-Browne et al. (eds.), *The Idea of the Vernacular: An Anthology of Middle English Literary Theory, 1280–1520* (University Park, Pa., 1999); Rosalynn Voaden, *Prophets Abroad: The Reception of Continental Holy Women in Late-Medieval England* (Cambridge, 1996);Alastair Minnis and Rosalynn Voaden (eds.), *Medieval Holy Women in the Christian Tradition c. 1100–c. 1500* (Turnhout, 2010); and Kathryn Kerby-Fulton, 'The 15th Century as the Golden Age of Women's Theology in English', in Stephen Kelly and Ryan Perry (eds.), *Devotional Culture in Late Medieval England and Europe: Diverse Imaginations of Christ's Life* (Turnhout, 2014), 573–91.

Gg: Cambridge, University Library, MS Gg.1.6. England, s. xv²

Catalogue 1401. Paper. ff. iv + 146 + iv. 205 × 140 mm. Written space 146 × 92 mm. 25 long lines. Collation: a⁴, 1¹⁴ (wants i and xiv; xiv replaced by a parchment singleton), 2–3¹⁶, 4¹² (wants vii, viii, ix, x; two leaves have fallen out of the quire), 5–7¹⁶, 8¹⁰, 9¹⁶, 10¹² (wants xiii and xiv), b⁴. The bottom outer corner of the last leaf of each quire is numbered to indicate the proper order of the quires for the binder. Although the first quire originally contained sixteen leaves, two have been cut out with no apparent loss of text. A parchment singleton, in a second hand, is inserted into the first quire to replace ff. 13ᵛ and 14ʳ. Two leaves have fallen out of the fourth quire between ff. 54ᵛ and 55ʳ, leaving a lacuna that can be recovered using N. Signs of correction appear throughout, as do words inserted interlineally.

1. Ff. 1ᵛ–144ʳ. *Mirror to Devout People* or *Speculum Devotorum* begins 'Here begynnyth a prefacyon to the boke folowynge. Gostly syster in Ihesu cryste I trowe hyt be not 3ytt fro 3our mynde that whene we spake laste togyderys I behette a medytacyon of the passyon of our lorde . . .'; ends 'to whom be all worschype ioye and preysynge now and withoute endynge. Amen. Deo gracias.' (See Pl. 1.)

2. Ff. 144ʳ–145ʳ. *O intemerata.*[7] The Latin prayer entitled 'Oracio bona et deuota ad sanctam mariam matrem domini et beatum Iohannem apostolum et euangelistam' begins 'O intemerata et in eternum benedicta singularis atque incomparabilis virgo dei genitrix . . .'; ends 'qui patri et filio consubstancialis et coeternus cum eis et in eis viuit et regnat omnipotens deus per omnia secula seculorum. amen.'

O intemerata was a popular prayer to the Virgin Mary and John the Evangelist. It originally appeared in the twelfth century. By the fifteenth century, *O Intemerata* was frequently found in books of hours and devotional texts. The prayer's placement following the *Mirror* is unique because the final chapter of the *Mirror* relates a number of miracles that occured from the devout reading of *O intemerata* in order to encourage the reader to study it diligently.

3. Ff. 145ʳ–146ʳ. Middle English translation of *O intemerata.* Unique to Gg, begins with 'O vndefulyd and withoute ende blyssyd syngler

---

[7] The standard edition of *O intemerata* is found in André Wilmart, *Auteurs spirituals et textes dévots du moyen âge latin*, reproduction de l'édition parue en 1932 (Paris, 1971), 474–504.

Notre Dame, University of Notre Dame, Hesburgh Library,
MS Eng d. 1, f. 1ʳ

and incomparable vyrgyne the mothyr of god marye moste kynddest temple of god . . .'; ends 'with hem euyrlastynge with hem and in hem lyuyth and regnyt all mygthty god withoute ende. Amen.'

There are two hands in the manuscript. The first hand is a loose, at times messy, fifteenth-century anglicana while the second hand is a tidier, yet still loose, anglicana.[8] Capital letters in red begin each chapter, with brown ink from a fine pen used for decoration. Paragraph marks, underlining, and erasures are done in red ink; occasionally, a scarlet manicule appears in the margin to indicate an important point in the text or indicate a correction. Marginal additions to the text are usually placed in small shields.

There are numerous correction marks written between the lines and in the margins. They are used to correct word order, highlight key passages, provide alternative words, indicate chapter numeration, and occasionally insert missing text. There are also a number of notes for clarification in the margins. Manicules are used in a similar manner throughout to highlight key passages and make corrections. An important example occurs in f. 83^v, where the scribe copied a paragraph of text on the wrong folio. A small symbol is next to a manicule that points to where the text should appear. In the margin a note reads, 'Turne to þe iiii lef to sueche a syne', followed by a small marker to direct the attention of the reader. The matching sign appears at the top of f. 87^v, where the missing paragraph is in the text. Another manicule appears in the margin of f. 87^v with a small matching symbol and the words 'turne aȝen were þu leftyst & rede at sueche a syne'.

The binding of the manuscript appears to be mid-twentieth century. In the upper left corner of the first pastedown is a hand-written note stating 'Douglas Cockerell & Son; Grantchester; July, 1969'. Sydney Cockerell (d. 1987), son of the bookbinder Douglas Cockerell (d. 1945), continued the family bookbinding business after his father's death. One of the first universities to seek his services was Cambridge University and they remained a long-standing customer.[9]

There are two watermarks: (1) an anvil design that closely resembles Briquet 5952 (c.1408/1419), 5953 (c.1416/1426), and

---

[8] See A. I. Doyle, 'Book Production by the Monastic Orders in England (c. 1375–1530): Assessing the Evidence', in Linda L. Brownrigg (ed.), *Medieval Book Production: Assessing the Evidence* (Los Altos Hills, Calif., 1990), 1–19 at 13, plate 8.

[9] See David McKitterick, 'Cockerell, Sydney Morris (1906–1987)', *ODNB*, accessed 3 June 2015.

5959 (*c*.1462/1472) and (2) a balance type that resembles Briquet 5904 (*c*.1451/1459) and 5905 (*c*.1450/1454). The watermarks suggest paper of Italian origin. There are typically twenty-six pricks visible down the outer edge of each page.

A contemporary note on f. iii, which differs from the main hand of the text, locates the book at the Sheen Charterhouse and identifies the scribe: 'Speculum Devotorum : et est liber domus Ihesu de Bethleem ordinis cartusiensis de shene et nomen scriptoris Willelmus plenus amoris. Quicunque in hoc libro profecerit oret pro scriptore pure et caritative. Sunt meditaciones deuote et motiue de vita domini Ihesu cristi.' The first part of the phrase is the common formula used to indicate book ownership in a Carthusian library.[10] 'Willelmus plenus amoris' may be a possible reference to William Mede, a monk at the Charterhouse of Sheen who copied a number of manuscripts; he was ordained as an acolyte in 1417, spent the majority of his career at Sheen, and died as a sacrist in 1474.[11] He writes in what A. I. Doyle describes as an 'unpretentious and sometimes untidy' anglicana.[12] The hand of Mede corresponds to typical anglicana scripts actively in use during the mid-fifteenth century and suggests that Gg was produced some time early in the second half of the fifteenth century. Further, Mede copied all or part of four other Sheen manuscripts: London, British Library, MS Cotton Vespasian D. ix; Oxford, Bodleian Library, MSS Bodley 117 and Hatton 14; and Dublin, Trinity College, MS 241. Each of these was copied in the second half of the fifteenth century, which suggests this was when Mede was most active as a copyist at Sheen. It appears that Gg was created between 1450 and 1460.

Little is known of the provenance of Gg after it left Sheen. On the third flyleaf is written 'For John Powell is a knaue and so hi ys (?)' in

---

[10] See E. M. Thompson, *The Carthusian Order in England* (London, 1930), 333.

[11] For more on Mede, see Doyle, 'Book Production'. Doyle provides a plate of Gg's note concerning William Mede at p. 13, fig. 8. *Medieval Libraries of Great Britain: A List of Surviving Books, edited by N. R. Ker: A Supplement to the Second Edition*, ed. Andrew G. Watson (London, 1987) provides the date of Mede's ordination but not the record of his death; see *The Chartae of the Carthusian General Chapter: Paris, Bib. Nat. MS Latin 10888*, ed. M. Sargent and J. Hogg, Analecta Cartusiana, 100:6, II (Salzburg, 1985), 211. For more information on the other MSS he copied, see N. R. Ker, *Medieval Libraries of Great Britain*, 2nd edn. (London, 1964), 305; Thompson also discusses Mede in *The Carthusian Order in England*, 332–3, as does A. S. G. Edwards, 'The Contexts of Notre Dame 67', in Jill Mann and Maura B. Nolan (eds.), *The Text in the Community: Essays on Medieval Works, Manuscripts, Authors, and Readers* (Notre Dame, Ind., 2006), 107–28 at 123 n. 6.

[12] Doyle, 'Book Production', 13.

what appears to be a fifteenth-century hand and the name Robert Tipper, in what appears to be an early sixteenth-century hand. Margaret Deansley suggested that the names John Ffarmer, which is written three times on f. 146^v, and Margarett Ffarmer, which appears on f. 147^r, are the names of early owners of the manuscript.[13] Below the name Margarett Ffarmer is a possible date, 1516, and three sequences of numbers. On the pastedown sheet of vellum at the end of the manuscript is the name Robert Farmer in a large, elegant sixteenth-century hand. In her 1956 edition of the *Mirror*, Bridget Ann Wilsher states that the 'book was given to the Cambridge University Library in 1715', which suggests it was part of the library of John Moore, Bishop of Ely.[14] Moore's library came to the University following his death in 1714, at which point King George I purchased the library; he gave it to Cambridge University in 1715.[15] However, Wilshire gives no source for the date of 1715. J. C. T. Oates does not include Gg in his 'Index of Manuscripts'.[16] If one follows Wilshire in her estimation of the date of Gg, then it would seem likely that the manuscript was part of the gift of King George I of John Moore's library.

N: Notre Dame, University of Notre Dame, Hesburgh Library, cod. Eng. d. 1 (*olim* MS 67)[17]. England, s. xv^I

Vellum. ff. ii + 127 + i. 300 × 210 mm. Written space *c.*210 × 140 mm. 27 long lines. Collation: 1–15^8, 16^8 (viii cancelled blank). Gatherings 1–13 contain catchwords in horizontal scrolls drawn with red and black ink. All or part of the word *examinatur* is visible at the bottom of the leaf on ff. 16^v, 24^v, 48^v, 64^v, 80^v, 88^v, 96^v, and 104^v. These supervision marks, along with corrections throughout the text of the *Mirror*, provide evidence that the manuscript was checked for accuracy. The book is bound in a contemporary doeskin binding

---

[13] See Margaret Deansley, 'Vernacular Books in England in the Fourteenth and Fifteenth Centuries', *Modern Language Review*, 15 (1920), 349–58 at 355.

[14] Wilsher, 'An Edition of "Speculum Devotorum"', 116.

[15] For Moore and his library, see David McKitterick, *Cambridge University Library: A History. The Eighteenth and Nineteenth Centuries* (Cambridge, 1986), 47–86 and Jayne Ringrose, 'The Royal Library: John Moore and his Books', in Peter Fox (ed.), *Cambridge University Library: Great Collections* (Cambridge, 1998), 78–89.

[16] See J. C. T. Oates, *Cambridge University Library: A History from the Beginnings to the Copyright Act of Queen Anne* (Cambridge, 1986), 493–5.

[17] A description of N also appears in *The Library of William Foyle. Part I: Medieval and Renaissance Manuscripts: Tuesday 11, July 2000 / Christie's* (London, 2000), Lot 73, 221–3. Edwards gives an account of the sale in 'Contexts', 107.

over wooden boards, with two brass catches and pin from clasp strap, modern red morocco lettering-piece. Brown morocco-backed box.

1. Ff. 1ʳ–108ʳ. *Mirror to Devout People* or *Speculum Devotorum* begins 'Gostely sustre in Ihesu criste I trowe it be nought ȝit from yo mynde . . .'; ends 'To whome be all worship ioye and preysynge nowe and with oute ony endynge. AMEN.' (See Frontispiece.)

2. F. 108ʳ. A Latin colophon immediately follows the *Mirror*:

> Ffinito libro sit laus et gloria Christo.
> Soluite nunc mentem pro W. H. ad omnipotentem.
> De uita Christi libro finis datur isti
> Paruos lactabit solidos quasi pane cibabit
> De Bethlem pratum dedit hos Ihesu tibi flores
> Et post hunc ergo statum reddas sibi semper honores

3. F. 108ʳ⁻ᵛ. *O intemerata*. Latin prayer titled 'Oracio bona et deuota ad beatam uirginem mariam matrem domini nostri Ihesu Cristi et beatum Iohannem Euangelistam'; begins 'O intemerata et in eternum benedicta singularis atque incomparabilis uirgo dei genitrix . . .'; ends 'qui Patri et Filio consubstancialis et coeternus cum eis et in eis uiuit et regnat omnipotens Deus per omnia secula seculorum. AMEN.'

4. F. 109ʳ. A Latin colophon follows *O intemerata*:

> Nos tibi uirgo pia semper commendo maria
> Nos rogo conserues Christi dilecte Iohannes.
> Virgo maria dei genetrix quam scriptor honorat
> Sis pia semper ei prout hic te sperat et orat
> Ex aliaque uice Iohannes christi dulcis amice
> Da sibi solamen cum sanctis omnibus. Amen.

In omni tribulacione temptacione necessitate et angustia succurre nobis piissima uirgo maria.

5. Ff. 109ᵛ–126ʳ. *The tretise of the craft of dying* (*The Craft of Dying*) begins 'For als miche as þe passage of dethe . . .'; ends 'by þe meditacyon of our Lorde Ihesu cryste þat is mediatour betwix god and man. amen.'

The Craft of Dying, a popular work in the *ars moriendi* tradition, concerns itself with the proper preparation for death. It survives in thirteen manuscripts but does not appear in Gg. It initially may have been written in Latin by a Dominican at or near the time of the Council of Constance in 1418. Following its composition, *The Craft of*

Dying was translated into a number of vernacular languages.[18] *The Craft of Dying* is followed by three Latin colophons at f. 126[r]:

> Esto memor mortis nam porta fit omnibus ortis
> Sepe sibi iuuenes accipit ante senes.

> Non homo leteris tibi copia si fluat eris
> Hic non semper eris memor esto quod morieris
> Es euanebit quod habes tunc alter habebit
> Corpus putrebit quod agis tecum permanebit.

> Finem siste pia mortis michi virgo maria
> Es quia regina Manfeld defende ruina. Amen.

The initial two lines are the opening of a macaronic poem in Latin and Middle English, followed by four lines of which a longer version (nine lines) exists.[19] Finally, the last two lines refer to Manfeld, a likely reference to William Manfeld, the personal secretary of John Scrope, 4th Baron Masham. Scrope owned N, and Manfeld is described in Scrope's will, dated 18 March 1453, as 'my secretar' and also designated as one of the executors of Scrope's estate.[20] In N, running vertically along the right-hand side of the Latin colophons in a large hand are the initials 'W. M.' It is possible that Manfeld is the scribe of *The Craft of Dying*; however, the Latin lines do not explicitly state that he copied the text.

There are two hands in N. The first hand appears in *Mirror to Devout People* and *O intemerata* and uses two distinct styles with identifying features, most notably the dotting of his *y*'s. In the *Mirror to Devout People* (ff. 1[r]–108[r]), the hand is a predominantly Secretary

---

[18] For a more detailed account of the treatise, see P. S. Jolliffe, *A Checklist of Middle English Prose Writings of Spiritual Guidance* (Toronto, 1974), L 4(a) and *Index of Printed Middle English Prose*, ed. R. E. Lewis, N. F. Blake, and A. S. G. Edwards, Garland Reference Library of the Humanities, 537 (New York, 1985), 234. See also Mary C. O'Connor, *The Art of Dying Well* (New York, 1942), 50–60 and Nancy Lee Beaty, *The Craft of Dying: A Study of the Literary Tradition of the Ars Moriendi in England* (New Haven, 1970), 7–53.

[19] For the first two lines, see *A Manual of the Writings in Middle English, 1050-1500*, ix, ed. Albert E. Hartung (New Haven, 1993), XXII.356; *The Index of Middle English Verse*, ed. Carleton Brown and Rossell Hope Robbins (New York, 1943), 3211; Hans Walther, *Initia carminum ac versuum Medii Aevi posterioris Latinorum* (Göttingen, 1969), 5892; and Edwards, 'Contexts', 121. For the next four lines, see Walther, *Initia*, 12072; and for the longer version, see *Yorkshire Writers: Richard Rolle of Hampole and his Followers*, ed. C. Horstmann, 2 vols. (London, 1895–6; repr. Rochester, NY, 1999), i. 431, lines 496 ff.; and Edwards, 'Contexts', 121.

[20] See *Testamenta Eboracensia: or, Wills Registered at York, Illustrative of the History, Manners, Language, Statistics, &c., of the Province of York, from the Year 1300 downwards*, ed. J. Raine, Part II, Surtees Society, 30 (Durham, 1855),192.

hand in a mixed style with anglicana two-compartment 'a', an 8-like 'g', and a long 'r', while in *O intemerata* (f. 108^{r-v}) it is a Gothic Book hand. The second hand is in *The Craft of Dying* (ff. 109^v–127^r) and is similar to the first, with a Secretary hand in a mixed style with anglicana features.[21]

The first hand is anglicana with Secretary features, including an open-looped 'W' that became common in the second half of the fifteenth century. The second hand, which copied *The Craft of Dying*, writes in a more fluid, loose anglicana and names 'Manfeld' in a Latin colophon following the work:

> Finem siste pia mortis michi virgo maria
> Es quia regina Manfeld defende ruina. Amen.

As noted above, William Manfeld was the personal secretary of John Scrope, and it is possible he was tasked with copying out the work. If he did copy the second half of N, then it is likely the manuscript was copied not in London, but closer to the home of the Scropes.

Three armorial initials are found in N beginning at f. 1^r, where an armorial initial 'G' with arms of Scropes *azure*, a bend *or* with label *argent* impaling those of Chaworth opens the *Mirror* (see the Frontispiece).[22] The second initial opens the *O intemerata* on f. 108^r. It is a historiated initial 'O' containing an image of the Virgin Mary holding the Christ child with John the Evangelist standing nearby holding a palm and chalice. The final initial opens *The Book of the Craft of Dying* on f. 109^r. It is a historiated initial 'F' with a bishop in the lower part of the stave giving last rites to a man tucked into bed. The border surrounding f. 1^r matches the style of illuminations common in London scriptoria of the early 1430s, but the figures in the historiated initials are not as sophisticated as manuscripts dating to London in the early 1430s. Rather, they resemble illuminations found in manuscripts that date slightly later to the late 1430s to mid-1440s.[23] Paragraph marks, underlining, and deletions are done in red ink. Some initials are also done in blue ink.

---

[21] See Edwards, 'Contexts', 124 n. 13.

[22] See Jessica Brantley, 'The Visual Environment of Carthusian Texts: Decoration and Illustration in Notre Dame 67', in Jill Mann and Maura B. Nolan (eds.), *Text in the Community: Essays on Medieval Works, Manuscripts, Authors, and Readers* (Notre Dame, Ind., 2006), 173–216 at 204 and Edwards, 'Contexts', 110.

[23] Similar illuminations survive in the Brut Chronicle in Chapel Hill, North Carolina, believed to have been illuminated in London in 1430–40. For a description and images of this Brut manuscript, see Kathleen L. Scott, *Dated and Datable English Manuscript Borders c. 1395–1499* (London, 2002), pl. XVIIII and colour frontispiece, 1445/6.

These illuminations provide insight into the early ownership of N. The opening initial with the impaled arms of the families of John Scrope, 4th Baron Masham and his wife Elizabeth Chaworth suggests lay ownership. John and Elizabeth were married some time before 24 August 1418 and John died in 1455. A mark of cadency in the opening initial complicates the dating of the manuscript. John inherited his title when his brother Henry was executed for his role in the Southampton Plot against King Henry V in 1415. John was not knighted until 1424 and the mark of cadency may be related to his impending knighthood. Elizabeth took the veil shortly after John's death and lived until 1466/7. As mentioned, N also contains a copy of *The Craft of Dying*, which follows the *O intemerata*. While it is likely that N was commissioned some time between the marriage of the Scropes and the death of John, it is possible that Elizabeth commissioned it for her own use after taking the veil. If John commissioned it, then it was most likely near the end of this period. This would date N some time between 1455 and 1466/7, making it later than Gg.

The family connections of the Scropes to Syon Abbey certainly allowed John Scrope and his wife Elizabeth access to a Carthusian text intended for a fairly limited female religious audience. Syon Abbey was known for its public mission of preaching, and through those connections, books were often made available to a small group of powerful friends and supporters.[24] And considering the apparently limited circulation of the *Mirror to Devout People*, it does not appear that it was known outside the circles of religious and well-connected aristocracy. The well-established family connections of the Scropes to Syon Abbey and English book collecting aided them in acquiring the *Mirror*.[25]

On the Chaworth side, the father of Elizabeth, Thomas Chaworth,

---

[24] See Vincent Gillespie, 'Dial M for Mystic: Mystical Texts in the Library of Syon Abbey and the Spirituality of the Syon Brethren', in Gillespie (ed.), *Looking in Holy Books: Essays on Late Medieval Religious Writing in England* (Turnhout, 2011), 185.

[25] Baron Henry Fitzhugh (1363?–1425), a Knight of the Garter, was the son of Henry Fitzhugh and Joan, daughter of Henry Scrope, 1st Baron Scrope of Masham, and sister of Archbishop Richard Scrope of York. In the early 15th c. he made plans for an English Birgittine community while in Sweden for the wedding of Henry IV and Philippa, daughter of Eric XIII of Sweden. He offered his estate at Cherry Hinton for the use of the Birgittines, but it was not until Henry V bequeathed land at Twickenham that Syon Abbey was established.See A. C. Reeves, 'Fitzhugh, Henry, third Baron Fitzhugh (1363?–1425), administrator and diplomat',*ODNB*, accessed 10 July 2014. Similarly, Henry Scrope, 3rd Baron Masham and brother of John, had a will that suggested similar religious commitments. He was very generous in his gifts to religious houses and he owned copies of the *Revelations of St Bridget*, the *Prick of Conscience*, the works of Richard Rolle, and a

had one of the largest book collections in the north-east Midlands, including a copy of the Middle English *Horologium Sapientiae* and a number of other sources used in the *Mirror*.[26] It is likely that a woman such as Elizabeth, who was raised in a powerful family with interests in book collecting and devotional practice, was literate and, like many women in the aristocracy during this time, interested in religious devotional reading. The connections of both the Scrope and Chaworth families to the Birgittine Order, the founding of Syon Abbey, and the connections to the English book trade allowed John and Elizabeth Scrope unprecedented access to the *Mirror to Devout People*.

Little is known of the history of the manuscript until the mid-twentieth century, at which point N was included in the sale of the Borthwick collection at Sotheby's, 3 June 1946, lot 112, where it sold for £280 to Mrs Bertram Bell. It was passed to William and Christina Foyle, who maintained their impressive book collection at Beeleigh Abbey. Following the death of William Foyle, his family sold much of the collection at auction. N was sold at Christie's on 11 July 2000, lot 73, to Quaritch. The University of Notre Dame then acquired the manuscript from Quaritch. N had received only limited scholarly attention due to its private ownership.[27]

3. THE RELATIONSHIP OF GG AND ND

Variations between Gg and N seem to confirm that they were copied with specific audiences in mind: a religious audience for Gg and a lay audience for N. In the Preface to the *Mirror*, the author discusses his rationale for writing the text when he states that he nearly gave up the project upon discovering that another Carthusian had already translated the *MVC*.

---

collection of verses to the Virgin Mary. See Brigette Vale, 'Scrope, Henry, third Baron Scrope of Masham (*c.*1376–1415)', *ODNB*, accessed 16 July 2014.

[26] When Thomas Chaworth died in 1459 at the age of 79, he left substantial evidence of his interests in book collecting. For his will, see *Testamenta Eboracensia*, ed. Raine, 227. See also Thorlac Turville-Petre, 'Some Medieval English Manuscripts in the North-East Midlands', in Derek Pearsall (ed.), *Manuscripts and Readers in Fifteenth-Century England* (Cambridge, 1993), 125–41.

[27] In his *Check-List of Middle English Prose Writings of Spiritual Guidance*, 225, Joliffe states that he was unable to examine the manuscript.

Gg: 'And most of all whenne I herde telle that a man of oure ordyr of charturhowse had iturnyd the same boke into Englyische.'

N: 'And moste of all when I herde tell þat a man of our Ordoure hadde turned þe same booke into Englysshe'

The omission of the phrase 'of charturhowse' in N may indicate an intended lay audience by omitting the Carthusian origins of the text, a detail perhaps deemed unnecessary for a text circulating within a wider readership. It may also be a sign that the secular family who owned the manuscript was familiar with the origins of the text and had no need to be reminded from which order it originated.

A second variation provides further evidence that N was created specifically for a lay audience. Chapter 14 contains a discussion of both the uneducated and the learned men Jesus chose to be his disciples and preach his message. According to the *Mirror*, Jesus chose learned or 'lettered' men so none could argue that simple men were fooled into following him. The simple men, however, were chosen to affirm the wisdom of God over the wisdom of man: 'the feythe of þe gospel schulde more be redressyd to þe wysedom of God thanne to þe wysedom of man'. If they were already 'grete clerkys' when they were called, then 'men wolde haue redresse`d´ here wysedom to þe wysedom of men'.

Following this discussion in N is a short passage, which does not appear in Gg:

And þis is ayeyns some nowe adayes þat when þei here or rede ony thynge ydo of a grete clerke, as of a maistre of dyuynyte or a doctour of lawe, anone þei haue grete deynte þerof and comenden it gretely. And ʒif it were ydo of a comon letterde man or of a deuoute man not a graduate, þat is to seye, noght degreede in scoles, þei dispise it or elles haue lytell deynte þerof. And ʒit it is a sygne of more grace of God when suche a man doth a thynge þan a grete clerke, not þat þei bene blameable for þai comende þat that a clerke doth, bot for þei take not vertuousely þat a symple man doth, so þat it be withoute heresye. (69/95–104)

This passage directs the lay reader to acknowledge the importance of devotional works written by 'symple' authors such as Carthusians and recognizes the broader outreach available to the Birgittine brethren and other orders that were highly educated and maintained public ministries. The Birgttine brethren had a public ministry of preaching, which put them in contact with aristocratic lay people, while the Carthusian monks at Sheen lived ascetic lives removed from the public and were often from humble backgrounds, having joined the order without the advanced degrees of the Birgittine men.[28]

Another similar example occurs on f. 74^r of Gg, where a paragraph-length passage appears in the margin, written in the same hand as the main text, with corresponding marks to indicate its insertion. The insertion marks are in the same style as other corrections that are confirmed by the text of N. However, this passage does not appear in N:

Also hyt ys wryte in the lawe to put aweye the errowrs þat unrygth falle in the peple þat ys they mygth wene þat hyt mygth not be mynystryd but vndyr bothe lyknessys for hyt ys suffycently vndyr þat one & therfore also hyt ys ordeynyd of holy chyrche to be resceyuyd so of the commune peple for to put a wey the forseyde errowrs but preests be bownde to resceyue hyt vndyr bothe lyknessys for our lorde ordeynyde hyt so as to hem. (92/153–9)

It is not clear if this paragraph is a scribal insertion or if it was omitted and added as a correction. The passage is inserted in the midst of a larger discussion concerning the role of the priest in the Eucharistic celebration, through which the author carefully guides the intended female reader with a series of questions. However, it shifts the discussion from the role of the lay reader to the role of the priest and what is expected of him. Its omission from N could be a scribal insertion or an indication that the manuscript was copied for a lay reader, while its inclusion in Gg might suggest a text directed to the broader community at Syon Abbey.

In addition to the intentional variations discussed above, there are a number of minor variations between Gg and N that appear to be the result of scribal error. At the bottom of f. 23^r in Gg, during a discussion of the insignificance of Bethlehem before the birth of Christ that relies on the *Historia Trium Regum*, the text reads, 'hyt ys fro Ierusalem too smale myle' (29/25–6). The same passage in N (f. 16^r) states 'eghte smale myle'. Both the English and Latin versions of the *Historia Trium Regum* confirm the readings in Gg.

---

[28] For more on the spirituality of the Birgittine brethren, see Roger Ellis, 'Further Thoughts on the Spirituality of Syon Abbey', in William F. Pollard and Robert Boenig (eds.), *Mysticism and Spirituality in Medieval England* (Cambridge, 1997), 219–43. Vincent Gillespie, 'The Haunted Text: Reflections in *The Mirror to Deuout People*', in Jill Mann and Maura B. Nolan (eds.), *The Text in the Community: Essays on Medieval Works, Manuscripts, Authors, and Readers* (Notre Dame, Ind., 2006), 129–72 at 146–8; ' "Hid Diuinite": The Spirituality of the English Syon Brethren', in *The Medieval Mystical Tradition in England: Exeter Symposium VII*, ed. E. A. Jones (Cambridge: Boydell & Brewer, 2004), 189–206; and 'Dial M for Mystic', 185 ff.

A similar variation that confuses the number of years Joseph, Mary, and Jesus spent in Egypt appears later in the text. At the end of f. 42^r, Gg reads 'and there they duellyde vii ʒere vnto the deth of Kynge Herowde' (51/60–1). N reads 'eght yhere'. The *Legenda Aurea*, which is the main source for this passage, and the *MVC* both confirm seven as the commonly accepted number of years.[29] This particular error could be a scribal misreading of 'vii' for 'viii'.

Later, in a discussion of the role of Joseph as the father of Jesus, Gg reads, 'Lyre seyth, thowgth Ioseph were iseyde oure Lordys fadyr, neuyrdeles he was not hardy to vndyrneme hym for he beleuyde hym stedfastly godys sone' (55/72–4). N replaces 'vndyrneme' with 'displese'. The use of 'vndyrneme' (rebuke or chastise) in Gg is supported by the source, Nicholas of Lyre's *Postilla*, while the reading in N seems to miss the point of the passage, which is the inability of Joseph to chastise the young Christ.

While the variations discussed above are important evidence of the possible different audiences for the *Mirror*, Gg and N are consistently similar. Two errors highlight this consistency. In the Preface, a misreading of a passage from Henry Suso's *Horologium sapientiae* results in the same significant error in both manuscripts:

Gg: 'The ofte thynkynge of my Passyon makyth an vnlernyde man a ful lernyd man and vnwyse men and ydyotys hyt makyth to profyte into maystrys' (f. 3^r)

N: 'The ofte thynkyng of þe Passioun maketh an vnlerned man and vnwyse men and ydiotes it maketh to profyte into maistres' (f. 2^r)

An eyeskip error occurs in N when the scribe omits 'a ful lernyd man'. However, the more interesting error is the reading 'to profyte into maystrys', which matches Gg but does not align with the *Horologium*: 'Frequens passionis huius memoria indoctum quemque reddit doctissimum, et imperitos ac idiotas facit proficere in magistros' ('The frequent recollection of this Passion makes any dullard most learned, and it turns amateurs and simpletons into teachers').[30] The same misreading of the Latin source in both Gg and N could mean that the later N was copied from Gg or that an earlier copy of the *Mirror* existed from which one or both manuscripts were copied.

---

[29] Jacobus de Voragine, *Legenda Aurea*, ed. Giovanni Paolo Maggioni, 2 vols. (Florence, 1998), i. 98–9; Iohannis de Caulibus, *Meditaciones Vitae Christi, olim S. Bonauenturo attributae*, ed. Mary Stallings-Taney, CCCM 153 (Turnhout, 1997), 51.85–8.

[30] Henry Suso, *Horologium Sapientiae*, ed. Pius Künzle (Fribourg, 1977), I.14, p. 494; Trans. Edmund Colledge, *Watch upon the Hours* (Washington, DC, 1994), 202.

Another connection between Gg and N is that the correction marks in Gg used to correct word order consistently match the word order found in N. Since Gg pre-dates N, the scribe of Gg could not be using N as a guide to make corrections. It seems likely that another copy or copies existed from which the Gg scribe made his corrections. While numerous examples of corrections in Gg align it with N, the correction of an error of metathesis on f. 15^r (21/125) of Gg illustrates the point. Gg reads 'trewthe the knowynge of' with the construe marks '*d, a, b,* and *c*' placed interlineally over each word respectively. In the left margin is written 'the knowynge of trewthe' with further construe marks, '*a, b, c,* and *d* ', over each word, which instruct the reader to rearrange the order of the words, and the marginal comment affirms the corrected order.[31] The corrected order aligns the text with N. Since Gg pre-dates N, the consistent use of correction marks that align Gg with the text in N suggests the existence of an earlier copy of the *Mirror*.

4. LANGUAGE OF THE TEXTS

Gg

It is often difficult to place mid- to late fifteenth-century texts such as Gg accurately using *LALME*, but in the case of Gg, the text reliably uses forms associated with the region from which it originates. The text of Gg was written somewhere in the Surrey area, which can be adduced from a number of linguistic features. More specifically, Gg can be located on the Surrey/Essex border near Richmond, which places it in very close proximity to the Sheen Charterhouse and Syon Abbey. Both Gg and N are fairly plain texts with strikingly dialectal linguistic features sprinkled throughout, which is probably a result of both originating from a lost archetype.

Within Gg there are consistent uses of forms that place the text along the Surrey/Essex border near Twickenham, the location of the two religious houses. For example, Gg consistently replaces ⟨d⟩ with

---

[31] Construe marks are not always corrective, but were also used to show students how a Latin passage would appear in the vernacular. For more on construe marks, see Fred C. Robinson, 'Syntactical Glosses in Latin Manuscripts of Anglo-Saxon Provenance', *Speculum*, 48 (1973), 443–75; Mildred Budney, 'Assembly Marks in the Vivian Bible and Scribal, Editorial, and Organizational Marks in Medieval Books', in Linda L. Brownrigg (ed.), *Making the Medieval Book: Techniques of Production* (Los Altos Hills, Calif., 1995), 199–239; and Daniel Wakelin, *Scribal Corrections and Literary Craft: English Manuscripts 1375–1510* (Cambridge, 2014), 116–18; 150–3.

⟨þ, th⟩ in words such as *elthyr*, 'elder', *abythynge*, 'abiding', and *therkenesse*, 'darkness', *thebate*, 'debate'. Gg also consistently replaces ⟨i⟩ with ⟨y⟩. Examples include words such as *thyse*, 'these', *yf*, 'if', *addyr*, 'adder', *arethy*, 'aredy', *aftyr*, 'after', *bothely*, 'bodily', and *hylle*, 'hill'. Further examples that are consistent in Gg are the addition of ⟨c⟩ to ⟨sl⟩ in order to form ⟨scl⟩ and the replacement of ⟨ght⟩ with ⟨gth⟩. These forms appear in words such as *sclaundre*, 'slander', *sclain*, 'slain' and *mygth*, 'might'. One sees these forms throughout southern England and particularly in the region near the Surrey/Essex border.

Other forms that are not as consistent in Gg are ⟨ȝ⟩ for ⟨y⟩ and ⟨g⟩ as in *ȝelde* for 'yelde' and *aȝenste* for 'against' as well as the omission of ⟨g⟩ in 'strength' as *strenthe*. These forms are also indicative of texts found along the Surrey/Essex border. Each of these linguistic forms takes on the plain nature of the dialect of Gg and they securely place it within close proximity to Sheen.

THESE	these (thyse)
SHE	sche
IT	hytt, hyt
THEM	hem
THEIR	her*e* (theyr*e*)
SUCH	sueche
EACH	eche ((vche))
ANY	eny
MUCH	myche
FROM	fro
AGAINST	aȝenste, aȝenst, ((^{a}ȝenste))
YET	ȝytt
STRENGTH	strenthe
ADDER	addyr
BURN	bre*n*n
DREAD	adrad
GATE	gate, ȝate
SLAIN	sclayne
WHO	hoso, hooso, hoo
YIELD	ȝelde

N

LALME does not analyse N.[32] In N, the dialect in which the *Mirror to Devout People* is written provides a text that contains several distinct features of an East Anglian dialect, specifically in East Norfolk. While it lacks some forms typically associated with the East Anglian area such as *xall* for 'shall' and ⟨qu-⟩ spellings of 'which', it does contain *friste* for first, *sustre* for sister, and *ony* for 'any'. Forms in N that prove somewhat problematic are *efter* for 'after' and *mykyll* for 'much', though both do appear in East Norfolk on a limited basis. However, *yhe* for 'ye' appears frequently in N and is a more characteristically northern form, though it is still not very common. Some other problematic forms within N can generally be placed in the Lincolnshire/Rutland/Leicestershire border, such as the scribe's confusion of 'þ' and 'y'. This was a common feature in this area.[33] However, forms such as *chirche* and *togidre* are indicative of the East Norfolk region and are predominant throughout the manuscript. Ultimately, N is a text containing so many areas that it becomes a plain, colourless text and while it cannot be definitively placed, the predominant dialect of the text originates in the East Norfolk area.

THESE	þese, these
SHE	she, shee
IT	it, hit
THEM	hem
THEIR	her
SUCH	suche
EACH	yche
ANY	ony
MUCH	mykel(l), myche
FROM	from, fro
STRENGTH	strenthe
AFTERWARDE	aftrewarde
BLESSED	blessede, blissede
DAUGHTER	doghter
YE	ye, yhe, ȝe

---

[32] I am indebted to Jeremy J. Smith for pointing out many of the dialectical features of N in a personal email of 5 May 2004.

[33] See Michael Benskin, 'The Letters ⟨þ⟩ and ⟨y⟩ in later Middle English, and Some Related Matters', *Journal of the Society of Archivists*, 7 (1982), 13–30.

ADDER	adder
BURN	brenn
DREAD	adrade
GATE	gate, yate, ȝate
WHO	hoso, hooso, hoo

5. SOURCES

The *Mirror to Devout People* dates to the early 1430s, which situates it in the initial decades of Syon Abbey. Henry V founded the Carthusian monastery at Sheen in 1414 and Syon Abbey in 1415. He constructed both centres of religious life in an unrealized plan to build three religious houses on the royal manor of Sheen, but the planned Celestine abbey was never built. Both Syon and the Carthusian monastery were royally sanctioned institutions in close proximity to London, which made them a spiritual and intellectual hub of English culture. Books played a central role in the daily devotional lives of those residing at the two houses. Carthusians were famous for their commitment to the written word and the sisters of Syon were held to a Rule that encouraged non-liturgical reading.[34]

In the years following their founding, Syon and the Sheen Charterhouse relied on each other for access to Latin and vernacular texts, with the Carthusians possibly providing mentoring to the sisters of Syon through commissioned texts in exchange for access to the impressive Syon library. Syon received its first professed inhabitants in 1420. In 1431, Syon moved from Twickenham to Isleworth, which placed it directly across the Thames from the Carthusian monastery.[35] The proximity of the two houses allowed them to become central in the creation and dissemination of Latin works translated into the vernacular. Shortly after Syon moved closer to the Carthusian monastery, the *Mirror to Devout People* was written.

This close relationship inspired the creation of a number of

---

[34] Ann Hutchison, 'What the Nuns Read: Literary Evidence from the English Bridgettine House, Syon Abbey', *Medieval Studies*, 57 (1995), 205–22.

[35] The standard account of the foundation of Syon Abbey remains G. J. Aungier, *The History and Antiquities of Syon Monastery, the Parish of Isleworth and the Chapelry of Hounslow* (London, 1840) as well as M. B. Tait, 'The Brigittine Monastery of Syon (Middlesex) with Special Reference to its Monastic Uses'(D.Phil. thesis, Oxford University, 1975). See also N. Beckett, 'St. Bridget, Henry V and Syon Abbey', in J. Hogg (ed.), *Studies in St. Birgitta and the Brigittine Order*, 2 vols., Analecta Cartusiana, 35:19 (Salzburg, 1993), ii. 125–50.

important translations and works of guidance during the early decades of the fifteenth century. In the 1420s and 1430s the Birgittine brethren and the Carthusians translated the works of important female religious figures, lives of Christ, and devotional guides, all for the Birgittine sisters at Syon. Along with the *Mirror to Devout People*, these works included the *Liber Celestis* of Birgitta of Sweden; the *Orcherd of Syon*, a Middle English translation of the *Dialogo* by Catherine of Siena; and the *Myroure of Oure Ladye*, which outlined a reading plan for the sisters at Syon. The *Mirror* author states that he promised the Birgittine sister for whom he wrote the text 'a medytacyon of the Passyon of oure Lorde, the whyche promysse I haue not putte fro 'my' mynde but be dyuerse tymys, be the grace of God, I haue parformyd hyt as I mygthte' (3/3–6). Thus it seems likely that the *Mirror* was written for Syon Abbey while possibly relying on sources found in the libraries of both religious houses.

   Near the conclusion of the Preface, the author gives a precise overview of the sources he uses in the *Mirror*:

And specyally I haue folowyd in þys werke tueyne doctorys, of the whyche þat one ys comunely called the Maystyr of Storyis, and hys boke in Englyisch the *Scole Storye*; that othyr maystyr, Nycholas of Lyre, þe whyche was a worthy doctur of dyuynytee and glosyde all the Byble as to the lettural vndyrstandynge. And therfor I take these tueyne doctorys most specyally as to thys werke, for they goo neryste to the storye and the lettural vndyrstandynge of eny doctorys that I haue red. Notwythstandynge, I haue browgth inne othyr doctorys in diuerse placys, as to the moral vertuys, and also summe reuelacyonys of approuyd wymmen (6/117–27).

The list provided by the author of the *Mirror* points to a reliance on the *Historia Scholastica* of Peter Comestor and the *Postilla* of Nicholas of Lyre for the majority of his commentary on the life of Christ. He also draws extensively from the *Legenda Aurea*, particularly to offer accounts of events in the life of Christ that are not found in the Scriptures, as well as the writings of St Birgitta of Sweden, St Mechtild of Hackeborn, and St Catherine of Siena, the 'approuyd wymmen' that he mentions.

   Carthusians were known for the importation of devotional works from the Continent and the sources in the *Mirror* do reflect the type of texts one might expect to find in a charterhouse library. The author of the *Mirror* uses works such as John of Hildesheim's *The Three Kings of Cologne*, Henry Suso's *Horologium Sapientiae*, and Mechtild of Hackeborn's *Liber specialis gratiae*, all of which correspond with existing evidence of the Carthusians' involvement in introducing German mystical works into England.[36] Since the earliest days of the Order, the preserving, collecting, copying, and correcting of books were central activities of the Carthusian Order.[37] The importance of Carthusian book production makes the intellectual and literary exchange between the two religious houses central to the book trade in fifteenth-century England. As a result, the variety of sources used in the *Mirror to Devout People*, which were available at both Sheen and Syon libraries, places the work in a prominent position within the broader context of English devotional writing.

a. *Meditaciones vitae Christi*

Although he nearly abandoned the writing of the *Mirror to Devout People*, the author consulted his Prior for advice and decided to write the *Mirror* despite the existence of the *MVC* and *The Mirror of the Blessed Life of Jesus Christ* by Nicholas Love, the 'man of oure ordyr of charturhowse'. He did not, however, produce another translation of the *MVC*, but instead wove together a life of Christ assembled from a variety of sources in order to fill in and supplement the details of the *MVC* and its English translations. The *Mirror* author distances his work from the *MVC* by never unequivocally drawing on it as a source, instead relying on the Bible, the Church Fathers, and a select group of female authors to compose a life of Christ. As a result, the *Mirror* acts as a companion to the *MVC* that includes details not found in the pseudo-Bonaventuran work while also offering spiritual guidance and direction to its audience.

At nearly every point that the *Mirror* author discusses a detail of the life of Christ found in the *MVC*, he chooses a different source to follow. For example, in lines 33/155–8, the *Mirror* states that the

---

[36] Clare Kirchberger, *The Goad of Love* (London, 1952) writes: 'The Carthusian houses provided the "open door" between Flanders and England, and it is from their libraries that come some of the mss. of Middle English translations of Ruysbroeck, Tauler and Suso, together with the Revelations of some of the German nuns' (p. 23).

[37] See Mary A. and Richard H. Rouse, 'Correction and Emendation of Texts in the Fifteenth Century and the Autograph of the *Opus Pacis* by "Oswaldus Anglicus"', in Sigrid Krämer and Michael Bernhard (eds.), *Scire Litteras: Forschungen zum Mittelalterlichen Geistesleben* (Munich, 1988), 333–46; James Hogg, 'Oswald de Corda, a Forgotten Carthusian of Nördlingen', in Hogg (ed.), *Kartäusermystik und Mystiker, III*, Analecta Cartusiana, 55:3 (Salzburg, 1982), 181–5; and Michael Sargent, 'The Problem of Uniformity in Carthusian Book Production from the *Opus Pacis* to the *Tertia Compilatio Statutorum*', in Richard Beadle and A. J. Piper (eds.), *New Science out of Old Books: Studies in Manuscripts and Early Printed Books in Honour of A. I. Doyle* (Aldershot, 1995), 122–41.

shepherds who were informed of the birth of Christ by angels were one mile from Bethlehem 'as the Mayster of Storyis seyt' (33/157–8). The *MVC* also tells us that the shepherds were one mile from Bethlehem, but the *Mirror* never cites the *MVC* as its source. When it does rely on the *MVC* for a detail, the *Mirror* does not give the *MVC* credit. For example, in chapter 30, at line 152/85, Mt Thabor is named as the place of the Transfiguration of Christ. The *Mirror* author directs the reader to chapter 15, where he had already discussed the details of the Transfiguration. Chapter 15 states that the event occurred on a 'hye hylle . . . as Lyre seyth' (73/63–4). Nicholas of Lyre's *Postilla* never mentions Thabor, so it seems probable that the *Mirror* found the item in the *MVC*, which locates the Transfiguration at that place.

The *Mirror* author discusses the relationship of his text to the *MVC* in the Preface when he addresses those who might question the worthiness of a text written by a 'sympyl man' after the work of 'Bonauenture' (4/59–60). He draws on the example of the Evangelists, who wrote the Gospels from different perspectives, each of which provided valuable insights:

Ther ben foure euangelyst that wryten of the manhede of oure Lorde Jhesu Cryste and зytt alle wryten 'wel' and trewly and that one leuyth anothyr supplyeth. Also the doctorys of Holy Chyrche exponen the same euangelyis þat they wrote diuerse wysys to the conforte of Crystyn peple, and зytt all ys goode to Crysten peple and necessarye and profytable. And so thowgth he that wrote fyrste the medytacyonys folowynge were but a sympyl man and of no reputacyon in comparyson of so worthy a clerke as Bonauenture was, зytt the medytacyonys, be the grace of God, mowe be ful goode and profytable to devout Crystyn soulys. (4/53–62)

The *MVC* does not work as a primary source for the *Mirror*, but rather as a framework for much of the discussion of the Passion of Christ, which allows the *Mirror* author to create a new perspective on the familiar. Particularly from chapter 19 to the end, the author frequently draws on passages from the *MVC* without attribution. Details such as how Christ wiped his face before rejoining his disciples in the Garden of Gethsemane (98/87–90) or that the length of the cross was 15 feet (113/114) may appear to originate with the *MVC*.

Longer discussions of key moments in the Passion also follow the *MVC*. When the *Mirror* describes the reaction of Mary, her sister, and Mary Magdalene to seeing Christ being led by Romans through the city, it closely follows the *MVC* (114/133–49). Additionally, in a discussion of the upright and supine methods of crucifixion, the *Mirror* again follows the *MVC*; unlike the *MVC*, however, the *Mirror* gives preference to the upright option (117/45–118/83). Despite relying on the *MVC* for much of the information included in its account of the Passion of Christ, the author of the *Mirror* maintains a noticeable distance from the *MVC*. The desire he expresses in the Preface to create a work that is 'ful goode and profytable to devout Crystyn soulys' also requires him to create a work distinct from the *MVC*.

b. The Vulgate Bible and Biblical Commentaries

Unlike the *MVC*, the Bible and, specifically, the Gospel accounts of the life of Christ are cited repeatedly throughout the entire thirty-three chapters of the *Mirror*. Not surprisingly, the story of the Passion relies heavily on scriptural accounts, often quoting biblical passages in full or paraphrasing so closely that the quotations are frequently indistinguishable from the words of the author. However, such subtle inclusion of scriptural sources is not always the case, and occasionally the *Mirror* falls into a digression after using a verse in order to make a point about the previous meditation or lesson. A pattern emerges as the *Mirror* author introduces scriptural passages into the text: a brief exhortation to the readers urging them to closely examine his words, followed by a small selection of verses, often seamlessly interwoven into the text, which introduces additional material to encourages readers to meditate.

There are 260 references to and quotations from the Bible inserted throughout the text of the *Mirror*. These references often summarize verses or borrow language from verses without quoting them directly. Occasionally, the references are part of another source that mentions the biblical passage. For example, in a discussion of the return route taken by the Wise Men after being warned not to return to Herod, the text reads: 'Ferthyrmore also ʒe schal [vndyrstande] that Seyint Gregory seyth vpon that texte of the gospel of thys same daye: "Per aliam viam reuersi sunt in regionem suam." Thys ys to seye: "Be anothyr weye they turned aʒen in here contry"' (44/234–7). The reference to Matthew 1: 23 is intermingled with the Latin quotation from Gregory the Great's *Homily 10*, which comments on the passage.

However, the majority of biblical allusions are in the form of direct quotations or summaries of the passage. Direct quotations of

Scripture vary in length, ranging from a single line up to full paragraphs. The majority of the quotations, 226, are taken from the Gospel accounts to provide the framework for the narrative of the life of Christ found in the *Mirror*. All but twenty of the biblical quotations are in Middle English. Those twenty selections appearing in Latin are followed immediately by a Middle English translation. Fifteen of the twenty Latin passages are from the Old Testament. Of the other five, three are general summaries of the contents of the verses and two are prophecies concerning Christ.

With so many verses intermingled throughout the text of the *Mirror*, the author relies on commentaries to provide context for the numerous biblical passages. The *Mirror* often turns to commentaries to provide background about names, to explain unfamiliar customs, and to fill in the narrative gaps found in the biblical extracts. Throughout the *Mirror*, three works are consistently utilized to enhance the account of the life of Christ by adding detail to the well-known story: Nicholas of Lyre's *Postilla*, Peter Comestor's *Historia Scholastica*, and Jacobus de Voragine's *Legenda Aurea*. Anecdotal selections from the works are placed throughout the *Mirror* to add depth to the accounts of important events in the life of Christ. This is done by borrowing little-known aspects of the story from commentators, such as using Nicholas of Lyre's *Postilla* to assert that the pinnacle on which the Devil tempts Christ was, in actuality, a flat roof (63/46–7), or retelling an anecdote concerning King Herod from Peter Comestor's *Historia* (51/62–74). In another instance, the *Mirror* author uses Jacobus de Voragine's *Legenda* to comment on how the Church of Rome honoured the Virgin Mary for being the first person to whom Christ appeared following his resurrection (142/57–60). Drawn from the three commentaries, these accounts weave together rich details that allow readers to picture the events being portrayed and, in turn, attempt to induce affective responses from them. In following the two masters of biblical exegesis and the popular collection of saints' lives, the *Mirror* brings to the forefront a commentary on the literal meaning of the text, only occasionally relying on other reputed authorities to arrange an allegorical or anagogical interpretation of the scriptural passage in question.

As the narrative structure of the *Mirror* progresses, Nicholas of Lyre's *Postilla* emerges as an important source. The *Postilla* was a popular biblical commentary and the *Mirror* author uses it for this purpose. He draws on Nicholas of Lyre for everything from a discussion of the apparent unease of Mary at seeing an angel in chapter 3 to an anecdote found in chapter 11 about the King of France being pricked by rushes that were as sharp as the thorns used on the crown of thorns worn by Christ. The reliance on the commentary of Nicholas of Lyre throughout the text places him in a position of authority within the text while providing English translations of relevant passages from the *Postilla*. Another reason the *Mirror* author may have chosen Nicholas of Lyre was the latter's reputation as an expert on Jewish custom and history. He was believed to have befriended and disseminated the works of important Rabbis and the *Mirror* author uses Nicholas of Lyre's explanation of Jewish custom to explain Caiaphas's rending of his garments at the words of Jesus, which the high priest perceived to be blasphemous.[38]

Peter Comestor's *Historia Scholastica* was probably chosen for similar reasons. The *Historia* is a guide to the historical books of the Bible, which quotes from them while commenting on difficult and important points. Much of the popularity of the *Historia* derived from its focus on the literal sense of the Bible, a reason the *Mirror* author mentions for choosing the work when he says that Nicholas of Lyre and Peter Comestor both adhered to the 'lettural vndyrstandynge' (6/122). Much like Nicholas of Lyre, Peter Comestor was also recognized as an authority on Jewish custom, and that belief probably became a key factor in the use of his work.

While the author of the *Mirror* often quotes directly from the three sources, many quotations attributed to other doctors and works were often taken directly from Peter Comestor and from the *Legenda*. The *Legenda* was used by the *Mirror* author to access sources such as St Bernard of Clairvaux, Richard of St Victor, Peter of Ravenna (also known as Peter Chrysologus), Remigius, and the *Gospel of Nicodemus*. In a discussion of the sweetness of the name of Christ, for example, the *Mirror* author writes:

Thys ys the name that ys so suete and confortable to the louyers of God, for as Seyint Bernarde seyth hyt ys hony in the mowthe, melodye in the ere, and in the herte a suetnesse þat maye not be tolde. Thys name also, as Seyint Bernarde seyt, as oyle schynyth iprechyd; hyt fethyth ithowgth; hyt esyeth and an vnvctyth icalled into helpe. (37/71–6).

---

[38] See Beryl Smalley, *The Study of the Bible in the Middle Ages*, 3rd edn. (Notre Dame, Ind.:, 1983), 189–91.

Both passages, which are attributed to St Bernard, originate with the
Legenda.[39] Another example occurs when the discussion turns to the
topic of how King Herod committed suicide. The *Mirror* attributes
the account to St Remigius. However, the passage derives from the
Legenda:[40] 'Aftyr thys ʒe maye thynke how Kynge Herowde for thys
synne and othyre þat he hadde doo, be þe suffraunce of God sclewe
hymselfe wyth the same knyfe þat he paryde an appyl with, as Seyint
Remygye seyth' (52/97–100).

Throughout the *Mirror*, the *Legenda* provides various additions to
the narrative. For example, chapter 8 offers a discussion of the Virgin
Mary's purification following the birth of Christ. It relies on a
number of sources, including the *Legenda*, but it follows the
discussion of Mary with an exact translation of the passage concerning a noble lady who experiences a vision of the Virgin Mary (48/
113–32). It is a verbatim translation from Latin to English of the
passage that concludes the same discussion in the work of Jacobus de
Voragine.[41]

Peter Comestor's *Historia Scholastica* is used in a similar manner as
the *Legenda* when it provides references to the *Epistle of Clement*, the
Book of Rightful Men, and, on occasion, St Jerome. The *Mirror* relies
on the *Historia* when discussing Jerome's account of Judas hanging
himself: 'and in þat he offendyde God more, as Seinte Ierom seyth,
`þenne' whenne he betrayede hym' (105/52–4). At the same point in
Peter Comestor's commentary, the following is found: 'Dicit Hier-
onymus super CVIII psal. quia magis offendit Iudas Deum, quando
se suspendit, quam in hoc quod cum prodidit.'[42] The *Mirror* author
also alludes to an otherwise unknown source when describing Mary's
choice to stay with Elizabeth until John the Baptist was born: 'and as
hyt ys red in the Boke of Ryghful Men sche was the fyrste that lefte
hym vp fro the erthe' (28/231–2). The *Book of Rightful Men* has not
been identified, but a passage at the same point in a similar discussion
within the *Historia* states that it was a book with which Peter
Comestor was familiar: 'Et legitur in libro Iustorum, quod beata
Virgo eum primo levavit a terra.'[43]

---

[39] 'Nomen quod secundum Bernardum est in ore mel, in aure melos et in corde
iubilus;nomen quod, sicut dicit idem Bernardus, instar olei lucet praedicatum, pascit
recogitatum, lenit et ungit inuocatum'; Jacobus de Voragine, *Legenda Aurea*, ed. Maggioni,
i. 121.

[40] Ibid. 102.   [41] Ibid.249–50.

[42] Peter Comestor, *Historia Scholastica*, PL 198: 1625, cap. CLXII.

[43] Ibid., col. 1538B, cap. III.

It seems that the *Mirror* author's intention in drawing on these three main sources was to interweave well-recognized religious authorities in a detailed and accessible account of Christ's life. This approach facilitated the transmision of the familiar story of the thirty-three years of Christ in a way that shows fidelity to biblical sources while emphasizing seemingly insignificant details that inspire readers to meditate upon the humanity and suffering of Christ. Drawing on established authorities like Peter Comestor, Nicholas of Lyre, and the *Legenda* allowed the author to provide an authoritative text that relates the life of Christ while providing details not found in the *MVC* or Nicholas Love's *Mirror of the Blessed Life of Jesus Christ*.

c. Approved Women

When the author of the *Mirror to Devout People* says he will incorporate the writings of some 'approuyd wymmen', he refers to the works of St Birgitta of Sweden, St Catherine of Siena, St Mechtild of Hackeborn, and Elizabeth of Töss.[44] The popularity of these four mystics flowered during the fifteenth century. Their writings were some of the first works of women's theology translated into English. Within a decade of the founding of Syon Abbey translations of their works appeared in English and it is likely that several of these texts were translated at Syon.[45] Their works, along with the founding of Syon Abbey and its outreach to the laity, were central to the increased demand for women's theological writings in the early decades of the fifteenth century.[46] Within a few years of their translation they were regularly circulating in devotional texts and seemed to be some of the most popular theological works in circulation. They were regularly paired with native English contemplative and devotional materials and their works were frequently circulated in Syon-related and Carthusian writings.[47]

[44] For the life of St Brigitta in Middle English, see *The Liber Celestis of St. Bridget of Sweden*, ed. Roger Ellis, 2 vols., EETS os 291 (1987). The life of Elizabeth of Töss is used in the thirty-third chapter of the *Mirror*. It is taken directly from Jacobus de Voragine's *Legenda Aurea* (ii. 1157) and is used as an illustration of miracles for which John the Evangelist is responsible.

[45] Hope Emily Allen discusses this possibility in the introduction to *The Book of Margery Kempe*, ed. S. B. Meech and H. E. Allen, EETS os 212 (1940), p. lxvi.

[46] See Kerby-Fulton, 'The 15th Century', 574–5.

[47] For the circulation of the works of the four female saints, see Rosalynn Voaden, 'The Company She Keeps: Mechtild of Hackeborn in Late-Medieval Devotional Compilations', in Voaden (ed.), *Prophets Abroad: The Reception of Continental Holy Women in Late-Medieval England* (Cambridge, 1999), 51–69; 'Mechtild of Hackeborn', in Alastair Minnis

While the *Mirror* uses Mechtild twice and Catherine once, Birgitta of Sweden is used extensively throughout four chapters. The cult of Birgitta proliferated in England during the early fifteenth century when her revelations and the devotional writings associated with her order became an integral part of English devotional writings. The author draws on Birgitta's *Revelaciones* to inform readers about events in Christ's life and to provide them with an account of Christ's childhood. This information concerning the life of Christ is only available through Mary's accounts of her son as given to Birgitta in a series of visions. In the fifth chapter, Mary is portrayed as an author who passes on her material to those who will tell her story. The *Mirror* author writes about the birth of Christ; however, the birth is told entirely from the perspective of St Birgitta, who emphasizes its miraculous nature by stressing the magnificence of the Christ child, who outshone the candles, and the way in which the body of Mary returned to its immaculate state immediately following the delivery.

In addition to aiding Birgitta through the rewarding of visions, Mary also relates the information necessary for the evangelists to give an accurate account of the story of the birth of Christ. The role of Mary as *auctor* is established when we are told, in chapter 5 of the *Mirror*: 'But oure lady kepte wel all in here herte haply þat sche mygth the bettyr telle hyt to hem that schulde wryte hyt aftyrwarde' (34/200–1).[48] In chapter 11, drawing on Book 6, chapter 58 of the *Revelaciones*, the *Mirror* uses the visions of Birgitta to fill in the details of the life of Christ from the age of 12 until his baptism in the River Jordan. According to Birgitta, these lost years were occupied in preparation for his later ministry as she recounts miracles performed by a young Christ.

However, the most important use of Birgitta's *Revelaciones* occurs in the twenty-second chapter of the *Mirror* when the Crucifixion is described in detail. Birgitta's account vividly portrays the dying Christ and provides a focal point upon which readers can meditate

and Rosalynn Voaden (eds.), *Medieval Holy Women in the Christian Tradition c. 1100–c. 1500* (Turnhout, 2010), 431–52; Claire Sahlin, 'Holy Women of Scandinavia',ibid. 697–703; Suzanne Nofke, 'Catherine of Siena', ibid. 601–24.

[48] Rebecca Selman, 'Spirituality and Sex Change: *Horologium Sapientiae* and *Speculum devotorum*', in Denis Reveney and Christiania Whitehead (eds.), *Writing Religious Women: Female Spiritual and Textual Practices in Late Medieval England* (Toronto, 2000), 63–79, points out how this passage from the *Mirror* presents Mary in an authorial role providing the information to those who will hear and Birgitta as the ideal reader whose 'modes of acting and seeing, if followed by a nun . . . enable[ed] her to strive towards spiritual insights and understanding' (p. 74).

in order to experience the Saviour's suffering. Small details gain significance and allow for an increasing intensification of the reality of Christ's suffering. The reader is repeatedly told 'beholden' as Christ's body is broken through torture after torture. As the text continually calls upon readers actively to look at the suffering of Christ, it increases the intensity with which they experience the Passion.

Prior to the visions of Birgitta, the *Mirror* incorporates details from the life of Catherine of Siena, found in the *Legenda Maior* by Raymond of Capua, to discuss the proper discernment of visions. In chapter 3, following a long description of the Annunciation, Catherine of Siena is used to guide a discussion of how to discern godly visions from devilish ones. The lengthy quotation is often misidentified as coming from the *Dialogue*, which is understandable since the *Dialogue* also takes up the discernment of spirits. There are no extant manuscript copies of the *Legenda Maior*, and the first full English copy is Wynkyn de Worde's printed edition in the sixteenth century. However, the passage found in the *Mirror* does circulate in other manuscripts, including British Library, MS Harley 2409.[49] The passage provides readers with the knowledge to recognize God-given visions, whose initial bitterness becomes sweet, from those of the Devil, which begin sweetly but end with bitterness. Its advice is fairly standard and gives readers direction in preparation for the forthcoming visions of St Birgitta.

Mechtild of Hackeborn is used in a short passage found in chapter 29 of the *Mirror* that deals with the resurrection and first apocryphal appearance of Christ:

And att thys gloryus Resurreccyon ȝe maye thynke was a gret multytude of angyllys, for hyt ʻysʼ conteynyd in a reuelacyon of Seyint Mawte þat here semyde sche seygh sueche a muʻlʼtytude of angyllys aboute the sepulcre þat fro þe erthe vp to the skye they ʻwenteʼ aboute oure Lorde as hyt hadde be a walle. (141/27–31)

The passage relates Mechtild's vision of a wall of angels filling the sky following Christ's resurrection and is taken from the Middle English translation of her *Liber specialis gratiae*, titled *The Booke of Gostlye Grace* in its English form.[50] Mechtild (or St Maute, as she is called in

[49] See Jennifer N. Brown, 'The Many Misattributions of Catherine of Siena: Beyond the Orchard in England', *Journal of Medieval Religious Cultures*, 41 (2015), 67–84.

[50] See *The Booke of Gostlye Grace of Mechtild of Hackeborn*, ed. Theresa A. Halligan (Toronto, 1979), 181.2–6. While this is the only modern edition of the Middle English

many Middle English translations including the *Mirror*) was a popular figure in late medieval English religious writing, and her work was frequently excerpted in devotional texts, often with links to Syon Abbey.[51]

Along with the *Mirror to Devout People*, Mechtild's *Booke* also appears in *The Myroure of oure Ladye*, a Middle English guide for the nuns at Syon concerning the liturgy.[52] *The Myroure of oure Ladye* contains an English translation of the Birgittine Breviary, Hours, Masses, and Offices, along with an account, written in Latin by Birgitta's confessor Master Peter, concerning how the Birgittine service was revealed to her by an angel. It is uncertain when the *Myroure* was written since the only surviving copy is a manuscript dating to the late fifteenth or early sixteenth century. It is likely, however, that the original copy of the work was composed between 1420 and 1448.[53] *The Myroure of oure Ladye* contains two excerpts from Mechtild's *Booke*: one to inform readers that they can miss confession before Mass or divine service with a legitimate reason and the second to recommend the reading of the prayers Christ gave to Mechtild.[54] Not only does Mechtild's work appear in Syon's library, the Syon Abbey library catalogue lists seven copies of it.[55] Three of the books are sixteenth-century printed editions, but the other four are manuscripts that contain Mechtild's work in varying stages of completion. Three manuscripts are in Latin, only one of which contains a complete copy of the *Liber*; however, the fourth manuscript, entitled *Reuelaciones beate Matildis in anglico*, contains the entire English translation of the *Liber*.

The choice of the three female saints reveals an awareness by the author of the *Mirror* of what writings by female saints were palatable

translation of Mechtild's text, there are some problems with it that are spelled out in a review by N. F. Blake in *Speculum*,56 (1981), 386–9.

[51] For a list of Middle English manuscripts in which Mechtild's book appears, see *The Booke*, ed. Halligan, 47–59.

[52] *The Myroure of Oure Ladye containing a Devotional Treatise of the Offices Used by the Sisters of the Brigittine Monastery of Sion at Isleworth during the Fifteenth and Sixteenth Centuries*, ed. John Henry Blunt, EETS ES 19 (1873).

[53] Ibid. pp. vii–viii and Ann M. Hutchison, 'Devotional Reading in the Monastery and in the Household', in Michael G. Sargent (ed.), *De Cella in Seculum: Religious and Secular Life and Devotion in Late Medieval England* (Cambridge, 1989), 215–28 at 220.

[54] Voaden, 'The Company She Keeps', 54–5; *The Booke*, ed. Halligan, 50.

[55] *Syon Abbey*, ed. Vincent Gillespie, Corpus of British Medieval Library Catalogues, 9 (London, 2001) which supersedes *Catalogue of the Library of Syon Monastery Isleworth*, ed. Mary Bateson (Cambridge, 1898).

for his intended audience. Within the library at Syon Abbey were numerous copies of the writings of Birgitta of Sweden, Catherine of Siena, and Mechtild of Hackeborn and their popularity among the Birgittines made them an obvious choice for inclusion in the *Mirror*.

d. 'Othyr Doctorys'

The sources the *Mirror* author describes as the 'othyr doctorys' that he will use 'in diuerse placys, as to the moral vertuys' are primarily made up of the Venerable Bede, St Bernard, Henry Suso, Adam the Carthusian (Adam of Dryburgh), St Bernard of Clairvaux, and Walter Hilton. For the most part, these authors are used sparingly, sometimes clearly taken from a *florilegium* and applied briefly for context or to make a point about a scriptural passage. Richard of St Victor and Peter of Ravenna are quoted second-hand and not from original texts, while nearly all of quotations attributed to Bernard are taken from the *Legenda*. Other authors are used more extensively, such as Henry Suso, whose *Horologium Sapientiae* had gained popularity in England after being translated, abridged, and rearranged as *The Seven Poyntes of Trewe Wisdom*.[56]

In the Preface to the *Mirror*, the author draws on a large passage from Suso, introducing the work as the 'Orlege of wisdom' (5/77) before providing a lengthy quotation (5/77–92). The *Horologium* and the *Seven Poyntes* share a great deal with the *Mirror*, such as the latter's familiar and largely conventional preface. The author of the *Seven Poyntes* relates his desire to assist others in their spiritual journey by exposing them to a variety of manuals offering spiritual guidance.

Another use of sources that provides a unique outcome differing from the original texts occurs in the final chapter of the *Mirror* when the author departs from his normal *modus operandi* in order to prepare the reader for the Latin prayer *O intemerata*, which follows the *Mirror* in both manuscripts. The final chapter of the *Mirror* is taken from a sermon by Peter Damien attributed to Bede, a sermon by Adam the Carthusian, and a grouping of three or four Mary legends. Following a brief description of the Apostles' vision of Christ rising to Heaven, the author says he will fulfil an earlier promise made in chapter 22 to recount how St John the Evangelist earned certain 'graces': (1) the special love of Jesus who loved John more than any other; (2) the

---

[56] See Henry Suso, 'Orologium Sapientiae or The Seven Poyntes of Trewe Wisdom, aus MS. Douce 114', ed. K. Horstmann, *Anglia*, 10 (1887), 323–89.

grace of virginity; (3) access to God's 'priuytees'; and (4) the privilege
of watching over Mary after the death of Christ. The *Mirror* author
spends nearly three hundred lines relating numerous instances in
John's life that earned him this distinct honour. He interweaves the
Legenda with the sermons by Bede, Peter Damien, and Adam the
Carthusian so effortlessly that his sources are nearly indistinguishable
and, as a result, creates a hybrid narrative voice that differs noticeably
from the previous thirty-two chapters. Along with the three sermons,
the *Mirror* author adds the Mary legends to the mix, incorporating
them briefly near the end of the chapter to show the importance of
reciting *O intemerata* on a daily basis. The miracles relate how
different people from varying walks of life were saved from eternal
damnation or lengthy purgatory because of their faithfulness in
repeating this prayer.

6. EDITORIAL METHOD

The edition relies on Gg as its copy text. All spelling from Gg is
reproduced and all interlineations are noted (marked ʽ. . .ʼ in the text).
Marginal corrections in Gg are marked in the same manner in the
text. The marginalia from N are listed in the Explanatory Notes,
unless they are a correction introduced into the text. Such corrections
are marked in the text and noted in the apparatus. In transcribing, I
have taken a loop on final -*r* as -*re* based on a number of instances in
which the final -*e* was necessary for spelling (e.g. *thr*- is followed by a
pronounced loop to indicate *thre*). Punctuation, paragraph divisions,
and capitalizations are my own. However, the capitalization of
marginalia is preserved as it appears. Manuscript *i/j* and *u/v* are
retained.

Abbreviations, including ampersands, are expanded silently with
the most commonly used unabbreviated spelling found in Gg. The
contraction *ihu* with a macron over the *u* is transcribed *Ihesu*.
Alterations and emendations are signalled in brackets ([. . .]). All
omissions are noted in the apparatus but not in the text. Scribal
corrections are accepted and noted in the apparatus. Emendations are
made where the manuscript is illegible or where scribal error or
omission has occurred (e.g. due to eye skip). All decisions regarding
emendations are based on reference to the source, usage in the two
manuscripts, or an attempt to correct scribal error. Minor emendations are not discussed in the Explanatory Notes. All lengthy

emendations and cruxes, along with conjectural emendations, are discussed in the Explanatory Notes.

The apparatus includes a full account of variants for the text. All substantive and grammatical variations, with a few exceptions, are included. I have taken as non-substantive many common examples of variation: between *was* and *were* (often used interchangeably with plural subjects), between *y-* or *ȝ-* and *yh-* (for example, *yhe* and *ye* or *ȝe*), between *will* and *wole*, between *afforeseyde*, *beforeseyde*, and *forseyde*, between *tofore* and *afore*, and between *before* and *afore* (in every instance the Gg scribe uses *before* and the N scribe *afore*). Linguistic variations, such as when the Gg scribe uses *th* for *d* (e.g. *theserte* for *desert* and *drethe* for *drede*), are not noted in the apparatus.

Conventions and abbreviations used throughout the variants are as follows:

]	separates a lemma from its variant(s)
canc.	cancelled, cancellation
con. em.	conjectural emendation
corr.	corrected, correction
exp.	expunged
fol.	followed
eras.	erased, erasure
illeg.	illegible
inser.	insertion
marg.	margin, marginal
om.	omitted
prec.	preceded

BIBLIOGRAPHY

A. EDITIONS OF THE *MIRROR TO DEVOUT PEOPLE*

Banks, John Patrick, '*Speculum Devotorum*: An Edition with Commentary' (Ph.D. diss., Fordham University, 1959).

The 'Speculum Devotorum' of an Anonymous Carthusian of Sheen, Edited from the Manuscripts Cambridge University Library Gg. 1.6 and Foyle, with an Introduction and a Glossary, ed. James Hogg, Analecta Cartusiana, 12–13 (Salzburg, 1973–4).

Wilsher, Bridget Ann, 'An Edition of "Speculum Devotorum," a Fifteenth Century English Meditation on the Life and Passion of Christ, with an Introduction and Notes' (M.Phil. thesis, University of London, 1956).

B. PRIMARY TEXTS AND SOURCES

Adam the Carthusian, *De Quadripartito Exercitio Cellae*, in *PL* 153: 787–884.

—— 'Sermo 33', *Sermones*, in *PL* 198: 91–440.

Ambrose, Saint, *Expositio Euangelii secundum Lucam*, in *Sancti Ambrosii Mediolanensis Opera*, ed. M. Adriaen, CCSL 14 (Turnholt, 1957).

The Apocryphal New Testament: A Collection of Apocryphal Christian Literature in an English Translation, ed. J. K. Elliott (Oxford, 1999).

Augustine, St, *In Iohannis Euangelium Tractatus CXXIV*, ed. Augustino Mayer, CCSL 36 (Turnhout, 1954).

—— *Sancti Aureli Augustini De fide et symbolo, De fide et operibus, De agone christiano, De continentia, De bono coniugali, De sancta virginitate, De bono viduitatis, De adulterinis coniugiis lib. II, De mendacio, Contra mendacium, De opere monachorum, De divinatione daemonum, De cura pro mortuis gerenda, De patientia*, ed. Joseph Zycha, CSEL 41 (Vienna, 1900).

—— Sermo CVIII (*PL* 38).

—— 'Sermo 98', in *Sancti Aurelii Augustini Hipponensis Episcopi Opera Omnia*, in *PL* 38: 591–5.

—— 'Le sermon LI de saint Augustin sur les généalogies du Christ selon Matthieu et selon Luc', ed. Pierre Verbraken, *RB* 91 (1981), 20–45.

Augustine, (pseudo) St, *Liber Soliloquiorum Animae ad Deum*, in *PL* 40: 863–902.

—— *Sermo* 370, *De Natiuitate Domini*, in *PL* 39: 1657–9.

Bede the Venerable, *In Marci Euangelium Expositio*, CCSL 120, ed. D. Hurst (Turnhout, 1960).

—— 'In primam partem Samuhelis libri iiii', in *Opera*, ed. D. Hurst, CCSL 119 (Turnhout, 1962).

—— *Opera homiletica*, ed. D. Hurst, CCSL 122 (Turnhout, 1955).

Bernard of Clairvaux, St, *Sancti Bernardi Opera*, ed. Jean Leclercq, Charles H. Talbot, and Henri Rochais, 8 vols. (Rome, 1957–79).

Biblia Sacra: iuxta Vulgatam versionem, ed. B. Fischer et al., 4th edn. (Stuttgart, 1994).

Bridget, St, *Revelaciones, Book VI*, ed. Berger Bergh (Stockholm, 1991).

—— *Revelaciones, Book VII*, ed. Berger Bergh (Stockholm, 1978).

—— *Revelaciones, Book VIII*, ed. Hans Aili (Stockholm, 2002).

The Chartae of the Carthusian General Chapter: Paris, Bib. Nat. MS Latin 10888, ed. Michael G. Sargent and James Hogg, Analecta Cartusiana, 100: 6, II (Salzburg, 1985).

Chrysostom (pseudo), St John, *Opus imperfectum in Matthaeum*, in *PG* 54: 611–946.

Concilia Magnae Britanniae et Hiberniae, iii, ed. D. Wilkins (London, 1737).

Damian, Peter, *Sermones*, ed. Giovanni Lucchesi, CCCM 57 (Turnhout, 1983).

Gregory I, Pope, *Homiliae in Evangelia*, ed. Raymond Etaix, CCSL 141 (Turnhout, 1999).

—— *Moralia in Iob*, ed. Mark Adriaen, CCSL 143, 143A, 143B (Turnhout, 1979–81).

Hilton, Walter, *The Scale of Perfection*, ed. Thomas H. Bestul (Kalamazoo, 2000).

Iohannis de Caulibus, *Meditaciones Vitae Christi, olim S. Bonauenturo attributae*, ed. Mary Stallings-Taney, CCCM 153 (Turnhout, 1997).

Jacobus de Voragine, *Legenda Aurea*, ed. Giovanni Paolo Maggioni, 2 vols. (Florence, 1998).

Jerome, St, *De perpetua uirginitate Beatae Mariae aduersus Heluidium*, in *PL* 23: 183–206.

—— *Opera*, ed. D. Hurst and M. Anastos, CCSL 72–80 (Turnhout, 1969).

Josephus, *The Jewish War*, ed. and trans. Gaalya Cornfeld (Grand Rapids, Mich., 1982).

Kempe, Margery, *The Book of Margery Kempe: The Text from the Unique ms. Owned by Colonel W. Butler-Bowdon*, ed. Sanford Brown Meech and Hope Emily Allen, EETS OS 212 (1940).

Love, Nicholas, *Mirror of the Blessed Life of Christ: A Full Critical Edition Based on Cambridge, University Library, Additional MSS 6578 and 6686 with Introduction, Notes and Glossary*, ed. Michael Sargent (Exeter, 2005).

Mandeville, Sir John, *Mandeville's Travels, Translated from the French of Jean d'Outremeuse. Edited from MS. Cotton Titus C. XVI in the British Museum*, ed. P. Hamelius, 2 vols., EETS OS 153–4 (1919–23).

Matthew Paris, *The Life of St. Edmund*, ed. C. H. Lawrence (Oxford, 1996).

Mechtild of Hackeborn, *The Booke of Gostlye Grace of Mechtild of Hackeborn*, ed. Theresa A. Halligan (Toronto, 1979).

The Myroure of Oure Ladye Containing a Devotional Treatise of the Offices

Used by the Sisters of the Brigittine Monastery of Sion at Isleworth during the Fifteenth and Sixteenth Centuries, ed. John Henry Blunt, EETS ES 19 (1873).

Nichodemus his gospel, ed. John Warrin ([Rouen], 1635).

Nicholas of Lyre, *Postilla super totam Bibliam* (Strasbourg, 1477).

Peter Comestor, *Historia Scholastica*, in *PL* 198: 1537–1644.

Pseudo-Matthew, *Libri de Nativitate Mariae*, ed. Jan Gijsel, CCSA 9 (Turnhout, 1997).

Quodvultdeus, St, *Opera Quodvultdeo Carthaginiensi Episcopo Tributa*, ed. René Braun, CCSL 60 (Turnhout, 1976).

Radbertus, Paschasius, *Expositio in Matheo libri XII*, ed. Beda Paulus, CCSM 56–56B (Turnhout, 1984).

——*Pascasii Radberti Epistula Beati Hieronymi ad Paulam et Eustochium de Assumptione Sanctae Mariae Virginis*, ed. Albert Ripberger, CCCM 56C (Turnhout, 1985).

Raymund of Capua, *Legenda Maior*: 'De S. Catharina Senensi virgine de poenitentia S. Dominici', in *Acta Sanctorum*, ed. Johannes Bolland, Godefridus Henschenius, and Daniel van Papenbroeck, rev. Jean Baptist Carnandet, April, vol. 3 (Paris, 1866), 862–967.

Sarum Missal: Edited from Three Early Manuscripts, ed. J. Wickham-Legg (Oxford, 1969).

Suso, Henry, *Horologium Sapientiae*, ed. Pius Künzle (Fribourg, 1977).

——'Orologium Sapientiae or The Seven Poyntes of Trewe Wisdom, aus MS. Douce 114', ed. K. Horstmann, *Anglia*, 10 (1887), 323–89.

——*Watch upon the Hours*, trans. Edmund Colledge (Washington, DC, 1994).

Testamenta Eboracensia: or, Wills Registered at York, Illustrative of the History, Manners, Language, Statistics, &c., of the Province of York, from the Year 1300 downwards, Part II, ed. J. Raine, Surtees Society, 30 (Durham, 1855).

Thomas de Cantimpré, *Bonum universale de apibus*, ed. George Colvener (Douai, 1627).

The Three Kings of Cologne: An Early English Translation of the 'Historia Trium Regum' by John Hildesheim. Two Parallel Texts, Edited from the MSS., Together with the Latin Text, ed. C. Horstmann, EETS OS 85 (1886).

The Two Middle English Translations of the Revelations of St. Elizabeth of Hungary, ed. Sarah McNamer, Middle English Texts, 28 (Heidelberg, 1996).

Yorkshire Writers: Richard Rolle and his Followers, ed. C. Horstmann (1895–6, repr. Rochester, NY, 1999).

C. SECONDARY SOURCES

Aungier, G. J., *The History and Antiquities of Syon Monastery, the Parish of Isleworth and the Chapelry of Hounslow* (London, 1840).

Barratt, Alexandra, 'The Revelations of Saint Elizabeth of Hungary', *The Library*, Sixth Series, 14 (1992), 1–11.

Beaty, Nancy Lee, *The Craft of Dying: A Study of the Literary Tradition of the Ars Moriendi in England* (New Haven, 1970).

Beckett, N., 'St. Bridget, Henry V and Syon Abbey', in J. Hogg (ed.), *Studies in St. Birgitta and the Brigittine Order*, 2 vols., Analecta Cartusiana, 35: 19 (Salzburg, 1993), ii. 125–50.

Benskin, Michael, 'The Letters ⟨þ⟩ and ⟨y⟩ in later Middle English, and Some Related Matters', *Journal of the Society of Archivists*, 7 (1982), 13–30.

Brantley, Jessica, 'The Visual Environment of Carthusian Texts: Decoration and Illustration in Notre Dame 67', in Mann and Nolan (eds.), *The Text in the Community*, 173–216.

Brown, Jennifer N., 'The Many Misattributions of Catherine of Siena: Beyond the Orchard in England', *Journal of Medieval Religious Cultures*, 41 (2015), 67–84.

Budney, Mildred, 'Assembly Marks in the Vivian Bible and Scribal, Editorial, and Organizational Marks in Medieval Books', in Linda L. Brownrigg (ed.), *Making the Medieval Book: Techniques of Production* (Los Altos Hills, Calif., 1995), 199–239.

de Hamel, C. F. R., *Syon Abbey: The Library of the Bridgettine Nuns and their Peregrinations after the Reformation* (Roxburghe Club, 1991).

Deansley, Margaret, 'Vernacular Books in England in the Fourteenth and Fifteenth Centuries', *Modern Language Review*, 15 (1920), 349–58.

Doyle, A. I., 'Book Production by the Monastic Orders in England (*c.*1375–1530): Assessing the Evidence', in Brownrigg, Linda (ed.), *Medieval Book Production: Assessing the Evidence* (Los Altos Hills, Calif., 1990), 1–19.

Edwards, A. S. G., 'The Contexts of Notre Dame 67', in Mann and Nolan (eds.), *The Text in the Community*, 107–28.

Ehrman, Bart D., and Plunkett, Mark A., 'The Angel and the Agony: The Textual Problem of Luke 22:43–4', *Catholic Biblical Quarterly*, 45 (1983), 401–16.

Ellis, Roger, 'Further Thoughts on the Spirituality of Syon Abbey', in William F. Pollard and Robert Boenig (eds.), *Mysticism and Spirituality in Medieval England* (Cambridge, 1997), 219–43.

Forrest, Ian, *The Detection of Heresy in Late Medieval England* (Oxford, 2005).

Gillespie, Vincent, 'Dial M for Mystic: Mystical Texts in the Library of Syon Abbey and the Spirituality of the Syon Brethren', in Gillespie (ed.),

Looking in Holy Books: Essays on Late Medieval Religious Writing in England (Turnhout, 2011), 175–207.

—— 'The Haunted Text: Reflections in *The Mirror to Deuout People*', in Mann and Nolan (eds.), *The Text in the Community*, 129–72.

—— ' "Hid Diuinite": The Spirituality of the English Syon Brethren', in E. A. Jones (ed.), *The Medieval Mystical Tradition in England: Exeter Symposium VII* (Cambridge, 2004), 189–206.

Hogg, James, 'Oswald de Corda, a Forgotten Carthusian of Nördlingen', in Hogg (ed.), *Kartäusermystick und Mystiker, III*, Analecta Cartusiana, 55: 3 (Salzburg, 1982), 181–5.

Hutchison, Ann M., 'Devotional Reading in the Monastery and in the Household', in Michael G. Sargent (ed.), *De Cella in Seculum: Religious and Secular Life and Devotion in Late Medieval England* (Cambridge, 1989), 215–28.

—— 'What the Nuns Read: Literary Evidence from the English Bridgettine House, Syon Abbey', *Medieval Studies*, 57 (1995), 205–22.

The Index of Middle English Verse, ed. Carleton Brown and Rossell Hope Robbins (New York, 1943).

Index of Printed Middle English Prose, ed. R. E. Lewis, N. F. Blake, and A. S. G. Edwards, Garland Reference Library of the Humanities, 537 (New York, 1985).

Johnson, Ian, 'Prologue and Practice: Middle English Lives of Christ', in Roger Ellis et al. (eds.), *The Medieval Translator: The Theory and Practice of Translation in the Middle Ages* (Cambridge, 1989), 69–85.

Jolliffe, P. S., *Check-List of Middle English Prose Writings of Spiritual Guidance* (Toronto, 1974).

Ker, N. R., *Medieval Libraries of Great Britain*, 2nd edn. (London, 1964).

Kerby-Fulton, Kathryn, *Books under Suspicion: Censorship and Tolerance of Revelatory Writing in Late Medieval England* (Notre Dame, Ind., 2006).

—— 'The 15th Century as the Golden Age of Women's Theology in English', in Stephen Kelly and Ryan Perry (eds.), *Devotional Culture in Late Medieval England and Europe: Diverse Imaginations of Christ's Life* (Turnhout, 2014), 573–91.

Kirchberger, Clare, *The Goad of Love* (London, 1952).

The Library of William Foyle, Part I: Medieval and Renaissance Manuscripts: Tuesday 11, July 2000 / Christie's (London, 2000).

McKitterick, David, *Cambridge University Library: A History. The Eighteenth and Nineteenth Centuries* (Cambridge, 1986).

—— 'Cockerell, Sydney Morris (1906–1987)', *ODNB*, accessed 3 June 2015.

Mann, Jill, and Nolan, Maura B. (eds.), *The Text in the Community: Essays on Medieval Works, Manuscripts, Authors, and Readers* (Notre Dame, Ind., 2006).

A Manual of the Writings in Middle English, 1050–1500, ix, ed. Albert E. Hartung (New Haven, 1993).

Meale, Carol M. (ed.), *Women and Literature in Britain, 1150–1500*, 2nd edn. (Cambridge, 1996).

Medieval Libraries of Great Britain: A List of Surviving Books, edited by N. R. Ker: A Supplement to the Second Edition, ed. Andrew G. Watson (London, 1987).

Minnis, Alastair, and Voaden, Rosalynn (eds.), *Medieval Holy Women in the Christian Tradition c. 1100–c. 1500* (Turnhout, 2010).

Nofke, Suzanne, 'Catherine of Siena', in Minnis and Voaden (eds.), *Medieval Holy Women*, 601–24.

Oates, J. C. T., *Cambridge University Library: A History from the Beginnings to the Copyright Act of Queen Anne* (Cambridge, 1986).

O'Connor, Mary C., *The Art of Dying Well* (New York, 1942).

Panofsky, Erwin, *Early Netherlandish Painting: Its Origin and Character*, 2 vols. (Cambridge, Mass., 1953).

Reeves, A. C., 'Fitzhugh, Henry, third Baron Fitzhugh (1363?–1425), administrator and diplomat', *ODNB* (accessed 19 August 2011).

Riehle, Wolfgang, *The Middle English Mystics*, trans. Bernard Standring (London, 1981).

Ringrose, Jayne, 'The Royal Library: John Moore and his Books', in Peter Fox (ed.), *Cambridge University Library: Great Collections* (Cambridge, 1998), 78–89.

Robinson, Fred C., 'Syntactical Glosses in Latin Manuscripts of Anglo-Saxon Provenance', *Speculum*, 48 (1973), 443–75.

Rouse, Mary A. and Richard H., 'Correction and Emendation of Texts in the Fifteenth Century and the Autograph of the *Opus Pacis* by "Oswaldus Anglicus"', in Sigrid Krämer and Michael Bernhard (eds.), *Scire Litteras: Forschungen zum mittelalterlichen Geistesleben* (Munich, 1988), 333–46.

Sahlin, Claire, 'Holy Women of Scandinavia', in Minnis and Voaden (eds.), *Medieval Holy Women*, 697–703.

Sargent, Michael G., 'The Problem of Uniformity in Carthusian Book Production from the *Opus Pacis* to the *Tertia Compilatio Statutorum*', in Richard Beadle and A. J. Piper (eds.), *New Science out of Old Books: Studies in Manuscripts and Early Printed Books in Honour of A. I. Doyle* (Aldershot, 1995).

Scott, Kathleen L., *Dated and Datable English Manuscript Borders c. 1395–1499* (London, 2002).

—— *Later Gothic Manuscripts 1390–1490*, Survey of Manuscripts Illuminated in the British Isles, 6 (London, 1996).

Selman, Rebecca, 'Spirituality and Sex Change: *Horologium Sapientiae* and *Speculum Devotorum*', in Denis Renevey and Christiania Whitehead (eds.), *Writing Religious Women: Female Spiritual and Textual Practices in Late Medieval England* (Toronto, 2000), 63–79.

Silver, Larry, 'Nature and Nature's God: Landscape and Cosmos of Albrecht Aldorfer', *Art Bulletin*, 81 (1999), 194–214.

Smalley, Beryl, *The Study of the Bible in the Middle Ages*, 3rd edn. (Notre Dame, Ind., 1983).

Somerset, Fiona, 'Censorship', in Alexandra Gillespie and Daniel Wakelin (eds.), *The Production of Books in England 1350–1500* (Cambridge, 2011), 239–58.

Sticca, Sandro, *The Planctus Mariae in the Dramatic Tradition of the Middle Ages* (Athens, Ga., 1988).

Syon Abbey, ed. Vincent Gillespie, Corpus of British Medieval Library Catalogues, 9 (London, 2001).

Tait, M. B., 'The Brigittine Monastery of Syon (Middlesex) with Special Reference to its Monastic Uses' (D.Phil. thesis, Oxford University, 1975).

Thompson, E. M., *The Carthusian Order in England* (London, 1930).

Tuckett, Christopher M., 'Luke 22, 43–44: The "Agony" in the Garden', in Adelbert Denaux (ed.), *New Testament Textual Criticism and Exegesis: Festschrift J. Delobel*, Bibliotheca Ephemeridum theologicarum Lovaniensium, 161 (Sterling, Va., 2002), 131–44.

Turville-Petre, Thorlac, 'Some Medieval English Manuscripts in the North-East Midlands', in Derek Pearsall (ed.), *Manuscripts and Readers in Fifteenth-Century England* (Cambridge, 1993), 125–41.

Vale, Brigette, 'Scrope, Henry, third Baron Scrope of Masham (*c.*1376–1415)', *ODNB*, accessed 16 July 2014.

Voaden, Rosalynn, 'The Company She Keeps: Mechtild of Hackeborn in Late-Medieval Devotional Compilations', in Voaden (ed.), *Prophets Abroad: The Reception of Continental Holy Women in Late-Medieval England* (Cambridge, 1996), 1–70.

—— 'Mechthild of Hackeborn', in Minnis and Voaden (eds.), *Medieval Holy Women*, 431–52.

Wakelin, Daniel, *Scribal Corrections and Literary Craft: English Manuscripts 1375–1510* (Cambridge, 2014)

Walther, Hans, *Initia carminum ac versuum Medii Aevi posterioris Latinorum* (Göttingen, 1969).

Watson, Nicholas, 'Censorship and Culture Change in Late Medieval England: Vernacular Theology, the Oxford Translation Debate, and Arundel's Constitutions of 1409', *Speculum*, 70 (1995), 822–64.

Wilmart, André, *Auteurs spirituals et textes dévots du moyen âge latin*, reproduction de l'édition parue en 1932 (Paris, 1971).

Wogan-Browne, Jocelyn, et al. (eds.), *The Idea of the Vernacular: An*

Anthology of Middle English Literary Theory, 1280–1520 (University Park, Pa., 1999).

Woodward, Michael Scott, 'Nicholas of Lyra on Beatific Vision: A Dissertation' (Ph.D. diss., University of Notre Dame, 1992).

A MIRROR TO DEVOUT PEOPLE
(SPECULUM DEVOTORUM)

Here begynnyth a prefacyon to the boke folowynge   f. 1^r

Gostly syster in Ihesu Cryste, I trowe hyt be not ȝytt fro ȝoure mynde
that whenne we spake laste togyderys I behette ȝow a medytacyon of
the Passyon of oure Lorde, the whyche promysse I haue not putte fro
`my´ mynde but be dyuerse tymys, be the grace of God, I haue ₅
parformyd hyt as I mygthte. Oure Lorde graunte hyt be to hym
pleseable and to ȝow profytable or to eny othyr deuot seruant of God.
But I do ȝow to wyte that be conseyle I `haue´ put to myche more
thanne I `be´hette ȝow, to more encresynge of ȝoure loue to God and
vertuys or eny othyr that mygth be grace of God profyte be the same, ₁₀
as ȝe maye see schortly in the tabyl folowynge thys prefacyon. For I
haue dyvydyd the boke folowynge in thre and thyrty chapetelys to the
worschype of the thre and thryty ȝeres that oure Sauyoure lyuyde in
erthe. And I haue sette tytyllys of hem alle in a tabyl aftyr thys
prefacyon afore the boke, that hosoeuere lykyth to rede hyt maye see ₁₅
schortly there all the matere of the boke folowynge and rede where
hym lykyth best, and that he mygthte þe sonnyr fynde that he
desyryth moste and the bettyr kepe hyt in mynde, and also redylokyr
fynde hyt yf hym lyste to s|ee hyt aȝen. Notwythstondynge hyt were f. 1^v
best, hoso myght haue tyme and laysyr therto to re`de´ hyt all as hyt ys ₂₀
sette.

Also, I haue besteryd ofte tymys to haue lefte thys bysynesse, bothe
for my vnworthynesse, and also for Bonauenture a cardynal and a
worthy clerke, made a boke of the same matere the whyche ys callyd
Vita Cristi. And most of all whenne I herde telle that a man of oure ₂₅
ordyr of charturhowse had iturnyd the same boke into Englyische.
But er I began thys occupacyon, I askede conseyil of spiritual and
goode men I hope and leue of my Pryoure. And ȝytt aftyrward
whenne I was `moste´ in dowte of all and hadde proposyd to haue lefte
all togyderys and no more vttyrly to haue do therto, ȝytt I thowgth I ₃₀
`wolde´ aske conseyil of my Pryoure, the whyche I specyally louyde
and truste myche to. And I trowe I tolde `hym´ what mevyde me, and

Preface   1 Here . . . folowynge] *om*. N   5 God] our Lorde N   6 hyt²] þat it
myght N   6–7 to hym . . . profytable] to your profyte N   7 to¹] of N   God] our
Lorde N   10 vertuys] of vertues N   eny] of ony N   grace of God] þe mercy N
11 see] *fol. by canc.* there Gg   13 Sauyoure] Lorde N   15 afore] of N
16 where] when N   17 mygthte] maye N   18 redylokyr] þe redyer N   20 best]
þe beste N   26 of charturhowse] *om*. N   28 I hope and leue] and most in specyall N
30 thowgth] thoghte þat N

he ful charytably comfortyde me to perfo`r´me hyt wyth sueche
wordys as cam to hys mynde for the tyme. And so on the mercy of
35 God trustynge, to whom ys nothynge vnpossyble, wyth drede of my
vnkunnynge and vnworthynesse, also sumwhat bore vp be the
conseyil of goostly fadrys and the merytys of hem that be þe mercy
of God mowe be profytyd be my sympyl traveyle, in sueche tymys as I
mygth traueyle be my conscyence wythoute lettynge of othyr
40 excersysys and othyr dyuerse occupacyonys and lettyngys that
f. 2ʳ mygth falle in dyuerse wysys, I thowgth be the grace of God | to
make [an] ende therof. And so att the laste oure Lorde of hys mercy
ȝaf me [grace as] I hope to performe hyt. In the whyche, yf ȝe or eny
othyr devout seruant of God fynde eny thynge profytable or
45 edificatyf, hyt ys to be redressyd to the mercy of God and the merytys
of hem þat mowen profytyd therby. And yf enythynge be founde the
contrarye hyt ys to be redressyd fully to my vnabylnesse and
vnkunnynge.

Fe`r´thyrmore lest eny man that mygth aftyrwarde rede the `boke´
50 folowynge schulde conseyue temptacyon that a sympyl `man´ schulde
do sueche a werke aftyr so worthy a man as Bonauenture was, sygth he
wrote of the `same´ matere; hyt mygth be ansueryd to þe satysfaccyon
of hys conscyence thus: Ther ben foure euangelyst that wryten of the
manhede of oure Lorde Jhesu Cryste and ȝytt alle wryten `wel´ and
55 trewly and that one leuyth anothyr supplyeth. Also the doctorys of
Holy Chyrche exponen the same euangelyis þat they wrote diuerse
wysys to the conforte of Crystyn peple, and ȝytt all ys goode to
Crysten peple and necessarye and profytable. And so thowgth he that
wrote fyrste the medytacyonys folowynge were but a sympyl man and
60 of no reputacyon in comparyson of so worthy a clerke as Bonauenture
was, ȝytt the medytacyonys, be the grace of God, mowe be ful goode
f. 2ᵛ and profytable to devout Crystyn | soulys. And therfore I hope the`r´
wole none meke and deuot seruaunt of God conseyue mysly therof,
for thowgth the werke be but symple, ȝytt the entent `of hym´ that
65 dede hyt was ful goode. And therfore ho so cunne not escuse the
werke lete hym escuse the entent.

And for the entent of hym þat dede hyt was to sympyl and deuout

33 ful] *om.* N   wyth] *fol. by canc.* a sc Gg   40 dyuerse] *om.* N   41 thowgth]
purposede N   42 an] and Gg   43 grace as] *om.* Gg   45 the] to þe N
46 mowen] *fol. by canc.* be Gg   49 Fe`r´thyrmore] and N   50 temptacyon] *fol. by*
canc. þat Gg   that] I þat am bot N   53 hys] her N   54 Jhesu Cryste] *om.* N
61 goode and] *om.* N   63 mysly] no mys N

soulys þat cunne not or lytyl vn`dyr´stonde Latyn and also for the
deuout thynkynge of oure Lordys passyon and manhede ys the
grounde and the weye to all trewe deuocyon, thys boke may be 70
callyd a *Myrowre to Deuout Peple.*

Ferthymore, ȝe schal vndyrstande þat the dylygent `thynkynge´ of
oure Lordys manhede ys a trewe weye wythoute dysseyte to vertuys
and to the gostly knowynge and trewe louynge of God and suetnesse
in grace to a deuot soule that canne deuoutly and dylygently occupye 75
hym therinne. For Euyrlastynge Wysedom seyt, in the boke þat ys
called the *Orlege of Wysedom,* to hys dyscypyl thus: 'Be hyt knowe to
the that hyt ys not ȝeue to come to the hynesse of the godhede or
vnvsyd suetnesse but to folke drawe be a manyr meke affeccyon of
feythe and loue be the byttyrnesse of my manhede and Passyon. And 80
þe hyer eny man goeth, thys forsclewde, the lower he falleth. For
forsothe þys ys the weye be the whyche me goeth; thys ys the gate be
the whyche an en|trynge ys grauntyd to the desyryd ende.' And in f. 3ʳ
anothyr place of the same boke he seyt also thus: 'The ofte thynkynge
of my Passyon makyth an vnlernyde man a ful lernyd man and vnwyse 85
men and ydyotys hyt makyth [into perfyte] maystrys, not of the sciens
that bloweth a man wythinne but of charyte that edyfyeth; hyt ys a
maner boke of lyf, in the whyche ben founden all thyngys necessarye
to helthe.' And sone aftyr he seyt thus: 'Blyssyd ys he or sche that
sadly takyth hede to þe studye of hytt, for he schal profyte in the 90
dyspysynge of the worlde and in þe loue of God and all vertuys, and
he schal take the encresyngys of gracys.'

Also, hoso wole dylygently beholde þe manhede and the Passyon of
oure Lorde, he schal fynde confort in aduersytee, mekenesse and
drede in prosperytee, and the perfeccyon of vertuouse lyuynge, not 95
only in wordys but also in perfyte workys. And the oftyr and
dylygentlokyr he lokyth therinne, the more grace schal he fynde.
For whatsumeuere perfeccyon maye be founde in seyintys and holy
fadrys lyuynge, ther maye none be lykned to that that oure `Lorde´
dede in hys owen personne, `so´ edyfycatyf schulde be to a trewe 100
Crystyn soule. And therfore, hoso wole deuoutly and dylygently

68 or lytyl] wele N 69 deuout] *om.* N 74 to the] *om.* N louynge] lyuynge N
76 the] *om.* N 77 dyscypyl] disciples N 79 of] by N 81 eny man] þat ony N
For] *om.* N 84 place of the] *prec. by canc.* place of the Gg also] allso to his disciples N
85 my] þe N a ful lernyd man] *om.* N 86 into perfyte] *con. em.* to profyte into Gg, N
maystrys] maistres I seye maistres N, *om.* Gg the] þat N 87 a] *om.* N 89 or sche]
om. N 90 the] *om.* N 92 the] *om.* N 94 mekenesse] meke N 95 and²]
om. N 97 dylygentlokyr] þe more diligently N

beholde oure Lordys lyuynge and werkys and folow aftyr þe hys
_{f. 3^v} powere, as he byddyth hymself, seyinge | thus: 'He þat seruyth me
lete hym folow me and were I am there schal my seruaunt be,
105 hosoeuyr do so, he schal fynde in thys lyf grace, and aftyr thys lyf
ioye wythoute ende and be wyth hym'; as he behetyth, the whyche
worschype ys aboue all the worschype that a chosyn soule maye haue.
For what maye God ȝeue bettyr to a chosyn soule thanne hymself, and
to be wyth hym ther he ys?
110 Also, the medytacyonys folowynge be not to be red negligently and
wyth hastynesse, but dylygently and wyth a goode avysement that þe
redare maye haue the more profyte therof; for hyt ys bettyr to rede oo
chapetele dylygently and wyth a goode delyberacyon thanne thre wyth
negligence and hastynesse, for ȝe schul 'not' consydere how myche ȝe
115 rede, but how wel.
Ferthyrmore, gostly syster, ȝe schal vndyrstande that þe grounde of
the boke folowynge ys þe gospel and doctorys goynge thervpon. And
specyally I haue folowyd in þys werke tueyne doctorys, of the whyche
þat one ys comunely called the Maystyr of Storyis, and hys boke in
120 Englyisch the *Scole Storye*; that othyr maystyr, Nycholas of Lyre, þe
whyche was a worthy doctur of dyuynytee and glosyde all the Byble as
to the lettural vndyrstandynge. And therfor I take these tueyne
doctorys most specyally as to thys werke, for they goo neryste to
_{f. 4^r} the storye and the lettural vndyrstandynge of eny docto|rys that I
125 haue red. Notwythstandynge, I haue browgth inne othyr doctorys in
diuerse placys, as to the moral vertuys, and also summe reuelacyonys
of approuyd wymmen. And I haue put nothynge too of myne owen
wytt but that I hope maye trewly be conseyuyd be opyn resun and
goode conscy'e'nce, for tha't' I holde sykyrest. For thowgth ther
130 mygth haue be put to sum ymagynacyonys þat haply mygth haue be
delectable to carnal soulys ȝytt that þat ys doo aftyr conscyence ys
sykerest thowgth the medytacyonys mygth haue be, be sueche
ymagynacyonys, haply more confortable to some carnal folke.
Also I haue prayde ȝow in the fyrste chapetele of the boke
135 folowynge, or eny othyr devout seruaunt of God that maye aftyrwarde
be the grace of God rede the boke folowynge, to seye thre Pater

102 be] at N   103 he] our Lorde N   105 thys] his N   106 behetyth] seyth N
107 the] *om.* N   108 bettyr] more N   110 and] *om.* N   112 to] *om.* N
117 doctorys goynge] þe doctores N   119 þat] *om.* N   of²] of þe N   123 neryste]
moste nerest N   124 the] to the N   126 the] *om.* N   128 hope] trowe N
129 sykyrest] þe sikereste N   132 sykyrest] sikerer N   ??? or] and by yow or N
134–5 the boke folowynge] þis boke N

Noster, thre Aueys and a Crede to þe worschype of the Holy
Trynytee, the whyche ys oo verry God, of oure Lady and of all
seyintys; and for grace þat ys necessarye in redynge of the sympyl
medytacyonys folowynge, and also for the forȝeuenesse of the synnys 140
of the fyrste wrytare of hem. And the same prayere I haue askyd aȝen
abowte the myddyl afore the Passyon, and also in the laste ende, in
betokenynge þat the Holy Trinytee ys the begynnynge, the mydyl,
and the ende of all goode werkys. To whom be all worschype, ioye, 144
and | preysynge now and wythoute endynge. Amen. f. 4ᵛ

TABLE OF CONTENTS

Here folowyn the cʻhʻapetelys of þe boke folowynge, the whiche is
called *A Myrroure to Deuote Peple*.

Capitulum primum. How man was fyrste made only of þe goodnesse
of God, and what worthynesse he was inne bothe in body and soule,
and how he loste hyt be hys owen wylful synne in brekynge the 5
commaundment of God.

Capitulum secundum. How mannys soule that was lost be hys owen
synne and wrecchydnesse mygth be restoryd aȝen be the mercy and
goodnesse of God and how þe incarnacyon of oure Lorde Ihesu
Cryste was betokenyd afore be sygnys, fygurys, and proʻpʻhecyis. 10

Capitulum tertium. Of the salutacyon of oure Lade Seyint Marye, and
of the incarnacyon of oure Lorde Ihesu Cryste. And also a lytyl
techynge how a man or a woman mygth know goode vysyonys fro
badde aftyr the techynge of oure Lorde to a blyssyd virgyne that ys
called Kateryne of Sene. 15

Capitulum quartum. Of the Salutacyon of oure Lady to Elyȝabeth,
and of diuerse degreis of mekenesse. And how Ioseph wolde haue lefte
oure Lady whenne he perseyuyde here wyth chylde.

Capitulum quintum. Of the byrthe of oure Lorde Ihesu Cryste. Of
the apperynde of the angellys and of þe comynge of the shepherdys. 20

Capitulum sextum. Of the cyrcumsysyon of oure Lorʻdʻ and of the
suete name Iesus.

137 thre Aueys] Aue Maria N   139 seyintys] þe seintes N   grace] goode grace N
145 endynge] ende N

Table of Contents   1–2 the whiche . . . Peple] *om*. Gg   3 Capitulum primum] *see*
note   4 in] *om*. N   8 and²] and þe N   16 to] and N   17 haue] *fol. by* l *and a*
canc. descending stroke Gg   21 Lorʻdʻ] Lord Ihesu Criste N   Iesus] Ihesu Criste N

Capitulum septimum. Of the Apparycyon of oure Lorde Ihesu
f. 5ʳ Cryste | thaʽtʼ we calle þe tuelthe daye and of the comynge of the
25 thre kyngys wyth here offryngys.

Capitulum octauum. Of the Puryfycacyon of oure Lady, the whyche
we calle Candelmasse.

Capitulum nonum. Of the goynge of Ioseph wyth oure Lorde and
oure Lady into Egypte and of the scleynge of þe Innocentys and of hys
30 comynge aȝen into þe londe of Israel.

Capitulum decimum. Of the tuelthe ȝere of oure Lorde Ihesu Cryste
and how he was founde in the temple in the mydyl of doctorys.

Capitulum undecimum. What oure Lorde dede fro þe tuelthe ȝere of
hys bodyly age into the tyme of hys Baptyme aftyr the reuelacyon of
35 Seynt Brygytte.

Capitulum duodecimum. Of the Baptyme of oure Lorde, of mekenesse, and of othyr werkys þat maye be consyderyd þerabowte.

Capitulum tertium decimum. How oure ʽLordʼ was ledde of a spyryt
into theserte that he mygth be temptyd of the fende and how he
40 fastede wyth othyr edyfycatyf materys acordynge therto aftyr the
seyingys of doctorys.

Capitulum quartum decimum. How oure Lorde Ihesu Cryste aftyr
hys fastyinge in desert wente into the worlde and prechede the
kyngedom of God and callede hys apostyllys, and whyche of hem
45 were of ʽhysʼ kynne as in the kynde of man. And also of hys othyr
dyscyplys wyth othyr materys that maye be consyderyd therabowte.

Capitulum quintum decimum. Of oure Lordys myraclys that he
wrowthe and othyr dyuerse ʽwerkysʼ that he dede in hys manhede,
f. 5ᵛ of hys go|ynge abowte in prechynge and techynge, of the scrybys and
50 the Pharyseyis and what they were and why he toke mankyn[d]e wyth
othyr materys þat longyn therto.

Capitulum sextum decimum. How oure Lorde Ihesu Cryste amonge
othyr myraclys þat he wrowthe specyally araysyde thre deede, too
men and oo damesele. And ʽwhatʼ ys betokenyd be hem gostly and
55 how þe byschoppys and the Pharyseyis toʽkeʼ here conseyil togyderys
aȝenst hym and be the conseyil of Cayphas dyffynyde to scle hym as
sone as they mygthte.

----

24 thaʽtʼ] þe whiche N   27 Candelmasse] candelmesday N   44 God] heuen N
46 be] also be N   50 the] of þe N   mankyn[d]e] mankynge Gg   53 araysyde thre
deede] thre dede þat is to say N   54 ys] *prec. by canc.* ys Gg

60 aftyr] *om.* N   61 also] *om.* N   65 Hooly] holy *eras. and replaced with* sher N
69 also] *om.* N   70 and dyssese] *om.* N   72 þe] of the N   74 þe²] of þe N
76 þe²] of þe N   78 þe²] of þe N   88 A] off the N   90 apostyllys] apostelles of our lorde N

Capitulum vicesimum octauum. Anothyr deuout medytacyon how þe soule of oure Lorde, ionyd to þe Godhede, wente to Helle.

Capitulum vicesimum nonum. Of the Resurreccyon of oure Lorde, and how he apperyde fyrste to oure Lady.

95 Capitulum tricesimum. Of þe fyue apperyngys that ben conteynyd in the gospellys, the whyche were doo the same daye of the Resurreccyon. And of othyr too tha`t´ be [tolde] to haue falle also the same daye, that be not conteynyd in þe gospellys, and to what personys they were and how.

100 Capitulum tricesimum primum. Anothyr medytacyon of othyr fyue apperyngys þat ben conteynyd also in the gospellys þat were idoo aftyr the daye of the Resurreccyon, and to what personys they were. And also anothyr þat Seyint Poule tellyth of in one of hys pystyllys.

Capitulum tricesimum secundum. Of the Ascencyon of oure Lorde, 105 and of the werkys that maye be consyderyd therabowte.

Capitulum tricesimum tertium et vltimum. Of the comynge of the f. 6ᵛ Hooly Gost and sumwhat | what the apostyllys dede aftyr they hadde resceyuyd hym in a vysyble sygne and also a specyal commendacyon of the worthy apostyl Seyint Iohn Euangelyste.

CHAPTER I

Here foloweth the boke that ys called *A Myrowr to Deuot Peple*. How man was firste made only of the goodnesse of God, and what worthyne`sse´ he was inne, bothe in body and soule, and how he lost hyt be hys owen wylful synne in brekynge the commaundment of 5 God. Capitulum primum.

Relygyus syster, in the begynnynge of these symple medytacyonys, I pray 30w firste to wythdrawe 30ure thowgth fro all othyr thowgthtys and affeccyonys that mygth lette 30w, and thanne deuoutly to lefte `vp´ 30wre herte to God and seye hertyly thre Pater Noster, thre 10 Aueys, and a Crede to the worschype of God, of oure Lady and alle

95 fyue] fyfte N   ben] *fol. by canc.* red   97 tha`t´] *om.* N   tolde] N, red Gg
99 were] here N   100 fyue] þe fyfte N   103 also] *om.* N.   107 hadde] *fol. by canc.* they   108 hym] þe holy goste N

Chapter 1   1 Here foloweth . . . *Deuot Peple*] *om.* N   4 owen] *om.* N   the] of þe N
8 and affeccyonys] *om.* N   deuoutly] *om.* N   9 hertyly] deuoutely N   Noster] *fol. by canc.* no   10 Aueys] Aue Maria N   of] and of N   alle] of alle þe N

seyintys for grace that ys necessarye to ȝow and also for forȝeue`ne´sse
of þe synnys of the fyrste wrytare of these present medytacyonys.

And thanne fyrste in the begynnynge ȝe maye thynke how all
mygthty God made heuene and erthe and all that þat ys conteynyd in
hem of nowgth, frelyche of hys euyrlastynge goodnesse. And in the 15
sexte daye, he made the firste man the whyche ys callyd Adam and he
made hym | of sclyme of the erthe as to the body, as we rede in the f. 7ʳ
fyrste boke of holy wryt, þe whyche ys callyd Genesys, where hyt ys
wryte thus: 'Formauit Dominus Deus hominem de limo terre.' Thys
ys to seye: 'Oure Lorde God made man of the sclyme of the erthe.' 'Et 20
inspirauit in faciem eius spiraculum vite.' Thys ys to seye: 'And he
inspyryd in hys face þe spyracle of lyf', þe whyche ys no more to oure
opyn vndyrstandynge, but that he made and put in the same body that
he hadde formyd of the erthe a resounable spiryt, the whyche ys of
thre pryncipal mygthtys, þat ys to seye, of mynde, resun, and wyll to 25
the lyknesse of the Holy Trinytee, the whyche ys oo perfyth God. For
hyt ys `wryte´ in the forseyde boke of Genesys thus: 'Et creauit Deus
hominem ad ymaginem et similitudinem suam.' Thys ys to seye: 'And
God made man to hys owen ymage and lyknesse', vndyrstondyth as to
the soule. And thus was Adam the fyrste man made a perfyth man in 30
body and soule, the whyche man God putte in the paradyse of luste
and lykynge. For hyt ys seyde in the forseyde boke that oure Lorde
hadde isette a paradyse of luste and lykynge fro the begynnynge in the
whyche he putte man that he hadde made. And thanne he sente a
sclepe into Adam and whyle he sclepte he toke out one of hys rybbys 35
and fylde vp the place | wyth fleyisch therfore, and made therof a f. 7ᵛ
womman and browgth here to Adam. For he hadde seyde afore that
hyt was not goode man to be alone, and therfore he seyde: 'Lete vs
make hym an helpe lyke to hym', and so he made womman to the
helpynge of man. And ferthyrmore he made hem lordys of all othyr 40
vysyble creaturys, the whyche he hadde imade, seyinge to hem thus:
'Dominamini pis[c]ibus maris et volatilibus celi et vniuersis anima-
ntibus que mouentur super terram.' Thys ys thus myche to seye:
'Beyth lordys of the fyischys of the see, and of all the byrthys of the

11 for] *om.* N   14 that] *om.* N   15 in] *om.* N   17 sclyme] þe slyme N
17–18 in the fyrste . . . ys callyd] Gg, in holy wrytte in þe boke of N   18 hyt] *om.* N
20 the] *om.* N   22 spyracle] brethe N   ys] *om.* N   25 pryncipal] *om.* N
34 man] þe man N   36 vp the place] it vppe N   therfore] as it was before N
38 man] a man N   39 and] a N   womman] a woman N   40 all] *om.* N
42 piscibus] N, pissibus Gg   44 Beyth lordys] haue yhe lordeship N   all] *om.* N

45 eyre, and of all maner lyuynge creaturys that ben meuyd vpon the
   erthe.'
      Now 3e maye thynke firste how gret goodnesse hyt was of God to
   make man whenne he was not frely of hys euyrlastynge goodenesse
   and thanne to make hym a resounable man there ʽhe mygthte' haue
50 made hym a beste vnresounable as [an oxe] or a kow, or a worme or a
   tode or sueche anothyr vyle thynge, or what othyr he hadde wolde of
   vnresunnable creaturis. But he made hym none of all these, but he
   made hym a resunnable 3 man and lorde of all sueche creaturys vndyr
   hym, and 3ytt þat, that ys more worthynesse to hys owen ymage and
f. 8ʳ lykenesse as in soule the whyche ys of | thre pryncipal mygthtys as ys
   forseyde, þat ys, of mynde, resun, and wyll to the lyknesse of the Holy
   Trynytee as I haue tolde 3ow afore. Of mynde, to haue God in mynde,
   and hys commaundmentys stedfastly and stably wythoute eny
   oblyuyon or for3etynge. In resun, to know hym gostly, trewly, and
60 clerely wythoute eny bestly or carnal beholthynge, ignoraunsce, or
   errur. In wyll, to wylle þat God wyllyth and to not wylle that God
   wyll not wythoute eny contraryustee of eny weywarde wyll, and to
   loue hym clenely, feruently, suetly, wysely, and contynually wythoute
   cessynge or eny mysse coueytyse of eny othyr thynge vaynely. Thys
65 worthynesse hadde mannys soule be grace of þe firste makynge, the
   ʽwhyche' he mygthte euere haue hadde, yf he hadde wolde. But he
   corrupte[d] and defulyde þys ymage of ʽGod' in hymself and in hys
   chyldryn whenne he wyʽl'fully brake the commaundment of God and
   chese luste and lykynge in hymself and in othyr creaturys vycyusly
70 a3enst the wyll of God and the worthynesse of hys owen soule. For
   God badde hym ete of euyreche tre in paradyse, out take of the tre of
   knowynge of good and euyl, the whyche he forbadde hym seyinge to
   hym thus: 'De omni ligno paradisi comede; de ligno autem sciencie
f. 8ᵛ boni et mali ne comedas. | In quacumque die ex eo comederis, morte
75 morieris.' Thys ys in Englyische: 'Of eueryche tre of paradyse ete, but
   of the tre of knowynge of goode and euyl loke þu ete not, for in what
   daye þu etyste þerof, thow schal deye a deth', þat ys to seye, thow
   schalt dye in soule be lesynge of the rygthwysenesse þat þu arte sette
   inne, in soule, and also thow ʽschalte' nethys dye bodyly. The
80 ʽwhyche' commaundment he brake be suggestyon of the womman,

      50 an oxe] ane oxe N, a noxe Gg   or] *om.* N   51 vyle] *om.* N   55–6 as ys
   forseyde þat ys] that is to sey N   57 tolde] tolde to N   61 to wylle] *om.* N
   67 corrupted] N, corrupte Gg   69 luste] loue N   71 euyreche] euere N   75 in]
   þe N   eueryche] iche N   76 loke] loke þat N   77 a] by N

and sche be suggestyon of the addyr, in the whyche þe fende was meuynge þe tunge of the addyr to seye tho worthys. For the feend was chef autor of þys werke, the 'whyche' apperyde in the addyr, for he hadde enuye that man was sette in sueche blyssydnesse and worschype, for the wyse man seyt thus: 'Inuidia diaboli mors introiuit 85 in orbem terrarum.' Thys ys to seye: 'Be the enuye of the feende deth cam into all the worlde', þat ys, into all mankynde be the trespasse of the fyrste man. But ȝytt, not wythstandynge that, they fylle bothe be here owen defaute for they dede hyt wylfully and were not compellyd. For the feende mygth in the addyr and be the addyr, be the 90 suffraunsce of God, suggeste euyl to hem, but he mygth not compelle hem to euil. And therfore hyt 'was' here owen defaute in as myche as they | wyllfully consentyde thorow the whyche consentynge and f. 9ʳ aftyrwarde fulfyllynge the same euyl consentynge in wyrkynge, they deyed fyrste in soule be lesynge of the rygthwysenesse þat 'they' were 95 sette inne, as ys foreseyde, þe whyche was specyally in the gostly knowynge and loueynge of God be stabylnesse of mynde, clerenesse of knoyng, and feruoure of blyssyd charytee. Thys worthynesse they loste be the brekynge of the commaundment of God for they fylle fro the stabylnesse of mynde into vnstabylnesse of mynde and forȝetynge 100 of God; ffro the clerenesse of knowynge that was in resun into the therkenesse of ignoraunce and errur; and fro the feruoure of perfyth loue and charytee into coueytyse and carnal affeccyonys of vysyble and worldly thynges, and we in hem.

Of þys fallynge of the fyrste man Dauyd seyt in the *Sautyr* thus: 105 'Homo cum in honore esset non intellexit comparatus est iumentis insipientibus et similis factus est illis.' Thys ys in Englyisch: 'Man, whenne he was in worschype, vndyrstode hyt not, and therfore he loste hyt.' He ys lykened to vnwyse bestys, þat ys, to vnresunnable bestys be carnal beholdynge, and made lyke to hem in bestly louynge 110 of hymself and othyr creaturys vycyusly. And besy|de all thys, an f. 9ᵛ angyl, at the byddynge of God, throfe hem out of paradyse into thys wrecchyd worlde here to lyue in traueyle and sorowe all here lyf tyme, and aftyr to dye bodyly, and alle that cam of hem. All thys was for the

81 was] *fol. by canc.* chef auter of þys werke   84 enuye] grete envye N   man was] *prec. by canc.* man was   86 to] *om.* N   the¹] *om.* N   87 ys] is to saye N   90 the] *om.* N   91 euyl to hem] to hem wille N   92 to euil] *om.* N   94 euyl] wille N   96 as] as it N   100 into] in N   102 perfyth] blessed N   103 charytee] clene charite N   103–4 vysyble and] *om.* N   105 the²] *om.* N   108 vndyrstode] he vnderstode N   109 ys lykened to] was lykened vnto N   110 louynge] leuynge N   114 aftyr] afterwarde N

115 fyrste synne of man, the whyche ys called orygynal, for the whyche
synne as Hylton seyt: 'We mygth 'neuyr' haue 'be' sauyd thowgth we
hadde neuer doo othyr venyal ne deedly but only thys, that 'ys' called
orygynal (for hyt ys the fyrste synne, and that 'ys' nothynge ellys but
lesynge of þe rygthwysenesse 'þe' whyche we were [made] inne) but
120 yf oure Lorde Ihesu Cryste be hys precyouse Passyon hadde
delyueryd vs and restoryd vs aȝen.'

CHAPTER 2

How mannys soule that 'was' lost be 'hys' owen synne and
wrecchydnesse mygth be restoryed aȝen be the mercy and goodnesse
of God. And how the incarnacyon of oure Lorde Ihesu Cryste was
betokenyd afore be sygnys, fygurys, and prophecyis. Capitulum
5 secundum.

I haue sumwhat, relygyus syster, tolde ȝow in the cha'pe'tele nexte
afore thys of the fyrste makynge of man, and what worthynesse he was
inne of the fre endelese good'n'esse of God, and also what wrecchydnesse he fylle inne be hys owen wylful synne, and we in hym. Now hyt
10 were conforttable, I trowe, to ȝow or to eny othyr deuout seruaunt of
God to here how the forseyde man and tho þat cam of hym mygth
f. 10ʳ be | restoryd aȝen to the dygnytee and worthynesse þat he hadde be
the grace of the firste makynge, and to more be the mercy and
goodnesse of God. Fyrste thanne 'ȝe' schal vndyrstande that we were
15 alle defulyd and so acloyede in the fyrste synne of oure fadyr Adam
that none of vs mygth helpe othyr. Wherefore, yf we schulde be
delyueryd ther muste come one þat mygth haue the same kynde and
not the synne. And he mygth make satysfaccyon to God in dyinge for
the synne of mankynde, for the propyr payne for the synne of
20 mankynde was deth, the whyche he owede not to haue þat mygth
haue the same kynde and not the synne. And therfore, yf he dyde, he
payde that he owed not, and so yf he wolde frely dye and paye that he
owede not, he mygth make satysfaccyon to God for the synne of the

116 Hylton] Maistre Walter Hiltoun N   119 'þe'] þis N   made] N, om. Gg; N's text
aligns with the source

Chapter 2   2 goodnesse] þe godenes N   6 I] om. N   12 be] fol. by canc. resto
14 Fyrste thanne] nowe firste N   15 alle] also N   so acloyede] yclothed N
16 Wherefore] and þerfore N   18 And] and so N   21 the same] prec. by canc. the
same   22 he¹] fol. by canc. dyde

kynde that he hadde take, yf God wolde accepte that maner
satysfaccyon.   25

Be suesche a maner wyse oure mercyful Lorde God seynge the
wrecchydnesse of mankynde and the sorowe that hyt was falle inne be
hys owen synne, hauynge pytee and compassyon that the kynde that
he of hys endles goodnesse fyrste made schulde peryische, of the same
goodnesse, be hys vnscryptyble wysedom, wolde ordeyne a remedye   30
and a weye how the kynde `that´ he mercyfully lo|uyde, mygth   f. 10ᵛ
rygthfully `be´ bowgth aȝen fro the bondage of the feende to whom
hyt was `made´ soget be synne. And so the all mygthty fadyr,
werkynge wyth hym the Hooly Gost, wolde sende hys owen sone,
oure mercyful Lorde Ihesu Cryste, to take oure kynde wythoute the   35
synne of a clene vndefulyd virgyne and to dye in the same kynde. And
so be hys precyouse deth delyuere vs fro euyrlastynge deth, that rygth
as we dyde in Adam, so we mygth lyue aȝen in Cryste as Seyint Poule
wytnessyth, seyinge thus: 'Sicut enim omnes in Adam moriuntur ita
et in christo omnes viuificabuntur.' Thys ys in Englyisch: 'Forsothe,   40
rygth as alle men dyen in Adam, so alle schul be quyked in Cryste.'

All thys was betokened afore be sygnys, fygurys, and prophecyis for
hyt was worthy that so excellent a werke schulde be betokenyd afore.
And fyrste be sygnys and figurys in patriarkys, of the whyche I schal
telle ȝow one to ȝoure confort that was schewde loonge afore þe lawe   45
be the hooly patriarke Abraham and hys sone Ysaac. God bad
Abraham take hys one begeten sone Ysaac, the whyche he specyally
louyde, as we reede in the boke of Genesys, and offre hym in a
sacrifyce vpon an hylle that he wolde schewe hym. And thanne thys
hooly patryarke, at þe | byddynge of God, aroose be nygthte and   f. 11ʳ
arayde hys asse, takynge wyth hym too ȝonge men and hys sone Ysaac.   51
And whenne he hadde kytte wode for the sacryfyce, he wente to the
place þat God hadde hym goo too and the thyrde daye he seygth
the place afer. And thanne he badde hys chyldryn abyde there wyth
the asse and he and hys sone, he seyde, wolde go thethyr and   55
worschype God and come aȝen to hem. And thanne he toke the
wode that he wolde offre the sacryfyce vpon and leyde hyt vpon hys
sone Ysaac, and so he bare the wode that he schulde be offryd vpon.
And thus in thys was betokenyd that oure Lorde Ihesu Cryste, the

26 Be suesche a maner wyse] right so N   27 sorowe] sorowe and þe desese N
30 vnscryptyble] vncircumscriptible N   31 `that´] þe whiche N   36 delyuere] to
deliuer N   37 in] in in Gg   41 alle schul] shall all men N   45 þe] the þe Gg
47 one] owne N   48 a] om. N   51 too] fol. by canc. chyldryn   55 and¹] for N

60 whyche ys the one begetyn Sone of God, schulde bere the crosse
    hymself vpon the whyche he schulde be offryd to hys fadyr in heuene
    for the helthe of mankynde. For the gospel makyth mencyon that oure
    Lorde bare the crosse hymself vpon the whyche he dyde for the
    saluacyon of mankynde.

65   How oure Lorde schulde be borne of a mayde, I schal telle ʒow
    anothyr fygure that was schewde aftyr the lawe was ʒeue to the
    seruaunt of God, Moyses, and be hym to all the peple of Israel, and
    that was schewed in the rood of Aaron that borgenyde. God badde
f. 11ᵛ Moyses, as we rede in the boke of | Numery, that he schulde take of
70 euyreche trybe of þe peple of Israel a rood and wryte the name
    of eueryche trybe vpon the rood of the same trybe. But the name of
    Aaron schulde be in the trybe of Leuy, and whom he wolde chese to
    the presthode hys rood schulde borgene. Now ʒe schal vndyrstande
    that there were xii trybys of the peple of Israel, outtake the trybe of
75 Leuy þat Aaron was of, and so ther were xiii rooddys of the whyche
    sexse were at þat oo syde and vi at that othyr syde whenne they were
    browgth into tabernacle afore God. And so Aaronys rood was in the
    myddyl, the whyche rood meruelyusly borgenyde and bare froyte, and
    be þat myracle was the presthode of Aaron confermyd. And in that
80 rood Aaron ʻwasʼ betokenyd, as Seynt Ihonn Crysosteme seyt, oure
    Lady Seynt Marye, þe whyche wythoute eny moʻyʼstenesse of the
    erthe browgth forth a ful suete froyte. For sche, wythoute eny seed of
    man, browth forth a sone, þe whyche ys made the froyte of mannys
    helthe and be the whyche the verry and euyrlastynge presthode of
85 Holy Chyrche ys confermyd.

        These and manye othyr fygurys were ischewde afore in olde tyme
    þat oure Lorde Ihesu Cryste schulde come to saluacyon of mankynde.
f. 12ʳ But these that I haue schortly tolde ʒow here I hope suffyce as | for
    example. Also hyt was forseyde be prophetys, of the whyche one,
90 Ysaye, that spekyth moste opynly of the Incarnacyon of oure Lorde
    seyde thus: 'Ecce virgo concipiet et pariet filium et vocabitur nomen
    eius emanuel.' Thys ys in Englyisch: 'Loo, a mayde schal conseyue
    and brynge forth a sone and hys name schal be callyd Emanuel', that
    ys exponed as the Euangelyst seyt, God ys wyth vs. Thys and many

60 the¹] his N   62 mankynde] all mankynde N   65 ʒow] to yowe N
68 God] for god N   69 the] om. Gg   om. N   70 eueryche] yche N
71 eueryche] yche N   72 he] þat he N   76 sexse] sex roddes N   77 Aaronys]
note in marg. the rood of Aaron   80 Ihonn] om. N   81 Seynt] om. N   82 a]
om. N   86 fygurys] signes and figures N   87 to] to þe N   88 suffyce] be
sufficient N   92 emanuel] emanuel et cetera N

othyr were forseyde be the forseyde prophete of the incarnacyon and ₉₅
the byrthe of oure Lorde and also manye othyr propheciys were seyde
before [by] the same prophete and othyre of the Incarnacyon, the
Byrthe, Passyon, Resurreccyon, and Ascencyon of oure Lorde Ihesu
Cryste, and also `of´ the comynge of the Holy Goste, the whyche were
to loonge to telle here. But thys that I haue compendyu`s´ly `seyde´ I ₁₀₀
trowe be inowgth as for example, for hyt was worthy `and resunyable´,
as I haue forseyde, þat so excellent werkys schulde be betokenyd and
prophecyed afore.

CHAPTER 3

Of the salutacyon of oure Lady Seyint Marye and of the incarnacyon
of oure Lorde Ihesu Cryst and also a lytyl techynge how a man or a
womman mygth knowe goode vysyonys fro euyl aftyr the techynge of
oure Lorde Ihesu to a blyssyd vyrgyne þat ys callyd Kateryne of Sene.
Capitulum tertium.   5

Whenne oure mercyful Lorde God hadde forordeynyd the helthe of f. 12ᵛ
mankynde, firste in hys owen euyrlastynge wy`se´dom and goodnesse,
and sygth befortokenyd hyt be fygurys and prophecyis in the Olde
Lawe and afore, as I haue sumwhat tolde ȝow in the chapetele nexste
afore thys, and the tyme was come that so excellent a werke schulde be ₁₀
fulfyld in trewthe, ȝe maye thynke how the angyl Gabryel was sente
fro God as the gospel makyth mencyon, into [a] cytee of Galyle whas
name was Naȝareth to a vyrgyne dyspowsyd to a man `whas name´ was
Ioseph, of the mayne of Dauyd and the `name´ of the vyrgyne was
Marye. Here vndyrstondyth fyrste that Galyle was the contre and ₁₅
Naȝareth a cytee of the same contre in the whyche oure Lady
duellyde, and that sche was dyspowsyd to a man, merueylyth not
therof, for hyt was a gret dyspensacyon of the goodnesse of God for
dyuerse causys. One ys that yf sche hadde be wyth`oute´ a man, the
peple wolde haue seyde þat tyme that sche hadde conse`y´uyd amysse ₂₀
aȝenste the lawe of God, and that schulde haue be a gret schame to the
blyssyd vyrgyne, and be `the same´ lawe cause of deth. And therfore to

97 by] N, of Gg   97–8 the Byrthe] *om.* N   102–3 and prophecyed afore]
before N

Chapter 3   4 Ihesu] Ihesu criste N   6 mercyful] *om.* N   7 mankynde] man `and´
of mannes soule N   9 ȝow] to yow N   10 so] that N   a] *om.* N   12 a] N, *om.*
Gg   15 Here] nowe N   the] a N   19 that] *om.* N   21 the] þat N

exclude that sclaundyr and pereel, hyt was necessarye that sche
schul|de be cowplyd to a man. Anothyr ys that sche mygthte haue
the solace of a man to helpe here, to comforte here, and to do here
seruyse, for the Euangelyste beryth wyttnesse that he was a rygtful
man. And also anothyr cause maye be that the mysterye or pryuyte of
oure Lordys incarnacyon schulde be hyd fro the fende.

Now thanne, beholdyth deuoutly how the angil entryth in the
forseyde cytee of Naȝareth and into the place þat oure Lady duellyde
inne. And ʻhyt ysʼ wel lykly he fond here in here deuout preyerys, for
sche was alwey wel ocupyed. And fyrste he knelyth downe ʻreuer-
entlyʼ merueylynge the excellence of here that he salutyth as Seyint
Ierom seyith, and thanne he seyith thys fayre salutacyon to here:
ʻHayle Marye ful of graceʼ, thys ʻwordeʼ Marye thowth ys not there in
the texte but hyt ys vndyrstonde and sone aftyr expressyd, ʻoure
Lorde ys wyth the, blyssyd be þu amonge wymmenʼ. That ys to seye,
þu arte synglerly blyssyd afore alle wymmen or þu arte more blyssyd
thanne alle wymmen. And whenne sche herde þys salutacyon sche
was dystroblyd in that manyr speche and thowgthe what that manyr
ʻsalutacyonʼ schulde mene. And thanne the angyl ansueryde and
seyde: ʻDrede not Marye for forsothe þu haste founde grace att
God loo þu schalt conseyue and brynge forth a sone and þu schalte
calle hys name Ihesu Chryste.ʼ Ihesu Chryste, [ytornede] out of Latyn
into Englyisch, ys as myche to seye as Sauyoure and thys ys a
conuenyent name to hym for þe werke þat he cam fore, for he cam
specyally for helthe and saluacyon of mankynde.

And thanne ȝe maye | thynke how the blyssyd virgyne askyth hym
what wyse hyt schulde be doo sygth sche knewe no man, þat ys to
seye, be carnal medlynge togyderys ne purposyde, and so sche was a
clene virgyne bothe in body and soule and purpose. And thanne the
angyl seyde aȝene þat ʻscheʼ schulde not conseyue of eny man be the
wyrkynge of the Holy Gooste. Also for more certeyne confort of here,

24 schulde] *see note*   25 a] *om.* N   to²] and N   26 seruyse] *prec. by canc.* sery
the] *om.* N   wyttnesse] wytnesse of hym N   27 or] and N   28 schulde] myght N
29 entryth in] enterede into N   30 the] þat N   31 hyt ys] *marked for inser. from
marg.* Gg   And hyt ys wel lykly he fond] and happely he fyndeth N   deuout] *om.* N
32–3 reuerently] *marked for inser. from marg.* Gg   35 worde] *marked for inser. from marg.*
Gg   35–6 thys worde . . . expressyd] *om.* N   41 salutacyon] *corrects* spehe *with*
salutacyon *from marg.* Gg   thanne] *om.* N   42 for] *om.* N   44 ytornede] N, *om.* Gg
45 ys²] *caret mark for inser. from marg.* Gg   47 for] for þe N   and] *prec. by canc.* of Gg
48 thanne] *om.* Gg   49 man] man ne noght purposede N   50 ne purposyde] *om.* N
51 thanne] *om.* N   52 sche] *caret mark for inser. from marg.* Gg   be the] bot be N
53 Also] and also N   certeyne] *om.* N

he tolde her that Ely3abeth here olde barayne cosyn hadde conseyuid
`a sone´ in here age, the whyche ys callyd Seyint Iohnn baptyste, for 55
he seyde ther `ys´ nothynge impossyble to God. And thanne 3e maye
thynke þat the meke virgyne lystynge vp here handys to heuenewarde
and here eyin devoutly to God wyth a ful meke [herte] and a lowe
spyryt seyde these wordys: 'Loo the handemayde of oure Lorde! Be
hyt to me aftyr thy worde.' Now beholdyth deuoutly in 3owre 60
ymagynacyon the holy speche betuene the blyssyd virgyn and the
holy angyl, as ys forseyde. And att the laste the meke consentynge of
the blyssyd virgyne a`n´d also how mekely sche callyth hereself but a
seruaunt whenne sche wyste hereself be hym that sche schulde be
werkynge of the Holy Gooste brynge forth to be Quene of Heuene, 65
Lady of þe Worlde, and Empresse of Helle. And takyth example of
here mekenesse, for `yf´ sche that was so excellently chose afore all
othyre creaturys were | so meke, how meke thanne schulde we be þat f. 14ʳ
ben so synneful and wrecchyd and `vn´worthy eny benfeet or 3yfte of
God, sauynge hys owen fre endles goodnesse and mercy. And thanne 70
3e maye thynke whenne the angyl hadde do hys message and herde
the consent of that blysful lady and God`ys´ sone was conseyuyed, he
toke hys leue of that worschypful vyrgyne and modyr oure Lady
Seyint Marye and wente hys weye. For doctorys seyin that anone as
sche hadde seyde the wordys of consentynge, anone oure Lorde Ihesu 75
Cryste was conseyuyd of the vyrgyne Marye, perfygth God and man
in soule and fleyisch.

Now vn[der]stondyth here that rygth as deth entryde fyrste into
mankynde be synne, in the same wyse entryde lyf be grace; for rygth
as the feende in the addyr dysseyuyde Eue be false suggestyon, | rygth f. 14ᵛ
so the grace of God be a goode angyl and trewe suggestyon browgth 81
oure Lady to þe consentynge to bere hym þat all oure helthe schulde
come of. And so oure Lady, be obedyence to the grace of God and
goode suggestyon, foonde grace and helpe to alle mankynde. For
Seyint Austyn seyt thus: 'Eue inobedyent deseruyde payne, Marye 85
obedyent foonde grace. Sche in tastynge that þat was fo`r´bode,
acursyd'; thys, þat ys to seye oure Lady in beleuynge the angyl,
blyssyd. 'Sche browgth vs deth, thys bare lyf. And so rygth as deth
cam fyrste into mankynde be a womman, rygth so lyf cam a3en be a

---

54 olde barayne] *om. N*   55 a sone] *caret mark for inser. from marg.* Gg   56 `ys´]
was N   56–7 3e maye ... virgyne] þe meke virgyne as yhe may thynke N   57 the]
fol. by canc. illeg. word Gg   58 herte] N, *om.* Gg   61 blyssyd] holy N   62 as] as
it N   64 wyste] knewe N   68 were] was N   *so] see note*   78 vn[der]stondyth]
vnstondyth Gg   85 thus] *om. N*   88 rygth] *om. N*

90 womman. And rygth as the womman be suggestyon desseyuyde the
man, be þe whyche [man] alle men dyede, in the same wyse thys
vyrgyne browgth forth a man that alle men mygth be sauyd by. `And
so as myche sorowe as we hadde fyrste be a womman´, as myche ioye
ys now come to vs be a womman, and more yf we lyue trewly aftyr the
95 feythe that we haue take.´

Now hyt were goode here, I trowe, to haue summe informacyon or
techynge how a man or a womman mygthte knowe a goode vysyon fro
a badde and `whenne´ reuelacyonys or vysyonys ben of God or of the
enmy. For ȝe haue herde afore in thys chapetele that oure Lady was
100 dystrublyd or abaschyd in the speche of the angyl, not but `that´ sche
f. 15ʳ hadde seyn | angyllys afore tyme, for sche `was´ kepte of angyllys fro
here byrthe, but for they were not wounde to seye sueche thyngs to
here. For Lyre seyt þer ys nothynge more merueylus to a verry `meke´
man or womman as the exaltacyon of hymself. How a man or a
105 womman mygth knowe a goode vysyon fro a badde, and whenne they
be of God and of an euyl spyryt, oure Lorde taugth Kateryne of Sene
a prophytable lore, seyinge thus: 'Doctorys that I haue taugth seyin,
and soth hyt ys that my vysyonys begynnyn wyth a threde, but
euyrmore be processe they ȝeuyn more sykyrnesse. They begynnyn
110 also wyth a maner bettyrnesse but alwey be processe they wexe more
suettyr. The vysyon of the enmy hath the contrarye, for he ȝeuyth in
the begynnynge, as hyt semyth, a maner gladnesse, syky`r´nesse, or
suetnesse, but alwey be processe threde and byttyrnesse growen
contynuwally in the mynde of hym or here that seyth. Thys ys
115 verry trewe, for my weyis dyscorden fro hys be the same maner
dyfferrence, fforsothe the weye of penaunce and of my commaundmentys semyth in the begynnynge scharpe and harde, but the more a
man or a womman goyth therinne, the sue`t´tyr hyt wexyth and the
f. 15ᵛ more esy hyt ys. But `þe´ weye of vycys | semyth in the begynnynge
120 rygth delectable, but alweye be processe hyt ys `made´ byttyrer and
dampnablyr.´

'But I wole ȝeue the anothyr tokene more vndeseyuable and
sykerer. Hau`e´ þu for a certayne þat sygth I am trewthe alwey of

90 desseyuyde] om. N   91 man¹] N, om. Gg   92–3 And so as . . . womman]
written in marg. in a shield with mark for placement in text Gg   93 as¹] om. N   32²
myche] fol. by canc. ys Gg   98 badde] euyle N   101 tyme] om. N   of] with N
102 wounde] wonte N   104 How] Nowe þan N   105 badde] euyl N   106 of
God and] gode and when N   107 lore] word N   110 also] om. N   maner] maner
of N   be processe] om. N   112 maner] maner of N   114 in the] in the in the Gg
122 ȝeue] ȝeue to N   123 a] om. N

my vysyonys reboundyth in the soule more knowynge of trewthe, and
for the knowynge of trewthe ys most necessarye abowte me and 125
abowte hytself, þat ys to seye, þat hyt knowe me and hytselfe, of þe
whyche knowynge euyrmore comyth oute þat hyt dysspysyth hytself
and worschypyth me, the whyche ys the propyrtee of mekenesse, hyt
ys necessarye thanne that 'of' my [v]ysyonys the soule be made more
meke and more to knowe hytself and hys owen vylytee and 130
wrecchydnesse and so to dyspyse hytself. The contrarye comyth of
the vysyonys of the enmy, for in as myche as he ys fadyr of falsnesse
and kynge vpon alle the chyldryn of pryde and maye not ȝeue but that
he hath, alweye of hys vysyonys reboundyth in the soule a maner
propyr reputacyon or a presumptuousenesse of hytself, the 'whyche' 135
ys the propyr offyce of pryde and hyt abydyth isuolle and yblowe wyth
the wynde of pryde. Thow, therfore, alwey dylygently be examynynge
mayste perseyue fro whennys the vysyon cam, fro trewthe | or fro f. 16ʳ
falsnesse. For trewthe alweye makyth the soule more meke, but
forsothe falsnesse makyth hyt prowde. Thys same rule ȝe maye take 140
of gostly vysytacyonys, whethyr they bee in knowynge or in affeccyon
or in bothe, and thys ys a prophytable 'rule' and a trewe, as me semyth
of sueche maner materys.'

CHAPTER 4

Of the salutacyon of oure Lady to Elyȝabeth and of diuerse degreys of
mekenesse and how Ioseph wolde haue lefte oure Lady whenne he
perseyuyde here wyth chylde. Capitulum quartum.

Aftyr the angyl was go, ȝe maye thynke how oure Lady Seyint Marye
arose vp fro the reste of 'deuocyon and' prayere, the whyche was 5
afore-goynge of alle here werkys, as Lyre seyt, and with haste, as the
Euangelyste makyth mencyon, sche wente in the mounteyne, for hyt
ys the hyer Galyle as the forseyde doctur seyt, and into a cytee of
Iurye foure myle fro Ierusalem where, as hyt ys seyde, that tyme
ȝacharye duellede. And thanne sche entryde into the howse of the 10
forseyde ȝachary and salutyde Elyȝabeth. Thys ȝachary was an holy

---

125 the knowynge of trewthe] *see note*   128 the propyrtee] to profite N
129 vysyonys] wysyonys Gg   134 in] into N   136 isuolle] ybolned N
141 whethyr] where N

Chapter 4   6 Lyre] þe doctour Lire N   7 in] into N   8 ys] was N   9 Iurye]
þe Iewry N

prophete and Seyint Ihonn Baptystys fadyr, and Ely[ʒa]beth hys wyf
and oure Ladyis cosyn, of the whyche the angyl hadde made mencyon
to oure Lady afore and tolde here how sche hadde conseyuyd a chylde
f. 16ᵛ in here age. And | that made oure meke Lady to goo vysyte here,
bothe as summe doctorys seye, to do here seruyse and also for sche
was ʒongyr of age.

   Now ʒe maye beholde the mekenesse and the charytee of oure
Lady, how sche goeth out of Galyle into the forseyde cytee of Iurye.
20 And ʒe maye thynke that ther was a gret weye betuene and ʒytt not
wythstandynge the len`g´the of the weye ne the traveyle of the iorneye
and also sche, a tendyr virgyne, ʒytt sche wente thethyr and that in
haste. For Seyint Ambrose seyt that the grace of the Holy Goste can
no loonge taryinges, and also sche was \not/ wonde to be seyn myche
25 in opyn, and that `made´ here happly to hye the fastyr and also to
schewe be `þat´ example that a virgyne schulde not tarye loonge in
opyn ne holde no colloquyis in sueche placys.

   Now thanne beholdyth gostly how sche entryth into the howse of
þe forseyde ʒacharye and lowly and mekely sche salutyth the olde
30 woman Elyʒabeth here cosyn and anone, as Elyʒabeth herde the
salutacyon of oure Lady, the chylde that sche hadde conseyuyd ioyede
in here wombe. Thys chylde was Seyint Ihonn Baptyste, the whyche
not ʒytt borne, merueylusly knewe be the Holy Goste the presence of
f. 17ʳ oure Lorde in the virgynys wombe, | as doctorys seyin. And hym that
35 he mygth not ʒytt be speche, he knowlechede and worschypede be
sueche maner ioyinge. And also ʒe maye thynke þat Elyʒabeth hys
modyr was fu`l´fyld wyth the Holy Goste and seyde to oure Lady
thus: 'Blyssyd be þu amonge wymmen'; þat ys to seye, aboue alle
wymmen. 'And blyssyd be the froyte of thy wombe, and whennys ys
40 thys to me that my Lordys modyr schulde come to me? Loo, forsothe,
anone as I herde thy `salutacyon´ a chylde ioyede in my wombe and
blyssyd be þu that beleuydyst, for tho thynges þat haue be seyde to
the fro oure Lorde schulde be parformyd.' And thanne oure Lady
wyth gret ioye in the Holy Goste seyde: 'Magnificat anima mea
45 dominum. Et exultauit spiritus meus in deo salutari meo. Quia
respexit humilitatem ancille sue. Ecce enim ex hoc beatam me
dicent omnes generaciones.' Thys ys to seye: 'My soule magnyfyeth

---

12 and¹ . . . fadyr] *in marg.* in th`e´ fadyr of Seyint Ihonn baptyste Gg   Elyʒabeth]
Elybeth Gg   15 here] hir for she had herde þat of hir N   19 Iurye] þe Iewry N
22 also] *fol. by canc.* the traueyle of Gg   virgyne] mayden N   41 ioyede] ioyede with
ioye N

oure Lorde and my spyryt hath ioyed in God my Sauyoure. For he
hath gracyusly beholde the mekenesse of hys handmayde. Loo,
forsothe, fro hennys forwarde ʻall kynredys' schul seye ʻme' blyssyd.' 50
And so sche made an ende of the Holy Psalme *Magnificat*, the whyche
we vse to synge and rede in Holy Chyrche, specyally att euynsonge.

Gostly systyr, here I trowe | hyt were goode to seye sumwhat of f. 17ᵛ
mekenesse, for the mekenesse that ʒe maye beholde here in oure Lady
and othyr places also, the whyche ys a perfyth example and a trewe 55
merowre of perfeccyon to alle wymmen, as oure ʻLord' Ihesu Criste to
alle men. And therfore purposyth to folow aftyr as myche as God wole
ʒeue ʒow grace and kunnynge, and namely in mekenesse. For sche
seyt, as ʒe haue herde afore, that oure Lorde gracyusly behelde here
mekenesse. For hosoeuere be wel growndyd in mekenesse he ys abyll 60
to alle othyr vertuys and werkynge of the grace of God, and therfore I
wole sumwhat schewe ʒow of mekenesse, as God wole ʒeue me grace.
And fyrste of mekenesse of spyryt, of the whyche as of a rote all othyr
muste come.

Fyrste thanne ʒe schal vndyrstande that mekenesse ʻof spiryt' hath 65
dyuerse degreys, of the whyche foure I schal telle ʒow here be rowe.
The fyrste degre of mekenesse of spyryt ys in a goode wyll to God,
wythoute the whyche all ys nowgth that a man or a woman maye do in
the whyche goode ʻwyll' a man or woman [pleiseth God], for God
hateth all maner synne and vycys and louyth all goodnesse and 70
vertuys, and so in hys wyll for to plese God wolde veryly be meke
and beleuyth stedfastly alle hys synnys of hymself. And therfore he
cryeth God mercy, and doeth mekely penaunce for hem aftyr the
ordenaunce | of Holy Chyrche and byddynge of hys gostly fadyr; thys f. 18ʳ
ys the fyrste degre of mekenesse of spyryt and hyt loongyth to 75
begynnares and to the leste chosyn soule that ys.

Aftyr thys, to a soule that ys chosyn to more grace, oure Lorde
ʒeuyth a praktyc in knowynge of hys owen synnys and wreccheyd-
nesse bothe inwarde and outwarde, and that they be veryly of hymself,
and also a maner knowynge and an inwarde beholthynge of oure 80
Lordys goodnesse and benfetys frely doo to hym and to othyres. And
so of the consyderacyon of oure Lordys goodnesse and kyndnesse be
schewynge of hys benfetys to mankynde, hyt ys steryd to loue hym

50 forsothe] *om.* N   all kynredys] *line runs into marg.* Gg   54 mekenesse]
lowenesse N   56 Criste] *om.* N   65 Fyrste thanne] Nowe N   69 pleiseth God]
N, *om.* Gg   72 beleuyth] lyueth N   74 and] *fol. by canc.* bydynthe Gg   byddynge]
bydynge N   75 ys] *om.* N   76 to] *om.* N   81 doo] to do N

and to worschype hym and to desyre hym to be louyd and
85 worschypyd of alle othyres. And of `þe´ consyderacyon of hys
synnys and wrechydnessys, hyt ys steryd to despyse hytself and to
desyre to be despysyd, in that þat hyt ys so synneful and vnkynde to
God. And in thys degre the soule hath a trewe knowynge of hytself as
hyt ys be synne. And thys ys the secunde degre of mekenesse of
90 spyryt, and hyt ys in profytarys and sueche as growen and encresyn in
the loue of God and in the weye of vertuys. Aftyr thys comyth the
thyrde degre of mekenesse of spyryt and the beste and that ys whenne
a man or a woman be the grace of `God´ trewly knoweth and felyth
f. 18ᵛ hymself as he ys not only be synne, | but also as he ys in hys owen
95 beyinge in trewthe. And thys comyth of a gostly inwarde beholthynge
of the endles beynge of God, as a creature maye [haue] be the grace of
God aftyr hys capacytee in thys lyf. And hyt ys a practyke in goostly
knowynge, be the whyche hyt felyth and knowyth hytself as hyt ys in
trewthe, and alle othyr creatuyrs also and hyt ys a begynnynge of that
100 þat schal be parformyd in the blysse of Heuene. Hosoeuer haue þys
mekenesse veryly he nedyth no conforte in erthly thynges vaynely, for
he schal fynde confort inowgth in God and gostly thynges. And also
hyt bryngyth a man or a womman to perfyth charytee and to the very
loue of God as maye be felt or hadde in thys lyf. And thys maye be
105 callyd pouerte of spyryt in as myche as hyt makyth the soule poure
and nakyd fro all carnal affeccyonys and to nowgthte hytself in Godys
sygth and hys owen, as a man that hath rygth nowgth but ys bore vp
be the mercy of God. And sothly he can nowgth in trewthe exalte
hymself as of hymself afore the leste worme in the erthe ne no creature
110 that euyr God made. Of thys degre of mekenesse oure Lorde seyth in
the gospel thus: 'Beati pauperes spiritu quoniam ipsorum est regnum
celorum.' Thys ys in Englyisch: 'Blyssyd be poure in spyryt for here
f. 19ʳ ys the kyngedom | of Heuene.' Thys mekenesse hadde oure Lady
whenne sche seyde: 'My soule magnyfyeth oure Lorde and my spyryt
115 hath ioyed in God my sauyour.' For Seyint Austyn seyt that
`eueryche´ hy man or womman and e`uery´che proude man or
womman wole be ioyed in hymself and not in God and so the
sygne of mekenesse of spyryt ys ioye in God.
   The iiii degre of mekenesse of spyryt ys whenne a man or a woman

88 knowynge] syght N   96 haue] N, *om.* Gg   98 knowynge] knowynge of
God N   107 and] and in N   110 thys] *fol. by canc.* maner Gg   112 poure] pore
men and wymmen N   116 `eueryche´] yche N   hy] hyeth *with* eth *canc.* Gg
e`uery´che] yche N   118 spyryt] *prec. by canc.* sy Gg   ioye] ioyed N

for vnsykyrnesse that he hath of the knowynge of the rygthwyse 120
domys of God and that we be inne in thys lyf, holdyth hymself benede
alle men and wymmen. For the Wyse Man seyt: 'Noo man wote
whethyr he 'be' worthy loue or hate, but all thynges ben kepte
vncertayne into þe tyme þat ys to come.' And therfore he holdyth
hymself in the loweste place and thare not sette hymself in hys owen 125
sygth afore eny man or womman, ne pere hymself to eny, but mekely
holdyth hymself benede alle men and wymmen as yf he holde hymself
in the numbyr of chosyn, he holdyth hymself the leste amonge
synnares, the moste synneful. And so he kepyth hymself in the
loweste place aftyr the techynge of oure Lorde Ihesu Cryste in the 130
gospel of Luke, where he seyth thus: 'Whenne þu arte bode to the
feste goo sytt downe in the lowest place.' What ys thys to | seye gostly f. 19ᵛ
but whenne þu arte bode to the feste of Holy Chyrche feythe be grace,
holde thyself in thyne owen sygth benethe alle othyr and ke'pe' the
therinne into the tyme that trewthe be opynly and certaynely knowe 135
be ioye in the lyf that ys to come. And 'so' the sykyreste weye in thys
lyf ys to a man or a womman that kepyth not to be dysseyuyd to kepe
hymself in the loweste place, that ys to seye, to meke hymself benethe
alle men and wymmen.

How thanne maye ȝe seye schulde I meke myself benethe a Iewe or 140
a Sarsyn or the moste synful man in erthe? For'so'the rygth wel.
Poteth forth to example a Iewe or a Sarsyn or the moste synful man
that 'þe' cowthe ymagyne in erthe lyuynge in a body and preferryth
ȝowself afore hym. And I wole seye that hyt maye be that thys man be
the mercy of God maye be turnyd and become perfyther thanne euere 145
ȝe were. Thanne ys he afore ȝow that ȝe putte benethe ȝow, and
thanne haue ȝe offendyd the rygthwyse dome of God and exaltyd
ȝowself afore hym that 'God' knewe afore ȝow. For whatsumeuer he
be now, he ys sueche in Godys sygth as he ys to be in tyme to come.
And 'so' in the 'same' wyse yf ȝe wolde preferre ȝow afore eny man or 150
womman, the same that 'ȝe' preferre ȝow afore mygth be, be the
forseyde wyse, afore ȝow. And thanne schulde ȝe offende the
rygthwyse | dome of God and exalte ȝowself, and that were perlus. f. 20ʳ
And therfore the sykyreste weye in thys lyf in the whyche we be in no
sykyrnesse ys as ys forseyde to holde vs self in the loweste place, for yf 155
we 'be' so in Godys sygth we holde vsself as we be, and yf we be hyer

121 holdyth] beholdeth N   125 thare] þere N; see note   127 as] and N
131 the¹] a N   135 therinne] their N   140 meke] make N   142 synful]
symple N   156 in] in the sygh of God in marg. Gg

in Godys sygth att the hardyste we be so myche the ferthyr fro pride
and exaltacyon of vsself and so be that to be exaltyd in tyme to come.
For oure Lorde seyt in the gospel: 'He that exaltyth hymself ʼschalʼ be
160 mekyd and he that mekyth hymself schal be exaltyd.'

Thys degre of mekenesse ys necessarye and profytable to eche man
or womman in thys lyf in the whyche we be in no sykyrnesse. Also in
the too fyrste degreys of mekenesse of spyryt þat I haue tolde ȝow of
afore, thowgth a man or a womman hold hymself wers thanne ʼheʼ ys,
165 hyt ys no harme to hym but rathyr more sykyrnesse and cause of more
goode. Also, ȝe schal vndyrstande that ther ʼysʼ mekynge and
mekenesse. Mekynge ys the weye to mekenesse. And mekynge I
calle ʼwhenneʼ a man or a woman hath eny sueche lowgth consyderacyon or meke felynge, as ys forseyde, be the whyche he mekyth
170 hymself for the tyme in hys owen consyderacyon. But aftyrwarde, yf
he haue eny occasyon and thanne fallyth therfro, thanne was that but
f. 20ᵛ me | kynge and not mekenesse for he but mekyde hymself be sueche a
consyderacyon for the tyme and whenne he hadde occasyon he fylle
therfro. But yf he hadde sueche meke knowynge or felynge and
175 abydyth stedfastly thervpon and ys not putt therfro be eny occasyon,
thanne wolde I seye that he ys meke for he abydyth stedfastly ther
vpon and ys not mevyd there fro be eny occasyon. For oure Lorde
seyt in the gospel forseyde: 'Goo sytt in the lowest place.' And not
stande ne goo thethyr only, but ʼalsoʼ goo sytt in the lowest place. For
180 ʼȝeʼ wyte wel þat whenne a man syttyth he castyth hym to abyde and
therfore oure Lorde badde: 'Goo sytt in the lowest place', in
betokenynge that we schulde abyde stedfastly in mekenesse.

Thys degre of mekenesse and othyr forseyde or eny othyr lyke to
eny of these, in the whyche the vse of resun ys in gostly thynges, I
185 calle mekenesse of spyryt for as myche as hyt standyth in gostly
knowynge and vndyrstandynge of God and gostly thynges wythinne
in the mygthtys of the soule be resun and vndyrstandynge and not
wythoute in the bothyly wyttys, and of thys maner mekenesse hyt ys
wryte in þe Sautyr thus: 'Iuxta est deus hiis qui tribulato sunt corde et
190 humiles spiritu saluabit.' Thys ys to seye: 'Oure Lorde ys nygth to
f. 21ʳ hem that ben trub | lyd in herte'; that ys, fore here synnys, and he schal
saue meke [men and women] in spyryt. Thanne of thys mekenesse of
spyryt, the whyche ys in knowynge be dyuerse consyderacyonys,

159 gospel] same gospell N   168 sueche] *om.* N   175 eny] none N   177 eny]
none N   179 only but ʼalsoʼ] bot N   185 for] in N   standyth] is N   187 in²]
om. N   190 Thys] that N   192 men and women] N, *om.* Gg

muste come mekenesse of herte. For whene `the´ soule hath sueche a
meke consyderacyon in knowynge ther muste nethys folowe a meke   195
felynge and that ys in herte. Thanne of mekenesse of herte muste
come meke worthys and meke werkys as ȝe maye see in oure Lady,
how sche callyth here`self´ an handmayde and in werkys how sche
wente to Elyȝabeth and as ȝe schal here aftyrward more.

Also mekenesse of herte ys whenne a man or a woman be the grace   200
of God and sueche knowynge and felynge as ys forseyde can for God
suffre   mekely   and   gladly   wythoute   grucchynge,   despytes,
reprouynges, detraccyonys, or eny sueche othyr and `ys´ not steryd
be eny sueche occasyonys to vnpacyence ne euyl wyl ne indygnacyon
to hem that do so to hym, but rathyr to pytee and compassyon and to   205
praye deuotly for hem, and also to schewe out that lownesse of herte
in meke wordys and lowgth werkys to the worschype of God,
encressynge of hys meryts and `goode´ example of hys euyn Cristyn.
And specyally yf [he] haue eny occasyon fro wythoute as yf [he] be
spoke [to scharpely], bustusly, weywardly, falsly, or vnkyndly too   210
thanne to suffre | pacyently and to ansuere mekely and lowely aȝen or   f. 21ᵛ
nowgth, neuere ȝeuynge one euyl worde for anothyr also in werkys yf
he be putt to eny lowe or abiecte werke too doo hyt mekely and gladly.

Also a gret tokene of mekenesse of spyryt and herte bothe ys
whenne a man or womman wole mekely leue hys owen wytt and wylle   215
aftyr the conseyil of elthyr and wyseere and mekely aske conseyil and
doo ther aftyr and thys ys necessarye and profytable to ȝow and othyr
men and wymmen that lyue in relygyon and haue forsake here owen
wyl and holde hemself vndyr the meke and syker ȝoke of obedyence.
Hoso be thus ouyral meke, that ys to seye in spyryt be knowynge, in   220
herte be felynge, and wythoute in worthys and werkynge and ys not
put ther fro be eny occasyon but abydyth `stedfastly´ therinne wyth
perseueraunce into hys lyuys ende, I hope þat thys man or womman,
whateuyr he be, be perfythly meke and schal haue a ful gloryus and `a´
worschypful crowne of God and be exaltyd ful hye in Heuene. Gostly   225
syster, I haue loonge taryed here at thys place because of mekenesse,
but now hyt ys tyme that I turne aȝen to the matere that I beganne of.

194 `the´] a N   196 of] in N   201 knowynge] meke knowyinge N   as] as
it N   204 to] or N   205 and¹] om. N   206 also] þan N   208 of] to N
209 he] N, he Gg   haue] prec. by canc. be spoke Gg   wythoute as yf] with and N   he]
con. em. he N, Gg   210 to scharpely] N, shaply Gg   or vnkyndly too] and
vnkyndely N   213 be] om. N   214 herte] of herte N   216 aftyr] at N
21 and¹] and to N   219 here] your N   220 Hoso] whosoeuer N   225 be] to
be N   in] in þe blysse of N

Now thanne beholthyth that whenne oure Lady hadde made an
f. 22ʳ ende of that hooly songe *Magnificat*, | sche abode stylle wyth here
230 cosyn thre monethys seruynge here tyl sche browgth forth here
chylde, and as hyt ys red in the *Boke of Rygthful Men* sche was the
fyrste that lefte hym vp fro the erthe. Here ȝe maye beholde the gret
lownesse of oure Lady, as I haue tolde ȝow afore, for sche was wyth
here cosyn three monethys, not that anothyr mannys house delytede
235 'here', as Seyint Ambrose seyt, but þat hyt dyplesyde here to be seyin
myche in opyn. And in that tyme ȝe maye thynke sche dede here
myche lowe seruyse and whenne Seyint Ihonn Baptyste was borne
sche wente home aȝen into Naȝareth.

Here hauyth compassyon of the grete labore that sche hath in
240 goynge in and out and thynkyth what seruyse ȝe wolde haue doo 'to'
here yf ȝe hadde be there present wyth here. And whenne sche was
come 'home' Ioseph perseyuyde that sche was wyth chylde and for
sche hadde be so loonge oute and he wyste wel also þat sche was a
mayde for hym, he was adrad and suspycyus that hyt 'hadde' not be a
245 rygth, but 'he' was not syker. For Cry[s]osteme seyt that Ioseph helde
þat opynyon of the holynesse of oure Lady that hym semyde
vnpossyble here to falle so. And ȝytt, for he dowtede for the causys
forseyde and wolde not make here opyn to the lawe as 'a' mysgouer-
f. 22ᵛ nyd woman, he wolde priuyly haue lefte here and goo fro | here. But
250 the 'goodnesse' of God wolde not suffre the rygthful 'man' to erre so,
ne to 'be' ygnoraunt of tha't' worthy priuytee. And therfore 'he' sente
an angyl that apperyde to hym in hys sclepe and bad hym that he
schulde not 'drethe' to take here, for he seyde that þat ys borne in here
ys of the Holy Goste and sche schal brynge forth a sone and þu schalt
255 calle hys name Ihesu Criste, for forsothe he schal make saf hys peple
fro here synnys. And thanne he arose vp and dede 'as' the angyl bad
hym. For he knew be tho worthys that the angyl had seyde [to] hym
that God schulde be borne of here, the whyche alone forȝeuyth
synnys. And thanne he abothe stylle a madye wyth here, for as
260 doctorys seyin, bothe togyderys vowede [virgynytee].

228 beholthyth] yhe may thinke N   230 cosyn] cosyn there N   232 vp] *om.* N
234 delytede] debite N   239 Here] nowe here N   grete] *om.* N   241 ȝe] he N   be
there] bene N   242 perseyuyde] aspied N   was²] *om.* N   247 here] *om.* N
252 sclepe] shepe N   255 for] *om.* N   257 to] N, *om.* Gg   260 virgyntee]
virgynytee Gg

CHAPTER 5

Of the byrthe of oure Lorde Ihesu Criste, of the apperynge of the
angyllys, and of the comynge of þe shepherdys. Capitulum quintum.

The byrthe of oure Lorde Ihesu Criste was in the too and fourethyeth
ȝere of Octouyan, the Emperoure of Rome, as doctorys seyin, the
whyche emperoure hauynge lorde'schype' of all the worlde wolde 5
knowe how manye prouynces, how manye cyteys, how manye
castellys, how manye townys, and how manye men were in all the
worlde. And he bad 'þat' alle men schulde come out of subarbys,
townys, and wyllages to here chefe cytee and specy|ally to that þat f. 23ʳ
they throwth eny begynnynge of. Thys dyscrypcyon was firste done of 10
the Iustyce of Syrye as the Euangelyste seyt, Syryne be name. Syrye
ys a contre, and as doctorys seyin hyt ys in the mydyl of the erthe abyl
to be duelde and therfore the forseyde dyscripcyon was begunne
there. And thanne ȝe maye thynke þat all maner men wente to doo
homage, eche man into hys owen cytee. And so amo[n]ge all othyre 15
Ioseph cam out of Galyle, fro the cytee of Naȝareth into Iurye into the
cytee of Dauyd, þe whyche ys callyd Bethleem, for 'as' myche as he
was of the house and the mayne of Dauyd, that he mygth doo homage.
And he browgth oure Lady wyth hym, for he wolde not leue so
worthy a tresure behynde hym that was of the endles mercy of God 20
commyttyd to hym.

Here ȝe schal vndyrstande, as hyt ys wryte in a boke þat ys drawe of
the *Thre Kyngys of Coleyne*, that Bethleem as hyt semyth was neuyre
of gret reputacyon or quantyte, but hyt hath 'a' precyouse foundmet,
for 'there' ben manye cauys and dennys vndyr the erthe and hyt ys fro 25
Ierusalem too smale myle of that contre and hyt ys no gret towne, but
hyt ys callyd the cytee of Dauyd, for Dauyd was bore there, and in
that place summetyme stode the house of Ysay | Dauydys fadyr, the f. 23ᵛ
whyche be anothyr name ys callyd also Iesse, in the whyche house also
Dauyd was bore and vunctyd kynge of Israel be Samuel the prophete. 30
Also in the 'same' place God and man was borne of the virgyne Marye
and that place was att the ende of a strete, the whyche was þat tyme
'callyd' the Kyuyred Strete. For, for gret heete the sunne as hyt ys

Chapter 5   1   of³] and of N   2   of the 'comynge'] *om.* N   3   the²] *om.* N
15   into] in N   so] þan N   amonge] N, amooge Gg   16   out of] vp fro N   18   and
the mayne of Dauyd] of Dauid and of þe menyhe N   26   too] eghte N   *see* N
28   Dauydys] the fadyr of dauyd *in marg.* Gg   31   Marye] or lady seinte marye N
32   a] þe N

ȝytt the maner there, hyt was kyuyred aboue wyth blac clothys and
35 sueche othyr thynges and att the ende of that strete was a lytyl cote
afore a denne in a rok imade in the maner of a lytyl seler, and in that
denne Ysay, Dauydys fadyr and othyr men aftyrwarde for heete of þe
sunne, put vp necessaryis. And aftyr Dauyd was made kynge of Israel
fro that tyme aftyr Ysayis house Dauydys fadyr abode to the
40 kyngedom, but be processe of tyme Ierusalem and alle the londe
aboute was dystroyed so that no man rofte of that house for hyt was
falle downe so that nothynge abode there but the stone wallys tobroke
and falle downe, and in the grounde therof brede was solde in
betokenynge that þat place abothe to þe vsys of the kyngedom. But
45 in the denne and cote treyn vessellys and sueche maner comyn
thynges that cam to the markett and mygth not be solde were putt vp.
f. 24ʳ   And when|ne, as hyt ys forseyde, all the peple bothe men and
wymmen cam to doo homage eche to the cytee and towne that he was
borne of 'or toke eny begynnynge', thanne Ioseph wyth oure Lady late
50 in the euynynge cam and for hyt 'was' late and also alle places and
innys were ocupyed wyth stronge folke and gystes, and for they were
poure folke they wente aboute all the cytee and no man wolde ȝeue
hem herborowe and specyally whenne they seygth þat oure Lady was
a ȝonge woman syttynge vpon an asse wery of the iorneye and gret
55 wyth chylde and nere to brynge forth. And therfore in alle the cytee
no man woulde resceyue here into hys house ne inne, wherefore
Ioseph ledde here into the cote and denne forseyde of the whyche no
man rofte that tyme, and in that denne that same nygth God for vs
was borne a man in myche pouertee of the virgyne Marye wythoute
60 eny sorowe of byrthe, as hyt was semely. And sche wrappede hym in
clothys as 'þe' Euangelyste seyt, and in þe cote afore the forseyde
denne ȝytt of olde tyme abode a cracche of stone aboute an elle of
lenthe and 'ther'to Ioseph tyde the oxe and the asse that 'they'
browgth wyth hem. The asse ȝe maye thynke he brou'g'th that oure
65 'Lady' mygth sytte vpon, for sche was wyth chylde and mygth but
febly goo the oxe to selle and wyth the pryse bye here lyflode for they

35 that] þe N   37 Dauydys] the fadyr of dauyd *in marg.* Gg   38 vp] vp some N
39 Ysayis] the house of Ysay *in marg.* Gg   Dauydys] the fadyr of dauyd *in marg.* Gg   to]
om. N   41 rofte] toke kepe N   43 in¹] *om.* N   45 cote] in þe cote N   47 the]
om. Gg   and²] a N   49 or toke eny begynnynge] *in marg., marked for corr.* Gg
51 they] men N   57 denne] to þe denne N   59 Marye] our lady seinte mary N
61 and] *fol. by canc.* afore Gg   afore] beforeseide N   62–3 of lenthe] longe N
63 the] his N   65 Lady] *in marg., marked for inser.* Gg   66 febly] ful febly N   bye]
to bye N

were | but poure folke as in thys passynge worldlys rychessys, but f. 24ᵛ
they were ful ryche in gostly and eurylastynge rychessys. And in the
forseyde cracche the blyssyd virgyne Marye in the heye as wel as sche
mygth sche leyde here chyld betuene þe oxe and the asse for ther was 70
no place for hym in the hospytal, as the Euangelyste seyt, the
ʻwhycheʼ oxe and asse worschyppede hym as hyt ys wryte in the
Boke of the Ȝougthe of Oure Lorde. And ȝe maye thynke ʻalsoʼ that he
was borne the Sondaye att nygth.

Ȝytt more opynly how oure Lorde was borne and all the maner ther 75
of oure ʻLadyʼ schewde to Seyint Brygytt ful fayre be reuelacyon the
whyche sche tellyth thus: ʻWhenne I was att oure Lordys cracche in
Bethleem, I seygth a fayre mayde wyth chylde iclodyd in a whyte
mantyl and a sotyl kyrtyl, be the whyche I mygth see clerly fro
wythoute the madenys fleyisch whas wombe was ful and myche aryse 80
vp, for sche was thoo aredy to brynge forth chylde. Wyth the whyche
was an honeste olde man, and they hadde bothe ʻbutʼ one oxe and one
asse. And whenne they were entryd into a denne, the olde man wente
out the oxe and the asse ityde to the cracche and brougthte the virgyne
a candyl lygth and stykede here in the walle and wente out aȝen that 85
he wolde not be present personally att þe byrthe. | ʻAnd thanne the f. 25ʳ
virgyne dede of here schone and sche putt of the whyte mantyl that
sche ʻwasʼ kyueryd wyth and sche remeuyde the vayle fro here heed
and leyde hyt besyde here, sche abydynge stylle only in here kyrtyl
and here fayre heerys as they hadde be of golde were ispred abrode 90
vpon here schuldrys, the ʻwhycheʼ thanne toke out too finale ʻlynnynʼ
clowtys and too clene wollen clothys þat sche hadde browgth wyth
here to wrappe inne the chylde whenne hyt was borne, and othyr too
smale lynnyn clowtes to keuere and to bynde wyth hys heede, and
hem sche leyde besyde here that sche mygth vse hem in dewe tyme.ʼ 95

Whenne all thys was thus aredy, thanne the virgyne knelyde downe
wyth gret reuerence puttynge hereself to prayere, and forsothe sche
helde vp here face to heuene, ilefte vp ʻtoʼ the estewarde, and thanne
sche lefte vp here handes and eyen lokynge intently into heuenewarde
and sche stode as thougth sche hadde be lefte vp into the extasye or 100
suowynge of contemplacyon filde wyth goostly suetnesse. And as sche
stode so in prayere I seygth thanne þe chylde meuynge in here wombe

67 as in thys . . . rychessys²] *om.* N   69 Marye] our lady seinte mary N
77 Whenne] Reuelacio beate brigitte de natunate deum *in shield in marg.* Gg   81 thoo]
doo N   chylde] a childe N   83 And] þe whiche N   84 broughte] broghte to N
85 here] it N   91 too] *fol. by canc.* smale Gg   94 hys] hir N   96 was] was
done N   97 hereself] hir N   100 into the] in ane N

and anone, in a moment and the stroke of an eye, sche brougth forth a
sone of the whyche cam out so vnspekeable lyght and brygthnesse þat
f. 25ᵛ the sonne was not to be lykned therto ne the candyl that | the olde
106 man hadde putt in the walle in eny manerwyse ȝaf eny lygtht, and that
godly lyght `had´ all brougth to nowgth the materyal lygth of the
candyl and that maner bryngynge forth was so sodeyne and in so
schorte tyme doo þat I mygth not perseyue ne dyscerne how or in
110 what membyr sche browgth forth chylde. Neuyrdeles, I seygth anone
þat gloryouse chylde lyinge vpon the grounde nakyd and rygth whyte,
was fleyisch was rygth clene fro all maner felthe and vnclennesse. I
seygth also the skynne þat hyt cam out in lyinge besyde hym wrappyd
togyderys and rygth schynynge.'
115 'Also thanne I herde angyllys songes of merueylus softenesse and
gret suetnesse and anone the virgynys wombe that afore the bryrthe
was suolle wythdrew hytself and thanne here bothy semyde of
merueylus fayrenesse and delycate. And whenne the virgyne felte
that sche hadde brougth forth chylde anone, sche enclynede here heed
120 and iunede here handes togydere and wyth gret honeste and reuerence
sche worschypede the chylde and seyde to hym: ȝe be welcome, my
God, my Lorde, and my sone. And `thanne´ the chylde wepynge and
`hyt´ as were makynge for colde and hardenesse of the panyment
the`re´ hyt laye turnede hytself a lytyl and straugth out hys lemys
f. 26ʳ sekynge to fynde refute and fa|uoure of the mothyr, the whyche the
126 mothyr thanne toke vp in here handys and streynyde hym to here
breste and wyth here cheke and here breste sche made hym hoote
wyth gret gladnesse and ful tendry modryly compassyon, the whyche
thanne satte downe vpon the grounde and putt here sone in here lappe
130 and toke wyth here fyngrys craftyly hys nauyl the whyche anone was
kytte aweye, ne ther cam `e´ny lykur or blode out therof. And anone
sche beganne to suade hym vp dylygently, fyrste in the lytyl lynnyn
clowtes and aftyr in the wollen, screynynge the lytyl body, the legges,
and the armys wyth a suadynge bonde, the whyche was so`w´ned in
135 foure partyis of the ouyr wollen cloth. Aftyrwirde, forsothe, sche
wrappede and bonde abowte þe chyldeys heed the othyr tueyne smale
lynnyn clowtes the whyche sche hadde arethy therfore. Thys idoo, the
olde `man´ cam in and fylle downe to the erthe on hys kneys and

106 and] bot N   107 all] om. N   110 chylde] þe childe N   111 grounde]
erthe N   116 afore] was before N   118 And] fol. by canc. thanne Gg
119 chylde] þe childe N   heed] body N   123 were] om. N   131 out] om, N
133 the¹] om. N   134 whyche] om. N   135 wollen] litel wollen N   137 hadde]
om. N   138 the] þat N

worschypede hym; neuyrdeles, he wepte for ioye. Ne the virgyne
thanne in that byrthe was chongyd in coloure or in sekenesse ne ther 140
faylede eny bodyly strenthe in here as hyt 'ys' wonde to be in othyr
wymmen whenne they brynge forth chylde but that here wombe that
was suolle wythdrew hytself into the fyrste state that hyt 'was' in ere
sche brougth forth | chylde. Thanne sche arose vp hauynge the f. 26ᵛ
chylde in here armys and bothe 'to'gyderys, that ys 'to' seye sche and 145
Ioseph, leyde hym in the cracche, and here kneys bowed they
worschypede hym wyth gret ioye and gladnesse.' Thys ys Seyint
Brygytteys reuelacyon how oure Lady schewde here all the maner
how sche bare oure Lorde, affermynge to here be reuelacyon also þat
certaynely in the forseyde maner sche brougth forth here blysful sone 150
oure Lorde Ihesu Criste, and wyth so mych ioye and gladnesse of
soule that sche felte no greuounesse whenne he wente out of here
body ne eny maner sorowe the whyche ȝe maye thynke as thowgth ȝe
were present and seygth hyt doo afore 'ȝow' as sche dede.

Aftyr þys ȝe maye thynke, as the gospel seyt, that ther were 155
schepherdys in the same contreye wakynge and kepynge the waych-
chys of the nygthte vpon here flok a myle fro Bethl'e'em, as the
Mayster of Storyis seyt. 'To' the whyche schepherdys the angyl of
oure Lorde apperyde and tolde hem þat oure Sauyoure was borne and
tolde hem also a tokene seyinge to hem thus: 'ȝe schal fynde a ȝonge 160
chylde iwrappyd in clothys and leyde in a cracche.' And thanne ȝe
maye thynke that sodeynely ther was made wyth [þe] same angyl a
mu'l'tytude of heuenly cheuolrye praysynge God and seyinge: 'Ioye |
be to God in hy thynges', þat ys to seye in heuenely thynges, 'and pese f. 27ʳ
in erthe to men and wymmen of a goode wyl.' 165

Loo, gostly syster, thys was a suete songe and a confortabele to alle
deuout men and wymmen, the 'whyche' alwey be the grace of God
haue a good wyl to hym with the 'whyche' goode wyl, wel ifolowed
and performyd in goode werkys aftyr a man or womma[n]ys powere,
he maye neuyr peryische and wythoute the whyche all ys nougth þat 170
we maye doo. And therfore hauyth alwey a goode 'wyll' to God,
whatsumeuyr falle of that othyr dele and doeth as ȝe maye. And
whenne þe forseyde angyllys were goo aȝen into heuene, ȝe maye
thynke how the schepherdys spake togyderys seyinge thus: 'Lete vs

142 chylde] a childe N   143 hytself] it N   145 chylde] þe childe N   147 gret
ioye and gladnesse] ioye and gret gladnesse *order corr. with marks* Gg   155 were] was N
158 Storyis] þe storyes N   162 maye] *om.* N   þe] N, *om.* Gg   169 wommanys] a
wommanes N, wommays Gg

175 goo vnto Bethleem and see thys that hath be seyde to vs þat oure
Lorde hath schewde vs.' And thanne ȝe maye thynke how the`y´ goo
thedyr wyth haste, and whenne they were come thedyr they fond oure
Lady and Ioseph and the chylde putte in the cracche as hyt was
forseyde to hem of the angyl.

180   Now beholdyth inwardly and ȝoure soule the vnspekeable charytee
and the euyrlastynge mercy of God, how he that ys Lorde of all the
vnyuersytee of creaturys wolde of hys incomprehensyble goodnesse
take oure kynde of that blyssyd virgyne, and be borne in so myche

f. 27ᵛ pouertee þat we mygth | be made euyrlastyngly ryche; and be leyde in
185 a cracche betuene too bestys, the kynge of angyllys and ȝeuare of all
rychesse, vndyr the `gouerenaunce´ of a mayden, the gouernoure of
alle creaturys, the Lorde of all thynges in the lykenesse of a se`r´uaunt,
þat we mygth be made hyth wyth angyllys. And in þis consyderacyon,
mekely and hertyly, thankyth hym that he wolde fucheasaf of hys
190 endles mercy and goodnesse, so worthy a Lorde, frely to take oure
kynde and be borne so powrely for oure euyrlastynge helthe of that
blyssyd virgyne.
        Aftyr thys ȝe maye thynke how the schepherdys whenne they
seygth hym, they knewe hym be the wordys that the angyl hadde
195 seyde to hem, and also be the grace of God that they were ilygthed
wyth. And thanne ȝe maye beholde how they lowly wyth myche
gladnesse and reuerence worschypede hym and haply offrede to hym
sueche good as they hadde. And alle folke merueylyde that herde
therof, þat ys to seye, of tho thynges that were seyde to hem of the
200 schepherdys. But oure Lady kepte wel all in here herte haply þat sche
mygth the bettyr telle hyt to hem that schulde wryte hyt aftyrwarde.
        Aftyr thys the schepherdys wente aȝen to here schepe, gloryfyinge
f. 28ʳ and preysynge God of that benfeet done to all the worlde ge|nerally
and specyally schewde to hem. In alle these thynges kepyth ȝowself
205 present as thowgth ȝe seygth al thys done afore ȝow and ymagynyth
also what reuerence worschype and seruyse ȝe wolde haue doo there
to oure Lorde, to oure Lady, and to Ioseph, and how hertyly haue
thankyth oure Lorde for thys gret benfeet idoo to mankynde and also
how gladly ȝe cowthe suffre pouertee and penaunce for hys loue, þat
210 thus myche toke and suffrede for ȝow for sueche affeccyonys ben

177 were] om. N   180 the¹] om. N   181 the¹] om. N   182 of²] of of Gg
192 virgyne] holy virgyne N   193 maye] om. N   202 Aftyr thys] and þan yhe
maye thenke howe N   205 seygth] hadde sene N   207 to] and to N
208 thys] his N

rygth profytable and merytorye and thys maye be the medytacyon of
oure Lordys byrthe.

CHAPTER 6

Of the Circumsysyon of oure Lorde Ihesu Criste and of the suete
name Ihesu Criste. Capitulum sextum.

The circumcysyon of oure Lorde Ihesu Criste was the viii daye fro
hys byrthe, the whyche þe euangelyste tellyth schortly thus:
'Aftyrwarde þat viii dayes were fulfylde that the chylde schulde be 5
cyrcumcydyd, hys name was called Ihesu Criste, the whyche was
called of the angyl ere he were conseyuyd in hys modrys wombe.'

Fyrste here ȝe schal vndyrstande that þe cyrcumcysyon was an
obseruaunce in the olde lawe, iȝeue fyrste of God to the holy patriarke
Abraham and so forth be hym to all the peple of Israel that cam of 10
hym. And hyt was aȝenste the orygynal synne | amonge hem as f. 28ᵛ
cristyndon amonge vs and be þe whyche also they were dyssernyd and
departyd fro othyr peple, as we be crystyndom fro hethyn folke. And
hyt was a ful gret payne for hyt was doo in ꞌaꞌ ful tendyr place of a
mannys body wyth a knyfe of stone. Now thanne beholdyth how gret 15
lownesse hyt was the Lorde of the lawe to meke hymself to the lawe
and namely to so payneful an obseruaunce of the lawe, and also how
gret charytee for here he schedde fyrste hys precyouse blode for the
helthe of mankynde. And in thys consyderacyon hauyth pytee and
compassyon to see that fayre tendyr chylde and ȝoure louely Lorde 20
iput to so gret payne so ȝonge. And also ȝe maye ꞌthynkeꞌ that for
payne of that kyttynge he wepeth and cryeth, as the maner of
chyldryn ys, for he hadde parfythly take mankynde in no wyse
leuynge the kynde of God in the whyche he ys euyrmore euyn to
the fadyr. And therfore he suffrede ful myche payne in oure kynde, 25
the whyche ys vnpassyble in hys owene, and so he suffrede in thys
cyrcumcysyon ful myche payne and therfore hauyth pytee and
compassyon of hym and of hys blysful modyr, also thynkynge how
gret heuynesse hyt was to here to see hym wepe and in so gret payne.
And therfore ȝe maye thynke sche comfortyth | hym wyth all the f. 29ʳ
dylygence that sche can in wypynge the terys fro hys eyin and 31

212 byrthe] birth Deo gracias N
Chapter 6   3 fro] of N   5 Aftyrwarde þat] aftre þat þe N   11 synne] synne
vsede N   15 beholdyth] thenke N   18 schedde] shewed N   26 thys] his N

kyssynge hym, wyth othyr `confortys´ that longen to a modyr to doo
to here one belouyd sone. For ther was neuyr modyr in erthe that euyr
louyd here chylde so myche a sche dede hym.

35 And in thys maner medytacyon blyssyth and thankyth hym of thys
gret benfeet and of alle othyre frely and mercyfully schewed and done
to mankynde and beyth `meke´ and kynde for hys loue that was thus
me`ke and´ kynde for ȝow. And rygth as he suffrede to be cyrcumcy-
dyd for ȝoure loue, rygth so cyrcumcydyth ȝoureself for hys loue,
40 bothe bodyly and gostly. For in too manerys we schulde cyrcumcyde
vsself, as seyint Bernarde seyt. One ys wythoute in the fleyisch and
that othyr wythinne in soule. The outwarde cycumcysyon stondyth in
thre thynges: þat ys to seye, in habyte, that hyt be not notable; in
dede, that hyt be not reprouable; and in worde, þat hyt be not
45 despyseable. The inwarde also standyth in thre thynges: þat ys to
seye, in thowgth, that hyt be holy; in affeccyon, þat hyt be clene; and
in intencyon, that hyt be rygth.

Also ȝe schal vndyrstande that for manye causys oure Lorde wolde
be cyrcumcydyd, after þe seyinge of doctorys of the `whyche´ I wole
50 telle ȝow summe to ȝoure gostly comforte. One ys that he wolde |
f. 29ᵛ schewe be that that `he´ hadde veryly take mankynde, for he wyste wel
that `ther´ schulde come aftyrwarde herytykys that wolde seye þat he
hadde take no verry body, but a fantastyke. And therfore, to dystroye
that heresye he wolde be cyrcumcydyd and schede hys blode, for a
55 fantastyke body maye schede no blode. Anothry ys that the Iewys
schulde be vnescusable for yf he hadde not be cyrcumcydyd they
mygth haue escusyd hem and seyde: 'Therfore we resceyue the not,
for þu [ert] not lyke to oure fadrys'; þat ys to seye, be cyrcumcydynge
thyself. Anothyr was to proue þat Moyses lawe was goode and holy,
60 `for´ he cam not, as he seyt hymself, to breke the lawe but to fulfylle
hyt. Anothyr ys that he wolde schewe be that that he was of the kynde
of Abraham as to the fleyysch the `whyche´ toke of God the
commaundment of cy[r]cumcysyon and to whom the beheste of
Cryste was made, þat ys to seye, þat he schulde come of hys blode.
65 Anothyr ys þat he wolde commende to vs be hys ensample the vertu of

---

32 that] as N 33 sone] childe N 33–4 For ther was . . . chylde] *om.* N
34 dede] louede N 35 maner] *om.* N hym] *fol. by canc.* and thankyth Gg
49 `whyche´] whiche childe N 50 ȝow summe] to yowe N 51 veryly take
mankynde] take verrey flesshe N 58 ert] N, *om.* Gg to¹] *om.* N 59 thyself] of
þiselfe N 60 to] *fol. by canc.* br Gg 63 cyrcumcysyon] circumcisioun N,
cycumcysyon Gg 65 the] of N

obedyence in kepynge the byddynge of the lawe that he was not bounde too.

Also, att thys cyrcumcysyon hys name was called Ihesu Criste, as ʒe haue herde afore of the euangelystes wordys. Thys name was fyrste iputt to hym of the Fadyr of Heuene and so schewde be the angyl to 70 oure Lady and Ioseph and be hem made opyn to othyre. Thys ys the name that ys so suete and confortable to | the louyers of God, for as f. 30ʳ Seyint Bernarde seyth hyt ys hony in the mowthe, melodye in the ere, and in the herte a suetnesse þat maye not be tolde. Thys name also, as Seyint Bernarde seyt, as oyle schynyth iprechyd; hyt fethyth 75 ithowgth; hyt esyeth and an vnvctyth icalled into helpe. Also anothyr worthy clerke seyt thus: 'Ihesu Criste ys a suete name and a delectable a name confortynge a synnar and a name of blyssyd hope therfore', he seyt, 'Ihesu be to me Ihesu Criste'; that ys [to] seye, a sauyoure for Ihesu Criste in Englyisch ys a myche to seye as a sauyoure, also, hyt ys 80 a name of gret vertu. Wherefore anothyr worthy clerke seyt thus: 'Thys ys þe name that ʒaf sygth to blynde, herynge to def, goynge to halte, speche to dowme, lyf to dede, in the vertu of thys name drafe out of bodyis itake or beseged all the powere of the fende. And in the name of Ihesu euery kne be bowed of heuenely thynges, erthely, and 85 helly', as Seynt Poule seyt, 'and ther `ys´ no name vndyr heuene vntake thys that we maye be sauyd by', as the [same] apostyl seyt. All thys commendacyon of the name of Ihesu and myche othyr that ys seyde and maye be seyde therof, vndyrstandyth ys not symply and barely for thys name Ihesu Criste I wryte or spoke, but for hym that 90 þys worscypful name betokenyth the whyche ys oure blysful Lorde Ihesu Cryste, God and man, the sauyoure of mankynde to whom thys | suete name ys specyally and trewly apropryed, and therfore hyt f. 30ᵛ ys so suete to the louyers of God and of so gret vertu as ys forseyde.

66 the byddynge] *om.* N   70 the¹] an N   74 also] *om.* N   75 as oyle schynyth iprechyd] *om.* N   77 clerke] Ricardi de sancto victore *in marg.* Gg   79 to²] N, *om.* Gg   81 clerke] Petrus Rauenas *in marg.* Gg   83 dede] dede men N   in] and N 85 erthely] erthly thynges N   87 same] N, sauyd Gg   89 ys] it is N 92 mankynde] all mankynde N   93 ys] *om.* N   94 as] as it N

CHAPTER 7

Of the Apparycyon of oure Lorde Ihesu Cryste, the whyche we calle
the xii daye and of the comynge of þe thre kyngys with here offryngys.
Capitulum septimum.

Aftyr the cyrcumcysyon of oure Lorde Ihesu Criste, ȝe maye thynke
5 ordynatly aftyr `þe´ forme of Holy Chyrche anothyr fayre medytacyon
of the Apparysyon or the Apperynge of oure Lorde, the whyche `we´
calle the Tuelfethe Daye. And hyt ys callyd the Apparysyon or
Apperynge, `for´ that daye oure Lorde fyrste apperyde to the peple
that was not fyrste chosyn, for the peple of Israel was `fyrste´ chosyn
10 and to hem was the lawe ȝeue, and they were specyally called the peple
of God, and alle othyre generally folke as we calle now paynemys. And
to thre kyngys of hem oure Lorde wolde fuchesaf thys daye fyrste to
apere and, be hem thre, was betokenyd the eleccyon or chesynge of all
Cristyn pepyl, and therfore hyt ys callyd the apperynge of oure Lorde.
15 Wherefore hyt muste nethys be a solempne feste amonge Cristyn
pepyl, for thys daye were we in these thre men fyrste callyd to be
eyrys of euerlastynge herytage. And thys daye was oure Lorde in hys
blyssyd manhede xiii dayis olde, but we Englyisch pepyl calle hyt the
xii daye, for hyt `ys´ the tuelfthe daye fro hys byrthe. And thys daye
f. 31ʳ `cam´ the thre forseyde | kyngys to Ierusalem out of the eeste in the
21 dayis of Kynge Herowde as `þe´ euangelyste makyth mencyon seyinge
thus: 'Where ys he that ys borne kynge of Iewys? We seygth hys sterre
in the eeste and we `come´ with ȝyftes to worschype hym.'
Of these thre kyngys myche thynge ys wryte in a boke that ys drawe
25 of hem, of the whyche sumwhat I wole telle ȝow in thys present
chapetele as God wole ȝeue me grace.
Fyrste ȝe schal vndyrstande aftyr the tellynge of the forseyde boke
that they were thre grete kyngys and of diuerse kyngedomys fer
atuynne, and none of hem wyste of othyr, but in oo tyme they were
30 enformyd of the sterre that apperyde in the nygthte of oure Lordys 1
byrthe, the whyche was prophecyed afore of an hethen prophete, þe
[whyche] ys callyd Balaam. And that sterre apperyde vpon an hylle
that ys callyd Vaus, loonge iwaytyd there of tuelue astronomerys
iordeynyd there thertoo. And that sterre was not made as sche ys

Chapter 7   2 the³] *om.* N   thre] *om.* N   6 or] or of N   11–12 as we calle now
. . . thre kynges] *om.* N   13 be] in N   17 Lorde] lore N   19 hys] þe N
22 kynge] þe kynge N   25 of¹] of of Gg   31 whyche] *om.* N   32 whyche]
whiche N, *om.* Gg   apperyde] appede N   34 there] *om.* N

paynttyd in thys contre, but sche hadde manye loonge bemys more 35
brennynges thanne brondys and the bemys were imeuyd as hyt hadde
be an egle fleynge and betynge the eyre, and the sterre hadde in here
`as hyt had be´ the face of a chylde and aboue a sygne of a crosse. And
ther was a voyce iherde in the sterre seyinge: 'Thys daye ys borne the
Kynge of Iewys, the whyche ys here abydynge | and here Lorde. f. 31ᵛ
Goeth to seke hym and to worschype hym.' 41

And whenne the forseyde kyngys were enformyd of the forseyde
sterre be ast[r]`o´nomerys, doctorys, and prophetys sueche as were
amonge hem, they ioyede ryght myche that they mygth see in here
tyme the sterre that was so loonge prophecyed afore. And thanne they 45
made hem aredy with gret araye as they mygth, fayreest and
nobylereste, as the voyce fro the sterre badde to seke the Lorde and
Kynge of Iewys iborne and to worschype hym. And so myche
nobyllokyr and worschypfullokyr þat they knewe iborne an hyer
kynge aboue hem, the whyche they purposyde to seke and worschype. 50
And thanne ȝe maye thynke how the sterre alwey wente afore hem and
whenne they wente, sche wente, and whenne they stode, sche stode,
and in here vertue, þat ys to seye, in here brygthnesse sche lyghttede
alle here weyis. And in alle cyteys that they cam by, the why`che´
nothyr daye ne nygthte were schytte for gret pese þat was that tyme 55
hyt semyde daye. And aftyr these gloryouse kyngys were come out of
the costys of here kyngedomys, they cam to othyr stroonge londys and
kyngedomys. And fro þat tyme forwarde they wente be watrys,
desertes, mounteynys, pleynys, valeyis, and horryble dychys
wythoute eny lettynge, for all was to hem playne, and that | that f. 32ʳ
was vnrygth and scharpe was made to hem in playne weyis, ne they 61
restede daye ne nygthte or toke eny innys, but bothe here `ostys´ and
bestes tyl they cam to Bethleem abode withoute mete and drynke, and
to hem alle in the weye hyt semyde but oo daye.

And whenne euyryche of these kyngys wyth here ostys were too 65
myle fro Ierusalem, a thycke myste and a therkenesse keuerede all the
londe, and in that myste and derkenesse they loste the sterre. And the
cause therof was, as summe doctorys seyin, þat they schulde be
compellyd to seke aftyr the place of oure Lordys byrthe þat so they

36 brennynges thanne] brennyge þat N   37 eyre] erthe N   38 `as hyt had be´] in
marg. with mark for inser. Gg   39 Thys] þis is N   43 ast[r]`o´nomerys]
ast`o´nomerys Gg   47 seke] sethe N   49 and] om. N   an] ne an N
50 worschype] to worshipe N   51 how] þat howe N   54 cyteys] þe cites N
61 in] It is to tell in marg., 17th-c. hand Gg   ne] om. N   63 and] or N   65 these]
þe N   of these kynges] twice, 2nd canc. Gg   66 a] om. N

70 'myghte' be made certayne of hys 'byrthe', bothe be the apperynge of
the sterre and also be the tellynge and assercyon of the prophecye þat
they schulde here in the cytee of Ierusalem. For there duellyde the
scrybys and doctorys of the lawe that cowde telle the scrypturys and
the prophecyis of oure Lorde Ihesu Criste, as ȝe schal here
75 aftyrwarde. And whenne the thre forseyde kyngys nygthede to the
cytee of Ierusalem, the fyrste kynge cam besyde the Mounte of
Caluary that oure Lorde was aftyrwarde crucyfyed vpon. And
besyde þat hylle was a place that thre weyis cam togydyr inne and
therefor the myste and therkenesse and ygnoraunce of the weye, the
80 fyrste kynge, þat ys callyd Melchyor, with hys companye abode and
f. 32ᵛ wente no fe'r'thyr. And a lytyl aftyrwarde in the same | myste and
therkenesse, the secunde kynge, þat ys callyd Balthaȝar, with hys oste
cam be a specyal weye and abode in the therkenesse besyde the
Mounte of Olyuete in a lytyl towne þat ys callyd there Galyle. And of
85 that same lytyl towne the gospel spekyth myche and holy wryt, for in
the same lytyl towne the apostyllys and the dyscyplys, afore the
Resurreccyon of oure Lorde and aftyr for threde of the Iewys,
wythoute the cytee of Ierusalem were wonde priuyly to come
togyderys. But ther ys a contre, the whyche 'ys' callyd also Galylye,
90 and that ys fro Ierusalem as hyt were thre dayis iorneye or therabowte.
Thanne whenne the tueyne forseyde kyngys, þat ys to seye Melchyor
and Balthaȝar, abode in the forseyde myste and therkenesse a lytyl,
the myste and therkenesse arose vp. And whenne they seygth that
they 'were' nere the cytee, thanne euery kynge, ȝytt vnware of othyr,
95 with here ostes toke the weye to the cyteewarde. And whenne they
cam to the place that thre weyis cam togyder inne besyde the Mounte
of Caluarye, thanne the thyrde kynge, that ys called Iaspar, cam with
hys oste. And so these thre gloryouse kyngys with here ostes in that
thre folde weye mette togydere, and thowgth no of hem hadde iseye
100 othyr afore, ȝytt they kyssede togyderes. And thowgth they were of
f. 33ʳ diuerse languages, ȝytt hem semyde that | euyry spake othyrys
language. And whenne they hadde exponyd euery to othyr the
cause of hyre comynge and acordyde alle in one, they were myche
the gladdyr and feruentyr to [do] that þat they cam fore.

70 the¹] *om.* N   77 aftyrwarde crucyfyed] *reversed in text with marks to make order*
match N   79 therkenesse] þe derkenes N   84 there] *om.* N   85 that] þe N
86 the²] *om.* N   96 cam] come to þe citewarde and when þei come N   the¹] *om.* N
thre] þe thre forseide N   101 euyry] eueryche of hem N   104 feruentyr] more
feruente N   do] N, *om.* Gg

Aftyr þys ȝe maye thynke how they go into the cytee and askyn 105
where the Kynge of Iewys schulde be borne, as the gospel makyth
mencyon. For haply they trowede þat so excellent a chylde schulde
nowher be borne 'but' in the chef cytee. And whenne Kynge Herowde
herde thys, he was gretly dystroblyd and all the peple of [þe] cytee
with hym. For haply he dredde þat the kynge that was newe borne 110
schulde pote hym out of hys kyngedom, for he was an alyene iturned
to the Iewys lawe and imade theyre kynge be the Emperowre and the
Romannys. Anothyr cause maye be for they cam so sodeynely vpon
hem and with so myche peple, for hyt 'ys' seyde in the forseyde boke
that here oste was so myche that the cytee wythinne mygth not 115
herborowe hem, but for the moste parte they abode wythoute and laye
abowte the cytee as thowgth hyt hadde be beseged.

And thanne ȝe maye thynke how Kynge Herowde callede togydere
alle 'þe' prynces of prestys and the scrybys of þe peple, for they were
chef amonge hem as byschoppys and gret clerkys amonge vs in the 120
spirualte of ho|ly chyrche and of hem he askede where oure Lorde f. 33ᵛ
Ihesu Criste schulde be borne and they tolde hym in Bethleem as they
knewe be scrypture and prophecye. Here ȝe maye vndyrstande the
blyndnesse of the Iewys, the whyche tolde be scrypture the place of
oure Lordys byrthe and 'ȝytt' they wolde not beleue in hym, and so 125
hyre knowynge as Seyint Gregory seyt was to hem wytnessynge of
dampnacyon, and to vs helpe of beleue. For, sygth they knewe that he
schulde be borne and the place, and beleuyde not in hym, hyt was the
'more' wytnessynge of dampnacyon to hem. And so be here tellynge
they openyde the weye to vs and be here mysbeleue they putte the 130
grace of God fro here hertys.

Thanne aftyr thys ȝe maye 'thynke' how Kynge 'Herowde' callede
the kyngys pryuyly to hym and dylygently lernyde of hem the tyme of
the sterre þat apperyde to hem, þat yf 'they' cam not aȝen to hym, be
knowynge of the tyme and of the place, he mygth knowe where 'he' 135
were and so scle hym. And 'þanne he' sente 'hem' into Bethleem
seyinge: 'Goeth and enqyryth dylygently aftyr the chylde, and
whenne ȝe haue founde hym brynde me worde that I maye come
also and worschype hym.' Thys he seyde but of falsnesse and dysceyte
that he mygth the lygthlokyr dysceyue 'hem' and make hem come 140

105 Aftyr þys] and þan N   109 þe] N, *om.* Gg   111 was] was bot N
113 maye be for] myght be þat N   118 Kynge] the kynge N   120 chef] chosen
men N   the] *om.* N   121 of holy chyrche] *twice, 1st canc.* Gg   136 were] was N
137 seyinge] *om.* N   140 'hem'] hym N   come] to come N

aȝen to hym as Lyre seyt, faynynge 'hymself' to worschype hym that
f. 34ʳ he wolde haue sclayne, as 'was' opynyly schewde aftyrwarde | be
scleynge of the innocentes as ȝe schal here be the grace of God in thys
boke folowynge in anothyr chapetele. Thanne whenne Kynge Her-
145 owde hadde seyde the forseyde worthys to hem they wente here weye
to Bethleemwarde, and anone the sterre that they hadde seyin in the
eeste and the whyche they hadde loste in the forseyde myste and
therkenesse wente afore hem as sche dede afore tyme tylle sche cam
and stode ouyr the place where the chylde was, and whenne they
150 seygth here, they ioyede wyth ful gret ioye. And thanne ȝe maye
beholde how they entre into the cote and denne þat oure Lorde was
borne inne, be the keuyred strete of the whyche I haue tolde ȝow in
the chapetele of the byrthe of oure Lorde, for oure Lady and Ioseph
were there into that tyme. And there they fonde the chylde with hys
155 modyr oure Lady Seyint Marye, and thanne thynkyth how they falle
downe on here kneys and reuerently worschype hym and here tresorys
iopened. They offre to hym ȝftes: Golde, 'encense, and' myrre. Golde
they offrede, aftyr the seyinge of Seyint Bernarde, to the blyssyd
vyrgyne for the helpynge of here nede, encense 'a'ȝenste the stenche
160 of the stabyl, myrre for the 'sadlynge' of the chyldys membrys and
also to put aweye euyl wormys.

f. 34ᵛ   Also Seyint Gregory seyt, in the omelye of þys | feste that be golde
they betokene hym a kynge; be encense, God; be myrre, deedly, for
the helthe of mannys soule. 'But ther be summe herytykys', he seyt,
165 'that beleue hym God, but they beleue hym not ouyrall regnynge.
These þat 'be'leuyn thus offre hym encense but they offre hym no
golde. Othyre ther be also that trowe hym a kynge, but they denye
hym God. These offre hym golde, but they wole not offre encense.
And summe othyre ther beyn the whyche beleue hym God and a
170 kynge, but they denye hym to haue take deedly fleyisch, these offre
hym golde and encense, but they denye to offre hym myrre, þat ys to
seye, they wole not beleue hym to haue take dedly fleyisch for the
helthe of mankynde. But lete vs', seyth he, 'offre to oure iborne golde';
þat ys to seye, that we knowleche hym ouerall regnynge. 'Lete vs offre
175 hym encense'; þat ys to seye, that we beleue þat he that apperyde in
tyme was God afore all tymys. 'Lete 'vs' offre hym also myrre'; þat ys

---

149 they] *fol. by canc.* cam thedyr Gg   151 Lorde] *fol. by canc.* oure Gg
157 ȝyftes] *om.* N   16129 euyl] *prec. by canc.* of euyl of Gg   163 a] *om.* N
167 golde] *prec. by canc.* glo Gg   172 not] *fol. by canc.* offre Gg   176 all] ony N
hym] to hym N

to seye, þat hym that we beleue in hys godhede vnpassyble, 'lete `vs´ beleue also to haue be in oure fleyisch deedly.' Also he seyth in the same omelye folowynge, schortly forto seye: 'That be golde also ys betokened wysedom; be encense, holy prayere and heuenely desyres; 180 be myrre, | mortyfycacyon of oure fleyisch; and all þys muste we offre f. 35ʳ gostly to oure Lorde.'

Also ȝe schal vndyrstande, as hyt ys wryte in the forseyde boke of the *Thre Kyngys of Coleyne*, that whenne they offrede the forseyde ȝyftes to oure Lorde, he was in hys manhede xiii dayis olde, as I haue tolde ȝow 185 afore in thys chapetele, and as in the persone of man aftyr hys age he was sumwhat fatt as chyldryn been and laye in the cracche and heye vp to the armys iwrappy`d´ in poure clothys. And hys modyr oure Lady Seyint Marye as hyt ys founde in manye othyr ensamplys and bokys was a ful persone and sumwhat brow`n´e. And in the presence of the 190 thre kyngys sche was clothed in a poure whyte mantyl the whyche sche helde closyd afore here wyth the lyfte hande, and here heed safe here face was all wrappyd abowte wyth a lynnyn clothe, and sche satt aboue the cracche and wyth here rygth hande sche helde vp the chyldeys heed. And `whenne´ the thre kyngys hadde kyssyd the erthe afore the 195 cracche and the chyldys handys and hadde also offryd deuoutly and reuerently to the chylde Ihesu here ȝyftes, they leyde hem deuoutly in the cracche besyde the chyldys heed and hys modrys kneys. And schortly for[to] seye aftyr þe menynge of the forseyde boke, aftyr the kyngys hadde worschypyd oure Lorde and offryd `þe´ forseyde | ȝyftes f. 35ᵛ and gloryusly performyd all þat that they cam fore out of [þe] eeste, fro 201 thennys forwarde bothe they and here ostes horse and othry bestes þat cam fro so fer contreys wyth`oute´ mete and drynke in here maner and othyr deedly men began to sclepe. And all þat daye in Bethleem and othyr places abowte they ȝaf hem to reste and solace and mekely tolde 205 and exponede to all folke in that contre þe cause why the sterres had ledde hem so merueylusly fro here kyngdomys.

And whenne they hadde take an ansuere in here sclepe that they schulde not goo aȝen to Kynge Herowde, as the euangelyste makyth mencyon, be anothyr weye they wente aȝen in`to´ here kyngedomys. 210 And fro þat tyme aftyr the sterre that wente afore hem apperyde no more, but as they wente aȝen into here kyngedomys, be þe maner of

181 we] vs N   187 sumwhat fatt] fatt sumwhat *with marks for correct order* Gg
196 offryd deuoutly] deuoutly offryd *with marks for correct order* Gg   199 forto] N, for
Gg   200 offryd] offerede to hym N   201 þe] N, *om.* Gg   203 and¹] or N
206 folke] þe folke N   had] *fol. by canc.* so Gg   212 þe] *om.* N

men they toke here innys be daye and nygthte in the weye and
vnnethe in too 3ere they mygth performe þe gydys and othyr to
215 expone to hem the weyis þat they wente [to] come a3en into here
kyngdomys. And whenne they cam to the hylle þat ys callyd Vaus, of
the whyche I have tolde 3ow afore in thys chapele þat the sterre
'fyrste' apperyde vpon, there they dede make a chapel in the
worschype of the kynge of Iewys that they hadde softe and
f. 36ʳ worschypyd | and offryd 3yftes too. And in a towne þat was benethe
221 the hylle they reste'de' of the traueylys of here iorneye, and there
rygth be one assent they chese the place of here beryinge. And aftyr
the ascencyon of oure Lorde, Seynt Thomas the apostil cam into that
contre be the sonde of God, and into þat tyme they were alyue. And
225 thanne Seyint Thomas, be the grace of the Holy 'Gooste', baptysede
hem wyth all here peple. And thanne they were iunyd to Seynt
Thomas to preche the worde of God, and aftyrwarde he made hem
archebyischoppys. And so aftyrwarde in goode age and holy lyuynge
they dyde and were byrryed att the forseyde hylle as they hadde 'made'
230 couenaunt, and fro thennys they were translatyd be Seyint [Helene] to
Constantynople and fro thennys to the cytee of Medyolane þat Seyint
Ambrose was summe tyme byischop of, and fro thennys to Coleyne,
and there reste here blyssyd bodyis into thys daye.

Ferthyrmore also 3e schal [vndyrstande] that Seyint Gregory seyth
235 vpon that texte of the gospel of thys same daye: 'Per aliam viam
reuersi sunt in regionem suam.' Thys ys to seye: 'Be anothyr weye
they turned a3en in here contry.' Summe gret thynge seyth he the'se'
kyngys betokene to vs that they turned a3en in here contrey be
anothry weye. And sc[h]ortly to ende aftyr the menynge of hys
f. 36ᵛ wordys | he seyth that paradyse ys oure contry and we wente thennys
241 be pryde and vnobedyence, be folowynge of vysyble thynges, and be
tastynge of the mete that was forbode vs, all thys 3e schal vndyrstande
was in the fyrste man for in hym we fylle in alle the forseyde synnys.
But hyt ys nedful he seyth we goo thedyr a3en be wepynge, be
245 obedyence, be dyspysynge of vysyble thynges, and be refraynynge the
appetyte of oure fleyisch, and thys maye be medytacyon of þe
apparycyon of oure Lorde, þe whyche we calle þe tuelfthe daye.

215 to²] N, *om.* Gg   218 whenne] whe N   218 dede make] maden N   220 a]
þe N   222 assent] accorde N   225 be] thurgh N   227 to¹] of N
230 Helene] N, Gleyne Gg   233 reste] lyen N   234 also] *om.* N   vndyrstande]
vnrdyrstande Gg   238 contrey] kyngedomes N   239 schortly] scortly Gg   to] for
to N   241 thynges] *twice, 1st canc.* Gg   243 forseyde] *prec. by canc.* for Gg
synnys] thynges N   244 we] þat we N   246 be] be þe N

CHAPTER 8

Of the puryfy`ca´cyon of oure Lady Seyint Marye, þe `whyche´ we calle Candylmasse daye. Capitulum octauum.

Aftyr the thre kyngys forseyde hadde offryd here ȝyftes to oure Lorde and were goo aȝen into here kyngedomys, as hyt ys wryte in the boke of the same kyngys, oure Lady abode stylle ȝytt a lytyl whyle in the 5 cote and denne þat oure Lorde was borne in. But þe fame of here and of the thre kyngys growynge, sche wente wyth here sone Ihesu into anothyr denne vndyr the erthe imade of a rok for drede of Iewys. And there sche abode into the daye of here purifycacyon. And that was `þe´ xl daye fro the byrthe of oure Lorde, and hyt ys called puryfycacyon, 10 þat ys to seye in opyn Englylisch, a clensynge. Not that sche `was´ clensyd of eny thynge, for | sche hadde conseyuyd of no man but of f. 37ʳ the Holy Goste, but for sche dede of here owen lownesse þe same obseruaunce that othyr dede þat hadde conseyuyd of men. For hyt was bode in the olde lawe þat whenne a womman hadde conseyuyd of 15 a man and bore a knaue `chylde´ sche schulde be vnclene vii dayis, vnclene þat ys to seye fro the felawschyp of men and fro the entrynge of the temple. But vii dayis fulfylde sche was clene as to the felawschyp of men, but ȝytt as to the entrynge of the temple sche was vnclene vnto the xxxiiiᵗʸ daye. And thanne att the laste, xlty dayis 20 fulfylde, the fourethyeth daye sche entrede the temple and offryde the chylde wyth ȝyftes. But yf sche bare a womman þe dayys were idublyd bothe as to the felawschyp of men and to the entrynge of the temple.

To thys lawe oure Lady was not bounde for sche hadde not conseyuyd of eny man `but´ be werkynge of the Holy Goste, and 25 therfore sche was not bounde to that lawe but of here owen lownesse, rygth as oure Lorde Ihesu Cryste of hys lownesse wolde be circumsydyd. And also haply for sche wolde not be seyin synglere ne ȝeue eny occasyon to the peple þat was that tyme to deme euyle and to seye that sche was vnobedyent to the lawe of Moyses. For yf sche 30 wolde haue escusyd here | and seyde þat sche conseyuyde neuere of f. 37ᵛ man and therefore sche was not bounde therto, hoo wolde haue leuyd here that tyme? No man, for hyt semyde vnpossyble. Wherefore hyt was necessarye þat sche schul`de´ conforme hereself to othyre to

---

Chapter Eight 1-2 þe `whyche´ we calle] þat is callede N   3 thre] *om.* N
5 kyngys] thre kynges N   8 Iewys] þe iewes N   14 othyr] other women N
20 xxxiiiᵗʸ] one and thirty N   22 But] and N   28 for] þat N   31 haue] *fol. by*
canc. seyde Gg   33 Wherefore] therefore N

35 exclude that sclaundyr and [fals] demynge þat mygth haue falle yf
sche hadde not do so.

Here, as me semyth, ys a fayre ensample to alle relygyus men and
wymmen how gladly they schulde obeye to the obseruaunces of here
rulys and the byddynges of here soueraynys þat they byn bounde to,
40 sygth oure Lorde Ihesu Criste and hys blysful modyr were so
obedyent to that þat they were not bounde to. And also hyt ys a
general ensample 'to' all Crystyn pepyl how gladly and lowly they
schulle obeye to the bydynges and ordenaunces of here modyr 'Holy'
Chyrche. And also thys ensample of oure Lorde and oure Lady ys
45 myche aȝenst sueche as byn synglere and wole not conforme hemself
to othyre in thynges þat be not euyl, but be here syngleretee ȝeue
othyres cause of grucchynge and to speke heuyly. Also thys feste ys
callyd amonge vs Candylmasse, for thys daye we vse 'to' bere taprys
and wexe candyllys lygth in the worschype of oure Lady and in
50 betokenyge of here clennesse and the lygth of grace þat was in here
and be here ȝeue to all þe worlde.

f. 38ʳ   Aftyr þys ȝe maye beholde wyth ȝoure | gostly eye how aftyr that
the dayis of the purgacyon of oure Lady were fulfylde aftyr þe lawe of
Moyses, as the euangelyste seyth, oure Lady and Ioseph bare oure
55 Lorde Ihesu Cryste into Ierusalem that they mygthte presente hym in
the temple to God as the maner of the lawe was, and that the'y'
mygthte also ȝeue for hym a sacryfyce as hyt 'ys' wryte in the lawe of
oure Lorde a peyre [of] turtures or tweyne chekenenys of dowuys.
Thys was the offrynge of poure pepyl be the lawe, but the offrynge of
60 þe ryche was a lombe. And in thys ȝe maye consydere þe mekenesse of
oure Lady in that þat sche chese the offrynge of poure folke and not of
ryche.

And in the same tyme ȝe maye thynke also þat ther was a man in
Ierusalem whas name was Symeon, and thys man, as the euangelyste
65 beryth wytnesse, was a rygthful man abydynge the conforte of the
pepyl of Israel and the Holy Goste was in hym. And 'he' hadde take
an ansuere of the Holy Goste in hys deuout prayerys þat he schulde
not dye tyl 'he' hadde seyin oure Lorde Ihesu Cryste. For he hadde
ful gret desyres to see hym as Seyint Austyn seyth in a sermone that
70 he makyth of thys same feste in the whyche he seyth that thys olde
rygthful man schulde seye euery daye in hys prayerys thus: 'Whenne

---

35 that] þe N   fals] N, flas Gg   haue] *om.* N   42 and] howe N   44 oure²] of
our N   45 as] þat N   55 Ierusalem] þe cite of ierusalem N   58 of¹] N, *om.* Gg
60 ryche] riche folke N   in thys] here N   63 the] þat N

schal he come and whenne schal he `be´ borne? Whenne schal I see
[hym]? | Trowest þu he schal fynde me here? Trowest þu [þat] I schal f. 38ᵛ
dure? Trowst þu the`se´ eyen schal see hym be whom the eyen of the
herte schal be openyd?' Thys, seyth Seyint Austyn, he seyde in hys 75
prayeres and for hys desyre he toke an ansuere of the Holy Goste that
he schulde not dye tyl he hadde seye oure Lorde Ihesu Cryste.

Thanne maye ȝe thynke how be reuelacyon of the Holy Goste he
entryth into the temple, and whenne he was come into the temple
thanne ȝe maye beholde also how oure Lady wyth the chylde and 80
Ioseph entryn into the temple þat they mygthte doo aftyr the custom
of the lawe for hym as ys forseyde. And thanne ȝe maye beholde how
the forseyde olde man wyth ful gret ioye of herte resceyuyth hym in
hys armys and blyssyth God, thankynge hym for that gret benfeett,
and seyth: 'Now Lorde, þu leuyste thy seruaunt aftyr thy worde in 85
pese', þat ys to seye, ffro hennys forwarde þu schalte lete me goo out
of þys lyfe in pese of herte, 'ffor my eyen haue seyen thyn helthe'; þat
ys, hym þat þu haste ordeynyd helthe to all mankynde. For Seyint
Austyn seyth: 'The helthe of God ys oure Lorde Ihesu Criste';
vndyrstondyth in that þat he ys ordeynyd of God the Fadyr the 90
helthe or sauyoure of mankynde.

Aftyr thys ȝe maye thynke also how oure Lady and Ioseph were
me`r´ueylynge vpon tho thynges that were seyde | of oure Lorde that f. 39ʳ
tyme of Symeon and afore of þe kyngys, of the schepherdes, and of
Zacharye and Elyzabeth. And in that `same tyme´ also ther was an 95
holy prophetesse, Anne be name, and in the `same´ oure ȝe maye
thynke that thys was do, sche cam into the temple be reuelacyon of the
Holy Goste. And sche was a deuout wydowe and fer goo into age, for
the euangelyste seyth þat sche hadde lyuyd vii ȝere wyth an husbunde
fro here maydenhode, and aftyr hys deth sche abode a trewe wydowe 100
vnto fourescore ȝere and foure, the `whyche´ wente not fro the temple
seruyuynge oure Lorde in fastynge and preyere daye and nygthte.
And thys holy wydowe knowlechede to oure Lorde thankynge hym of
so `gret´ a benfeet fulfylde, and sche spake of hym to alle tho þat abode
the redempcyon of Ierusalem tellynge hem þat oure aȝenbyare was 105
borne. And whenne they hadde performyd all that was to be done
aftyr Moyses lawe they wente aȝen into Galyle into here cytee of

---

73 hym] N, *om.* Gg   þat] N, *om.* Gg   81 þat] *twice* Gg   82 as] as it N
83 olde] holy olde N   87–8 þat . . . helthe] *om.* N   88 to] as to N   90 ys] *om.* N
91 sauyoure] þe sauyour N   95 Elyzabeth] of Elizabeth N   103 holy] same N
104 a] *om.* N   106 that] *om.* N   107 Moyses lawe] þe lawe of moyses N

Naȝareth. Thys ʽysʼ Galyle the contre þat I haue tolde ȝow of in the nexte chapetele afore thys, and also in the chapeʽteʼle of the Salutacyon of oure Lady. And Naȝareth ys the cytee þat the angyl Gabryel salutede oure Lady inne, as I haue tolde ȝow in the same chapeʽteʼle.

Here I maye telle ȝow a goode tale to ȝoure edyfycacyon acordynge to thys feste and hyt ys wryte in the | Legende that ys callyd Aurea aftyr thys feste. Hyt ys seyde there that there was a nobyl howsewyf that hadde a specyal ʽdeuocyonʼ to oure Lady, and sche hadde byldʽdydʼ a chapele besyde here howse, and sche hadde a preste of here owen and euery daye sche wolde here a masse of oure Lady. But the feste of the Puryfycacyon of oure Lady nygthynge, the preste for an erande of hys was fer thennys and so that daye the lady mygthte haue no masse. Wherfore whenne sche hadde sorowed myche sche wente into here owen chapel and afore an auter of oure Lady sche laye downe prostrate. Thanne sodeynely sche was made in an extasye or a suowynge of mynde and here semyde that ʽscheʼ was sette in a fayre chyrche. And thanne sche lokyde abowte and sche seygth a gret companye of maydenys comynge into the chyrche, and afore hem wente a fayre virgyne icrowned wyth a dyamonde. And whenne they were alle sette downe be ordyr, thanne ther cam in anothyr companye of ȝonge men and they satte downe also be ordyr, and thanne ther cam in one that bare a gret bundel of taprys, and he ȝaf to the fyrste virgyne that wente afore othyre a tapyr, and aftyrwarde to the othyr virgynys and ȝonge men also.

Aftyrwarde he cam to the howsewyfe and ȝaf here a tapyr the whyche sche toke gladly. Thanne sche lo|kyde abowte the quere and sche seygth tueyne tapyrberarys and a sodekene, a dekene, and a preste iclodyd in holy clothys goynge to the autyr as thowgth they wolde synge masse. And here semyde that the too collectes were Seyint Laurence and Seynt Vyncent, the dekene and the sodekene, too angyllys, the preste oure Lorde Ihesu Cryste. And whenne the *Confiteor* was seyde, too fayre ȝonge men wente into the myddyl of the quere and beganne the offyce of the masse wyth an hye voyce and deuocyon, and the othyres that were in the quere folowede aftyr. And ʽwhenneʼ hyt was come to the offrynge, the quene of the virgynys and ʽþeʼ othyre virgynys wyth othyre that were in quere knelyde downe

115 thys] þis same N   121 sorowed] weyled N   122 sche] and N   124 sette]
om. N   129 thanne] om. N   130 to] om. N   the] eueryche the *with* eueryche *exp.*
Gg   131 the] þat N   144 quere] þe quere N

and as the manyr ys offrede here taprys to the preste. And whenn`e´ 145
the preste abode the howsewyfe þat sche schulde offre here tapyr to
hym and sche wolde not come, the quene of virgynys sente to here be
a messangere that sche dede vncurteysly that sche made the preste
abyde so loonge. And sche ansueryde aȝen that the preste schulde goo
forth in hys masse, fore sche wolde not offre here tapyr to hym.   150

Thanne the quene sente anothyr messangere, to the whyche sche
ansueryde that the tapyr that was ȝeue here, sche wolde vttyrly ȝeue to
no man, but sche wolde kepe [yt] of deuocyon. Thanne the quene of |
virgynys badde the messangere þat he schulde goo to here aȝen and   f. 40ᵛ
praye here to offre here tapyr or ellys he schulde violently take [yt] out 155
of here handys. And whenne the messangere cam aȝen and prayde here
and sche wolde not, he seyde þat he hadde in commaundment þat he
schulde take [yt] vyolently fro here. And thanne he toke the tapyr wyth
gret vyolence and was abowte to take [yt] fro hyre, but sche wythhelde
strongly and manly defendyde hereself. And whenne ther hadde be   160
loonge stryfe betuene hem and the tapyr was drawe vyolently hedyr
and thedyr, sodeynely the tapyr tobrake and the haluyndele abode in
the messangerys hande and the othyr dele in the ladyis hande. And att
thys gret brekynge sodeynely sche cam to hereself aȝen and fonde
hereself besyde the autyr where sche hadde leyde hereself and the tapyr 165
in here hande tobroke, of the whyche sche merueylyde gretly and ȝaf
gret thankynge to the blyssyd virgyne þat lett here not be wythoute
masse that daye, but made here to be att sueche an offyce. And thanne
sche dylygently putt vp that tapyr and kepte [yt] for a gret relyke. And
hyt ys seyde that alle thoo that ben tuchyd therwyth, what sykenesse 170
that euer they beeholde wyth, anone they ben delyuered.

Of the goynge of Ioseph wyth oure Lorde and | oure Lady into f. 41ʳ
Egypte, and of the scleynge of the innocentes and of hys commynge
aȝen into þe londe of Israel. Capitulum nonum.

Whenne ȝe haue bethowgth ȝou of the puryfycacyon of oure Lady, as
ys forseyde, thanne maye ȝe thynke a newe medytacyon of the fleynge 5

---

145 offrede] offrede vpp N   148 that¹] seynge to hir þat N   152 here] to hir N
153 yt] it N, hym Gg   155 he] she N   yt] it N, hym Gg   158 yt] it N, hym Gg
159 yt] it N, hym Gg   wythhelde] helde it N   164–5 fonde herself . . . leyde herself
and] om. N   169 yt] it N, hym Gg   171 delyuered] deliuerd Deo gracias N

Chapter 9 1 oure²] with our N   29 of²] om. N   5 medytacyon] medydytacyon,
second dy *canc.* Gg

of oure Lorde into Egypte, and that 3e maye thynke in thys wyse.
Whenne þe Kynge Herowde seygth that the kyngys cam not a3en to
hym as he badde hem, he trowede þat they hadde be dysseyuyd be the
apperynge of the sterre. And therfore he trowede that they hadde ʻbeʼ
10 aschamyd to come a3en to hym, and so he sesyde of sekynge aftyr oure
Lorde. But whenne he herde telle what þe schepherdys hadde seyde,
and what the holy man Symeon and the holy wydowe Anne hadde
prophecyed of hym, he was ʻsoreʼ adrad and thowgthte hymself fowle
dysseʻyʼuyd of the kyngys. And thanne he purposyde to scle alle the
15 chyldryn that were in Bethleem, þat he mygth amonge hem scle hym
þat he knewe not.
      Thanne 3e maye thynke how the angyl of oure Lorde apperyde to
Ioseph in hys sclepe, and badde hym take the chylde and hys modyr
and flee into Egypte, and be there into the tyme þat he warnede hym,
20 for forsothe he seyde in tyme to come Herowde schal seke the chylde
f. 41ᵛ to dystroye hym. Thanne 3e maye thynke how he tellyth oure Lady |
therof, and thanne sche ʻwasʼ sore adrad and happly prayeth hym that
ʻheʼ schulde hye faste to parforme the byddynge of þe angyl. And
thanne maye 3e beholde how the goode olde man arysyth vp be
25 nygthte, haply that he wolde not be aspyde and also for he wolde
fulfylle the byddynge of the angyl anone. And in þys ys hys trewe
obedyence and dylygence schewed, and therfore takyth ensampyl of
hym and lernyth to doo gladly and anone, wythoute eny taryinge or
grucchynge þat God byddyth 3ow be 3oure soueraynys.
30   Now thanne beholdyth how Ioseph wyth all the haste þat he maye
takyth the chylde and hys modyr, as ys forseyde, be nygthte, for he
was sore adrad of that he hadde herde of the angyl and goeth forth into
Egypte and that 3e maye thynke in thys wyse. Fyrste ymagynyth, as
thowgth 3e were presently wyth hem, and thanne beholdyth how ʻheʼ
35 settyth here vpon an asse and the chylde in here armys and hymselfe
goeth forth afore and haply ledyth the brydel, and so they goo forth in
here iorneye. And as they wente 3e maye thynke they cam be a palme
tre, as hyt ys seyde in a lytyl boke þat ys wryte of the 3ongethe of oure
Lorde vndyr the whyche oure Lady for werynesse desyryde to reste of
40 here. And whenne sche seygth þat ther was fʻrʼoyt þeron, sche
f. 42ʳ desyryde to haue þerof; and so att the byddynge of oure Lorde | he

8 be dysseyuyd] desceyuede hym N   10 of] of þe N   12 holy¹] forseide holy N
15 that were] om. N   20 for] om. N   25 that] for N   26 of] of god by N   hys]
om. N   30 Ioseph] þat Ioseph N   31 as] as yt N   38 þat] þe whiche N   of¹]
in N   39 Lorde] seuyoure N   41 so] om. N   he] þe tre N

enclynyde hymselfe downe to oure Ladyis feete. And so sche toke
therof what here lyste, and aftyr þat att the byddynge also of oure
Lorde, he arose vp aȝen as he was. And att þe rote of the same tre, as
yt ys seyde in the forseyde boke also, att þe byddynge of oure Lorde   45
spronge ʻvpʼ a welle of clene watyr, of the whyche they dranke and
here bestes also. And whenne they hadde doo they wente forth in here
iorneye. In all þys kepyth ȝowselfe in ȝoure ymagynacyon as thowgth
ȝe were present hauynge pytee of here labors in thys iorneye and
doynge sum seruyse to hem as ȝoure affeccyon wole ȝeue ȝow.   50

And so att the laste wyth myche labore they cam into the londe of
Egypte and in the comynge inne of oure Lorde into the londe of
Egypte, ȝe maye thynke how alle þe ydolys fylle downe aftyr the
prophecye of Ysaye. And hyt ys seyde also þat rygth as in the goynge
out of the chyldryn of Israel of Egypte þer was no howse ilefte in the   55
whyche ther ne laye deed the fyrste begotyn thynge, rygth so in the
commynge of oure Lorde into Egypte ther was no temple but ther
ʻwereʼ falle downe an ydole inne, þat ys to seye, a false god. And
thanne ȝe maye thynke that they toke a duellynge place in a cytee þat
ys callyd Hermopolym, and there they duellyde vii ȝere vnto the deth   60
of Kynge Herowde.

Aftyr þys | turnyth aȝen to the storye of Kynge Herowde and   f. 42ᵛ
thynkyth how, whyle he purposyde to scle the chyldryn, he was sente
aftyr be a pystyl fro the Emperowre to ansuere to certeyne accusacyonys that hys owen sonys hadde accusyd hym of to the Emperowre.   65
And so he lefte the persecucyon of the innocentes and wente to Rome
to ansuere to þat he was accusyd of. Thanne whenne the fadyr and hys
sonys streuyn togyderys afore the Emperowre, hyt was dyffynyd that
the sonys schulde obeye to the fadyr in all thynge and he schulde leue
hys kyngedom to whom he wolde, for therfore was here stryuynge.   70
Thanne whenne thys was done he cam home aȝen into hys kyngedom.
And of þys confyrmacyon of the Emperowre he thowgth hymselfe
more sykyr to doo þat wykked dede þat he purposyde er he wente out
to Rome, þe whyche was to scle the innocentes as ys forseyde.

Thanne aftyr ʻheʼ was come ʻhomeʼ, ȝe mayʻeʼ thynke how in gret   75
angyr he sente forth hys mayne and dede scle alle the chyldryn þat
were in Bethleem and in the costes therabowte fro the spase of too

42 hymselfe] *om.* N   Ladyis] lordes N   44 he arose] it rose N   he was] it was
before N   51 wyth] by N   the londe of] *om.* N   54 And] and as N   60 vii] eght
N; *see note*   62 Aftyr] Than aftre N   63 whyle] whilely N   64 to²] of N
71 home] *om.* N   73 out] *om.* N   74 þe whyche] þat N   ys] it is N   75 in] in
in Gg

ȝere and benede, aftyr the tyme that he hadde askyd of the kyngys.
For he hadde herde of the kyngys þat þe same day`e´ that the sterre
80 apperyde to hem oure Lorde was borne, and hyt was a ȝere whyle [he]
wente to Rome and cam aȝen. And therfore he trowede oure Lorde
f. 43ʳ were a ȝere | olde and summe dayis more, and therfore he dede scle
alle the chyldryn that were of that age and aboue þat age into too ȝere,
and benede into chyldryn of oo nygthte þat he mygthte be sekyr of
85 hym, and also leste the chylde that sterrys dede seruyse to mygthte
make hymselfe now to seme ȝongyr and now elthyr. But all thys
wylynessee profytede hym not, for ther ys no wysedom aȝenste oure
Lorde, as the Wyse Man seyth. Thys þat I haue seyde of Kynge
Herowde the Maystyr of Storyis tellyth in the *Scole Storyis*.
90 Thanne aftyr þys ȝe maye beholde wyth ȝoure gostly eye a pyteful
sy`g´th, how Kynge Herowdys mayne þat were sente forth cruelly scle
the ȝonge chyldryn. For some haply they bere thorow wyth here
sperys and of some they smyte of the heed, and some they hewe haply
halfe a too. And thanne maye ȝe beholde also how the modrys rennyn
95 aftyr here chyldryn, waylynge and wepynge wyth here brestes opyn
and all toterynge here heere for sorowe, and that was a rewful sygthte.
Aftyr thys ȝe maye thynke how Kynge Herowde for thys synne and
othyre þat he hadde doo, be `þe´ suffraunce of God sclewe hymselfe
wyth the same knyfe þat he paryde an appyl with, as Seyint Remygye
f. 43ᵛ seyth. Aftyr the deth of Kynge Herowde ȝe maye thynke how | the
101 angyl of oure Lorde apperyde to Ioseph aȝen in the londe of Egypte,
seyinge to hym thus: 'Aryse vp and take the chylde and hys modyr
and go aȝen into the londe of Israel for forsothe they be dede that softe
þe chyldys lyf.' And thanne thynkyth how he takyth the chylde and
105 hys modyr aftyr þe byddynge of the angyl and goeth aȝen into the
londe of Israel.
Hyt ys seyde in the boke þat ys wryte of the *Thre Kyngys of Coleyne*,
that be alle þe weyis þat oure Lady wyth oure Lorde Ihesu wente by in
the goynge into Egypte and comynge aȝen, `fownde´ growen drye
110 rosys, the whyche ben callyd Rosys of Ierico. And hem þe Sarsyn
wymmen gladly and myche vsyn. And thyke rosys gadre men þat ben
callyd there Bedewynys, þe whyche goo abowte þat deserte wyth
bestes fro place to place and selle hem for brede in gret multytude and

80 he] N, *om.* Gg 83 and . . . into] *om.* N 84 chyldryn] þe children N be] *prec. by canc.* he Gg 89 Storyis] þe stories N 90 Thanne . . . þys] now þan N 99 knyfe] *prec. by canc.* ky Gg 100 Aftyr] than aftre N 108 be] in N Ihesu] *om.* N by] *om.* N 109 `fownde´] *in marg. with inser. marks* Gg; *om.* N 111 thyke] þo N 112 þat] in þat N

quantytee to folke of that contre and pylgrymys. And be hem they ben
solde and bore forth abowte the worlde and the forseyde rosys growen   115
be ʾþeʾ weyis þat oure Lady wente by as ys forseyde and nowre ellys.

Also hyt ys seyde in that same boke þat the place þat oure Lady wyth
here chylde Ihesu duellyde inne in Egypte ys fro Bethleem xii dayis
iorneye. And therfore ȝe maye thynke þat they hadde ʾful gretʾ traueyle
in goynge in and out. And therfore hauyth pytee and compas|syon of   f. 44ʳ
hem, and takyth ensample of here mekenesse and pacyence and lernyth   121
to suffre mekely, and pacyently alle tribulacyonys þat fallen to ȝow in
thys lyfe for oure Lordys loue, forʾsoʾ dede they.

Aftyr thys thynkyth that whenne Ioseph wyth oure Lady and here
suete ʾsoneʾ Ihesu were icome into the londe of Israel, and Ioseph   125
herde telle þat Archyllaye regne in Iurye for Herowde hys fadyr, he
dred to goo thedyr leste he wolde haue pursued oure Lorde as
Herowde hys fadyr dede. And so ȝe maye thynke þat he was in gret
dowte what he mygthte beste doo. And thanne he was warnyd in hys
sclepe be a goode angyl þat he schulde goo into Galyle, and so he   130
wente forth into the partyis of Galylee and there he duellyde in a cytee
þat ys callyd Naȝareth. Thys was Naȝareth þat I haue tolde ȝow of in
the nexste chapeʾteʾle afore thys, and also in þe chapeʾteʾle of the
salutacyon of oure Lady, and Galyle the contre.

CHAPTER 10

Of the tuelfthe ȝere of oure Lorde Ihesu Cryste and how he was
founde in the temple in the myddyl of doctorys. Capitulum decimum.

Aftyr the forseyde medytacyon, ȝe maye thynke anothyr deuout
medytacyon how oure Lorde Ihesu Cryste grew vp in body and age
as ʾtheʾ comyn course of ma[n]kynde ys, thaʾtʾ in hys godhede ys   5
euyrmore the same wythoute eny | mutabylytee. And that ȝe myghte   f. 44ᵛ
the more conuenyently thynke þe medytacyon folowyinge, thynkyth
fyrste how hys modyr, oure Lady Seyint Marye and Ioseph, þat was
trowed hys fadyr, as deuout folke were iwonte to goo euery ȝere into
Ierusalem in the solempne feste of Estyr. For Ierusalem was þe chef   10

116 as ys forseyde] *om.* N   117 seyde] *fol. by canc.* also Gg   that] þe N
122 tribulacyonys] tribulacions and diseses N   126 Iurye] þe Iewry N   127 to] for
to N   thedyr] thider haply N   131 into] to N

Chapter 10   1 Lorde] *om.* N   2 temple] temple salamoun N   doctorys] doctoures
sittynge disputynge N   5 mankynde] makynde Gg; mankynde N   þe] þis N
7 folowyinge] *om.* N   10 feste] day N   þe] the þe Gg

cytee of Iurye and ther was the temple of God, and therfore they
wente thedyr euery ȝere onys aftyr the byddynge of the lawe, as ys
forseyde in the solempne feste of Estyr. But ȝe schal vndyrstande þat
Estyr was not amonge hem as hyt ys amonge vs. What Estyr was
15 amonge hem ȝe may`e´ here in the xvii chapetele of þys boke
folowynge. And so in a tyme whenne they wente thedyr aftyr the
custum of þe festful daye, oure Lorde Ihesu Cryste whenne he was
tuelue ȝere olde as in the kynde of man, wente thedyr wyth hem. And
whenne they hadde be there a certayne tyme as the manyr was, and
20 the dayis were fulfyld of here abythynge there, ȝe maye thynke how
they wente home aȝen and how the chylde Ihesu Cryste abode stylle in
Ierusalem, and oure Lady and Ioseph wyste not therof, wenynge þat
he hadde be in the falawschyp. As to the vndyrstandynge of these
worthys, ȝe schal vndyrstande that Lyre seyth vpon thys same texte
f. 45ʳ that to thys | solempne feste of Estyr men wente in oo companye be
26 hemselfe, and wymmen wente in anothyr companye be hemselfe, and
cam home aȝen in the same wyse, þat they mygthte the more
relygyu`s´ly solempne here haly daye in kepynge hem fro here
wyuys. But chyldryn mygthte goo indyffrently whethyr they wolde
30 goo in the companye of men or wymmen. And so whenne Ioseph
seygth not oure Lorde in the companye of men, he wende he hadde be
wyth Marye hys modyr in the companye of wymmen, and þe same
wyse oure Lady wende `þat´ he hadde `be´ in the companye of men
wyth Ioseph. And therfore they softe not aftyr hym att that tyme, but
35 wente forth a dayis iorneye fro Ierusalem, and wyste not þat he abode
stylle in Ierusalem. And whenne they were come to the iorneyis ende
þe ne`x´ste daye aftyr, thynkyth they softe hym bothe in the
companye of men and wymmen also, and amonge here cosynys and
othyre of here knowleche.
40   And `whenne´ they fonde hym not, ȝe maye mekely thynke þat they
were rygth sory and heuy, thynkynge hemselfe bothe vnkynde and
necglygent þat they ne hadde take bettyr hede to hym. And so the
thyrde daye they wente all þe dayis iorneye aȝen to Ierusalem wyth
gret heuynesse `to´ seke hym. And therfore hauyth pytee and
f. 45ᵛ compassyon of hem, for they ben `in´ gret heuynesse and | mowe
46 not be merye tyl they haue founde hym. Be thys ensample maye ȝe

11 Iurye] þe Iewry N   12 ys] it is N   15 xvii] threttene N   16 whenne] as N
20 ȝe] the N   25 wente] *om.* N   27 in] *om.* N   30 so] also N   33 `þat´]
om. N   37 thynkyth] thenketh howe N   41 hemselfe] hymselfe N   42 ne
hadde] hadden not N   43 iorneye aȝen] priuely aȝen N   44 `to´ seke] sechynge N

lerne þat yf oure Lorde be absent fro ȝow for synne or eny
mysgouernaunce of ȝoure`selfe´, not to be merye tyl ȝe haue founde
hym aȝen be meke wepynge and waylynge for ȝoure synnys and othyr
penaunce doynge, for so wole he be founde aȝen yf `he´ be loste be 50
synne.

Thanne aftyr thys ȝe maye thynke how att the laste aftyr thre dayis
they fonde hym in the temple, not in the market as Lyre seyth, ne in
pleyinge as chyldryn be wonte to be founde, but in an holy place
iordeynyd to holy prayeres and doctrine, syttynge in the my`d´dyl of 55
doctorys þat he mygthte the bettyr here hem alle and aske questyonys.
Here ys anothyr ensample also how goode chyldryn and ȝonge men
wel isette to Godwarde schulde drawe to holy placys, and where they
mygthte here holy doctrine, and in sueche placys they schulde here,
aske, and lerne and not teche.   60

Thanne thynkyth also how alle thoo þat herde hym merueylyde of
hys wysedom, for they herde neuer chylde of that age speke so wysely,
and therfore they wondryde gretly of hym. Aftyr thys, thynkyth how
aftyr hys modyr and Ioseph were icome into the temple and lokyde
aftyr hym there, they aspyde hym syttynge in the myddyl of 65
doctorys, | as ys forseyde, and thanne they merueylyde gretly. And f.46ʳ
whenne he perseyuyde hys modyr and Ioseph he cam to hem and
thanne they `were´ passyngly glad, for the more `sorowe´ they hadde
of hys absense and `in´ sekynge aftyr hym, the more ioye they hadde in
the fyndynge of hym. And thanne ȝe maye thynke how hys modyr 70
seyde to hym thus: 'Sone, why haste þu doo to vs thus? Loo, thy fadyr
and I sorowynge haue isofte the.' Lyre seyth, thowgth Ioseph were
iseyde oure Lordys fadyr, neuyrdeles he was not hardy to vndyrneme
hym for he beleuyde hym stedfastly godys sone. But oure Lady Seyint
Marye, hys modyr, of gret loue þat sche hadde to hym, dede hyt for 75
ouyrpassynge loue canne no lorde.

Also, gostly syster, takyth hede how oure meke Lady preferryth
Ioseph afore here, seyinge: 'Thy fadyr and I, and not I and thy fadyr
sorowynge haue isofte the.' Vp`on´ thys texte, Seyint Austyn seyth
thus: 'Fyrste hyt ys not to be ouyrpassyd, moste for the lernynge of 80
wymmen, oure systryn, so holy a mesurabylnesse of the virgyne

49 waylynge] sorowynge N   50 be³] for N   57 and] a N   58 placys] places
where N   63 thynkyth] yhe may thenke N   65 the myddyl] myddes N
66 doctorys] þe doctoures N   ys] it is N   thanne] *om.*N   68 they] þat thei N
69 of hys absense and] *om.* N   70 the] *om.* N   fyndynge] fyndyngynge; gyn *canc.* Gg
73 vndyrneme] displese N; *see note*   76 no lorde] no man shewe our lorde N; *see note*
79 texte] same texte N   80 the] *om.* N

Marye. Sche hadde ibore Cryste, an angyl cam to here and seyde: Loo, þu schalte conseyue and brynge forth a sone, and þu schalte calle hys name Ihesu Cryste. Thys schal be gret and he schal be callyd the

f. 46ᵛ sone of hym þat ys hyeste. Sche hadde deseruyd to bryn|ge forth the
86 sone of hym þat ys hyeste, and ȝytt sche was rygth meke for sche preferryde not hereselfe afore here hosebunde, in so myche as in the ordyr of name, þat sche wolde seye I and thy fadyr, but sche seyth thy fathyr and I. Sche beholdyth not the dygnytee of here wombe, but
90 sche beho`l´dyth the ordyr of maryage, for `for´sothe meke Cryste, he seyth, hadde not taugth hys modyr to wexe prowde.'

And a lytyl aftyr he seyth thus: 'How myche lasse, thanne, schulde othyr wymmen wexe prowde?' And therfore be thys ensample of oure meke Lady, lett wymmen lerne to be meke and not to preferre
95 hemselfe afore men in enythynge, and namely sueche as haue hosebundys. For oure Lady ys a parfyth ensample to alle wymmen, as oure Ihesu Cryste to alle men. And þat sche callyth Ioseph oure Lordys fadyr, me`r´ueylyth not þerof. For sche mygthte trewly calle hym oure Lordys `fadyr´ in as myche as he was cowplyd to here þat
100 was hys verry modyr, and also the comyn trowynge and seyinge was so, and therfore sche callyde hym as the comyn trowynge and seyinge was.

ftyr thys thynkyth how oure Lorde seyth to here aȝen thus: 'Why haue ȝe softe me? Wyste ȝe not þat I muste be in sueche thynges as
105 longen to my Fadyr?' Thys he seyde of hys heuenely Fadyr, for Seyint

f. 47ʳ Austyn seyth | that he wolde not so be knowe here sone, but þat he wolde be knowe Godys sone also. And Lyre seyth þat he was more affectyd to hys natural fadyr and euyrlastynge in heuene thanne to hys natural modyr in erthe or to Ioseph þat was tro`w´ed hys fadyr. But
110 they vndyrstode not thys manyr speche of oure Lorde Ihesu Cryste; for, as the forseyde doctur seyth, they were not wonde to here sueche wordys of hym. Thanne aftyr þys thynkyth how mekely and lowly he goeth wyth hem home aȝen to the cytee of Naȝareth. And as the euangelyste seyth: 'He was sogett to hem', bothe, as the forseyde
115 doctur Lyre seyth, for here conforte for they were heuyed of hys absence, and also to the informacyon of vs and to the confusyon of oure pryde.

Loo, gostely syster, here beholdyth dylygently how gret schame

---

82 an] and an N   seyde] seide to hir N   91 hadde] he had N   wexe] be N
93 wexe] be N   97 oure²] our Lorde N   99 he] *om.* N   cowplyd] couplede and
ioynede N   100 seyinge] seyinge þat it N

and confusyon hyt schulde `be´ to vs þat ben but synful wrecchys to
be inobedyent to oure gostly fadrys or modrys, or natural othyr, so 120
that they bydde vs not to doo eny thynge þat ys aȝenste the wyll of
God or contrarye to oure verry helthe. For in sueche thyngys we schul
in no wyse obeye to hem, sygth that we rede þat oure Lorde and God
was sogett to hys modyr in erthe, and not only to hys modyr, but also
`to´ hym þat was trowed hys | fadyr. For the euangelyste seyth þat he f. 47ᵛ
was not only obedyent to here, but to hem; that ys to seye, to oure 126
Lady Seyint Marye þat was hys verry modyr and to Ioseph þat was
trowed hys fadyr.

What oure Lorde Ihesu Cryste dede fro the tuelfthe ȝere of hys
bodyly age into the tyme of hys baptyme aftyr the *Reuelacyon* of
Seyint Brygytte. Capitulum undecimum.

Gostly syster, in the begynnynge of þys chapetele ȝe schal vndyrstande þat fro the xii ȝere of oure Lorde Ihesu Cryste into þe tyme of 5
hys baptyme no euangelyste makyth eny mencyon what he dede. And
that tyme, as summe doctorys seyin, he was xxixᵗʸ ȝere ful and
begynnynge the thyrtyeth ȝere, of the whyche he hadde xiii dayis, as
Lyre seyth. But ȝe maye haue for certayne þat he was synglere holy
afore eny man þat euer was. For he was vttyrly clene fro all maner 10
synne and neuer dede eny and so all þat euer he suffrede of hys endles
goodnesse in oure kynde in thys worlde, hyt was for vs and nothynge
for hymselfe, but that he wolde haue oure soulys to be eurylastyngly
wyth hym in ioye. Ȝytt not wythstandynge þat no euangelyste makyth
eny mencyon what he dede al that tyme, oure goode Lady, thowgth be 15
the mercy of God to þe conforte of deuout soulys, tolde Seyint
Brygytt be reuelacyon sum|what what he dede. Whereof be the grace f. 48ʳ
of God sumwhat I wole telle ȝow in thys present chapetele, for what
was do abowte hym tyl he were xii ȝere olde as in þe persone of man,
ȝe haue herde suffycyen[t]ly, I trowe, in othyr medytacyonys afore. 20
    Now hyt ys to be tolde what he dede for the xii ȝere forwarde into
þe tyme of hys holy baptyme, aftyr þe *Reuelacyon* of Seyint Brygytte,
as oure Lady, þat k[n]ewe best nexte God alone, tolde here.

121 that] *om.* N   123 that] *om.* N   128 fadyr] fader deo gracias N
Chapter 11 6 eny] *om.* N   And] bot N   9 was] *om.* N   12 nothynge] *fol. by*
canc. thy Gg   19 man] man and what he dede when he was twelfe yhere olde N
20 suffycyen[t]ly] suffycyenly Gg   23 k[n]ewe] kewe Gg

'Forsothe', sche seyde, 'whenne he cam to more age', vndyrstondyth,
25 thanne ys seyde afore, 'he was contynuant in preyere and he wente
obedyently wyth vs to festys iordeynyd in Ierusalem and othyr placys.
Whas sygthte `and speche´ was so merueylus and acceptable þat
manye folke dessesyd seyde: Lete `vs´ goo to Maryeys sone, of whom
we maye be confortyd. Forsothe he, encressynge in age and wysedom,
30 of the whyche he was ful fro the begynnynge, laboryde wyth hys
handys othyrwhyle sueche thyngys as were semely. And he spake to
vs', vndyrstondyth oure Lady and Ioseph, 'seperatly', þat ys `to´ seye,
departyd fro othyr, 'confortable wordys and wordys of dyuynytee so
þat `we´ were fulfyld co[n]tynually wyth vnspekeable ioye.'
35   'And forsothe whenne we were in pouertee, dredys, and dyffycul-
teys, he made vs no golde and syluyr but he steryde vs to pacyence,
and oure necessaryis cam to vs, othyrwhyle of campassyon of meke
f. 48ᵛ soulys, and othyr whyle of | oure owen traueyle, so þat we hadde
`oure´ necessaryis only to oure nede and not to superfluytee, for we
40 softe not ellys but only to serue God.'
'Aftyr thys he talkede homely in the howse wyth hys frendys that
cam to hym of þe lawe and of the sygnyfycacyonys and fygurys þerof
also `he´ dysputyde in opyn wyth wyse men, so þat they merueylyde
seyinge: Loo, Iosephys sone techyth maystrys. Sum gret spyryt
45 spekyth in hym. And in a tyme whenne I thowgth on hys passyon
and he seygth me ful heuy he ansueryde to me Beleuyst not þu modyr
þat I am in the Fadyr and the Fadyr in me were þu defulyd att my
comynge in or were þu dysesyd att my goyinge out why art þu so
dystracte wyth heuynesse forsothe hyt ys my Fadrys wyll þat I suffre
50 deth also hyt ys my wyll wyth the Fadyr that I haue of the Fadyr maye
not suffre but the fleyisch þat I haue take of the schal suffre that the
fleyisch of othyre maye be bowgthte aȝen and the spyryt sauyd.'
'Also he was `so´ obedyent þat whenne Ioseph by happe seyde to
hym do that or þat anone he dede hyt for he hydde so the mygth of
55 hys Godhede that but of me and othyr whyle of Ioseph hyt mygth not
be knowe the whyche þat ys to seye I and Ioseph seygth ofte tymys
merueylus lygth schyne abowte hym and we herde angyllys voysys |
f. 49ʳ syngynge vpon hym and we seygth that vnclene spyrytys the whyche

24 seyde] in margin þat ys oure lady to seyint brygytte   25 thanne] þan þat N
26 obedyently] om. N   28 to] in marg. to þe son of Marye Gg   31 sueche] in
suche N   as] þat N   33 wordys²] worde N   34 co[n]tynually] cotynnally Gg
36 and] nor N   43 merueylyde] merueylynge and N   44 Iosephys] in marg. þe sone
of Ioseph   51 take] om. N   52 of] om. N   53 whenne] om. N
57 merueylus] merueylouse syghtes and N   58 vpon hym] superscript ouyr hym Gg

mygth not be put out be prouyd exorcystys in oure lawe wente out att
the sygth of the presence of my sone loo thowgthtyr lett these thyngys 60
be contynually in thy mynde and thanke God clenly for be the I wolde
make opyn to othyre hys ʒougthe.'

These be the wordys þat oure Lady hadde to Seyint Brygytt of þe
ʒougthe of oure Lorde Ihesu Cryste, and namely fro the tuelfthe ʒere
forwarde, as hyt ys wryte, hoo lyste to see in the sexte Boke of 65
Reuelacyonys of the forseyde hooly lady Seyint Brygytt, in the lviii^{ty}
chapetele the whyche I haue drawe here into Englyische tonge almoste
worde for worde, for the more conuenyent forme and ordyr of these
sympyl medytacyonys, and to ʒoure edyfycacyon or eny othyr deuout
creature þat cannot vndyrstande Latyn; the whyche ʒe maye thynke 70
vndyr forme of medytacyon as I haue tolde ʒow of othyre afore. For,
thowgth hyt be schortly seyde here vndyr a compendyus maner, ʒytt
hyt maye be drawe ful loonge in a soule þat can deuoutly thynke and
dylygently beholde the werkys of oure Lorde that be conteynyd
therinne. And in sueche maner thynkynge, beholde inwardly and 75
wysely the gret mekenesse, charytee, and obedyence of that
worschypful | Lorde, and also the pacyence and pouertee of oure f. 49ᵛ
Lady and Ioseph, and so be the grace of God to caste hym to folowe
aftyr in lyuynge be hys powere and kunnynge.

CHAPTER 12

Of the baptyme of oure Lorde Ihesu Cryste, of mekenesse, and of
othyr werkys þat maye be consyderyd þerabowte. Capitulum duo-
decim.

The baptyme of oure Lorde Ihesu Cryste, as ʒe maye thynke was aftyr
the seyinge of summe doctorys, whenne he was xxx^{ty} ʒere ful and 5
begynnynge the thyrtyeth ʒere, of the whyche he hadde xiii dayis, as I
haue tolde ʒow in the chapetele nexte afore thys. And att þys tyme of
hys bodyly age, ʒe maye thynke how he cam out of the contre þat ys
callyd Galyle and fro the cytee of Naʒareth, to þe flode of Iordan, to
Seyint Ihonn to be baptysyd of hym. Iordan, as Seyint Ierom seyth, 10
takyth hys name of too wellys of þe whyche þat one ys callyd Ior and

65 hoo] whoso N   see] see it N   67 into] in N   71 vndyr forme] by þe maner N
othyre] om. N   73 soule] soule to hem N
Chapter 12 1 of³] and of N   4 was] fol. by canc. sum Gg   5 ʒere¹] yhere old N
7 haue] om. N

that othyr Dan. And ʻtheseʼ to medlyd togydyrys make þys name
Iordan, and hyt ys fro Ierusalem, as Bonauenture seyth, xviii myle.

To thys flode of Iordan ȝe maye thynke how oure Lorde Ihesu
15 Cryste, lorde of all the worlde, cam fro the forseyde cytee of Naȝareth,
mekely all alone as for the companye of eny man. For he hadde not ȝytt
þat tyme callyd hys dyscyplys. And ȝe maye beholde þat he goeth haply
barefoot or ellys werynge sandalyis, the whyche were as they hadde bee
f. 50ʳ solys of schone, | and hem he weryde vndyr hys feete for hete of the
20 erthe, for hyt ys seyde þat hyt ys ful hoote in that contre, and they were
fastenyd aboue þe foot wyth a maner fastenynge to holde hem faste.

Now thanne beholdyth hym wele, and in ȝoure consyderacyon
hauyth pytee and compassyon of hym how he goeth al that weye
alone, and merueylyth hys mekenesse and charytee. The persone and
25 lyknesse of oure Lorde as in the persone of man, ȝe maye thynke thus,
Beholdyth hym a man of the myddyl syse and of the age forseyde,
and, as Seyint Berna[r]de seyth: ʻMeke, lowgth, benyngʻnʼe, sobyr,
chaste, mercyful and in all clennesse and holynesse synglerly fayre,
and the same all mygthty God.ʼ And also as hyt ys wryte in the
30 *Legende of Symon and Iude*, ȝe maye thynke hym wel ieyed, and wel
ibrowed, and hauynge a loonge face and bowed, þe whyche ys a sygne
of sadnesse. Also, ȝe maye thynke hym a sangueyne man, and
sumwhat browne, lyke hys modyr. And beholdyth hym vndyr thys
forme, ʻþe fayrest manʼ that euyr was, for hyt ys wryte of hym in the
35 Psalme thus: ʻSpeciosus forma pre filiis hominum.ʼ Thys ys to seye:
ʻHe was fayre in forme or lyknesse afore the sonys of men.ʼ

Also, oure Lady tolde Seyint Brygrytte, as hyt ys seyde in the fyrste
chapetele of the viii boke of here *Reuelacyonys*, þat whenne ʻscheʼ
f. 50ᵛ noryischede hym he was so | fayre that hosoeuer behelde hym, he was
40 confortyd of the sorowe of herte þat he hadde. Wherfore manye
Iewys, as sche seyth also, there seyde togyderys: ʻLete vs goo see
Maryeys sone, þat we maye be confortyd.ʼ And thowgth they wyste
not þat he was Godys sone, neruyrdeles they resceyuyde gret conforte
of the seyinge of hym. Also, hys body was so clene þat ther ʻcamʼ
45 neuer there vpon eny lows or othyr worme for the worme dede
reuerence to hys Makere. Ne ther was founde eny knyttynge
togyderys or vnclennesse in hys heere ʻor norschydʼ.

16 all] *om.* N   17 ȝytt] *om.* N   18 they] it N   21 maner] maner of N
23 that] þe N   26 the] *om.* N   27 Berna[r]de] Bernade Gg   29 as] *om.* N
34 in the] *twice* Gg   36 or] and in N   39 so] *om.* N   45 othyr] ony N
46–7 Ne ther . . . norschyd] Ne ony knyttynge togidre, ne vnclennes was founded in his ere
ne norischede N

These be the wordys þat oure Lady seyde to Seyint Brygytte of the fayrenesse of oure Lorde. Aftyr thys beholdyth deuoutly in ȝoure soule how thys moste worthy Lorde comyth to hys trewe seruant 50 Seyint Ihonn Baptyste where he was baptysynge as ys forseyde att þe `flode´ of Iordan to be baptysyd of hym. Thanne thynkyth how Seyint Ihonn, seyinge hym comynge to hymwarde, anone be the Holy Goste he knewe hym. And thanne merueylynge hys lownesse he seyde these wordys to hym: 'Lorde, I schulde be baptsysd of þe and þu comyste to 55 me?' Thanne thynkyth how oure Lorde Ihesu Cryste ansueryth ful mekely aȝen, seyinge thus: 'Suffre now, for forsothe thus we muste fulfylle all rygtwysenesse'; þat ys to seye, all mekenesse.

And here I wole telle ȝow thre degreys of mekenesse þat I tolde ȝow `not´ opynly of in the iiii chape|tele, where I tolde ȝow myche of f. 51ʳ mekenesse. Aftyr the seyinge of doctorys, ther ben thre degreys of 61 mekenesse. The fyrste ys whenne a man or woman ys obedyent to hys souerayne, and that ys necessarye to verry helthe. For a man or a woman þat wole be sauyd and come to euyrlastynge ioye muste nedys obeye to hys souerayne. The secunde ys whenne a man or a woman ys 65 obedyent to hys falawe or pere, and that ys more mekenesse, and in þat more medeful, and hyt ys but of a mannys owen fre wyll. The thyrde ys whenne a man or a woman, for God and perfeccyon, ys obedyent to hys seruaunt or hym þat `ys´ lower thanne he and that ys moste mekenesse, and so be that moste medeful, and hyt longyth to 70 perfeccyon; thys degre of mekenesse fulfylde oure Lorde Ihesu Cryste, whenne he mekede hymselfe to hys good seruaunt Seyint Ihon Baptyste. And myche perfythlokyr he fulfylde hyt whenne so mekely and pacyently he toke so myche despyte and dyssese of hys vntrewe seruauntys, the wyckede Iewys. 75

Also for thre causys prin[ci]pally oure Lorde wolde be baptysyd of Seyint Ihon Baptyste, as the Mayster of Storyis seyth: the fyrste ys þat he wolde approue the baptyme of Seyint Ihon; the secunde ys þat he wolde fulfylle all mekenesse, and be hys ensample teche hyt to be fulfylde of hys parfyth seruauntys; the thyr|de ys þat he mygthte be f. 51ᵛ the tuchynge of hys holy body ȝeue to the watyr strengthe of getynge 81 aȝen, þat ys to seye, to halowe the watyr that hyt `mygth´ haue aftyrwarde powere, be the worde of God, men and wymmen to be

51 where] there N   as ys forseyde] *om.* N   52 `flode´] forseide flode N
62 woman] a woman N   64 come] wole come N   67 a] *om.* N   owen] *om.* N
69 hym] to hym N   73 hyt] *om.* N   75 vntrewe] vntrewe and vnkynde N
wyckede] cursede N   76 prin[ci]pally] prinpally Gg   77 of] of þe N
81 tuchynge] techynge N   the²] *om.* N

baptysyd inne, and so be the sacrament of baptyme and crystyndom to
85 be borne aȝen of watyr and the Holy Goste, and be made eyrys of
euyrlastynge herytage.

Aftyr `þys´ beholdyth how the meke Lorde doeth of hys clothys and
goeth into the watyr. And thanne hauyth pyte of hys tendyr fleyisch,
for hyt was haply payneful to hym to stande so or knele in the colde
90 watyr. And thanne beholdyth also how Seyint Ihonn baptysyth hym
in helynge watyr vpon hys blyssyde body. Aftyr thys thynkyth þat
anone as he was baptysyd he cam out of the watyr aȝen. And whenne
he was come out of the watyr ȝe maye beholde a merueylus sygth, how
heuene was openyd and how Seyint Ihonn sawgth the Holy Goste
95 comynge downe in the lyknesse of a dowue and abydynge vpon hym.
And also a voyse was herde fro heuene seyinge thus: 'Thys `ys´ my
belouyd sone in the whyche I am plesyd'; þat ys to seye, as Lyre seyth,
in the whyche my wyll schal be fulfyld of þe helthe of mankynde.

Here in the baptysynge of oure Lorde Ihesu Cryste, ȝe maye
100 vndyrstande þat all the Holy Trynytee apperyde, þat ys to seye, the |
f. 52ʳ Fadyr in the voyse, the `Sone in the´ persone of man, the Holy Goste
in the lyknesse of a dowue, the whyche Trynytee ys to verry God, to
whom be all worschype, ioye, and preysynge now and withoute
endynge. Amen.

CHAPTER 13

How oure Lorde Ihesu Cryste was led of a spyryt into deserte þat he
mygthte be temptyd of the fende, and how he fastede xl^{ty} dayis wyth
othyr edyfycatyf materys acordynge therto aftyr the seyinge of
doctorys. Capitulum tredecimum.

5 Aftyr the baptyme of oure Lorde, ȝe maye thynke ordynatly anothyr
medytacyon how he was led into deserte of hys owen spyryt, þat ys
the Holy Goste, that he mygthte be temptyd of the fende. And
whenne he hadde fastyd xl^{ty} dayis and xl^{ty} nygthtys, aftyr that he
hungrede. Here ȝe schal vndyrstande fyrste þat oure Lorde fastede in
10 a deserte þat was be`tuene´ Ierusalem and Ieryco, as the Mayistyr of
Storyis seyth. Now thanne beholdyth fyrste how the goode Lorde was

---

89 payneful] ful paynefull N   91 helynge] heldynge N   92 as] after N   aȝen]
anone N   94 sawgth] *prec. by canc.* seyg Gg   97 belouyd] welbolouede N
99 ȝe] þe N   102 the^1] *om.* N

Chapter 13   8 aftyr that] afterwarde N   11 Storyis] þe Storyes N   thanne] *om.* N

ledde into 'the' deserte forseyde of hys owen spyryt. And there he
fastede fourthy dayis and xl^{ty} nygthtys, that, as Lyre seyth, he
mygthte punysche hys innocent fleyisch for vs, and that he wolde
ȝeue exsample to hys trewe seruauntys. And in that he dede sueche
thyngys aftyr hys baptyme, he schewde to vs that he þat begynnyth
anewe lyf muste offre hymself to God be prayere and fastynge.

Also in that 'he' ȝaf exsample that men that wole teche and preche
Godys worde schulde fyrste vse hemselfe to be myche alone fro the
companyis of folke, where they | myghte ȝeue hem conuenyently to
holy medytacyon and preyere, fastynge, wakynge and othyr holy
excersysys, be the whyche, helpynge the grace of God, they mygth
ouyrcome vicys in hemselfe and the sotyl temptacyonys of the fende;
lest, yf they do not so, they hyndre moo be here badde lyuynge thanne
profyte be here prechynge. For hyt ys wryte also of oure Lorde Ihesu
that he beganne to do and teche, so he dede fyrste, and aftyrwarde
taugthte. And so wolde God alle precharys wolde do now a dayis. For
Lyre seyth vpon the same texste that to teche wel and lyue euyll ys
nothynge ellys thanne to dampne hymself be hys owen voyce. And
therfor hyt ys goode that they doo hemselfe that they teche othyre.
But lete vs goo to oure purpose aȝen.

Aftyr thys ȝe maye thynke that whenne oure Lorde hadde fastyd all
the forseyde tyme, he hungrede, but for he wolde so of hys owen
goodnesse to schewe hymselfe be that þat he was 'a' verry man, and to
ȝeue the fende occasyon to tempte hym. Thanne beholdyth how the
fende comyth to hym in the lyknesse of a man, for so hyt ys to
beleuyd, as the Mayistyr of Storyis seyth. And thanne thynkyth how
he seyth to hym thus: 'Ȝyf þu be the sone of God, seye that these
storiys 'maye' be louys.' And thanne oure Lorde ansueryth aȝen,
seyinge: 'A man leuyth not only be brede but in euery worde þat
comyth out of the mowth of God.' Here vndyrstondyth that he
temptyth oure Lorde fyrste in glotenye. But oure Lord ansueryth
hym aȝen, so that neythyr he mygth perseyue | hys godhede ne
brynge hym to glotenye

Aftyr thys the deuyl toke hym into the holy cytee, þat ys Ierusalem,
and sette hym vpon a pynnacle of the temple. Thys pynnacle, a[s]
Lyre seyth, was the rofe of the temple, the whyche was flatt aboue.

Marginal references: f. 52^v (line 20), 21, 25, 30, 35, f. 53^r (line 43), 45
Line numbers: 15, 40

14 wolde] myghte N   15 exsample] *fol. by canc.* ensample Gg   24 badde]
euyle N   25 profyte] *in marg.* Nota Gg   Ihesu] Ihesu Criste N   26 aftyrwarde]
after N   32 Aftyr] Than aftre N   36 the lyknesse of a man] a mannes lyknes N
38 the sone of God] God son N   43 aȝen] *om.* N   so] so as Lyre seyth N   46 a[s]]
a Gg, as N

And the entent of the deuyl berynge ʽhymʼ thedyr was, as the same
doctur seyth, þat the peple of the cytee schulde haue wende hym to
50 haue flowen, and so he schulde haue be lyfte vp into vanyne glorye.
But, be þe vertu of hys godhede, he dede so þat no man seygth hym,
for hyt was in hys powere to be seyin and not to be seyin. And
ʽthanneʼ thynkyth þat the deuyl seyde to hym eftesonys: 'Yf þu be
Godys sone, falle downe'; as ho seyth, þu maʽyiʼste wythoute eny
55 perel be thyne owen vertu, and also for the seruyse of angyllys that
seruyn the. And thanne oure Lorde seyde to hym aȝen: 'Thow schalt
not tempte thy Lorde God.' Vpon thys texte þe forseyde doctur seyth
thus: 'Forsothe to tempte God ys ʽtoʼ seke experyence of the vertu of
God wythoute vnfleable nede, and þat ys synne.' For whenesoeuere a
60 man hath eny thynge þat he maye doo aftyr the weye of man to flee
perel, he schal ʽnotʼ leue þat and seke experyence of God. Therfore
oure Lorde Ihesu Cryste ansueryde the feende temptynge hym that
þat he seyde. For whenne he mygth come downe fro the pynnacle of
the temple be the ʽweyeʼ of man, þat ys to seye, be þe grecys þat were
65 made therfore in þe temple, he owgthte ʽnotʼ to come downe be
anothyr weye, for that hadde be to tempte God. And in thys
temptacyon vndyrstondyth þat the feende temptyth hym in vayne
f. 53ᵛ glorye, | but be the ansuere forseyde he avoydede þat temptacyon.

Aftyr þys ȝe maye thynthe how the feende toke hym vp into a ful hy
70 hylle and schewde hym alle the kyngedomys of the worlde and the
ioye of hem, and seyde to hym: 'All thys I wole ȝeue the yf þu wolt
falle downe and worschype me.' Thane oure Lorde seyde to hym
aȝen: 'Goo thy weye, Sathanas, fforsothe hyt ys wryte, thow þu
schalte worschype thy Lorde God and serue hym alone.' Thane the
75 deuyl forsoke hym, and angyllys cam to ʽandʼ seruyd hym. 'Here oure
Lorde blamyth hym', þat ys whenne ʽheʼ seyde, 'goo forthe Sathans',
and not in othyr temptacyonys afore, to schwew þat a ʽmanʼ schal bere
hys owen wrongys, but in no wyse he schal suffre Godys wronge.
Forsothe, þat ys do moste whenne the worschype dew to God ys ȝeue
80 to the feende, the whyche the feende suggestede oure Lorde to doo.
And whenne oure Lorde hadde ȝeue hym the forseyde ansuere, and

49 haue wende] wene N   53 þat] how N   33 deuyl] fende N   54 Godys
sone] þe sone of God N   59 a] ony N   62 the] to the N   that] be þat N
64 the²] om. N   65 he] hym N   67 temptyth] temped N   68 the] om. N   þat]
þe N   69 into] in N   73 thy weye] forthe N   75 to] hand with finger pointing
in margin   cam to ʽandʼ seruyd] come and mynystrede vnto N   hym] hym thies bene þe
wordes of þe eungeliste apon thies wordes lyre seyth þus N; see note   79 do] to do N
80 feende¹] deuylle N

he, ouyrcome, hadde forsake hym, angyllys cam, as ys forseyde, and
dede hym seruyse as to here verry Lorde.

Here ʒe maye vndyrstande þat he was verry God and man. An
verry man, ʒe maye vndyrstande hym, þat hungrede but for he wolde,   85
God, þat angyllys dede seruyse too. In the forseyde ʻtemptacyon' ʒe
maye vndyrstande þat the feende temptyde oure Lorde in coueytyse,
but ouyrall he ouyrcome hym and att þys tyme vttyrly putte hym fro
hym. Thys, as me seiyth, schulde ʻbe' a gret exsample of conforte to
alle men and wymmen þat suffre temptacyon, to bere hyt esyly and   90
pacyently, sygth they maye here and rede wytnessynge the gospel,
þat | oure Sauyoure was temptyd hymselfe haply þat we that beleue   f. 54ʳ
in hym the esylokyr schulde bere oure temptacyonys þat we suffre in
thys lyf. For a trewe seruaunt suffryth the esylokyr hys dyssese and
trybulacyon, whateuer hyt bee, whenne he heryth or seeth hys meke   95
Lorde specyally for hys cause dyssesyd afore hym. And wytyth for
certayne that whatsumeuere temptacyon a man or a womman suffre in
thys lyf, as longe as they ʻbe' not ouyrcome therwyth, þat ys to seye,
nothyr wythinne be wylful cosentynge ne wythoute be euyl werkynge,
hyt ys no perel to hem but rathyr myche profyte and gret meryte. For 100
Seyint Iamys ʻþe Apostyl' seyth in hys pystyl: 'Blyssyd ʻbe' that man
þat suffryth temptacyon, for aftyr he hath be prouyd, he schal take the
crowne of lyf þat God hath behett to hem þat louyn hym.'

Ferthyrmore, gostly syster, ʒe schal vndyrstande that Seyint
Gregory seyth in the omelye vpon the lesson of the gospel in the   105
fyrste Sondaye of Lenton that whenne hyt ys seyde: 'God, a man,
itake vp or into an hy hylle, or into the holy cytee of the deuyl, the
mynde goeth therfro, the erys of man dredyn to here that. Whenne,
thowgth, we knowe these thyngys not to be vnbeleʻueʻable, yf we
beholde wel also othyr dedes in hym. Sykyrly the deuyl ys þe hede of 110
all wykkede and the menbrys of thys hede beyn alle wyʻkʻkede. Was
not Pylat a menbyr of the deuyl? Where not the Iewys pursuynge oure
Lorde membrys of the | feende? And the knygʻthʻtes crucyfyinge   f. 54ᵛ
hym? Therefore what wondyr was hyt yf he suffryde ʻhymʻselfe to be
ledde into þe hylle of hym þat suffryde hymselfe also to be crucyfyed 115
of hys membrys? Wherefore hyt was not vnworthy to oure aʒenbyere
þat he wolde be temptyd, the whyche cam to be sclayne. For forsothe

93 the esylokyr schulde] shulde þe more esier N   94 esylokyr] more esyer N
99 euyl] wilful N   103 to] vnto N   104 Ferthyrmore] also N   105 seyth] *fol. by
canc.* per Gg   107 holy] *fol. by canc.* holy Gg   109 vnbeleʻueʻable] beleuable N
111 wykkede] wykednes N   112 deuyl] feende N   116 vnworthy] vnconuenyent *in
marg.* Gg   oure] youre N   117 For] *om.* N

hyt was rygthful þat so he schulde ouyrcome oure temptacyonys be hys temptacyonys, rygth as he cam to ouyrcome oure deth be hys deth.'

But hyt ys to be knowe to vs that temptacyon ys doo in thre manerys: be suggestyon, in delytynge, and in consentynge. And whenne we be temptyd ofte tymys we sclyde into delytynge or also into consentynge, for we þat be browgth ʻforthʼ of synne of the fleyische here wythin vs selfe where ʻofʼ we suffre stryuyngys, þat ys to seye, euyl steryngys þe whyche we muste be reson and a vysement wythstande. But forsothe God þat toke fleysche in the virgynys wombe cam into thys worlde wythoute synne and therfore he suffrede nothynge contraryus wythinne hymselfe. Wherefore he mygth be temptyd be suggestyon, but the delyte of synne bote neuere hys mynde, and therfore all þat temptacyon of the feende was wythoute and not wythinne. Also the same doctur seyth in the forseyde omelye folowynge that the olde enmy that ys the deuyl lyfte hymʻselfeʼ vp aȝenste the fyrste man, oure fadyr, Adam in thre thynges. For he temptyde hym in glotenye, vayneglorye, and coueytyse. But be temptynge he ouyrcome hym, for he made ʻhymʼ sogett to hym be consentynge but be the ʻsameʼ manerys he ys ouyrcome of [þe seconde man, þat is our Lorde Ihesu Criste, by þe whiche he ioyede hymselfe to haue ouercome þe firste man, that he, ytake, go oute of our hertes by þe same enterynge, by þe whiche enterynge he was ledde in and [helde] vs. Bot þere is another thynge, dere systre, þat þe forseide doctour seith þat we shulde beholde in þis temptacioun of our Lorde. Ffor, when he was temptede of þe fende, he answerede by biddynges of Holy Writte; and in þat he was God sone myghte haue drownede his tempter in þe depnes of helle, shewede noght þe vertue of his myghte, bot broghte onely aȝeyns hym þe byddynges of Holy Writte, þat he myght shewe to vs ensample [of] paciens þat as ofte as we suffre ony thynge of shrewde men, we shulde be sterede rather to techynge þan to vengeance.

Taketh hede how mykell þe pacience of God is, and how mykel oure inpacience. If we be prouokede by wronges or by ony hurtynges, anone we be sterede with fersnes, and so, or as mykell as we may, wenge ourselfe, or þat we may not doo, we threte. Lo, our Lorde

sufferede aduersite of þe fende, and nothynge answerede hym bot
worde of softenes. He suffreth hym þat he myght punysshe þat that 155
myght growe hyer in þe preysynge of hym, ȝif he ouercome his
ennemy, not in sleynge hym, bot inwardely sufferynge. Thies bene þe
wordys of Seynte Gregore, þe Pope, in þe Omelye before-seide. And
þus I ende þis chapitle.

CHAPTER 14

How our Lorde Ihesu Criste, after his fastynge in deserte, wente into
þe worlde and prechede þe kyngedome of God, and callede his
apostels. And whiche of hem were of his kynne, as in þe kynde of
man, and also of his oþer | disciples, with other matiers þat may bene f. 40ʳ
considerede there aboute.   5

After our Lorde Ihesu Criste hadde fasted fourty dayes and fourty
nyghtes, and ouercome þe fende, as I haue tolde yow in þe chapitle
nexte before þis, yhe may thenke how he goth forthe into þe worlde
and precheth þe kyngedome of God and þe waye to euerlastynge lyfe.
And yhe shal vnderstonde þat he prechede thre yhere and a halfe vnto 10
his Passioun, as is moste comonly holde, as Lyre seyth. And in þat
tyme, he callede his disciples, and wroghte his myracles to þe
confirmacioun of his holy doctryne.

His twelfe chefe disciples, 'þe whiche' he callede appostelles, were
þies: the firste was Symon, þe whiche our Lorde named Petre, and 15
Andrewe his brother; Iames þe more, Zebedeus sone, and Iohn, his
brother. Thies two were our Lordis cosynnes as in þe kynde of man,
as yhe shal here more opynly afterwarde. Philippe and Bertholomewe;
Thomas and Mathewe; Iames þe lesse, Alpheus sone; Symon and
Iude, 'his brethren'. Thies three also were our Lordys cosynnes, as in 20
kynde of man. And Iudas Scarioth þe laste. This fals man betrayede
our Lorde and he is callede Scarioth of þe towne þat he was borne in,
þe whiche was a litell towne in þe Iury, as Lyre seyth.

Now 'þan', as to þe more 'open' vnderstondynge, howe þe fife
appostelles þat I haue tolde yow of before were our Lordys cosynnes, 25
yhe shall vnderstonde firste þat sometyme þere were two holy systren,
of þe whiche one was callede Emerye and þe tother Anne. Emorye had
a doghter, þe whiche was callede Elizabeth, and she bare Seynte Iohn
Baptiste and so was he our Lordis cosyn, bot not so nere as þe forseide
appostelles were, for þei were our Ladies systers sonnes. Seynte Anne, 30

þat other sister, yhe shall vnderstonde had thre housebondes, yche
aftre other, of þe whiche þe firste was called Ioachym, þe secunde
Cleophas, and þe thirde Salome. By þe firste she hadde a doughter, þe
whiche was called Marye, and she was compellede to a man whos
35 name was Ioseph. And þis Marye, þe which is our lady floure of all
women, bydynge stille a clene mayden bare oure Lorde Ihesu Criste,
þe sauyoure of mankynde. By þe seconde housebonde, þat is callede
Cleophas, she had another doughter, þe whiche was namede also
Marie and she was ioynede to a man whose name was Alphey. And by
40 hym she had foure sones, þat is to seye Iames þe lesse, Symon, Iude,
and Ioseph his brethren. Bot þis Ioseph was none of þe twelfe
apostels, bot afterwarde he was chosen with Mathias, we rede in þe
werkes of þe apostelles, to haue fulfillede þe twelfeth nowmbre aftre
Iudas þat betrayede our Lorde had hangede hymselfe. And þis same
45 Ioseph is callede also Barsabas and ryghtfull, for þe euydence of his
holynes, as Lyre saythe. By the thirde housbonde, þat is callede
Salome, she had þe thirde doughter, and hir also she callede Marye.
And she was wedded to a man þat is callede Zebedey, and by hym she
hadde two sones, þat is to seye, Iames þe more, and Iohn þe
50 euangeliste, his brother. Here yhe may vnderstonde þat þis Iames,
þat is callede þe more, was yonger þan þe other Iames, þat is callede
þe lesse. But he is callede þe more by seynge of doctours ffor he was
called firste to apostelhode, and for our Lorde toke more familiarite
with hym þan with þat other, as it semeth by þe Gospell, and also for
55 he was þe firste þat suffrede matirdome of þe appostelles. Also, þat
other Iames þat is callede þe lesse is callede also Iames þe ryghtfull for
his holynes, and he is callede also our Lordis brother, ffor it is seide
þat he was so lyke oure Lorde in face and in all disposicioun of body
þat a man shulde not wele haue knowe þe toone from þe other. And
60 þerfore Iudas kyssede our Lorde þat by þat þei þat come with hym
myghte knowe hym fro Iames þe lesse. Also, þis Iames, for worthines
of his lyuynge, was chose of þe other appostelles to by friste
Archebisshope of Ierusalem.

f. 55ʳ   Here, gostely systre, yhe] | maye vndyrstande be þat ys forseyde,
65 that oure 'Lorde' Ihesu Cryste chese fyue of hys owen cosynys as in
the kynde of man into apostlys, þat ys to seye: Iamys þe more and
Ihon hys brothyr; Iamys þe lasse; and Symon and Iude hys brethryn,
þe whyche Iude ys callyd also be anothyr name, Thadee. And þys, as

Chapter 14   64 maye vndyrstande] Gg *resumes*   maye] may firste N   þat] þat that N
67 Ihon] Seint Ihon N   brothyr] þe euangeliste N   and²] *om.* N

me semyth, ys a gret and an euydent exsample how a man or a woman
schulde stere a helpe hys kynne to goodenesse afore othyre. Also, hyt 70
ys the ordyr of charytee, the ˋwhycheˊ fyrste euyrmore begynnyth att
hytselfe as in the secunde boonde of charytee þat longyth to hymself
and to hys euery Crysten, and so goeth forth to othyre as they be
nexste hym in the orthyr of charytee. Also, the chefe of the apostlys,
þat ys to seye Petyr and Andrewe, Iamys and Ihon were icalled fro 75
fyischynge, for they were fyischarys as þe euangylyste beryth
wytnesse and no gret lordys of þe worlde, ne wyse phylosopherys.
For Seyint Poule seyth þat God chese the febyl thyngys of the worlde,
þat ys be pouertee, symplycytee, or vnkunnynge, þat he mygthte
confounde the stronge; þat ys be rychesse worˋlˊdyly, worschype, or 80
sotyl kunnynge.

Also, Lyre seyth þat rygth as oure Lorde fro the begynnynge
calleˋdeˊ summe symple, as ys opyn in hem forseyde, so also he callyde
summe letteryd fro þe begynnynge as Nathanael and Nychodeme.
For yf he ˋhadˊ callyd only sympyl men hyt mygth haue be | trowed f. 55ᵛ
þat they hadde ˋbeˊ dysseyuyd of symplycytee. Neuyrdeles, he 86
ordeynyde more sympyl men apostlys and precharys of gospel
thanne lettryd men that the feythe of þe gospel schulde more be
redressyd to þe wysedom of God thanne to þe wysedom of man. For
haply yf they hadde be grete clerkys afore oure Lorde callyde hem, 90
men wolde haue redresseˋdˊ here wysedom to þe wysedom of men.
But, sygth they were so sympyl whenne oure Lorde callyde hem to
apostylhode, and aftyrwarde so wyse hyt muste nethys be redressyd to
þe specyal werkynge of þe Holy Goste.

[And þis is ayeyns some nowe adayes þat when þei here or rede 95
ony thynge ydo of a grete clerke, as of a maistre of dyuynyte or a
doctour of lawe, anone þei haue grete deynte þerof and comenden it
gretely. And ȝif it were ydo of a comon letterde man or of a deuoute
man not a graduate, þat is to seye, noght degreede in scoles, þei
dispise it or elles haue lytell deynte þerof. And ȝit it is a sygne of 100
more grace of God when suche a man doth a thynge þan a grete
clerke, not þat þei bene blameable for þai comende þat that a clerke
doth, bot for þei take not vertuousely þat a symple man doth, so þat
it be withoute heresye.]

Also, þat oure Lorde hymselfe in thys ˋworldeˊ toke pouertee and 105
chese hym a poure modyr and poure dyscyplys, hyt ys a gret and an

70 to] in N   73 as they] þat N   74 in] and N   80 ys] is to seye N   83 as]
as it N   hem] þies N   87 of¹] of þe N   95–104 And þis . . . heresye] *om.* Gg

opyn exsample to alle þat desyre the state of perfeccyon to folowe
pouertee and to despyse the ioye of þys worlde. For Seyint Bernarde
seyth þat hyt ys a gret abusyon and to gret þat a vyle worme wolde be
110 ryche for whom God of Magestee and Lorde of Ostes wolde be poure.
Cryste chese pouertee, and therfore hyt ys to be chose of vs;
hoosoeuer seyth othyr, cursyd be he, thowgth he be an angyl of
heuene. And aftyrwarde also he seyth thus: 'He chese poure dyscyplys
and behette the kyngedom of heuene to poure folke.' Also Seyint
115 Gregory seyth in the *Moralys vpon Iob*, in the xiii boke, þat rygth as
oure Lorde Ihesu Cryste chese in hys prechynge poure men, ydyotes,
f. 56ʳ and sympyl so the con|trarye þat dampnyd man, þat ys to seye,
Antycryste, the whyche þe angyl iturnyd to schrewdnesse, þat ys the
deuyl, schal take to hym ys to chese to preche hys falsnesse, wyly men,
120 duble and hauynge the kunnynge of þys worlde.

    The tuelue apostyls þat I haue tolde ȝow of afore were oure Lordys
chefe dyscyplys and specyal apostyllys. And they, ȝe maye thynke,
wente wyth hym and seygth hys holy lyuynge, herde hys prechynge,
and seygth also hys worthy meraclys þat he wrowgth, of the whyche,
125 be the helpe of þe same Lorde, ȝe schal here in the tueyne nexte
chapetelys folowynge aftyr þys. To these tuelue also he ȝaf pouere to
arayse deed men, to hele seke, to clense leprys, and to pote out
deuyllys, seyinge to hem: 'Ȝe haue take frely, þat ys to seye, sueche
powere, frely doeth hyt'. Also, as ȝe schal here aftyrwarde, he toke
130 more famylyarytee wyth thre of hem thanne wyth the othyr apostlys,
þat ys to seye, wyth Petyr Iamys the more, and Ihon hys brothyr. And
in þat, as me semyth, he lafte vs exsample þat we maye take more
famyl`y´arytee wyth one thanne wyth anothyr so hys lyuynge be goode
and uertuus.

135   Ferthyrmore, besyde these tuelue þat were pryncepal he hadde ȝytt
othyr thre score and xii dyscyplys, as the euangelyste Luke beryth
wytnesse, the whyche he seyth he sente tueyne and tueyne afore hys
f. 56ᵛ face into eueryche cytee and | place whythyr he was to come. And he
seyde to hem: 'Forsothe, the corne ys myche but þe werke`men´ ben
140 fewe', as ho seyth, þe peple ys myche but ther ben but fewe precharys
þat maye werke in hem be techynge of Godys worde. 'Prayeth
þerfore', he seyde, 'þe Lorde of the corne that he wolde sende

    107 alle] all þo N   108 despyse] displese N   109 þat¹] *om.* N   111 of¹] to N
113 also] *om.* N   116 Ihesu Cryste] *om.* N   117 contrarye] contrey N   119 ys
to] his N   men] *om.* N   120 duble and] double men and men N   123 wente] wente
aboute N   127 to²] *om.* N   130 the] *om.* N   135 Ferthyrmore] also N
138 into eueryche] in yche N   142 wolde] *om.* N

wyrkemen into hys corne.' Vpon the`se´ wordys of oure Lorde I
conseyle ȝow to praye oure Lorde Ihesu Cryste, þat ys Lorde of
Crystyn peple, þe whyche ys `hys´ spyrytual corne, to sende wyrke-   145
men, þat ys to seye, precharys in wordys and werkys into hys corne,
þat ys to seye, amonge Crystyn peple. For thowgth ther ben manye
precharys, as hyt semyth now adayis in wordys, ther ben but fewe
thowgth in werkys, as a devout man seyth in metre thus: 'Multos
habemus doctores sed paucissimos factores in vita mortalium', þys ys   150
in Englyisch: 'We haue manye doctorys but rygth fewe doarys in the
lyf of deedly men.'

CHAPTER 15

Of oure Lordys myraclys þat he wrowthe and othyr diuerse werkys
þat he dede in hys manhede, of hys goynge `about´ in prechynge and
techynge of the scribys and þe Pharyseys and what they were, and
why he toke mankynde wyth othyr materys þat longen therto.
Capitulum quindecim.   5

Relygyus syster, I haue sumwhat tolde ȝow in þe chapetele nexste
afore thys how oure Lorde Ihesu Cryste, aftyr hys fastynge in deserte,
wente into the worlde and prechede, and also callede | hys dyscyplys. f. 57ʳ
Now in thys chapetele and the nexste aftyr thys I wole telle ȝow
sumwhat, be the helpe of the same Lorde, of hys worthy myraclys þat 10
he wrowthe to the confyrmacyon of hys holy doctryne and to the
schewynge of hys godhede, summe in specyal and summe in general,
wyth othyr werkys þat he dede. Fyrste thanne, ȝe maye thynke þat þer
was made a weddynge in a strete `of´ Galyle þat was callyd Chana
foure myle fro Naȝareth. And oure Lady `was´ there, for hyt ys   15
comynly seyde þat hyt was the weddynge of Seyint Ihon Euangelyste.
And therfore oure Lady `was´ there as hys aunte and a gouernoure of
the weddynge, for as myche as hyt was here cosynys weddynge. For
Lyre seyth þat hyt ys not lykly þat sche wolde haue come thedyr but
yf hyt hadde myche loongyd to here. And fro thys weddynge ȝe maye   20
thynke oure Lorde callyde Seyint Ihon and made hym one of hys
dyscyplys, and to hym oure Lorde schewde more tendyr loue thanne
to othyre, as ȝe schal here be þe grace of `God´ here aftyr, for he abode

144 of] of all N   146 and] and in N   147 thowgth] om. N
Chapter 15   3 þe] om. N   5 Capitulum quindecim] om. N   9 and the] om. N
13 thanne] om. N   16 Ihon] Ihon þe N   19 þat] om. N   22 more] more and N
23 here] here aftrewarde somewhat N   here aftyr] om. N

stylle a clene mayde. Also oure Lorde was callyd to þys weddynge and
25 hys dyscyplys. And att thys weddynge ȝe maye thynke 'he' turnede
watyr into wyne att þe askynge of hys modyr whenne hyt faylede, for
hyt loongyde to here 'to see' þat nothynge faylede there, for honestee of
f. 57ᵛ here neuew. And | in that myracle oure Lorde schewde þe mygthte of
hys godhede; and thys he doeth gostly in mennys soulys whenne he
30 turnyth the naked resun that was fyrste drye, fro gostly knowynge, into
lygth of vndyrstandynge, and the bare wyll þat was fyrste vnsauery fro
þe suetnesse of deuocyon into brennyge loue and affeccyon.

Aftyr thys ȝe maye thynke how he wente forth into the contre
mekely on hys feete and hys xii apostlys wyth hym. And so ȝe maye
35 beholde hym how he goeth abowte fro cytee to cytee, fro towne to
towne, and fro castel to castel, prechynge and techynge 'þe weye' to
euyrlastynge lyf, schewynge þe mygthte of hys godhede, and
appreuynge hys techynge be opyn myraclys, as in helynge seke
men, in clensynge leprys, in puttynge out of deuyllys, in makynge
40 blynde men to see, of þe whyche one he helyde þat hadde be blynde
fro hys byrthe, þat 'was' neuer herde afore that tyme. And schortly,
for to seye, he helyde all maner sekenesse be the vertu of hys godhede,
as he mygth do as he wolde.

Also, he wente vpon the watyr and commaunddyde the wynde to be
45 stylle and the see to cesse of tempeste and the wynde and the see obeyed
to hym as to here verry lorde and makare. Also, he fedde fyue
thowsende men, out take wymmen and chyldryn, wyth u louys & ii
fyischys and ȝyt there were fyld xii copherys of þe leuelys. Anothyr
tyme he fedde also four thowsende men, out take wymmen and
f. 58ʳ chyldryn, wyth vii louys and a fewe smale fyis | chys, and of the leuelys
51 were fylde vii baskettys. And manye othyre myraclys he wrowthte to
schewe hys godhede and to brynge men to þe rygth feythe, of þe whyche
summe I haue tolde ȝow in general wordys, for hyt were to longe to
make a medytacyon of euyryche werke þat the evangelystys telle of oure
55 Lorde. And also I trowe, hyt nede not, for a deuout soule maye be þe
grace of God, draue thys þat ys schortly seyde in to loonge medytacyon
yf he wole and be dysposyd þerto be grace. But ȝytt not wythstandynge,
I wole telle ȝow some werkys þat oure Lorde dede in specyal to ȝoure
more comforte in hym, and that ȝe maye the bettyr thynke othyre.

26 hyt¹] wyne N   30 into] into þe N   32 þe suetnesse of] om. N   of] fol. by
canc. the N   33 how] þat N   35 abowte] om. N   36 'þe weye' to] to þe weye
of N   41 herde] helede N; see note   42 the] om. N   43 as] what N
47–8 wyth u louys . . . and chyldryn] in marg. shield Gg   55 for] fol by canc. hyt nedyth
Gg   þe] om. N   59 othyre] transfigurio deum in marg. scroll Gg

In a tyme ȝe maye thynke, as the euangelyste Mathew makyth 60
mencyon, oure Lorde toke Petyr, Iamys, and Iohnn hys brothyr, for
these `thre´ were moste pryuy of hys conseyil and ledde hem into an
hye hylle. And he was transfygure afore hem, not þat he chongede þe
lynyamentys of hys `body´ or the fygurys, as Lyre seyth, but for the
Immensytee of the clerenesse of hys face. For hys face schone as þe 65
sunne and hys clothys were imade whyte as snowe. And Moyses and
Hely apperyde to hem, spekynge wyth oure Lorde of hys Passyon and
deth þat he schulde `suffre´ wythoute Ierusalem. And thanne ȝe maye
thynke how Petyr seyde to oure Lorde, for he was moste bol|dest to f. 58ᵛ
speke: 'Lorde, hyt ys goode to vs to abyde here; ȝyf þu wolt lete vs 70
make here thre tabernaclys: the one, Moyses one, and Hely one.' He
spake not of eny tabernacle for hymselfe and fore hys felawys, for as
Lyre seyth, he wolde haue be wyth oure Lorde in hys tabernacle and
haue hadde hys felawys þat one in Moyses tabernacle and þat othyr in
Helyis tabernacle. 75

And whyle he spake so, ȝe maye beholde how a schynynge clowde
beschone hem and out of þat clowde cam a voyce seyinge thus: 'Thys
ys my belouyd Sone in the whyche I am `wel´ plesyd; heryth hym.'
And thanne the dyscyplys herynge that fylle downe flatlynge and were
sore adrad for the infyrmyte of man mygth not bere the presence of 80
God. And thanne beholdyth how oure Lorde comyth to hem and
tuchyth hem ful famylyarly, suetly confortynge hem, and seyinge to
hem: 'Arysyth vp and thredyth not.' And thanne they lokyde vp, but
they seygth no man but oure Lorde alone. And as they cam downewarde of the hylle, oure Lorde badde hem telle no man that vysyon 85
tylle he arose fro deth to lyue.

And whenne he cam to the peple aȝen he helyde a lunatyke chylde
att þe prayere of hys fadyr. Here ȝe schal vndyrstande þat men that
ben callyde lunatyke aftyr the seyinge of doctorys ben not traueylyd so
be the vyse of the mone, ne the mone ys not cause of that dyssese þat 90
they suffryn, a some `vnwyse men´ seyin, | but hyt ys an euyl spyryt f. 59ʳ
þat traueylyth hem, so as doctorys seyin, to dyffame the mone þe
whyche ys þe creature of God; or God hymselfe þat ys makare of the
mone; or ellys to putte men into sueche false opynyonys. For hyt ys
seyde in the gospel of Mathew þat hyt was a deuyl þat oure Lorde 95

60 Mathew] *om.* N   61 oure] seinte mathew how N   62 `thre´] *om.* N
71 the] to þe N   72 not of eny] of no N   74 þat] *om.* N   þat othyr] another N
76 how] *om.* N   77 þat] þe N   78 belouyd] wele beloued N   79 were] *fol. by*
canc. were Gg   82 and] *om.* N   91 a . . . seyin] as som N   92 so] *om.* N
92–3 þe whyche] þat N   95 a deuyl] deuylles N

putte out of þat chylde þat hys fadyr callyde lunatyke, and therfore
they synne þat dyffame the mone so wythoute cause.

Also, ȝe maye thynke þat myche peple folowede oure Lorde and
cam to hym in diuerse placys were he prechede and helede in gret
100 multytyde bysyde hys dyscyplys, but for dyuerse causys: summe of
deuocyon and goode wyll to here hys holy doctryne; and summe of
curyosytee to see merueylys; and summe for nede to be helyd of here
sekenessys; and summe for enuye yf the`y´ mygthte take hym in hys
wordys or werkys and so accuse hym, as were the false scribys and
105 Pharyseys and here dyscyplys. And that ȝe mygthte the bettyr knowe
what they were, and also þat I haue no nede to expresse hem eny more
to ȝow in othyr medytacyonys folowynge for ȝe schal here myche of
hem in thys `boke´ folowynge, I wole telle ȝow what maner men they
were aftyr þe seyingys of doctorys.

110   The scribys were sueche men þat hadde moste letty`r´ature amonge
hem and were wyseest in þe lawe and they were ordynarye iuggys
amonge the peple. The Pharyseys were, as hyt hadde be, moste
f. 59ᵛ rely|gyus amonge the peple, and they weryde aboute here heedys as
hyt hadde be cha`r´turys in the maner of crownys, and the`r´inne were
115 iwryte the tenne commaundmentys of gret lettyrys. Also, they hadde
anothyr ibownde abowte here lyfte arme and they hadde pryckys in
the hemmys of here clothys to prycke hem as they wente to haue þe
commaundmentes of God in mynde. And for they were so diuerse fro
the comyn habyte of othyr men, they were callyd Pharyseys, as the
120 Maystyr of Storyis seyth. All þys they dede to be hadde in more
reuerence and worschype amonge men, for oure `Lorde´ seyth
hymselfe þat they dede alle here werkys to bee seyin of men, and
therfore they were false ypocritys.

These scrybys and Pharyseys were moste aȝenste oure Lorde and
125 chef chause of hys deth, for he reprouyde here vycys, ypo`cr´ysye, and
falsnesse. And therfore they bare hym an hande that he blasphemyde,
for he seyde þat he was Goddys sone, and that `he´ brake þe haly daye
for he helyde syke folke þerinne, and also þat he turnyde the peple fro
þe lawe, for he taugthte hem the weye of trewthe and the weye to

96 fadyr] moder N   99 were] þore N   101 deuocyon] gode deuocioun N
103 for] of N   take] kache N   104 so] so to N   107 in othyr . . . folowynge] here
afterwarde ffor yhe shall here mykel of hem in þe meditacions folowyinge N
108 maner] maner of N   110–11 amonge hem] om. N   114 crownys] a
crowne N   were] prec. by canc. wre Gg   116 anothyr . . . hadde] om. N; see note
120 All] and N   121 and worschype] om. N   125 of hys deth] þat he was dede N
126 an] apoun N   128 folke] men N

euyrlastynge lyf. And 'þat' ȝe mygthte þe bettyr knowe here enuye 130
and euyl wyll aȝenste hym, I schal schewe ȝow betueyne ensamplys
how sotylly they caste to haue dysseyuyd hym yf they hadde mygth
but trewthe and euyrlastynge wysedom maye not be dysseyuyd.

In a tyme the | Pharyseys ȝe maye thynke, to here conseyil f. 60ʳ
togyderys how they mygthte take oure Lorde in 'hys' speche, for 135
they mygthte 'not' take 'hym in' hys werkys, for a man ys soonyr take
in hys wordys thanne in hys werkys, as Lyre seyth, and so they sente
to hym here dyscyplys wyth Kynge Herowdeys knygthtys, seyinge to
hym be hem: 'Maystyr, 'we' wyte wel that þu arte trewe and techyste
the 'weye' of God in trewthe, and þu rekkyste of no man, 'for' 140
forsothe þu beho[l]dyst not þe persone of man. Seye vs what the
semyth: Ys hyt laweful moneye to be ȝeue to emperowre or none?'
Thys they mente of þe trybute that they bare to the Romaynys, for
they were that tyme trybutaryis to hem. But oure Lorde knewe here
falsnesse wel inowf, and therefore he seyde to hem: 'Where to tempte 145
ȝe me, ypocrytys?' And ypocryte ys he that schewyth outwarde
holynesse and ys inwarde the contrarye, and seyth one and menyth
anothyr, and 'so' dede these. For Lyre se'y'th þat they putte þys
questyon to hym malycyusly, þat yf he hadde seyde not 'to' be
laweful, anone the knygthtys schulde haue take hym as contrarye to þe 150
Emperoure; and yf he hadde seyde laweful hyt schulde haue semyd
contrarye to the fredom of the peple and the worschype of God. And
so 'he schulde' haue hadde þe euyl wyll and malycyusnesse of the
peple.

But all thys falsnesse was not vnknowe to hym þat knewe here 155
hertys. And therfore, þat he mygthte the 'more' conuenyently |
ansuere 'hem', he badde hem schewe hym the cune of the monye. f. 60ᵛ
And thanne they toke hym a penye þat was worthe x pence amonge
hem. And thanne oure Lorde, þat he mygthte the warelokyr ȝeue hem
a ful ansuere, askede hem whas 'the' ymage was þat was in the peny 160
and the wrytynge ther vpon, for the ymage of the Emperowre was
cunyd in the peny and hys name wryte abowte. And they seyde: 'The

130 mygthte] mygth somwhate N   enuye] ennemy N   132 they] þat þei N   hym]
hym and N   133 trewthe] trewe N   134 Pharyseys] in marg. shield Gg   to]
takenne N   136 soonyr take] taken lightlyer N   137 thanne] þat N   138 to
hym] om. N   Kynge] þe kynge N   139 techyste] þou techeste N   141 beho[l]dyst]
behodyst Gg; behodeste N   man] men N   142 to] to þe N   146 And] ane N
148 For] for as N   þat] om. N   149 'to'] om. N   153 and] and þe N   159 þat]
fol. by canc. oure Gg   warelokyr] more warely N   160 'the'] om. N   161 ther]
om. N

Emperowrys', and thanne oure Lorde badde hem ȝelde tho thyngys þat longyn to þe Emperowe to þe Emperowre, and tho thyngys þat
165 longyn to God to God.

Loo, gostly systyr, how perfyth an ansuere thys was to avoyde clerely alle perelys, be the whyche they were fully ouyrcome. And therfore, whenne they hadde herde þat ansuere they meruelyde that they hadde no weye in hym and so they wente here weye as confusyd.
170 Anothyr tyme the scribys and the Pharyseys browgth a woman itake in spouse breche, and they sette here in the myddyl of the peple, and seyde to oure Lorde thus: 'Maystyr, thys woman was now take in spouse breche. Moyses badde vs in the lawe to steyne to deeth suecheamanyr woman. What seyest þu therto?' Thys, ˈþeˈ euangelyste
175 seyth, they seyde temptynge hym þat they mygthte accuse hym, for yf he hadde seye: 'Naye, steynyth here not to deth', theˈyˈ wolde haue accusyd hym as rebell to Moyses lawe; for Moyses lawe byddyth þat sueche a woman schulde be steynyd to deth. Att þat othyr syde, yf
f. 61ʳ he | hadde seyde: 'Steynyth here to deth as the lawe byddyth', they
180 ˈwoldeˈ haue seyde þat he dede aȝenste hys owen prechynge and werkynge, for he prechyde pytee and mercy and dede hyt in werkynge, as ȝe maye here afore, in helynge of sekenessys and maˈnˈye othyr dyssesys, for he was ful suete and mercyful. And therfore, of the tueyne they trowede þat he wolde haue demyd here to
185 be lett goo, as Lyre seyth, and so they mygthte haue accusyd hym as a trespassare of the lawe.

Thanne ȝe maye beholde how oure Lorde stopyth downe and wrytyth wyth hys fyngyr in the erthe. And whenne they perseueryde askynge hym, ȝe maye thynke how he lyftyth vp hymselfe aȝen and
190 seyth to hem: 'He þat ys wythoute synne of ȝow, lett hym caste þe fyrste stone on here.' And thanne he enclynede hymselfe aȝen and wrote in the erthe. Some seyin þat he wrote here synnys, þat he mygthte schewe hem vnable to the execuscyon of hys sentence. And thanne ȝe maye beholde how they wente out one aftyr anothyr
195 begynnyge att the eldyste, for they were aschamyd haply of here synnys, that they seygth wryte there be the mygthte of God. And so oure Lorde abode there alone, vndyrstondyth, as for hem þat hadde accusyd the woman and the woman afore hym standynge in the

169 they²] þei lefte hym and N   confusyd] confoundede N   170 Anothyr] in marg. scroll Gg   175 they seyde] om. N   178 þat othyr] þe tother N   182 maye here] haue herde N   of sekenessys] of þe sekenesse N   186 of] aȝenste N   191 enclynede] inclynede downe N   hymselfe] hym fol. by canc. sefl Gg   192 þat] þat by þat N   196 synnys] owen synnes N   wryte] om. N

myddyl of the peple þat abode there wyth oure Lorde. For ȝe maye
thynke þat oure Lordys dyscyplys abode wyth hym and the | othyr ‎f. 61ᵛ
pepyl, outtake hem þat hadde accusyd þe woman, for they thurste no 201
lengyr abyde for schame of hemselfe. And thanne ȝe maye thynke how
oure Lorde lyfte vp hymselfe eftesonys and ful mercyfully seyde to
the woman: 'Woman, where bee they þat accusyde the? None of hem
hath condempnyd the?', and thanne sche seyde aȝen, 'No, Lorde'. 205
'Ne, I schal [not] condempne the. Goo forth and wyll no more to
synne.'

Loo, gostly systyr, what mercy thys was of oure mercyful Lorde þat
thus mercyfully delyueryde þys synful woman fro þat wykkede peple,
and so suetly and lowly spake to here, thanne louyth hym wyth all 210
ȝoure herte. For forsothe he ys ful worthy to be louyd þat so mercyful
was in hys domys, so holy in hys lyuynge, soo trewe and profytable in
hys techynge and soo mygthty in myraclys werkynge. Manye othyr
dyssesys, waytyngys, and wrongys thanne be forseyde oure Lorde
suffrede ful mekely and pacyently, specyally of the forseyde scribys 215
and Pharyseys and othyr vnkynde peple, for the helthe of hys chosyn
and to ȝeue exsample of perfeccyon to hys folowarys. Also, ȝe maye
thynke how in myche goynge abowte in prechynge and techynge he
was wery. Also, he fastede, he wakyde, he prayde, he sclepte, he
hungrede, he thurstede, and sueche othyre infyrmyteys of mankynde 220
he suffryde. 'But' all þys was for he wolde do so of hys euyrlastynge
goodnesse, and not aȝenste hys wyll for he þat ys allmygthty
mygthte | not be compellyd to doo othyrwyse thanne he wolde ‎f. 62ʳ
hymselfe. But all þys he dede to schewe hymselfe a verry man, and
that we schulde knowe how myche loue and charyte he hadde to 225
mankynde, þat wolde for the endles profyte of the same kynde take
hyt and therinne suffre soo myche tribulacyon and dyssese soo loonge
tyme, and, att þe laste, for the same loue and charytee, dye in þe same
kynde.

For foure 'causys' I consydere specyally þat oure Lorde wolde take 230
mankynde fore. The fyrste and þe pryncepal ys þat he wolde bye aȝen
mankynde that for hys owen synne and wrecchydnesse was loste, and
euyre schulde haue be but 'yf he' of hys endles mercy hadde bowgth
hyt aȝen for he seyth hymselfe in the gospel thus,: 'Venit filius

200 the] þat N   203 mercyfully] *fol. by canc.* seyde to the Gg   206 not] N; *canc.*
Gg   209 synful woman] woman þat was synfull N   211 he] *fol. by canc.* wo Gg
214 thanne be forseyde] þat N   217 hys] *fol. by canc.* to Gg   220 sueche] *fol. by
canc.* othyr Gg   221 euyrlastynge] owne N   231 fore] *om.* N   and þe pryncepal]
om. N   233 be] *om.* N

235 hominis non ministrari, sed ministrare et dare animam [suam]
redempcionem pro multis.' Thys ys to seye in Englyische: 'The
sone of the mayde cam `not´ to `be´ serued but to serue and to 3yue
hys lyf redempcyon for manye.' The secunde cause ys þat he wolde
3eue vs exsample of perfeccyon in hys owen persone, not only in
240 wordys but also in perfyth werkys, þat we schulde folowe hym here in
thys lyf be goode werkys, yf we wole be partenerys wyth hym in ioye
euyrlastynge. For he seyth in the gospel thus: 'Qui mihi ministrat, me
sequatur.' Thys ys to seye, 'He þat seruyth me lett hym folowe me';
f. 62ᵛ thys ys, not | only in outwarde goynge, for so folowede hym Iudas
245 that aftyrwarde betrayede hym, but also in mekenesse, pacyence, and
charytee, and othyr vertuus lyuynge inwarde and outwarde. And in
the same texste folowynge also he seyth: 'Et vbi sum ego, illic et
minister meus erit'; þys ys: 'And where I am there schal my seruaunt
be.' The thyrde cause maye be for the goode Lorde knewe afore þat
250 hys chosyn schulde suffre myche tribulacyon in thys worlde. And
therfore he wolde goo `the´ wey of tribulacyon and dyssese afore hem,
þat they schulde the esylokyr suffre tribulacyonys and dyssesys for
hys loue and for here owen profyte, sygth he suffrede soo myche for
hem and afore hem. For he seyth in the gospel thus: 'Si mundus uos
255 odit, scitote quia me priorem vobis odio habuit'; þys ys to seye: 'Yf þe
worlde hate 3ow, wyte 3e wel þat he hate me afore 3ow.' The foureth
cause ys that `he wolde´ dystroye þe vice of vnkyndnesse in
mankynde, for yf men and wymen wolde consydere dylygently
what kyndnesse oure Lorde hath schewde to hem, they schulde be
260 rygth sory to be soo vnkynde as [mony] be in these dayis. For the vyce
of `vn´kyndnesse ys a foule vyce and myche dysplesaunt to God, for
Seyint Austyn seyth in hys *Solyloquyis* to oure `Lorde´ of þat vyce
thus: 'I wote wel þat vnkyndnesse dysplesyth the, þe whyche ys roote
f. 63ʳ of all spyrytual euyl, | and a maner wynde dryinge and brennynge all
265 goode, stoppynge vp the welle of þe mercy of God to men, be the
whyche bothe euyl thyngys deed spryngynge a3en and lyuynge
werkys dyen and be not gett a3en.'
  Therfore, beeth 3e kynde to our Lorde þat 3e maye here fynde
mercy and grace, and in the lyf to come euyrlastynge ioye and

235 suam] N; *om.* Gg   236 to seye] *om.* N   237 to³] *om.* N   238 redempcyon]
om. N   wolde] wole N   242 thus] *om.* N   mihi] N; mihi michi Gg   244 thys]
þat N   248 ys] is to seye N   253 here] his N   254 and afore hem] *om.* N
255 ys] is þis N   260 mony] N; maye Gg   these] there N   264 euyl] wille N
wynde] of wynde N   265 stoppynge] *prec. by canc.* sp Gg   267 a3en] *om.* Gg
lyuynge] lyfely Gg   267 dyen] dryen N   269 come] come `to´ N

gladdnesse, þe whyche oure ʼLordeʼ mercyfully ȝeuyth to hem þat   270
kyndly, mekely, and trewly serue and loue hym here in þys present
lyfe.

CHAPTER 16

How oure Lorde Ihesu Cryste, [amoonge] othyr myraclys þat he
wrowgthe, specyally araysede thre deede, þat ys to seye too men and
oo damesele, and what ys betokenyd be hem gostly, and how þe
byischoppys and the Pharyseys toke here conseyil togyderys aȝenste
hym and be þe conseyil of Cayphas dyffynyde to sclee ʼhymʼ as sone as   5
they mygthte. Capitulum sedecim.

Amoo[n]ge othyr myraclys that oure ʼLordeʼ Ihesu Cryste dede here
in erthe, ȝe maye specyally take to mynde how he araysede thre deede
specyally and haply moo. But hyt ys not wythoute cause þat thre ben
specyally named for sumwhat they betokene to be doo in holy chyrche   10
gostly. For Seyint Austyn seyth þat manye men and wymen haue
bodyly eyen wyth the whyche they mygthte see yf a man or a woman
were araysyd bodyly, but manye kunne not see how men and
wymmen ben aray|syd fro deth to lyf gostly. And ȝytt he seyth hyt   f. 63ᵛ
ys more maystrye to arayse a man or a woman in soule euyrmore to   15
lyue thanne to arayse þe body that ʼschalʼ dye aȝen. And therfore I
wole telle ȝow fyrste of thre þat oure Lorde araysede bodyly, and
thanne what ys betokenyd be hem gostly. For Seyint [Austyn] seyth
þat oure Lorde wole þat we beleue the myraclys þat he dede here in
erthe, idoo in trowthe as we here red, and also he seyth he wole hem to   20
be vndyrstonde gostly.

   The fyrste of hem þat oure Lorde araysede bodyly was a ȝonge
damsele of xii ȝere olde. And sche was the dowgthtyr of þe prynce of
the synagoge whas name was Iayre, and here he araysede wythinne the
howʼseʼ of þe same prynce, no man beynge present but the fadyr and   25
the modyr of þe same damsele and thre of hys dyscyplys, þat ys to
seye, Petyr, Iamys, and Ihon hys brothyr. Be þys mayde ben
betokenyde men and wymmen that dye in thowgthte wythinne here
soulys be wylful consentynge to synne. But þe deth ys withinne, as

271 serue] seruen hym N

Chapter 16   1 amoonge] amonge N; amooge Gg   6 Capitulum sedecim] om. N
7 dede . . . erthe] here in erthe wroghte N   11 gostly] om. N   15 a] om. N   to²]
om. N   18 Austyn] N; Gregory Gg   21 be] om. N   22 bodyly] om. N
23 the] om. N   27 mayde] damesele N

30 Seyint Austyn seyth, for the euyl thowgth ys not ȝytt goo forth in
   dede. Sueche a soule, þe same doctur seyth, oure Lorde betokenynge
   hymselfe to arayse , `he´ araysede the forseyde damsele, þe whyche
   was `not´ ȝytt bore out but sche laye deed in the house for the synne
f. 64ʳ was | as hyt hadde be ȝytt pryuy.

35 The secunde was a wydowes sone, the whyche oure Lorde mette
   wythoute the ȝate of a cytee þat ys callyd Naym; thys was in the contre
   of Galylee, as the Maystyr of Storyis seyth. And the forseyde ȝonge
   mannys modyr, a wydowe, folowede the bere and myche peple of þe
   cytee wyth here, the whyche whenne oure Lorde seygth wepynge, of
40 gret mercy ȝe maye thynke he hadde `pytee´ and compassyon on here
   and badde `here´ not wepe. And thanne he wente `to´ and tuchyde the
   bere, and anone they that bare hym stode stylle. And `thanne´ oure
   Lorde seyde to hym þat laye deed: 'Ȝonge `man´, I seye to the, aryse.'
   And anone he þat laye deed satte vp and beganne to speke. And
45 `thanne´ he `be´toke hym `to hyer´ modyr, and alle the peple þat
   seygth thys dredde and magnyfyede God.

   Be thys man ben betokenyd men and wymmen þat not only dyen in
   soule be wylful consentynge to synne, the why`che´ ben betokenyd be
   the forseyde damsele, but also hem þat fulfylle here euyl consentynge
50 in dede. For Seyint Austyn seyth: 'Forsothe, yf þu not only haste
   consentyd to an euyl delyte, but also þu haste doo the `same´ euyl', þat
   ys to seye, in werkynge, 'þu haste, `as´ hyt were, bore out the deede
   wythoute the ȝate. Now þu arte wythoute and þu arte bore oute
   deede. Neuyrdeles', he seyth, 'oure Lorde also araysede hym and |
f. 64ᵛ ȝeldyde hym to hys modyr, the wydowe. Ȝyf þu haue synned', he
56 seyth also folowynge, 'forthynke hyt, and thanne `oure Lorde´ arasyth
   the and schal `ȝelde´ the thy Modyr holy chyrche.' Thys ben Seyint
   Austynys wordys vpo`n´ þe gospel of Seyint Ihon.

   The thyrde deede was Lasur, the brothyr of Marye Mawdeleyne
60 and Marthe here systyr, the whyche oure Lorde araysyde att þe
   preyerys of hys systryn aftyr he hadde `be´ foure dayis deed and beryd
   and a stone leyde vpon hym. And be thys man ben betokenyd men
   and wymmen þat not only dyen in thowgth and dede, the whyche ben
   betokenyd be the too deede forseyde, but also hem þat lyen stylle in
65 synne be lo`o´[n]ge custum. For they be as hyt were beryed be loonge

---

30 thowgth] thoght N; ithowgth Gg   32 arayse] aryse N   36 was] cite is N
37 of²] of þe N   40 on] of N   43 Lordeʳ] he N   laye] was N   47 man] man
and woman N   51 `same´] om. N   52 haste] haue N   57 thy] to þi N
59 Marye] Seint Mary N   65 hyt] þei N

and contynuant lyinge in the fylthe of synne, also they as hyt were
stynkyn be the badde name and fame þat arysyth of suechemanyr
folke. For hyt ys red also of Lasur þat he stanke, and the stone of euyl
custum lyeth so heuyly vpon hem þat vnnedys they maye aryse. But
ȝytt be the mygth of God, to whom nothynge ys impossyble, and the ₇₀
prayerys of oure Lady and othyr seyintys and the merytys of oure
'modyr' holy chyrche, summe sueche bee mercyfully araysyde fro
here badde custum and become ful goode and holy. Thus I haue I
tolde ȝow schortly | of the thre deede þat oure Lorde araysyde bodyly, f. 65ʳ
and what ys betokenyd be hem gostly.   75

Aftyr thys ȝe maye thynke how manye Iewys that seygth thys 'laste'
myracle doo, as the euangelyste beryth wytnesse, beleuyde in oure
Lorde Ihesu Cryste. For the same euangelyste seyth that there were
manye Iewys icome to Marye and Marthe to conforte hem of here
brothyrys deth. And so ȝe maye thynke þat they were present at the ₈₀
forseyde myracle, and therfore manye of hem aftyr they hadde seye
that gret myr'a'cle done beleuyde in oure Lorde, as ys forseyde. And
some wente to the Pharyseys and tolde hem what oure Lorde hadde
idoo, ellys þat they schulde beleue in hym or ellys, þat that ys more
lykelokyr, that they schulde sende and take hym. Fo'r' Lyre seyth þat ₈₅
'r'ygtht as goode chosyn of myraclys þat they seyin be turnyd to more
goode, rygth 'so' euylle oftetymys be more obdurat or harde in euyl.
And þat semyth 'of hem' more, he se'y'th be the lettyr folowynge,
where hyt ys tolde of þe gaderynge togyderys of the Pharyseys to trete
of oure Lordys deth, and therof wole I telle ȝow now.   90

Whenne the byischoppys þat were moste of autoryte amoonge the
Iewys and the Pharyseys þat semyde moste relygyus herde telle of the
forseyde myracle þat oure Lorde hadde idoo, | they gaderyde here f. 65ᵛ
conseyl togyderys aȝenste oure Lorde and seyde: 'What schal we doo?
For thys man doeth manye myraclys, yf we leue hym thus, all the ₉₅
peple schal beleue in hym. And thanne schul the Romaynys come and
take aweye oure place', þys they mente of the cytee of Ierusalem and
the temple for that was here chef cytee and abydynge, 'and oure peple
also', they seyde. For they trowede þat yf all the peple hadde beleuyd
in oure Lorde, the Romaynys wolde haue come and dystroyed the ₁₀₀
cytee and the temple, and haue take awey þe peple and made hem

66 also] and N   as hyt were] lye as þei were N   73 I] *fol. by canc.* haue I Gg
76 Aftyr] than aftre N   manye] mony of þe N   7728 beryth] *fol. by canc.* seyth N
79 manye] mony of þe N   80–1 the forseyde] þis doynge N   82 that] þis N   done]
om. N   as] *om.* N   83 wente] wente forthe N   87 be] made N   93 they] *om.* N
94 Lorde] Lorde Ihesu criste N   schal] shulde N   97 aweye] *fol. by canc.* oure Gg

dralle. And þat ȝytt fylle aftyrwarde for here synnys and vnkyndnesse
aȝenste oure Lorde, as ȝe schal heere in the xxi chapetele folowynge.

　　Aftyr þys ȝe maye thynke how one of hem, Cayphas be name, þat
105　was byischop þat ȝere, ȝaf hem wykkyd conseyil and seyde: 'Hyt ys
spedeful to ȝow þat one man dye for the pepyl and not all the pepyl
peryische.' Thys the euangelyst seyth he seyde not of hymselfe, but
for he was byischop 'þat ȝere' he prophecyede þat oure Lorde schulde
dye for the pepyl. Here we be taugwth, as Seyint Austyn, seyth that
110　othyrwhyle the spyryt of prophecye seyth thyngys þat bytgth to come
be euyl men. Wherfore, the spyryt of prophecye or myraclys
f. 66ʳ　wyrkynge or vysyonys or reuelacyonys | or sueche othyr ȝyftys þat
been ȝeue synglerly to some, bee not myche to be desyryd, but where
oure Lorde wole frely ȝeue hem wythoute eny sekynge of vs, for they
115　maye be hadde othyrwhyle of euyl 'men' and wymmen as wel as 'of'
goode, as ȝe maye 'here' afore of Cayphas.

　　Also oure Lorde seyth in the gospel of Mathew that manye schul
come to hym seyinge: 'Domine, Domine, nonne 'in nomine' tuo
prophetauimus, et in nomine tuo demonia eiecimus, et in nomine tuo
120　virtutes multas fecimus? Et tunc confitebor illis quia nunquam noui
uos, discedite a me omnes qui operamini iniquitatem.' Thys 'ys' to
seye in Englyische: 'Lorde, Lorde, prophecyede we not in thy name,
and in thy 'name' we caste out deuyllys, and in thy name we dede
manye myraclys?' 'And thanne schal 'I' knowleche to hem', he seyth,
125　'I knewe ȝow neuere'; þat ys to seye, as for my chosyn. 'Gooeth fro me
alle þat wyrkyn wykkednesse.' Hereby ȝe maye vndyrstande þat
manye maye haue the ȝyfte of prophecye, the puttynge out of
deuyllys, and of myraclys wyrkynge, and ȝytt he reprouyd. And
therfore they bee not myche to bee desyryd of hem that haue hem not,
130　and yf they be, hadde they bee not myche to be sett by wythoute
othyre holy vertuys and holy lyuynge therwyth. But mekenesse and
charytee, wyth feythe, hope, and perseueraunce in goode and all othyr
f. 66ᵛ　vertuus lyuynge inwarde and outwarde been gretly and con|tynually
to be desyryd of ȝow and alle othyre that wole be partenerys of
135　euyrlastynge herytage, for ȝe maye not haue hem and be reprouyd.

　　Aftyr thys ȝe maye thynke þat whenne the byischoppys and the

　　　103　as] at N　　　106　not¹] noght þat N　　　107　Thys] This is N　　　110　othyrwhyle]
while þat N　　come] fol. by canc. to Gg　　111　spyryt] ȝiftes N　　114　wole] wolde N
119　demonia] canc. me fol. de　　eiecimus] eicimus N　　121　discedite] discite N
122　in Englyische] om. N　　130　be] haue bene N　　131　holy¹] om. N　　134　alle] of
all N　　136　ȝe maye thynke] thenketh N　　byischoppys] forseide bisshopes N　　the²]
om. N

Pharyseys hadde take here conseyil togyderys, and Cayphas hadde
ȝeue hem conseyil vndyr the forme of the wordys forseyde, fro that
daye they thowgthte to scle oure Lorde as sone as they mygthte. For
thowgth afore they hadde wyll to sclee hym, as ȝe maye here be the 140
wordys þat they hadde whenne they cam togyderys, ȝytt whenne
Cayphas hadde ȝeue hem hys conseyil they fully dyffynyde to
performe hyt as sone as they mygthte. Be these wordys ȝe maye
vndyrstande þat I nygthhe faste to the Passyon of oure Lorde, þe
whyche ys the chef cause of þys sympyl labore, as I behette ȝow. And 145
therfore I beseke þe same mercyful Lorde, for hys Passyon and the
preyerys of oure Lady and Seyint Ihon Euangelyste, and alle the holy
courte of heuene, so bee hys grace to ȝeue me to trete therof as hyt
maye bee to hym pleesaunt and acceptable, to me spedeful and
merytorye, and to ȝow or eny othyr þat ys be the grace of God to 150
reede hyt or heere hyt, edyfycatyf and prophytable amen.

   [And here I praye ȝow of þe same preyere that I askede in þe fyrste
chapetele of 27 þys boke, þat ys, iii Pater Noster, iii Aueys, and a
crede.]

CHAPTER 17

Of the sopere þat was made to oure Lorde in Betanye in the
Satyr|daye afore Palme Sondaye, þat ys Palme Sondaye euyn. And f. 67ʳ
how in the nexste `daye´ aftyr þat ys callyd Palme Sondaye, he was
resceyuyd into the cytee of Ierusalem. And how in the Wedenysdaye
in the same wyke folowynge Iudas solde oure Lorde for xxx^ty pence. 5
Capitulum decimum septimum.

Gostly `systyr´, I haue tolde ȝow in the chapetele nexste afore thys
how the byischoppys and the Pharyseys toke here conseyil togyderys
aȝenste oure Lorde, and be conseyil of Cayphas purposyde to sclee
hym as sone as they mygthte. Aftyr þys ȝe maye thynke how oure 10
Lorde Ihesu Cryste, as the euangelyste Seyint Ihon beryth wytnesse,
vi dayis afore Estyr amonge the Iewys, þat ys Palme Sondaye euyn,
cam into Betanye, the whyche ys too myle fro Ierusalem. Here I wole

   138 the] *om.* N   139 to] forto N   Lorde] Lorde Ihesu Criste N   140 to] forto N
144 to] *om.* N   147 preyerys] prayer N   Ihon] Ihon þe   151 heere] to here N
152-4 And here . . . crede] *in marg. scroll* Gg   153 ys] is to seye N   iii²] and thre N
Aueys] Aue Maria N

Chapter 17 1 oure Lorde] hym N   8 conseyil] þe counseil N   9 purposyde]
om. N   10 Aftyr] sistre N   13 into] to N   the whyche ys] *om.* N

telle ȝow fyrste what thys Estyr was amonge hem, for ȝe schal
15 vndyrstande þat hyt was a gret festeful daye amonge þe Iewys, and
hyt ys as myche to seye as a passynge. Thys feste was vsyd amonge
hem, ȝe schal vndyrstande, in mynde of the grete benfeett þat God
schewde hem whenne be hys angyl he delyuerede hem out of þe londe
of Egypte fro the cruel bondage of Kynge Pharao. For the nygthte
20 afore þat they were delyuered, the angyl of God wente bee alle þe
f. 67ᵛ howses of Egypte and sclewe eche fyrste | begotyn thynge therinne,
bothe of men and of bestes, outtake of þe peple of Israel. And for the
angyl of God wente soo and smote eueryche fyrste begotyn thynge in
the londe of Egypte, and sauyde hem, hyt was callyd þe Passynge of
25 oure Lorde. And fro that tyme hyt was a solempne feste amonge hem
be þe commaundment of God, and hyt duryde vii dayis, but the fyrste
daye and the laste were moste solempne. And thys feste was callyed
Estyr amonge hem, þat ys to seye, þe Passynge of oure Lorde.

And so vi dayis afore þys feste amonge þe I'e'wys, ȝe maye thynke
30 as ys forseyde, how oure Lorde cam into Betanye where Lasur hadde
be deede the whyche he araysyde, as I haue schortly tolde ȝow in the
chapetele afore þys. And there men of þat place made hym a soper,
and Marthe, Marye Maudeleynys systyr, seruyde and Lasur, here
brothyr, was one of hem þat satt att sopere wyth oure Lorde. Thys
35 sopere, as some doctorys ˋseyinˊ comunely, whas in the house of a man
þat ys callyd Symon Lepyr, the whyche oure Lorde hadde helyd of þe
lepyr, but þe name abode in mynde of þat myracle. And the same
man, as Lyre seyth, was Marthys nygthbore, and therfore sche was þe
boldyr to doo seruyse to oure Lorde in hys house.

40   Also, ȝe maye thynke that Marye Maudeleyne, here systyr, toke a
f. 68ʳ pow|nde of ful precyouse vnement. And fyrste ȝe maye thynke sche
weische hys feete and thanne wypede hem wyth the heerys of here
heede, for sche louyde hym wyth all here herte, and aftyr that sche
anvnetyde hem wyth the forseyde vnement. And alle the house was
45 fylde wyth the sauoure þerof, for hyt was a ful precyouse vnement and
of gret pryse, and hereby ȝe maye vndyrstande the gret deuocyon of
þat blyssyd Lady to oure Lorde.

17 of] þat N   19 cruel] orbbell N   20 þe] *om.* N   22 of²] *om.* N
23 eueryche] yche N   25 And] and so N   tyme] tyme forewarde N   27 daye]
om. N   30 ys] it is N   into] in N   Lasur] *om.* N   32 chapetele] chapitle next N
33 Marye] *in marg.* þe systyr of Marye Mawdeleyne Gg   34 of hem] *om.* N   sopere] þe
sopere N   35 some] *om.* N   36 ys] was N   37 þat] þe N   42 thanne] þan
she N   the] hir N   43 aftyr that] afterwarde N   45 fylde] fulfillede N   46–7 of
þat] *prec. by canc.* of þat Gg

Aftyr thys ȝe maye beholde how Iudas Scaryot þe [whiche] aftyrwarde betrayede oure Lorde, grucchede seyinge: 'Why was not thys vnement solde for thre hundryd pence and ȝeue to poure men?' 50 Thys he `seyde´, the euangelyste seyth, not þat hyt longyde to hym of poure men (as hoo seyth, he roste not of hem) but for he was a thefe, hauynge pursys in the whyche he hydde þat that `schulde´ haue be spendyd in othyr vsys. For he bare þat that was ȝeue oure Lorde to the helpynge of hys bodyly nede and hys dyscyplys. And ȝytt, 55 thowgth he dede hyt falsly, oure Lorde pacyently suffryde hym, to ȝeue vs exsample þat we schulde suffre pacyently screwys, for Seyint Gregory seyth: 'He was neuer goode that recusyth to suffre euylle.' And thanne oure Lorde mekely and lowly ansueryde aȝen and seyde in escusynge of here: 'Why be ȝe heuy to thys woman? Sche hath doo 60 a goode | werke in me, for forsothe ȝe schul haue poure men alweye f. 68ᵛ wyth ȝow, and whenne ȝe wole ȝe maye do hem goode. But forsothe ȝe schul not alweye haue me'; þat ys to seye, in deedly fleyisch. Be these wordys or oure Lorde, hyt semyth wel þat some othyre of the dyscyplys grucchyde as wel as Iudas. Neuyrdeles, Lyre seyth they 65 were steryd be Iudas and also they dede hyt of pytee, but Iudas of couetyse.

Thanne aftyr thys ȝe maye thynke that myche peple of Iewys knewe þat oure Lorde was att Betanye, þe whyche ys too myle fro Ierusalem, as I haue tolde ȝow afore. And ther`fore´ they cam thedyr not only for 70 oure Lorde, but also þat they mygthte see Lasur þat he hadde araysyd for deth to lyue, for þat was a gret merueyle to hem. And therfore the prynces of prestys þat were chef gouernorys of the peple thowgthte to sclee Lasur also, for for hym manye of þe Iewys wente aweye fro hem and beleuyde in oure Lorde Ihes Cryste. Aftyr þys thynkyth how in 75 the mor`o´we aftyr, þe whyche we calle Palme Sondaye, myche peple þat was come to the forseyde halydaye, whenne they herde telle þat oure Lorde wolde come to Ierusalem, the`y´ toke bowys of palme treys and cam aȝenste hym. And some, as `a´nothyr euangelyste seyth, strowede here clothys in the weye. And hereby ȝe maye | vndyrstande f. 69ʳ the deuocyon of the peple to oure Lorde.   81

Thanne aftyr thys ȝe maye thynke also how oure Lorde Ihesu Cryste þat knewe all afore, whenne he nygthede to Ierusalem att þe

48 Aftyr thys] Than N   whiche] N; *om.* Gg   49 grucchede] grochynge and N
55 dyscyplys] disciples and to be ȝeue to pore men N   57 screwys] shrewes N
58 He was] he was he was N   recusyth] recoseth or forsaketh N   60 to] with N
68 Thanne aftyr] after N   of] of þe N   73 prestys] þe prestes N   75 Aftyr] than
aftre N   thynkyth] yhe may thenke N

Mount of Olyuetee, þe whyche ys myd weye betuene Ierusalem and
85 Betanye, he sente too of hys dyscyples to Ierusalem to feyiche hem an
asse and here colte that stode tyde att the townys ende, that he
mygthte sytte vpon. Thys asse and here colte were tyde there for
poure peple þat hadde none, for as doctorys seyin, hyt was a custum
att Ierusalem that ther was 'iiii' asse and here [colte] tyde att þe
90 townys ende, þat poure men þat hadde none mygthte take hem for a
tyme and vse hem and for here nede. And he þat occupyede hem
schulde fynde hem mete. And whenne he hadde doo hys nede, he
schulde brynge hem aȝen ther he foonde hem. And these hyt were þat
oure Lorde hadde.

95   Thanne ȝe maye thynke how hys dyscyplys leyde here clothys vpon
hem, haply for more honestee, and also þat he mygthte sytte þe
esylokyr. And fyrste ȝe maye thynke he sate vpon the colte, and
aftyrwarde vpon the asse. And thanne ȝe maye beholde how myche
peple þat was come to the halydaye, as ys forseyde, cam aȝenste hym.
100 And some wente afore hym, and some cam aftyr hym wyth grene
f. 69ᵛ bowys of palme | treys in here handes in betokenynge of gladnesse.
And they þat wente afore and they þat cam aftyr hym seyde thus: 'I
be'seke' the, saf', for they askede helthe of hym. And they seyde also
therwyth: 'Iblyssyd be he þat comygth in the name of oure Lorde, the
105 Kynge of Israel.' For they wende that he schulde haue regne'd'
temporally and delyuered hem of þe trybute þat they bare to þe
Romaynys, as Lyre seyth. And so wyth suechemaner songys of
preysynge, they browgth hym into the 'cyte' of Ierusalem. Also the
euangelyste seyth þat they cam aȝenste hym so, for they herde telle
110 þat he hadde araysyd Lasur fro deth to lyue.

Thanne thynkyth also þat the Pharyseys hadde gret indynacyon
that sueche reuerence schulde be doo to hym. Wherfore they seyde
amonge hemselfe thus: 'Ȝee see that we profyte not. Loo all the worlde
goyth aftyr hym.' Not that all þe pepyl of the worlde folowede 'hym',
115 but for myche pepyl folowyde hym as the comyn speche ys that
whenne myche pepyl goyth, some vsyn to seye all the worlde goyth.

Thanne aftyr thys ȝe maye thynke þat oure Lorde prechyde in the
cytee of Ierusalem, comynge and goynge into Tuysdaye att euyn. And
tho he wente aȝen into Betanye, where Marye Maudeleyne duellyde,

---

86 here] *fol. by canc.* cl Gg   88 þat] þat it N   89 colte] N; clote Gg   91 and²]
om. N   96 mygthte] shulde N   97 thynke] thenke þat N   99 þat] þer N   ys] it
is N   103 the] *om.* N   105 that] *om.* N   106 delyuered] haue deliuerde N
109 herde] had herde N   112 Wherfore] And þerfor N   114 the²] *fol. by canc.* of
the Gg   115 myche pepyl] mony N   119 tho] þan N   123 into] to N

and Marthe here systyr, and Lasur here brothyr, for he louyde hem, 120
and therfore he cam ofte thedyr. And there he abode stylle and
wente | not aȝen into Iersualem the nexste daye aftyr, that ys f. 70ʳ
Wedenysdaye, as he dede the othyr dayis afore, for Lyre seyth ʻþatʼ
he wolde ȝeue place to the Iewys to trete of hys deth. And thanne
thynkyth that the same ʻWedenysʼdaye the pryncys of prestys and the 125
eldyste men of the peple cam togyderys into the halle of þe chef
prynce, þat was callyd Cayphas, þe whyche hadde ȝeue hem conseyil
afore to putte oure Lorde to deth, as ȝe haue herde afore. And att thys
tyme they cam togyderys aȝen to aske conseyil how they mygthte doo
hyt pryuyly wythoute eny stryfe or thebate of the comyn peple, for 130
manye of hem beleuyde in oure Lorde. And therfore they wolde not
doo hyt in the halydaye, leste ther schulde be stryfe amonge the
comyn peple for hym.

Thanne ȝe maye thynke that ʻwhenneʼ Iudas Scaryot, þat false
traytur, herde telle þat they ʻwereʼ come togyderys to trete of oure 135
Lordys deth, he wente to hem and askede hem what they wolde ȝeue
hym and he wolde betraye hym to hem, ʻas ho seythʼ, pryuyly and
wythoute eny noyse. And thanne they were glad therof, for hem
semyde þat that was a conuenyent weye to take hym by. And so they
behette hym xxxᵗʸ pence, of the whyche eueryche was worthe x pence 140
of the comyn monye. And fro thennyʻsʼ forwarde he softe leysur tyme
and place whenne he mygthte betraye hym | pryuyly wythoute noyse f. 70ᵛ
or stryfe of the peple, for there ʻwasʼ myche peple drawynge to
hymwarde to here hys prechynge, and also for the myraclys þat he
wrowthe. And therfore the false schrewe wolde take a tyme whenne 145
ther was no man wyth hym but hys dyscyplys alone, and that was þe
nexste daye folowynge ʻattʼ euyn, þe whyche we calle Holy Thursdaye, of þe whyche I wole trete be the helpe of oure Lorde in the
nexste chapetele folowynge.

122 the²] þat N   ʻþatʼ] om. N   125 of] N; of of Gg   126 of¹] of þe N
129 aske] aske also N   139 that] om. N   140 eueryche] ilkone N   145 whenne]
fol. by canc. whenne Gg   147 ʻattʼ] fol. by canc. nygthte Gg   euyn] nyght N   Holy]
om. N   148 wole] shall N

CHAPTER 18

Of the sopere that oure Lorde hadde with hys dyscyplys on Holy
Thursdaye att euyn and of the werkys þat were doo there att.
Capitulum duodeviginti.

Relygyus syster, ȝe haue herde afore how Iudas the Wedenysdaye
5 nexste aftyr Palme Sondaye solde oure Lorde. Now thanne thynkyth
how in the nexste `daye´ folowynge, þe whyche we calle Holy
Thursdaye, and hyt was the euyn `of the euyn´ amonge the Iewys
of the haly daye folowynge, the whyche was here Estyr, of þe
`whyche´ I haue tolde ȝow in the chapetele nexste afore thys, bothe
10 what hyt was and how loonge hyt duryde, and in þat euyn they ate
here Estyr lombe. And therfore ȝe maye thynke that oure Lordys
dyscyplys cam to hym and askede hym where he wolde þat they
schulde make aredy to ete the Estyr lombe. And thanne thynkyth how
f. 71ʳ aȝenste euyn he sente Petyr and Ihon, and badde hem goo forth | and
15 make aredy for the sopere in the whyche they mygthte ete the Estyr
lombe. And thanne thynkyth þat they askede hym where, and he
badde hem go forth into [þe] cytee of Ierusalem and anone they
schulde mete wyth a man berynge a potte wyth watyr in hys hande,
and they schulde folowe hym into the howse þat he wente in att and
20 bydde the goode `man´ of the howse ordeyne therfore. For ȝe maye
thynke þat hyt was some worthy man of þe cytee þat beleuyde in hym
and wolde doo what he badde hym and he schewde hem a place
conuenyent þerfore, and there they made aredy þat that schulde
loonge to the sopere.
25   And att euyn he cam thedyr wyth hys dyscyplys and satte downe to
sopere, and hys xii apostlys wyth hym, and whenne they hadde
almoste sopyd, þat ys whenne they hadde ete the Estyr lombe; but ȝytt
vndyrstondeth þat brede and wyne stode vp on the borde and sueche
othyr thyngys as be wont to stonde stylle whenne men haue ete here
30 gret metys. Aftyr thys beholdyth how oure Lorde Ihesu arysyth `vp´
fro`m´ þe sopere and wole do seruyse to hys owyn seruauntys. And
fyrste thynkyth how he doyth of some of hys clothys þat he mygthte
the bettyr do that `he´ purposyde, and thanne beholdyth also how he

Chapter 18   1 Holy] shir N   3 Capitulum duodeviginti] om. N   5 nexste] om. N
6 Holy] shire N   7 the¹] at N   `of the euyn/´] in marg. with inser. marks Gg; om. N
10 and¹] and also N   þat] þis N   11–12 that . . . dyscyplys] howe þe disciples of our
Lorde N   13 thanne] om. N   16 and] and þan N   17 þe] N; om. Gg   18 in
hys hande] om. N   21 hyt] he N   22 and] and so N   25 to] to þe N
30 Ihesu] Ihesu Criste N   31 and] for he N   wole] wolde N

takyth a lynnyn cloth as a towayle and gyrdyth hyt abowte hym and
puttyth watyr in`to´ a basyn wyth | hys owyn holy handys, for he   f. 71ᵛ
wolde weyische hys dyscyplys feete.   36

And thynkyth fyrste how he comyth to Symon Petyr and Petyr,
seynge þat he cam to hymwarde to do suechemaner seruyse to hym.
He was sore abayischyd and astoyny`e´d, and seyde to hym: 'Lorde,
wolte þu weyische my feete?' As hoo seyth, that am but a synneful   40
man and þu Godys sone and my Lorde, hyt ys no wyse semely. And
thanne oure Lorde seyde to hym aȝen: 'That I do, now þu woste not',
as ho seyth, what hyt menyth, 'but þu schalte wyte aftyrwarde.' And
thanne Petyr, seynge þat oure Lorde algatys wolde do hyt, seyde to
hym aȝen: 'Thow schalte not weyische my feete wythoute ende'; as ho   45
seyth, þu schalte neuer doo hyt `to´ me, I wole neuer suffre hyt. Thys
seyde he of gret loue and reuerence þat he hadde to oure Lorde, for he
louyde hym wyth all hys herte and thowgthte as eny man mygthte þat
hyt was no wyse resunnable or conuenyent, ne to be suffryd, þat he
schulde do eny sueche seruyse to eny creature. But oure Lorde Ihesu,   50
maystyr and ȝeuare of mekenesse and of alle othyr vertuys, `wolde´
ȝeue vs prowde and synful wrecchys a parfyth exsample of mekenesse.
And therfore he seyde to hym aȝen: 'But I weyische the, þu schalte
haue no parte wyth me'; | þat ys to seye, in my ioye. And thanne Petyr   f. 72ʳ
seyde to hym aȝen: 'Lorde, not only my feete, but also my handys and   55
my heede'; as hoo seyth, Lorde, I hadde leuyr suffre the to weyische
all my body thanne to be departyd fro the. And so, thowgth he were
loth to see hys Lorde do hym seruyse, ȝytt he hadde leuyr suffre hym
to doo hys suete wylle thanne `to´ be departyd fro hym, and so he
suffryde hym to doo hys wylle. And `thanne´ beholdyth dylygently   60
how the Lorde of all the worlde knelyth downe att a poure fyischarys
feete and mekely and lowly weyischyth hem, and aftyrwarde wypyth
hem wyth the lynnyn cloth þat `he´ was gerde wyth, and aftyr þat he
weyische forth othyrys be rowe.

Loo gostly syster, here consyderyth what schame hyt schulde bee to   65
vs þat been but synneful wrecchys to forsake to doo seruyse to oure
euyn Crystyn, or to be hye in oure owen sygthe, whenne we maye
beholde thus myche mekenesse in God. Aftyr thys thynkyth how he

36 wolde] woll N   37 And¹] and þan N   and Petyr] om. N   40 that] fol. by canc.
arte godys sone Gg   41 ys] is in N   46 hyt] þat N   48 eny] mony N
51 of²] om. N   othyr] om. N   52 and] om. N   53 he . . . hym] thenketh þat oure
lorde seide to Seynte Petre N   54 þat] þis N   Petyr] Seinte Petre N   57 all] om. N
61 worlde] fol. by canc. worlde of all N   63 aftyr þat] þan N   66 doo] do lowe N
68 mekenesse] lownes N

takyth hys clothys to hym aȝen þat he hadde afore doo of and doyth
70 hem on aȝen. And thanne beholdyth how he syttyth downe aȝen and
seyth suechemanyr worthys to hem: 'Ȝe wyte what I haue doo to ȝow?
Ȝe calle 'me' Maystyr and Lorde, and ȝe seye wel þerof, for forsothe I
am soo. Ȝyf I thanne þat am Maystyr and Lorde haue weyische ȝoure
f. 72ᵛ feete, myche more thanne schull ȝe weyische eueryche | othyrys feete.
75 For forsothe I haue ȝeue ȝow ensample þat ryth as I haue doo to ȝow,
that ȝe doo 'so' also.

Aftyr thys beholdyth dylygently how oure Lorde Ihesu Cryste in
thys sopere also ordeynyde the worschyful sacrament of hys owen
precyouse fleyische and blode, and comunyde hys dyscyplys, the
80 whyche he wolde be vsyd in hys holy chyrche in the mynde of hym.
For hyt ys the condycyon of some louarys that whenne they be
departyd bodyly, they wole desyre summe memoryal or tokene that
they maye the bettyr thynke eueryche on othyr by. And so oure louely
Lorde Ihesu Cryste, whenne he knewe þat hys tyme was come be hys
85 owen ordenaunce, þat he wolde dye for mannys soule and aftyrwarde
gloryu's'ly aryse, and also merueylusly stye vp to þe rygth hande of
hys fadyr and 'soo' wythdrawe the bodyly forme, in the whyche he ys
lyke to vs, fro the bodyly beholdynge of hys dyscyplys, the whyche þat
tyme louyde 'hym' all manly, and also fro the bodyly beholdynge of
90 hys othyr chosyn þat were to come in holy chyrche, ȝytt he wolde 'be'
presently wyth hem in thys worthyest sacrament. For he seyde to hys
dyscyplys thus: 'I am wyth ȝow into the worldlys ende'; the whyche
maye be vndyrstande of hys gostly presence, be the whyche he ys
ouyrall present, and also of þys precyouse sacrament, in the whyche
f. 73ʳ he ys bodyly present. For he seyth to hys | dyscypyl in the boke þat ys
96 callyd 'þe Orlege of Wysedome thus: 'Sykyrly, trewly, and wythoute
eny doute, I am conteynyd in thys sacrament, God and man, wyth
body and soule, fleyisch and blode, as I wente 'out' of my modrys
wombe and hynge in the crosse and sytte att þe rygth hande of my
100 Fadyr.'

Loo, gostly systyr, how mygth hyt be seyde more opynly? Thanne
louyth thys moste excellent sacrament wyth all ȝoure herte and
worschypyth hyt, for of all thyngys that been in thys lyf, hyt schulde
be moste confortable to a soule þat veryly desyryth and louyth God.

74 eueryche] om. N   76 doo 'so' also Aftyr] also in the same manere that N
77 Aftyr] hand with finger pointing in marg. Gg   thys] þe N   78 hys] om. N   81 be]
om. N   83 eueryche on othyr] one N   by] therby N   84 þat] when N
87 wythdrawe] withdrewe N   88 fro] prec. by canc. for Gg   91 worthyest] worthi N
92 the] in marg. into ende of the world Gg   96 trewly] in marg. Nota bene Gg

For he ys there trewly present hymselfe, as ȝe haue herde afore; and 105
that hyt 'ys' so hydde vndyr the forme of brede and wyne, hyt ys a
gret and a mercyful dyspensacyon of the mercy of God for oure verry
and endles profyte. For, yf 'hyt' were ȝeue vs in hys owyn lyknesse, as
opyn fleyische and blode, or as a man or a chylde, hoo wolde be so
bolde to resceyue hyt into hys mowthe and suolowe hyt downe into 110
hys body, þat he ne schulde drede and lothe hyt? Therfore that we
'schulde not' lothe hyt, hyt ys ȝeue vs mercyfully vndyr the forme of
brede and wyne, and also þat we mygthe haue þe mede of oure
feythe, ffor yf we seygth hyt opynly afore vs as hyt ys, what mede were
hyt to vs to beleue hyt? Forsothe, rygth none. And therfore þat we 115
mygthte haue the mede of oure beleue and no | lothnesse to resceyue f. 73ᵛ
hyt, hyt was nedeful and spedeful to vs to resceyue hyt vndyr sueche
lyknesse.

Here, as me semyth, ȝe mygthte seye: 'Soth hyt ys þat prestys þat
seye here massys resceyue oure Lorde vndyr the forme of brede and 120
wyne, but I þat am a woman and othyr commune peple, whenne 'we'
be communyd, we resceyue hym vndyr the forme of brede only, and
ȝytt I hope and beleue þat we resceyue oure Lorde as wel as prestys
þat resceyue hym vndyr bothe lyknesse.' Soth hyt ys, but vndyrstondyth hyt thus: ȝe and sueche othyre folke as resceyue hym vndyr 125
þe forme of brede only, beleuyth forsothe and wythoute eny dowte þat
oure Lordys body ys there 'wyth alle' the membrys be the vertu of the
consecracyon the blode the soule and the godhede felawschypynge þer
wyth'be' the vertu of þe onehede, be the whyche they maye neuer be
departyd. And in the same 'wyse' ys hyt kepte ovyr the autyr be the 130
ordenaunce of holy chyrche. But prestys that resceyue hym vndyr
bothe lyknessys, vndyrstondyth þat bothe the body and the blode
been there be the vertu of þe consecracyon, þe soule and the godhede
felawschyppynge therwyth, þat ys to seye, vndepartably oned ther to
be the vertu of the onehede that maye neuer be departtyd. 135

Why thanne, maye ȝe seye, ys hyt not mynystryd to vs vndyr bothe
lyknesses as prestys | resceyue hyt? For hyt suffysyth to ȝow vndyr f. 74ʳ
the forme of brede only, for oure Lorde ys there presently, as I haue
tolde ȝow afore. Anothyr cause maye be, as me semyth, for hyt maye
not be mynyst'r'yd vndyr the lyknesse of wyne so esyly to the 140
commune peple wythoute perel, for hyt mygthte haply be sched or
sum lykur therof mygthte falle besyde in ofte takynge fro mowthe to

---

105 so hydde] do N   115 rygth] om. N   122 vndyr] vnde N   130 'wyse']
manere N   138 haue] om. N   140 so] so lightly and N   141 haply] lightly N

mowthe, and namely in sueche as resceyue hyt but selde, amonge the
whyche also othyr whyle come some ful ȝonge, and so mygthte perele
145 falle. And therfore hyt ys wel and resunnably ordeynyd in holy
chyrche that hyt be resceyuyd of sueche folke þat haue not the
ordyr and dygnytee of preshode vndyr that forme, in the whyche no
sueche perele, as ys forseyde, maye falle and þat also maye esylokyr be
mynystryd to sueche folke. Also holy chyrche hath iordeynyd hyt to
150 be resceyuyd of sueche folke þat haue not the ordyr of presthode
vndyr the forme of brede only, and þat ys inowf to eueryche meke
Crystyn soule.

[Also, hyt ys wryte in the lawe to put aweye the errowrs þat mygth
falle in the peple, þat ys þat they mygth wene þat hyt mygth not be
155 mynystryd but vndyr bothe lyknessys. For hyt ys [suffycently] vndyr
þat one, and therfore also hyt ys ordeynyd of holy chyrche to be
resceyuyd so of the commune peple for to put a wey the forseyde
errowrys, but preestys be bownde to resceyue hyt vndyr bothe
lyknessys for our Lorde ordeynyde hyt so as to hem.]

160 Fferdyrmore, I conseyle ȝow not [to] seke [mony] questyonys
abowte þys precyouse sacrament, but to holde ȝow payde wyth thys
lytyl þat I haue seyde [to] ȝow, and to putt ȝowre feythe generally in
f. 74ᵛ the feythe of holy chyrche, and in that feythe whenne ȝe rescey|ue hyt
wyth all the loue drede and reuerence þat ȝe kunne to rescey`ue´ hyt.

165 Thys moste worthy sacrament ys the worschypful memoryal þat oure
Lorde hath lefte vs in the mynde of hym and of hys Holy Passyon, be
the whyche Passyon he offryde hymselfe a sacryfyse to hys Fadyr in
heuene for the redempcyon of mankynde, and so there he ȝaf
hymselfe into oure redempcyon. And in þys precyouse sacrament
170 he ȝeuyth vs hymselfe into oure gostly strenthe and conforte in oure
weye goynge in thys lyfe. And aftyr þys lyfe he behetyth vs hymselfe
into oure euyrlastynge herytage in the blysse þat neuer schal haue
ende yf we trewly loue hym and serue hym whyle `we´ lyue here. And
I praye ȝow, how mygthte he haue schewde more kyndnesse?

175 Also, in thys precyouse sacrament of hys verry fleyische and blode,
he confermyde the newe lawe, there the olde was confermyd in the

143 as] þat N   but] om. N   144 ȝonge] thynge N   mygthte] myghte lightly N
147 in . . . no] þat none N   148 as] as it N   falle] falle in N   also] om. N
151 eueryche] yche N   153–9 Also . . . hem] in marg. of Gg; om. N   155 suffycently]
con. em. suffyently Gg, om. N   160 Fferdyrmore] also N   to] N; om. Gg   mony] N; maye
Gg   162 to] N; om. Gg   164 wyth] to receyue with N   kunne . . . hyt] kanne N
170 vs] to vs N   171 behetyth] beheth N   vs] to vs N   172 blysse] blysse of heuen N
haue] om. N   174 more] vs more loue or N   176 olde] olde lawe N

blode of vnresunnable bestys, as of kydys, lombys, and wederys, and
othyr vnresunnabyl bestys in betokenynge of þat that was to come.
And so þat that was but a fygure, but thys ys trewthe. Thys, belouyd
syster, ys the sacrament of holy chyrche þat oure Lorde hath lefte vs   180
in the mynde of hys Passyon, as ys forseyde, þat we schulde ʻnotʼ
forʒete hym and therfore hyt ys contynually offryd in holy chyrche,
for the verry helthe and helpynge | bothe of lyuynge and deede, and   f. 75ʳ
in betokenynge þat we schulde ʻhaueʼ hym contynually in mynde and
loue hym wyth all oure hole hertys, mygthte, and pouere þat thus   185
mercyfully and kyndly wythoute oure merytys fyrste louyde vs. And
þe same forseyde worschypful sacrament ys the refugye, conforte and
strengethe of Godys chosyn soulys, traueylynge in thys valeye of
wrecchydnesse and desyrynge to come to þe heuenely Ierusalem in
the whyche they schal see hym clerely face to face and preyse ʻhymʼ in   190
the companye of holy angyllys in reste and ioye wythoute ende. And
þat oure Lorde weyische hys dyscyplys feete er he ʒaf hem þe
worschyful ʻsacrament of hys precyouseʼ fleyisch and blode, hyt
maye be betokenyd þerby þat we schulde weyische oure soulys be
penaunce fro the fylthe of synne er we resceyue þat precyouse   195
sacrament, and so in lownesse of herte and clennesse of soule in the
drede of God resceyue hyt.

Aftyr þys ʒe maye thynke how amoonge othyr wordys þat oure
Lorde seyde att thys laste sopere, he seyde these wordys to hys
dyscyplys þe whyche heuyʻeʼde hem ful sore, and no wondyr: 200
ʻFforsothe one of ʒow schal betraye me. Not forthann, woo bee to
þat man þat I schal be betrayed by. Hyt hadde be bettyr ʻto hymʼ
neuer to haue be borne.ʼ Thanne thynkyth þat the apostlys were sore
astonyed and dredde ful myche, and beʻganneʼ to loke eueryche vpon
othyre, dowtynge hoo [f. 75ᵛ] hyt schulde bee. And thanne they   205
beganne to aske of oure Lorde be rowe ho hyt schulde bee. Thanne
beholdyth also how ther was one of þe apostlys þat restyde vpon oure
Lordys breste; thys apostly was Seyint Ihon euagelyste, the whyche
oure Lorde louyde so specyally þat he suffryde hym to restyde vpon
hys holy breste and schewde hym hys pryuyteys, and þat was a syne of   210
gret loue.

And thanne Seyint Petyr seygth þat he was ʻsoʼ nere oure Lorde

178 that] *om.* N   179 belouyd] welbelouede N   181 as] as it N   188 valeye]
om. N   192 dyscyplys] postels N   203 to] *om.* N   sore] so N   204 ful] ryght N
vpon] on N   205–6 And ... bee] *om.* N   207 also how] þat N   208 Ihon] Ihon þe N
209 restyde] rest N   vpon] on N   210 þat] þis N   212 thanne] þan thenketh þat N

and so famylyar wyth hym, he thowgth he mygthte aske what he
wolde and so he made a tokene to hym þat he schulde aske oure Lorde
215 pryuyly hoo hyt was for, as doctorys seyin, yf he mygth haue knowe
hym, he wolde haue scleyne hym anone, so feruently he louyde oure
Lorde. And thanne thynkyth how Seyint Ihon pryuyly askyde oure
Lorde hoo hyt was, and oure Lorde pryuyly tolde hym, seyinge to
hym þat hyt was he `to´ whom he toke þe brede þat he wente, for he
220 wette þe brede in wyne or in summe othyr lykur þat stode afore hym,
and toke hyt Iudas, ȝytt be thys mygthte none of the othyr dyscyplys
knowe hoo hyt was, for oure Lorde tolde hyt to Seyint Ihon but
pryuyly. And þat Seyint Ihonn tolde not forth, hyt semyth aparty
merueyle; but Lyre seyth þat he was so astonyed þat he toke no hede
225 what oure Lorde seyde. Also some `othyre´ holy men seyin þat he
seygth þat tyme þe pryuyteys of God, and therfore hyt mygthte bee
f. 76ʳ þat he | was soo raueyischyd þys inne be loue and knowynge þat he
fo`r´ȝete bothe Petyr and Iudas, in betokenynge þat men and wymmen
þat haue take vpon hem þe state `of´ contemplatyf lyuynge, the
230 whyche was betokenyd be Seyint Ihon, schulde be so bysyly and
dylygently occupyed in the louynge of God that they schulde forȝete
all worldly thyngys and othyr mennys dedys þat loonge not to hem
and tende only therto.

Here also ȝe maye merueyle þat obstenacye of þys repreuyd man
235 Iudas, þat for alle the benfeetys þat oure Lorde schewde to hym hadde
no grace to turne fro hys wykkydnesse. For he weyische hys feete as
he dede [to] othyrys, and fedde hym wyth the same precyouse
`sacrament´ þat he dede othyre, and also notyde hym be the brede
þat he toke hym and seyde: 'Woo be `to´ þat man that I schal be
240 betrayed by. Hyt hadde be bettyr to hym þat he hadde neuyr be
borne.' And ȝytt, for all þys he cesyde not of hys wykkyde purpose.
Also, att þat othyr syde ȝe maye merueyle the incomprehensyble
goodnesse of oure Lorde, that so lowly suffryde hym, and moreouyr
so myche charytee schewde to hym. For `ȝyf´ hyt were gret lownesse
245 and charytee that he dede to hys trewe seruauntys, myche more hyt
was þat he dede to hym þat he wyste wel hadde solde hym and aftyr
þat schulde betraye hym.

And also thys ys a gret exsample þat we þat ben but synful
f. 76ᵛ wrecchys schulde mekely and pacyently suffre schrewys sygth | we

220 wyne] þe wyne N   221 ȝytt] `and´ ȝyt N   223 þat] þan N   tolde] tolde it N
229 þe] þat N   234 man] om. N   235 to¹] om. N   237 to] N; om. Gg
246–7 aftyr þat schulde] afterwarde wolde N   247 schulde] wolde in marg. Gg

see þat oure Lorde thus mekely and pacyently suffryde hys traytur. 250
Thanne aftyr þys thynkyth þat anone as Iudas hadde itake the
forseyde brede of oure Lorde, he wente forth to fette men and
stroonge pouere to take oure Lorde. But þe othyre dyscyplys wende
he hadde igoo to bye þat that was necessarye to þe halydaye
folowynge, for he bare the purse and was oure Lordys procuratur. 255
And whenne he wente out so hyt was nygthte as the [euangelyste]
seyth, to schewe þerby that hyt was a conuenyent tyme for the traytur
to performe hys wykkyde purpose, and also in the betokenynge of the
therknesse of synne þat was in hys soule.

Aftyr thys ȝe maye thynke how oure Lorde tolde hys dyscyplys 260
afore that they schulde forsake hym þat nygthte euyrychone, and they
seyde: 'Naye', for they hadde leuyr dye wyth hym thanne forsake
hym. But Petyr, þat was boldyr thanne othyre, seyde to hym: 'And
thougth they alle forsake the, I wole neuyr forsake the. For I am aredy
rathyr to goo to persone wyth the and to deth also.' Thys, vndyr- 265
stondyth, he seyde of gret loue for he wende to haue doo so forsothe.
But he seyde false, for `he´ performyde not þat he seyde, but he lyede
not, for hyt was in hys herte as he seyde wyth hys mowgth. And for he
was more presumptuus thanne othyre and wende to haue do hyt of
hys owen streng|the, oure Lorde ansueryde more scharply aȝen to f. 77ʳ
hym and seyde þat ere the koc hadde icrowe tueys he schulde denye 271
hym threys.

Thanne oure Lorde made a fayre sermone to hem confortynge hem
for they were ful heuy of the wordys þat he hadde seyde afore. And
beholdyth also þat they `take´ goode hede what he seyth, and specyally 275
Seyint Ihonn euangelyste, for he wrote aftyrwarde þat he seyde there.
And some of hem thynkyth also askede hym questyonys, fyrste one
and aftyr anothyr. And oure Lorde `mekely´ and lowly ansueryde
`hem´ aȝen and also confortyde hem in here feythe and aftyrwarde
prayde to hys Fadyr in heuene, fyrste for hymselfe and thanne for hys 280
dyscyplys and att the laste for hem þat schulde beleue in hym be here
prechynge. And so in thys he ȝaf vs ensample þat we schulde fyrste
praye for vs selfe, and nexste for oure frendys, and att þe laste for oure
enmyis.

251 the] *prec. by canc.* the Gg   252 he] *om.* N   254 that] *om.* N   255 he]
Iudas N   256 euangelyste] euagelyste Gg; eungeliste N   258 the] *om.* N
263 boldyr] feruenter N   265 deth] dyeth N   266 forsothe] sykerly N
271 þat] *om.* N   hadde icrowe] crowe N   275 goode] gods N   276 Ihonn] Iohn
þe N   þat] *om.* N   280 in] of N   282 so] *om.* N

CHAPTER 19

Of the werkys that oure Lorde dede aftyr hys sopere in the euyn afore
hys Passyon, and how he was take in the nygthte, and how hys
dyscyplys forsoke hym, and also of the despyte þat was doo to hym in
diuerse placys þe same nygthte. And thys ys callyd the oure of
5   Matynys. Capitulum decimum nonum.

Gostly ʻsystyrʼ, praye ȝow takyth goode hede to that þat schal be
seyde, and kepyth ȝowselfe be ymagynacyon as thowgth ȝe were
f. 77ᵛ   present and seygth all | that I schal seye ȝow done afore ȝow. Ffyrste
thanne ȝe maye thynke þat whenne oure Lorde made the fyrseyde
10   sermone to hys dyscyplys in the place þat he hadde sopyd inne, he
seygth, as Lyre seyth, þat they were adrad of deth, bothe for the tyme,
for hyt was nygthte and also for the place, for ʻthey wereʼ ȝytt þat
tyme in the myddyl of the cytee of Ierusalem where they hadde ete þe
Estyr lombe. And ʻþerforeʼ they dredynge to be take of enmyis, as hyt
15   were, contynually caste here eyin to the dorewarde, and therfore oure
Lorde seyde to hem: 'Arysyth vp and goo we hennys'; as hoo seyth,
lete vs goo to anothyr place more sykyr and pryuyer were ȝe maye take
bettyr hede to þat that I schal seye ȝow. And soo, thynkyth he ledde
hem to anothyr place more pryuy, and there he endyde hys sermone.
20   And fro þat place he wente wyth hys dyscyplys ouyr the broke of
Cedron. Lyre seyth þat Cedron ys þe name of a broke betueʻneʼ þe
cytee of Ierusalem and the Mounte of Olyʻueʼte. And ouyr that broke
thynkyth oure Lorde wente and hys dyscyplys wyth hym towarde þe
Mounte of Olyuete, þe ʻwhycheʼ was a myle fro Ierusalem. And att
25   the foot of þat hylle was a lytyl towne þe ʻwhycheʼ ys callyd
Gessemany, and att þat townys ende was a gardyn into the whyche
oure Lorde wente wyth hys dyscyplys. And Iudas knewe þat place wel
f. 78ʳ   for oure Lorde was won|de to come ofte dedyr wyth hys dyscyplys.
Thanne thynkyth how he byddyth viii of hys dyscyplys sytte stylle
30   there and praye whyle he wente vp into the hylle to praye. And
beholdyth how he takyth wyth hym thre of hys dyscʻypʼlys, þat ys to
seye, Petyr, Iamys, and Ihon hys brothyr. And the othyr viii abothe
stylle in the gardyn, as oure Lorde badde hem. And ʻthanneʼ thynkyth
þat oure Lorde beganne to wexe all heuy and sory and seyde to hem

Chapter 19   3 also] *om.* N   þat] *om.* N   8 seygth] tell N   that] *om.* N   21 þeʼ]
fol. by canc. broke Gg   a] þe N   22–3 that broke thynkyth] þe broke þenketh þat N
24 was] is N   26 þat] þe N   30 And] and þan N   33 ʻthanneʼ] *om.* N
34 þat] howe how N

thre: 'My soule ys sory vnto deth'; as hoo seyth, aȝenste þe deth `þat´ I 35
wote wel I schal suffre tomorowe. 'Abydyth here and prayeth wyth
me.' Here prayeth wyth me.' Here hauyth pytee and compassyon of
ȝoure louely Lorde, for hoo mygth see or here telle þe `ioye´ of alle
chosyn in hys manhode sory and heuy, and not be sory and heuy also
of pure pytee and compassyon? Thanne beholdyth how he goeth fro 40
hem thre as hyt were a stonys caste, and prayeth `to hys Fadyr´ in
heuene þat yf hyt were possyble he wolde `lete´ þat Passyon passe
ouyr, for he dredde to dye `as´ a verry man, and also to schewe þerby
that he hadde trewly take mankynde. And ȝytt notwythstandynge all
thys, he commyttyde hyt to þe wylle of hys Fadyr in heuene to ȝeue vs 45
exsample þat we schulde ouyrall and in all thynge desyre the wyll of
God to be fulfylde and not oure owen carnal wyll, the whyche
euyrmore sekyth hys owen ese and sueche thynge as ys delec|table. f. 78ᵛ
And `thanne´ thynkyth how he comyth to hys dyscyplys aȝen and
fyndyth hem sclepynge, and thanne he seyth `to Petyr´ thus: 'Soo'; as 50
ho seyth, thow schewest not so myche feruour now in thy dede as þu
dedyste wel ere in thy worde. 'Mygtheste þu not wake one oure wyth
me?' And thanne he seyde to alle thre in generall: 'Why sclepe ȝe?
Wakyth and prayeth þat ȝe falle not into temptacyon'; þat ys to seye,
þat ȝe bee not ouyrcome wyth temptacyon. 'The spyryt ys rethy, but 55
the fleyisch ys feble'; as hoo seyth, ȝe were redy inowf to behete me to
dye wyth me, but now apperyth wel inowf þe infyrmytee of ȝoure
fleyische.

And thanne he wente aȝen the secunde tyme and prayde the same
wyse þat he dede afore. And thanne he cam to hys dyscyplys aȝen the 60
secunde tyme and fonde hem sclepynge for sorynesse, and also hyt
was wythinne the nygthte and here eyin were agreuyd for sclepe. And
so, what fo heuynesse and what for sclepe, they `were´ almoste
ouyrcome, and therfore hauyth pytee on hem for they were in gret
sorowe and heuynesse. Aftyr `þys´ beholdyth how oure Lorde goyth 65
aȝen the thyrde tyme and prayeth as he dede afore, but att þys tyme he
was putt in a stryfe and thys stryfe, as Lyre seyth, was betuene the
senseualyte dredynge deth and resun acceptynge hyt. For be the vertu
of God, he seyth, eueryche parte was suffryd to doo and to suffre þat

35 vnto] vnto þe N   36 wel] wele þat N   37 prayeth] waketh N   38 ȝoure]
our N   hoo] whoso N   40 pure] pore N   46 and] om. N   48 as] þat N
49 aȝen] om. N   52 Mygtheste] maye N   54 into] in no N   56 me] om. N
57 wel] it wel N   60 cam . . . aȝen] come agayne N   63 heuynesse] sorynes N
they] þe N   66 and prayeth] om. N   but] bot thenketh þat N   68 hyt] þat
thynge N   69 eueryche] yche N

f. 79^r that was propyr to | hym. And therfore he prayde the lengyr,
71 schewynge be þat that the more nede a man hath, the more he
schulde praye. And thys stryffe was so myche þat the suet þat cam fro
hym was as dropys of blode rennynge into þe ꞌgꞌrounde, and in thys ꝫe
maye vndyrstande what traueyle and heuynesse he was inne. And
75 thanne thynkyth þat ther cam an angyl fro heuene and confortyde
hym, and thys was done to þe confermynge of þe feyth of þe
dyscyplys, þat they mygthte see þat he was God þat the angyl dede
seruyse too, and also man þat was confortyd aꝫenste þe heuynesse þat
arose in þe senseualytee. And here hauyth also gret pytee and
80 compassyon to see ꝫoure suete Lorde and the sauyoure of mankynde
in thus myche ꞌheuynesseꞌ þat he mygthte delyuere vs fro euyrlastynge heuynesse.

And moreouyr thynkyth þat he gladly and lowly att þe wyll of hys
Fadyr chesyth deth for þe saluacyon of mankynde. And here
85 merueylyth hys charytee þat wolde come into all þys heuynesse and
chese deth for pure loue and clene charytee þat he mercyfully hadde
to soo vnworthy wrecchys as we bee. Aftyr þys beholdyth how the
goode Lorde wypyth hys face wyth sumthynge þat he hadde abowte
hym, and arysyth vp fro hys preyere and goeth fyrste aꝫen to the thre
90 dyscyplys þat were nexste hym. And thanne thynkyth he takyth hem
f. 79^v wyth | hym and comyth to þe othyr viii þat were in þe gardyn. And
thanne thynkyth how he byddyth hem all sclepe a whyle and reste
hem and soo he suffryde hem sclepe a whyle, tyll he knewe þat Iudas
cam.

95 And whenne Iudas nygthede, he awakyde hem, seyinge to hem:
'Arysyth vp and lete vs goo, for he nygeth þat schal betraye me.' And
whyle oure Lorde spake thus wyth hys dyscyplys, beholdyth how fro
the cytee of Ierusalemwarde comyth Iudas þat was one of þe xii
apostlys, and wyth hym a gret companye of men wyth suerdys, stanys,
100 and armys, and lanternys (for hyt was nygthte) þat they mygthte see.
And Iudas ꝫaf hem þat cam wyth hym a tokene whereby they mygthte
knowe oure Lorde, for ther was one of hys dyscypllys so lyke hym þat
they ꞌmyghtteꞌ not ellys wel haue knowe þat one fro þat othyr. And
thys dyscypyl ys callyd Iamys the Lasse, of þe whyche I haue tolde
105 ꝫow in the xiiii chapetele.

---

70 that] that þat N   72 stryffe] styfe N   the] his N   73 þe] *om.* N
76 confermynge] confermyge N   þe³] his N   80 ꝫoure suete Lorde] þoure swete N
87 Aftyr þys] and þan N   91 gardyn] gadyn N   92 hem . . . whyle] *om.* N
97 beholdyth] he beholdeth N   100 and²] *om.* N

Thanne thynkyth how oure Lorde goeth aȝenste hem wyth hys dyscyplys and metyth wyth hem and askyth hem whom they seke. And they seyin aȝen: 'Ihesu of Naȝareth'; for oure Lorde was noryischyd in Naȝareth, and therfore he ys callyd Ihesu Cryste of Naȝareth. And thanne oure Lorde seyde aȝen: 'I am he.' And anone 110 they fylle downe bakwarde vpon the grounde, for they | mygthte not f. 80ʳ here hys worde, for all here armys and wepenys þat they hadde. Here hyt ys to be hadde in mynde of how myche mygthte hys worde schal bee whenne he schal deme all þe worlde, sygth hys worde was of so myche mygthte whenne he wente to be demyd. And ʼthanneʼ 115 thynkyth þat they arose vp aȝen, and thanne oure Lorde askyde hem efte sonys whem they softe, and they seyde aȝen: 'Ihesu of Naȝareth.' And thanne he seyde to hem: 'I haue tolde ȝow þat hyt ys I. Thanne yf ȝe seke me, suffryth these (be hys dyscyplys) to goo here weye.' For he wolde not þat eny of hem schulde haue eny harme. 120

And ʼthanneʼ beholdyth how Iudas cam to hym and kyssyde hym, and thanne they þat stode abowte sette [handes] vpon oure Lorde for to take hym and lede hym forth. And amonge othyre ther was a knaue þat bare a lanterne, and how so hyt were he presyde nere to take oure Lorde or to lygth vp þat othyre mygth see to take hym. And Petyr 125 seygth þat and drew out hys suerde and smote att hym, purposynge haply to haue sclayne hym or to haue perlusly woundyd hym. But, be the dome of God, hyt fylle þat he faylyde of hys purpose and so smote of hys rygth ere. And þys seruauntys name was Malchys, as the euangelyste seyth. And thanne beholdyth | how oure benyngʼnʼe f. 80ᵛ Lorde takyth vp the ere and settyth here on aȝen. And so he dede good 131 for euyll, and thanne ʼheʼ seyde to Petyr: 'Put vp they suerde into þe schede aȝen, for he þat wyth suerde smytyth, wyth suerde schal peryische. Trowest þu not þat I mygth praye my Fadyr and he schulde now ȝeue me moo thanne xii legyonys of angyllys?' A legyon ys vi 135 thowsende, vi hundryd, sexty and syxe. Thys oure Lorde seyde not þat he nedyde helpe of angyllys, but to schewe therby þat he mygthte haue goo fro hem manye wysys yf he hadde wolde. Also he seyde: 'How schulde scripturys be fulfylde ellys, for thus hyt muste bee.'

And thanne he seyde to þe peple þat stode abowte hym: 'Ȝe come to 140 me as to a thef wyth suerdys and stauys to take ʼmeʼ. Whenne I was euery daye techynge in the temple amonge ȝow and ȝe helde me not,

109 ys] was N　　110 seyde] seide to hem N　　118 he] our Lorde N　　120 eny of hem] þei N　haue] haue hadde N　　122 handes] N; hande Gg　　123 knaue] knafe thenketh N　　128 so] so he N　　131 here on] it N　　137 schewe] shewe hem N

but thys ys ʒoure oure and the pouere of derkenesse'. And whenne he
hadde `seyde´ these wordys, beholdyth how the wykkyde peple sette
145 [hondes] vpon hym wyth fersnesse and angyr, as thowgth he hadde be
a mysdoare and so take hym and bynde hym faste. And hys dyscyplys,
seynge þat, they forsoke hym euyrychone and lefte hym in hys enmyis
handys and fledde, as oure Lorde hadde tolde hem afore.

f. 81ʳ   And thanne beholdyth how the wykkyde pe|ple lede hym forth
150 amonge hem boustusly ibounde, and fare foule wyth hym. And here
hauyth inwardly compassyon of ʒoure suete Lorde. For what deuoute
creature mygthte see hys Makare for hys loue bounde as a thef and
forsakyn of hys dyscyplys, and wyth myche despyte and repreue
ibrowgth bounde fyrste to Anne, wythoute terys? For to hym he was
155 browgth fyrste, as the `holy´ euangelyste Ihon seyth. Thys Anne was
Cayphasys wyuys fadyr, and he hadde be byischop the ʒere afore. And
so as they wente to Cayphasys housewarde, they muste goo be þys
Annys house. And therfore hem semyde hyt hadde be a velonye but yf
they had browgth oure `Lorde´ into hym as they wente for reuerence
160 þat he was Cayphas wyuys fadyr.

        Now thanne thynkyth also þat Petyr and Ihon euangelyste
folowyde oure Lorde afer, but fyrste they fledde as othyre dyscyplys
dede, but aftyrwarde ʒytt they cam aʒen and folowyde hym afer of, for
they louyde hym more thanne othyre apostlys dede. But Seyint Ihon
165 `was knowe´ in the byischoppys house and therfore he was suffryd to
goo in wyth oure Lorde, but `Petyr´ stode wythoute as a man vknowe.
Aftyr thys thynkyth þat Seyint Ihon cam out aʒen and prayde the
damesele þat kepte the dore to lete in Petyr, and soo Petyr was lete
f. 81ᵛ come in. And as he | cam inwarde the same damesele lokyde on hym
170 and hadde suspycyon þat he schulde be one of oure Lordys dyscyplys,
for how so hyt were he wente inwarde all heuyly and dredyngely. And
so sche askede hym whethyr he were eny of hys dycsyplys, and he
seyde: 'Naye.' And anone the koc crewe, but Petyr perseyuyde hyt
not, for he was so sore trublyd and agaste þat he toke no hede þerof.
175   And thanne he wente forth vp into þe halle and stode be þe fyre and
warmyde hym amonge othyre þat stode abowte the fyre, for hyt was

---

145 hondes] N; hande Gg   vpon] on N   146 a mysdoare] an euyle doer N   take]
tuke N   bynde] bonde N   And] and þan N   147 lefte] lete N   155 euangelyste]
eungeliste seynte N   156 Cayphasys . . . fadyr] þe fader of Cayphas wyfe N
Cayphasys] fadyr to þe wyf of Cayphas *in marg.* Gg   157 so] *om.* N   be] afore N
158 therfore hem semyde] so hem thoght N   163 of] *om.* N   166 goo] entre N
167 Aftyr thys] and þan N   168 Petyr¹] Seynte Petre N   169 inwarde] in N
174 sore] mykel N

colde wedyr. And wythin a whyle ther cam anothyr damesele þat
seygth hym standynge be the fyre, and anone sche seyde to hym: 'And
þu were wyth Ihesu of Naȝareth?' And thanne he denyde oure Lorde
aȝen wyth an othe and seyde þat he knewe hym not. And thanne he   180
beganne to drawe hym to þe dorewarede, for he was adrad to abyde
amonge the Iewys eny lengyr. And ʻthanne' the seruauntys began to
drawe abowte hym, for they were steryd be the dameselys speche and
hadde suspycyon to hym þat he schulde be one of oure Lordys
dyscyplys. And anone one of hem þat was Malchusys cosyn, whas ere   185
Petyr hadde smyte of, seyde to hym: 'Seygth I not the in the gardyn
wyth hym?'; as ho seyth, ȝys. And ʻthanne' Petyr beganne to suere and
curse þat he knewe not þe man. | And anone the koc crewe aȝen. And   f. 82ʳ
thanne thynkyth þat oure Lorde lokyde to Petyrwarde, as ho seyth,
now hyt ys fufylde þat I seyde to the afore. And thanne Petyr hadde 190
mynde of the worde þat oure Lorde hadde seyde to hym afore, how he
schulde denye hym threys er the koc hadde crowe tueys. And thanne
Petyr wente out and wepte byttyrly, goynge, as þe Maystyr of Storyis
seyth, into a caue þe whyche ys callyd koc crowynge.

Here, belouyd syster, ys a gret exsample to vs synful wrecchys how   195
myche we schulde drede to presume eny thynge of vs selfe, and how
sore oure Lorde ʻmyghtte' suffre vs to falle yf we presume eny thynge
of vs selfe, sygth he suffryde thys worthy apostyl to falle so foule for
he presumyde of hymselfe. And also, yf we falle of oure owyn
wrecchydnesse, how gret truste we maye haue of forȝeuenesse yf we   200
be verry sory for oure synnys as he was and mekely aske forȝeuenesse,
sygth ʻaftyrwarde' he hadde forsake oure Lorde thre tymys, hadde
forȝeuenesse, and also was browgth to so gret dygnytee þat he was
oure Lordys vycary in erthe and prince of þe apostlys.

Thanne aftyr thys beholdyth how oure Lorde standyth bounde   205
afore the forseyde Anne. And he askede oure Lorde of hys dyscyplys
and of hys doctrine, and oure Lorde ansueryde aȝen and seyde: 'I haue
spoke | opynly to þe worlde'; þat ys to, seye to men of þe worlde.   f. 82ᵛ
'And I haue alweye tawgth in the synagoge and in þe temple were alle
þe Iewys come togydere, and I haue doo nothynge in pryuy, þat ys   210
that was to be done in opyn. And therfore aske of hem þat haue herde
me what I haue seyde, for they wyte what I haue seyde.' And whenne

178 standynge] stonde N   185 And] an N   Malchusys] cosyn to Malchus *in marg.*
Gg   186–7 not . . . hym] ye not with hym in þe gardyne N   188 þe] þat N
193 of] of þe N   195 belouyd] welbelouede N   ys] it is N   196 vs selfe] ourselfe N
205 beholdyth] thenketh N   207 ansueryde] ansuerde hym N   210 pryuy] prevy
places but N

oure Lorde hadde seyde these wordys, a seruaunt þat stode besyde ȝaf
oure Lorde a stroke, seyinge to hym: 'Why ansueryste þu so the
215 byischop?', for hym semyde þat he ansueryde hym to schortly. And
thanne oure Lorde ansueryde hym mekely aȝen and seyde: 'Yf I haue
spoke euylle, bere wytnesse of euyl. And yf I haue spoke wel, why
smytyst þu me?'

Aftyr þys thynkyth that Anne sendyth oure Lorde forth ibounde as
220 a man worthy deth and afore hym condempnyd to Cayphas, þat was
chef byischop that ȝere. Thys Cayphas hadde weddyd the forseyde
Annys thowgthtyr, and he hadde 'ȝeue' þe Iewys conseyil to putte
oure Lorde to deth, as I haue forseyde in þe xvi chapetele. And att hys
house as chef byischop þat ȝere, the scribys and the Pharyseys and the
225 eldyste of the peple were icome togyderys. And there they softe alle þe
false wytnessys þat they coude aȝenste oure Lorde Ihesu Cryste, that
they mygthte putte hym to deth, and they coude none fynde
fol. 83ʳ suffycyent (vn|dyrstondyth, to pote hym to deth) fore whenne
manye false wytnessys were browgth forth. And att þe laste ther
230 cam ii false 'wytnessys' and seyde: 'Thys man seyde I maye dystroye
the temple of God þat was made wyth the handys of men and
withinne thre dayis arayse vp anothyr not made with the handys of
men.' And thanne thynkyth þat Cayphas arose vp and seyde to oure
Lorde: 'Why ansueryst þu not to þat that these men seye aȝenste the?'
235 But oure Lorde mekely helde hys pece and suffryde pacyently þat
they falsly accusyde hym of. And Cayphas seyde to hym aȝen: 'I
coniure the in the name of God þat þu telle vs yf þu be Cryste Godys
sone or not.' And thanne for reuerence of þat name, oure Lorde
ansueryde and seyde: 'I am.' And also he tolde hem of hys comynge to
240 þe dome in the clowthys and thanne 'Cayphas' rente hys clothys and
seyde þat he blasphemyde, for hyt was the maner amonge þe Iewys
þat whenne they herde eny blasphemye aȝenste God to rente here
clothys, and so dede thys Cayphas, for he wende þat oure Lorde
hadde 'blasphemyd' for he seyde þat he was Godys sone. And thanne
245 he seyde to hem þat stode aboute: 'Loo, ȝe haue herde the
blasphemye. What semyth ȝow?' And thanne they seyde anone þat
he 'was' worthy to be deed.
f. 83ᵛ   Aftyr thys beholdyth how the seruauntys that | were aboute take

213 these] þere N   215 þat] om. N   219 that] þan N   223 xvi] twelfe N
226 wytnessys] witnesse N   227 coude] myghte N   230 'wytnessys'] wytnes N
231 the] om. N   231–3 and . . . men] om. N; see note   236 And] and þan N
238 not] none N   241 þat] om. N   242 þat] om. N   244 hadde] om. N
245 stode] were N   246 thanne] om. N   247 thys] þis þan N

hym wyth haste and angrynesse, and sette hym downe wyth despyte
vpon a stole or sum sueche othyr thynge. And thanne beholdyth   250
dylygently how some helyn hys fayre face and some spete therinne
and some smyte hym and bydde hym rede hoo smote hym laste. And
thus was that worthy Lorde despysyd, þe whyche ys worthy all
worschype. Here dylygently wyth avysement ʽbeʼholdyth ʒoure suete
Lorde, how lowly and pacyently he suffryth all thys despyte for the   255
helthe of mannys soule and to ʒeue vs ensample how gladly we
schulde suffre despyte for hys loue and for oure owen profyte þat ben
but synful wrecchys and not ellys worthy, sygth he suffryde so myche
for vs þat ys worthy all worschype and presynge. And hauyth
inwardly pytee and compassyon of hym, for hoo mygthte see God   260
in all thys despyte and not merueyle hys mekenesse, pacyence, and
charyte and haue pure pytee vpon hym? And also takyth dylygently
exsample of the vertu ys forseyde, thynkynge how gret schame hyt
schulde be to vs yf we cunne not mekely take despytys and wrongys of
oure euyn Crystyn, whenne oure Lorde toke so myche despyte and   265
wronge of wykkyde peple, þe whyche he mygthte haue made sonke
downe into helle yf he hadde wolde ano|ne forthwyth. Myche more   f. 83ᵛ
thanne schame and confusyon schulde hyt be to vs, yf we cunne not
take mekely and pacyently rygthful correccyonys of hem þat been
aboue vs, and specyally of hem þat correcte vs for the profyte of oure   270
soulys.

Aftyr þys ʒe maye thynke þat the chef men wente here weye and
betoke oure Lorde to here seruauntys, þat they schulde kepe hym in
faste holde into the mornynge. And thanne beholdyth how they pote
hym in pryson or in sum sueche strayte kepynge and bynde hym to a   275
pyloure, and there they despysyde and scornyde hym wyth sueche
maner despytys as beforseyde into the mornynge. | And therfore ʒe   f. 84ʳ
maye thynke ʒowselfe to harde hertyd, but yf ʒe haue here pytee and
compassyon of ʒoure worthy Lorde, for all þat nygthte he was in
myche despyte, trybulacyon, and dyssese. And also thynkyth inwardly   280
what loue and charytee hyt was þe Lorde of all the vnyuersyte of

249 angrynesse] angrees N   downe] om. N   255 suffryth] suffrede N   the] om. N
260 of] on N   262 vpon] on N   also] om. N   264 take] om. N   266 made]
made forto haue N   267 anone] fol. the o in anone, Gg leaves out 12 lines. A marg. note
reads Turne to þe iiii lef to sueche a syne. The corresponding sign appears at the top of fol. 87ᵛ,
where the missing paragraph is copied. See note   272 Aftyr] than aftre N   275 bynde]
bonden N   a] om. N   276 dyspsyde] dispisede hym N   278 as] as it is N   And]
marg. sign where Gg rejoins N prec. by turne aʒen were þu leftyst and rede at sueche a syne
278 to] to haue to N   hertyd] hertes N   yf] om. N   280 myche . . . dyssese] grete
tribulacioun and dispite with disese N

creaturys for þe saluacyon of [mankynde] wylfully to pote hymselfe to
so myche despyte, tribulacyon, and dyssese. But thys ys but lytyl in
comparyson of þat that, be the grace of þe same Lorde, `ȝe´ schal here
285 folowynge.

CHAPTER 20

Of the oure of Prime and of þe werkys þat were `doo´ in that oure.
Capitulum vigintum.

Now beholdyth how in the mornynge the pryncys of prestys and the
eldyste men of the peple cam togyderys aȝen, and toke here conseyil
5 togyderys aȝenste oure Lorde how they mygthte pote hym to deth, for
hem semyde þat the wytnesse þat was browgth aȝenste hym the nygth
afore was not suffycyent to pote hym to deth fore. And therfore they
toke here conseyil togyderys aȝen att thys tyme to seke a suffycyent
cause to pote hym to deth fore, and be whyche they mygthte accuse
10 hym to Pylate as worthy deth, the whyche ȝe schal here aftyrwarde.
    And thanne thynkyth how they `bydde´ here seruauntys sett fortth
f. 84ᵛ that false prophete and dysseyuare of the peple, and sueche | othyre
foule worthys. And `þanne´ beholdyth how the wykkyde seruauntys
lose hym fro the pyloure þat he was boounde to, and eftesonys bynde
15 hym aȝen as hyt were a thef, and so lede hym forth amonge hem as a
meke lombe amonge a companye of lyonys and angry houndys. And
`thanne´ beholdyth also `how he´, wythoute eny wythstandynge or
grucchynge, goeth wyth hem. And `ther´fore he ys lyknyd resunnably
to a suete lombe in innocense, for Ysaye the prophete hadde seyde of
20 hym afore thus: 'Sicut ouis ad occisionem ducetur, et sicut agnus
coram tondente se obmutescet, et non aperiet os suum.' Thys ys in
Englysche: 'As a schepe he schal be ledde to deth, and as a lombe afore
hym þat scheryth hym he schal holde hys pece, and he schal not opyne
hys mowgth'; þat ys to seye, be grucchynge aȝenste hem that
25 dyspysyde hym and scornyde hym and ledde hym as a thef. Ne he
openyde hys mowgth be contradyccyon and reprouynge of hem þat
falsly accusyde hym afore Anne and Cayphas, as ȝe haue herde afore,

282 mankynde] N; mankynge Gg   283 But] bot al N   284 that] *om.* N

Chapter 20 2 Capitulum vigintum] *om.* N   9 to] ynoghe to N   be] be þe N
11 sett] to sette N   14 lose] lowsede N   bynde] bounden N   17 `thanne´] *om.* N
18 goeth] goth forth N   19 the] the holy N   22 deth] þe deth N   23 scheryth]
clyppeth N   25 dyspysyde] dispisen N   scornyde] scorne N   26 openyde] opynde
not N

and also afore Pylat and Kynge Heroude, as ȝe schal here aftyrwarde
be the grace of God. But all these wrongys, despytys, and false
accusacyonys, he mekely and pacyently suffryde for the helthe of 30
mannys soule, and to ȝeue vs exsample of verry mekenesse and
pacyence, and to schewe what loue and charytee he hadde to
mankynde.

And thanne thynkyth that wyth sueche maner despytys as ben
forseyde, they | brynge hym forth to Pylat, the whyche was ordeynyd f. 85ʳ
of þe Emperowre of Rome, iugge of the peple of Iewys, for they were 36
þat tyme trybutaryis to the Romanys. Wherefore they mygthte pote
no man to deth be here owen autoryte, and therfore they browgth hym
ibounde to hym into the mote halle, the whyche was a place þat he
demyde inne that he schulde pote hym to deth. But they wolde not 40
come in that place hemselfe, leste th`e´y schulde haue be defulyd be
the entrynge in the howse of a paynym. And in thys ȝe maye
vndyrstande the gret blyndnesse of hem þat made conscyence to
entre into þe house of a paynym, but they hadde no conscyence to put
oure Lorde to deth wythoute cause.   45

Aftyr thys beholde`th´ how Iudas þat hadde betrayed oure Lorde
can aȝen to princys of the prestys, for hym forthowgthe þat he hadde
betrayed oure Lorde and browgth aȝen the xxxᵗʸ pense and seyde þat
he hadde synned, for he hadde betrayed þat rygthful blode. And they
seyde `to hym´ aȝen: 'What ys þat `to´ vs? Besee the'; as hoo seyth, 50
'We rekke neuer'; avyse the what þu haste doo. And `thanne´ he caste
`þe´ monye fro hym and wente and hangy`de´ hymselfe. And in that
he offendyde God more, as Seyint Ierom seyth, `þenne´ whenne he
betrayede hym.

And thanne the princys of prestys toke þe moneye and seyde þat 55
hyt was `not´ laweful to pote hyt aȝen into the comune place where
inne the offryngys of þe | temple were igaderyd to þe repa`ra´cyon of f. 85ᵛ
the temple and othyr necessaryis. And therfore they toke here conseyil
togyderys and be a comune asente they bowgthte wyth þe same
moneye a pot`t´arys fylde to berye pylgrimys inne. Aftyr thys turnyth 60
aȝen to `þe´ Passyon of oure Lorde and beholdyth how oure Lorde
stondyth afore Pylat, and how Pylat goeth out to þe Iewys and askyth
hem `what´ accusacyon they brynge aȝenste hym, and they seyde aȝen

32 to²] in N   34 that] how N   despytys] dispite N   ben] it is N   41 in] into N
42 in¹] into N   in thys] here N   47 to] to þe N   forthowgthe] for þoffe N
49 And] and þan N   55 prestys] þe peple N   60 Aftyr] than aftre N
62 askyth] askede N   63 seyde aȝen] seye þan N

to hym: 'But yf he were a mysdoare we wolde not haue browgth hym
65 to the.' And thanne Pylat seyde aȝen to hem: 'Take ȝe hym thanne and
demyth hym aftyr ȝoure lawe.' And thanne they seyde to hym aȝen:
'Hyt ys not laweful to vs to scle eny man.'

And `thanne´ they accusyde hym of thre thyngys. The fyrste was
þat as they seyde he turnyde the peple fro Moyses lawe; the secunde
70 was þat he forbede they seyde the trybute to be ȝeue to the
Emperoure; the thyrde was for he seyde þat he was Cryste, a kynge
and Godys sone. And of þe fy`r´ste puncte þat they accusyde hym of,
Pylat rofte neuer, for he was a paynym and therfore he rofte not of
Moyses Lawe. And `as´ of the secunde, nothyr, for he hadde `herde´
75 telle haply þat oure Lorde hadde ibode þat the trybute schulde be
ȝeue to the Emperoure, as I haue tolde ȝow afore in the xv chapetele.
But of the thyrde puncte þat hym semyde was aȝenste the worschype
f. 86ʳ of the Emperoure, he askede hym | for hym semyde þat hyt was
aȝenste the worschype of the Emperoure, that eny man schulde be
80 callyd a kynge but he. And therfore he askyde hym thus: 'Thow arte
Kynge of Iewys'; as ho seyth, hyt ys soth that ys put vpon the, þat ys
to seye, þat þu woldyste take `þe´ kyngdom vpon the? And thanne
oure Lorde seyde to hym aȝen: 'Whethyr seyst `þu´ þys of thyselfe, or
haue othyre seyde hyt `to´ þe of me?' And thanne he seyde aȝen: 'Am I
85 a Iewe'; as hoo seyth, naye, and therfore, I seye hyt not of myselfe.
'But thy peple and thy byischoppys hau`e´ take the to me, accusynge
`þe´ therof. What haste þu doo?' As ho seyth, hyt semyth wel þat þu
arte sumwhat gylty, sygth they þat ben of thyne owen peple and of so
gret autoryte as byischoppys haue accusyd the. And thanne oure
90 Lorde seyde aȝen: 'My kyngedom ys not of þys worlde'; as ho seyth, I
seke not to regne temporally in thys worlde, but I am come to dye for
the helthe of mankynde. An`d´ `thanne´ Pylat seyde aȝen: 'Thanne art
þu a kynge?' And `thanne´ oure Lorde seyde aȝen: 'Thow seyst þat I
am a kynge'; as hoo seyth, so hyt ys in trewthe. 'And therfore I a`m´
95 come into the worlde to bere wytnesse to trewthe. Eueryche man þat
ys of trewthe heryth my wordys'; þat ys be obeynge to hem.

And `þanne´ Pylat askyde hym: 'What ys trewthe?' And whenne he
f. 86ᵛ hadde `askyd´ þat, he wente `out´ aȝen to the Iewys and seyde | that he

65 thanne] þan he seide N   69 as] *om.* N   70 was] *om.* N   71 was¹] *om.* N
þat] *om.* N   72 of¹] as for N   73 not] neuer N   74 And] *om.* N   of²] for N
77 semyde] thoughte N   78 for] whether N   hyt] is N   79 man] *om.* N
81 vpon] on N   85 of] *om.* N   90 kyngedom] *fol. by canc.* ys Gg   92 the] *om.* N
mankynde] mannes soule N   `thanne´] *om.* N   95 Eueryche] yche N   96 ys] is to
sey N   97 `askyd´] seide N

'fonde' no cause in hym, þat ys to seye, worthy to pote hym to deth
fore. And anone they cryde aȝen and seyde that 'he' steryde the peple,   100
as hoo seyth, he trublyth the comune 'peple' begynnynge fro Galyle
hedyr to. Galyle was the contre þat oure Lorde was inoryischyd vp
inne and there Kynge Herowde was lorde. And therfore Pylat,
whenne he herde telle þat he was of Galyle sente hym to Kynge
Herowde, as to þe Lorde of Galyle, þat he schulde delyuyre hym or   105
dampne hym, for he was att Ierusalem thyke dayis.

And 'thanne' thynkyth how they lede oure Lorde ibounde to
Kynge Herowde thorow the cytee of Ierusalem. And whenne he
sawgth hym he was rygth glad, for he hadde loonge desyryd to see
hym in as myche as he hadde herde telle myche of hym, and so he   110
hope'de' to haue seye hym doo sum myracle afore hym. And he
askyde hym manye questyonys, but oure Lorde ansueryde hym rygth
nowfte aȝen, ne he 'wolde' doo 'e'ny myracle in hys presence, for he
was 'vn'worthy for as myche as he desyryde hyt but of curyustee and
not of deuocyon. And the princys of the prestys and the scribys,   115
thynkyth, stode besyde stedfastly accusynge hym. And thanne Kynge
Herowde, seynge þat he wolde ȝeue hym no ansuere, dyspysyde hym
and so dede hys mayne also, holdynge hym but an ydyote or a fole,
and so he made hym be clodyd in a whyte cloth in | scorne, for so they   f. 87ʳ
vsyde to scorne folys þat tyme. And so he sente hym aȝen to Pylat, and   120
for that reuerence þat eueryche dede to othyr, they were made frendys
for afore þat tyme they were enmyis eueryche to othyr.

In all þys tyme takyth goode hede how mekely and pacyently oure
Lorde suffryth all þese false accusacyonys, despytys, and wrongys
afore Cayphas, Pylat, and Herowde, wythoute eny grucchynge, and   125
neuere ansueryth but mekely and lowly and þat ȝytt but fylde, and
ofte tymys he helde hys pece. And therfore takyth exsample of hym
and lernyth to suffre mekely and pacyently despytys, wrongys, and
othyre aduersyteys in thys worlde for hys loue and the prophyte of
ȝoure soule, þat thus myche suffryde for ȝow. But all þat that ys   130
forseyde ys but lytyl in rewarde of þat that ȝe schal here folowynge,
and therfore I praye ȝow takyth goode hede.

Now thanne beholdyth how he standyth bounde afore Pylat, and
how Pylat seyth to the Iewys that nothyr he ne Kynge Herowde fonde

101 'peple'] *prec. by canc.* pees N, Gg   104 sente] he sente N   to] *fol. by canc.* hym
Gg   106 thyke] in those N   11322 for] in N   115 the²] *om.* N
116 thynkyth] thenketh þat N   stedfastly] *om.* N   117 dyspysyde] he dispisede N
118 a] *om.* N   121 eueryche] yche N   122 eueryche] yche N   123 In] nowe
thenketh and in N   126 ansueryth] ansuerde N

135 eny cause in hym to put hym to deth fore, and therfore he wolde
correcte hym he seyde and lete hym goo hys weye. Also he seyde to
hem thus: 'Hyt ys a custum to ȝow þat I delyuyre ȝow one. Wole ȝe
þat I delyuyre ȝow þe Kynge of Iewys?' And `thanne´ they cryde aȝen
anone and seyde: 'Not hym, but Barraban.' And that Barraban was a
f. 87ᵛ thef, þe whyche for debate and sclaugthyr idoo in the | cytee was put
141 in prysone. As to the vndyrstondynge of þys ȝe schal vndyrstande that
the Iewys hadde a custum att the hy feste of Estyre amonge hem to
delyuere `one´ out of prysone whom they wolde þe whyche was
worthy to be deed, in mynde of here deliueraunce out of the londe of
145 Egypte. And `so´ for the more fauoure of the Iewys the Romanys
hadde grauntyd hem to vse that custum forth. And therfore Pylat
askyde hem whethyr he schulde delyuere hem oure Lorde or ellys the
forseyde thef, and they askyde obstynatly be sterynge of the
byischoppys þat were chefe amonge hem the delyueraunce of the
f. 88ʳ thef and that oure Lorde schulde be putt to deth. And | in thys ȝe
151 maye vndyrstande opynly here malyce aȝenste oure Lorde þat askyde
the delyueraunce of an opyn thef aȝenste þe commune profyte and
rygth also, and oure Lorde wythoute cause to be putt to deth.
      And thanne Pylat, seynge be here cryinge þat he mygthte in no
155 wyse lete hym vttyrly fre wyth here pece, and att that othyr syde `he´
was looth to scle an innocent, therfore to satysfye hem he made hys
knygthtys and othyre seruauntys to punyische hym, and that ȝe maye
thynke in thys wyse. Ffyrste, thynkyth how Pylat takyth oure Lorde
into hys howse, and thanne he betakyth hym to hys seruauntys to
160 scorge hym. And thanne beholdyth dylygently how they take hym
boystuly amonge hem as thowgth he hadde be a mysdoare, and drawe
of angryly and fersly hys clothys and so strype hym sterte nakyd. And
thanne they bynde hym faste to a pyloure wyth ropys or cordys and
thanne happly `they´ doo of here clothys, also into here dublettys þat
165 they mygthte smyte the soryr and not be lettyd wyth here clothys.
      And thanne beholdyth dylygently how wyth scharpe scorgys they
bete hym scharply, and how hys precyouse blode rennyth oute att
euery stroke, for hys fleyische and skyn was tendyrer `and softyr´
thanne euyr eny othyr mannys was, for hyt was the same þat he hadde
170 mercyfully take of þe blyssyd virgyne oure Lady Seyint Marye and

136 he seyde¹] om. N   138 `thanne´] om. N   141 the] þe more opyne N
144 in] in þe N   153 be] om. N   to] to þe N   155 lete] leue N   att that othyr] on
þe tother N   157 seruauntys] seuantes N   161 drawe] drewe N   162 strype]
strypede N   sterte] stone N   164 into] in N   167 scharply] smertely N
168 `softyr´ . . . was] om. N; see note

therfore hyt was tendyrer | and softyr ˋthanneˊ euyr eny othyr mannys   f. 88ᵛ
was a sonyr mygth be broke thanne othry mennys mygthe, and also
for gret tendyrnesse hyt was myche more payneful. But ȝytt
notwythstandynge, thynkyth þat theˋyˊ haue no pytee, ne compassyon
of hym, ne spare not, but angryly and scharply leye stroke vpon   175
stroke, and so wounde vpon wounde tyl ther were no hole skyn lefte
on hys blyssyde body, as Ysaye the prophete hadde seyde afore thus:
'Ffro the sole of hys foote to the toppe of hys heed þys was no helthe
on hym.' Ath, Ihesu Cryste mercy, what man or woman mygthte see
hys God and Lorde in thus myche payne for hys loue and not haue   180
ˋpyteeˊ and compassyon of hym, and merueyle the loue and charyte
þat he hadde to mannys soule.

   Now thanne beholdyth how hys precyouse blode rennyth downe on
euyry syde, and theˋyˊ lose hym fro the pylur and thanne they [knytte]
a crowne of ryischys of the see, the whyche be scarpe and harde as   185
thornys. And therfore the ewangelystys happly calle hem thornys for
the lyknesse þat they haue to thornys in scharpenesse and hardnesse,
or lygthly theˋyˊ be callyd ˋsoˊ in that contre, for the Maystyr ˋof
Storyisˊ seyth þat they þat dylygently ˋhaueˊ seyin hyt seye þat thyke
thornys were ryischyssys of the see, and Lyre also seyth the same.   190
And also he seyth þat ˋheˊ herde of a man þat hadde be bee ȝende the
see with Seyint Lodewyke, the Kynge of Fraunce, | þat in the   f. 89ʳ
brymmys of ˋþe seeˊ he hadde felte þe pryckyngys of suechemaner
ryischys thorow hys schone. And hereby ȝe maye vndyrstande how
scharpe they were. Also Maundeuelde, þat was a wel traueylyd   195
knygthte, seyth in hys boke, I trowe, þat oure Lordys crowne was
of sueche ryichys of þe see, þe [whiche] ben callyd iunˋcˊkys of þe see.

   And thys [crowne] they putte vpon hys blyssyde heed, as to a man
þat wolde regne and mygthte not. And ˋthanneˊ ȝe maye beholde how
the pryckyngys of þe crowne renne into hys heed þat the bloode   200
rennyth downe be hys suete face and all hys heed, and thys maye be a
pyteful sygth to a deuout soule. And also, as for more despyte, they
take a purpur cloth, olde and foule, and doo hyt aboute hym. And they
ˋtokeˊ also a reede and putt hyt in hys hande instede of a ceptur, and
thanne they knele downe afore hym and salute hym ˋinˊ scorne,   205
seyinge: 'Hayil, Kynge of Iewys.' And they spete also in hys

175 leye] leyde N   176 were] was N   179 Ath] a N   180 not] no N
184 knytte] N; kyntte Gg   187 haue] hadde N   189 thyke] þo N   191 And]
om. N   197 whiche] N; om. Gg   198 crowne] N; crowe Gg   199 beholde]
beholdeth N   200 pryckyngys] prikkes N   hys] fol. by canc. hys Gg   202 pyteful]
peynfull N

worschypful face, and ʻthanneʼ they take the reede out of hys hande
and smyte hym apon the heed ther wyth wyth the whyche smyteynge
they smyte the forseyde iunckys ferthyr into hys heed, the ʻwhycheʼ
210 was passyngly paynful. And thus they punyischyde and despysyde
oure worschyful Lorde as thowgth he hadde bee here seruaunt and a
mysdoare.

f. 89ᵛ   Aftyr thys beholdyth how Pylat goyth out to the Iewys where | they
stode, for they thurste not come in hys howse, as I haue tolde ȝow
215 afore lest they schulde haue be defulyd be entrynge into the house of a
paynym. And thanne Pylat seyde to hem: ʻLoo, I brynge hym out to
ȝow, þat ȝe knowe þat I fynde no cause in hym.ʼ And thanne
beholdyth how oure Lorde comyth out mekely att the byddyng of
Pylat wyth the forseyde crowne vpon hys heed and the purpur cloth
220 aboute ʻhymʼ, þat they mygthte see opynly how he was punyischyd,
and so they schulde be meuyd to compassyon. And thanne Pylat seyde
to hem also: ʻLoo, manʼ; as hoo seyth, yf he haue doo eny thynge
amys, he ys punyischyd suffycyently therfore and more thanne
worthy ys, and therʻforeʼ hyt schal suffyce to ȝow. Now beholdyth
225 deuoutly how ȝoure worthy Lorde stondyth afore all the peple so
ipunyischyd and despysyd, as ys seyde afore, wyth the forseyde
paynʻeʼful crowne vpon hys heed and the purpur cloth aboute hym.
And therfore hauyth inwardly compassyon of hym, for but ȝe haue
pytee on hym here, with þat that ys seyde afore, ȝe maye thynke ȝow
230 selfe ful vndeuout and vnkynde also.

CHAPTER 21

Of the oure of Terys and of þe werkys þat were do in þat oure.
Capitulum vigintum unum.

Now thanne takyth to mynde whenne the byischoppys of Iewys and
othyre þat were wyth hem seygth oure Lorde ʻsooʼ iscorgyd and
f. 90ʳ scornyd, | as ys forseyde, and also perseyuyde that be þat weye Pylat
6 wolde haue lete oure Lorde goo fre whythyr he hadde wolde and haue
doo no more to hym, they cryde and styryde othyre to crye also,
seyinge thus: ʻCrucyfye hym! Crucyfye hym!ʼ As hoo seyth, thys
payne suffycyth not to vs, but we aske þat he be do to deth. And

208 smyte] smote N   apon] on N   213 out] forth N   214 in] into N
215 be] by þe N   223 thanne] þan he N   226 as] as it N   227 vpon] on N

Chapter 21 5 as] as it N   that] how N   9 suffycyth not] is not ynoghe N   do]
putte N

thanne Pylat seyde to hem aȝen: 'Take ȝe hym thanne and crucyfyeth   10
hym, `for´ forsothe I fynde no cause in hym.' Thyse wordys he seyde
but of scorne and indynacyon, for they hadde no powere to pote eny
man to deth, as I haue tolde ȝow afore in the oure of Prime. But thyse
wordys he seyde, as hoo seyth, yf ȝe hadde powere to pote hym to deth
ȝe wolde sone and wythoute eny cause, but I wole not so.   15
    And thanne they cryde aȝen and seyde: 'We haue a lawe, and aftyr
þe lawe he schal dye, for he hath made hymself Goddys sone.' Thys
they putte vpon hym as for a blasphemye aȝenste God, for here `lawe´
hadde þat men that blasphemyde God schulde be put to deth, but
oure Lorde blasphemyde not in that he seyde he was Godys sone, but   20
he seyde soth, and whenne Pylat herde þat he was Godys sone he was
more agaste. And `thanne´ thynkyth how Pylat goyth in aȝen into hys
house and takyth oure Lorde wyth hym to examyne hym and wyte
more sykyrly whethyr he were Godys sone or | none, for he mygthte   f. 90ᵛ
not examyne hym amonge þe Iewys, so they cryde.   25
    And `thanne´ thynkyth how he askyth hym of whennys he ys, but
oure Lorde `ȝaf´ hym no ansuere aȝen, but mekely helde hys pece, for
Pylat was a paynym and therfore he was not worthy to knowe of the
generacyon of God, and also haply yf he hadde knowe, he wolde haue
lette oure Lordys Passyon. And thanne Pylat seyde to hym aȝen: 30
'Why spekyst þu not to me? Wost þu not wel þat I haue powere to
crucy`fy´e the, and also to lete the goo?' And thanne to refreyne hys
boste and pre`sump´tuou`s´nesse, oure Lorde ansueryde aȝen and
seyde: 'Thow shuldest haue no powere of me, but hyt were ȝeue the
fro aboue. And therfore he þat betrayede me to the hath the more   35
synne.' In thys worde betokenynge þat Iudas and the Iewys synnede
more thanne Pylat, for Iudas was `steryd´ of coueytyse and the Iewys
of rancoure and malyce, but Pylat was steryd of drede of man and
fauoure, as ȝe schal here aftyrwarde.
    And whenne oure Lorde hadde seyde the forseyde wordys, Pylat   40
softe to leue oure Lorde, for he seygth wel inowgf that oure Lorde
hadde conuyctyd hym of synne yf `he´ putte an innocent to deth. And
therfore he softe occasyonys to delyuere oure Lorde and lete hym goo
whythyr he wolde. And `thanne´ the Iewys seynge that, they cryde   44
seyinge thus: 'Yf þu leue | thys man, þu arte `not´ the Emperourys   f. 91ʳ

---

10 thanne Pylat] N; pylat thanne *with corr. marks* Gg   12 of scorne and] in scorne
and of N   15 eny] *om.* N   18 blasphemye] N; blasphemye a Gg   22 goyth]
wente N   23 hym] *om.* N   24 were] was N   30 Lordys] Goddes N
33 ansueryde] answerde hym N   34 but] bot ȝif N   36 betokenynge] betokenede N
38 drede] þe threte N   44 whythyr] where N

frende, for ʽhoˊsoeuere make hymselfe a kynge, he doyth aȝenste the
Emperoure.' And whenne Pylat herde these wordys he brougthte
ʽforthˊ oure Lorde and satt as for a iugge in a place þat ys callyd in
here language Galbata, and hyt was a place pauyd wyth stone afore
50 Pylatys place, and there he satt to deme. Here ȝe maye vndyrstande
þat Pylat thruste not do eny thynge þat semyde aȝenste the worschype
of the Emperoure, for anone as they seyde, yf þu leue thys man þu
arte not the Emperourys frende. Anone he brougth out oure Lorde
and satt for ʽtoˊ iugge, and as he satt forto deme, thynkyth how hys
55 wyf sente to hym seyinge be a messengere thus: 'Nothynge be to the
and that rygthful man'; as ho seyth, loke þat in no wyse þu
condempne þat ryghful man, but rathyr delyuere hym, 'For I haue
suffryd mayne thyngys', sche seyde, 'thys daye be vysyon for hym.'
Haply the ʽfeendeˊ perseyuyde þat be the Passyon of oure Lorde
60 mankynde schulde be sauyd, and therfore he dyssesyde the woman,
sterynge here þat sche schulde speke to here hosbunde to delyuere
oure Lorde. Butt thynkyth þat ʽþeˊ pryncys of þe preestys and the
eldyste men cryden and styryde the commune peple to crye also to
haue oure Lorde deed.
65   And thanne ʽPylatˊ, seynge þat he profytyde not and that ʽtheyˊ
f. 91ᵛ cryde more and more the contrarye | be styrynge of the preestys of
here secte, he weyische hys handys afore hem alle, seyinge thus: 'I am
innocent of thys rygthful mannys deth. Avyse ȝow.' And thanne all
the peple of Iewys ansueryde aȝen and seyde: 'Hys blode be vpon vs
70 and vpon oure chyldryn'; þys ys ʽtoˊ seye, the vengeaunce of hys blode
be vpon vs and vpon oure chyldryn. And so aftyrwarde hyt fylle ffor
xl^{ty} wyntyr aftyr oure Lordys Passyon, Veˋsˊpacyan and Tyte hys
sone, Princys of Rome, cam to Ierusalem and vttyrly dystroyede hyt.
And rygth as Iudas solde oure Lorde for xxx^{ty} pense, rygth so Tyte,
75 Vespacyanys sone, as hyt ys seyde in the Legende þat ys callyd Aurea,
solde xxx^{ty} Iewys for thyrty pense. And now theˋyˊ lyuyng in diuerse
ʽplacysˊ of the worlde and kyngedomys as trybutaryis and wrecchys in
thraldom, and myche of here lyuynge, as yt ys ʽseyde, ysˊ be vsurye.
      Now thanne lete ʽvsˊ turne aȝen to the Passyon of oure Lorde and
80 thynkyth þat whenne the Iewys hadde itake all the perele vpon hem,
Pylat seyde to hem: 'Schal I crucyfye ȝoure kynge?'; as ho seyth, hyt

46 make] maketh N   48 ʽforthˊ] oute N   52 of the Emperoure] emperours N
54 ʽtoˊ] a N   56 þat] om. N   62 þat²] how N   68 deth] blode N; blode in marg.
Gg   69 of] of þe N   74 for xxx^{ty} pense] alweye for a peny N   76 for thyrty
pense] alweye for a peny N   79 thanne] om. N   80 þat] om. N

ys a foule schame to ʒow to see ʒoure kynge crucyfyed. And ʽthanne´ the byischoppys seyde to Pylat aʒen: 'We haue no kynge but the Emperoure.' Loo, how thyse wrecchyde men forsoke God for here kynge and chese a deedly man. And thanne Pylat, seynge þat they bonde hem to perpetual bondage | to the Romaynys to haue oure Lorde deed, he dredde þat yf he ʽhadde´ forsake hyt, he schulde haue be accusyd to the Emperoure. And therfore, what for drede of þe Emperoure and what for fauoure of the peple of Iewys, aʒenste rygth he ʒaf the sentence of deth vpon oure Lorde and condempnyde hym to deth as they desyryde.

And thanne thynkyth þat the wykkyde peple made myche ioye and gladnesse þat they hadde here wykkyde entent. And thanne beholdyth also how Pylatys seruauntys take oure Lorde amonge hem and pullyn of the purpur cloth þat they fyrste hadde putt vpon hym, and wyth the pullynge of ʒe maye thynke they drawe of all the skynne of hys body and renne alle hys woundys. And ʽal´ thys, beholdyth, they doo scharply and angryly. And therfore now beholdyth how hys pry-cyouse blode rennyth downe be alle the placys of ʽhys´ blyssyde body, and ʽthanne´ they make hym do on hys owen clothys aʒen þat he mygthe be best knowe in hys owen clothys. And here ʒe maye thynke a newe payne, for ʒe maye wel wyte þat he mygthe not do on hys owen clothys aʒen vpon hys ʽbody´ so iwoundyd wythoute gret payne. And therfore beholdyth fyrste in thys consyderacyon how ʒoure suete Lorde stondyth nakyd afore all the peple scornynge and despysynge hym as thowgth he hadde be a mysdoare. And ta|kyth goode hede of hys merueylus charyte, mekenesse, and pacyence, how louly and pacyently he suffryth all thys despyte and payne for the helthe of mankynde. And thanne how he doyth on aʒen hys clothys softe and esyly, for hyt was ful paynful to hym. And thanne beholdyth how some of hem seygth þat he dede hyt but softe and esyly and sterte to hym fersly and drewe hem on faste and hastyly.

And thanne thynkyth þat they sette forth the heuy crosse, the whyche as hyt ys seyde, was xv feete longe, and that they leyde vpon hys schuldyr so ibeete as ys forseyde wyth sc'h´arpe scorgys, the whyche he mekely resceyuyde as thowgth he hadde ʽbe´ here seruaunt

85

f. 92ʳ

90

95

100

105

f. 92ᵛ

110

115

and worthy that payne. For as cruel and scharpe and schrewde as they
were in malyce, as suete and as lowly and benynge was he in pacyence
and charytee and myche more wythoute eny comparyson. And
120 'þanne' beholdyth also how they take too theues out of prysone and
lede hem wyth hym to be putt to deth also, and so was euyrlastynge
Trewthe icouplyd to tueyne theuys. And ȝytt they dede more despyte
and payne to hym thanne to the theuys, for we rede not of hem 'þat'
they bare eny crossys or were despysyd and beete as he was.

125   Now I praye ȝow, takyth goode heede and consyderyth dylygently
f. 93ʳ how oure Lorde Ihesu Cryste mekely goyth thorow the cytee of |
Ierusalem wyth the forseyde heuy crosse on hys schuldyr, and how
the peple goyth aboute hym, of the whyche some punyische hym and
lede hym to crucyfye hym, and þat were Pylatys men, Romaynys and
130 paynymys, and some were Iewys þat hadde pursuyd hym to the deth.
And they scornyde hym and despysyde hym and were glad þat they
hadde here badde purpose, and 'some' wondryde on hym and they
were the comune peple of the cytee. Now thanne beholdyth wyth gret
pyte and compassyon how oure worschypful Lorde goyth amonge all
135 the peple in so myche despyte and payne, as ys forseyde. And thanne
thynkyth also how, as he comyth out att sum ȝate of the cytee, oure
Lady wyth here felawschyp metyth wyth hym, for haply sche mygthte
not mete wyth hym in the cytee for prese of peple. And therfore
Seyint Ihon thynkyth ledde here be a nere weye where he trowede
140 sche schulde mete wyth hym, see hym, and speke wyth hym.

    And thynkyth also þat oure Ladyis systryn goo wyth here and
Marye Maudeleyne and manye othyre deuout wymmen þat hadde
folowyde oure Lorde fro Galyle. And whenne sche seygth oure Lorde
and here suete sone comynge amonge all the peple so dyspytfully led
145 wyth the heuy crosse vpon hys schuldyr and hys blyssyd face so
defulyd wyth blode and foule spetynge and hys handys blody and hys
f. 93ᵛ feete and icouplyd to tueyne theuys, ath, Ihesu | mercy, what herte
mygthte holy thynke wyth how myche sorwe and heuynesse here
herte was fylde in thys beholthynge of here suete sone? Ȝe maye
150 thynke forsothe þat sche fylle downe in Seyint Ihonnys armys a suowe
and mygthte nothyr stande ne speke to hym for passynge sorowe and
heuynesse. And also they þat were wyth here, ȝe maye thynke, made

118 and¹] *om.* N   125 takyth . . . and] *om.* N   128 punyische] pusshen N
131 And¹] and þan N   132 on] apon N   133 beholdyth] beholdeth deuoutely N
134 pyte] *om.* N   135 in] and N   as] as it N   136 as] *om.* N   139 Seyint] þat
seynte N   140 hym¹] hym and N   144 dyspytfully] dispitusely N   145 so]
om. N   146 hys¹] *om.* N   and] and also N   147 ath] a N   150 a] in N

myche sorowe and lamentacyon bothe for pytee and compassyon of
hym and here also. And 'so' doeth ȝe wyth hem, for ȝe muste thynke
ȝowselfe in ȝoure ymagynacyon as thowgth ȝe were present wyth hem   155
and one of hem.

And thanne thynkyth also þat whenne oure Lorde seygth hys
modyr in so myche sorowe and care for hys loue and othyre þat were
wyth here, he hadde gret pytee and compassyon of hem, and specyally
of hys modyr, the whyche he knewe a clene virgyne and moste ful of   160
sorowe for hym. And so what for compassyon of hys modyr and of
hem þat were wyth here and vnkyndnesse of the Iewys þat whyche
wytyngly and wylfully hadde pursuyd hym to the deth and also
ygnoraunce of the paynymys þat ledde hym and punyischyde hym
and othyr sympyl peple that wondryd on hym, ȝe maye mekely   165
conseyue þat he hadde gret heuynesse in hys herte þat neuere thowgth
mys, and so ȝe maye thynke þat he was in gret payne and heuynesse
bothe inwarde and outwarde. And | therfore wyth oure Lady and   f. 94ʳ
Seyint Ihon and othyr deuout folke þat were there, hauyth inwardly
pytee and compassyon of hym. For what deuout Crystyn soule   170
mygthte see hys Lorde Ihesu Cryste for hys euyrlastynge saluacyon
in all thys payne, and hys Lady so wepynge and waylynge, and othyre
deuout folke that were wyth here and not wepe wyth hem for pure
pytee and compassyon?

Aftyr þys thynkyth how they þat ledde oure Lorde mette there   175
wyth a man whas name was Symon, and hym they compellyde to bere
the crosse aftyr oure Lorde. For they seygth happly þat oure Lorde
was wery and wente but softe, and therfore they made hym to bere the
crosse aftyr oure Lorde, þat they mygthte the sonnyr come to the
place þat he schulde be crucyfyed inne, for they were adrad laste Pylat   180
wolde haue reuokyd the sentence. And therfore thynkyth that they
ledde hym forth amoonge 'hem' wyth gret haste as a suete lombe in a
companye of as manye houndys. In all 'þys' ȝe maye rygthfully
merueyle the vnspekeable charytee of oure Lorde, þat for so vnworthy
synnarys as we bee, wolde wylfully suffre all thys payne and dyspyte   185
and myche more, as ȝe schal here aftyr, to delyuere vs fro euyrlastynge
payne and to make vs eyrys of euyrlastynge ioye. Wherfore, here
thynkyth inwardly how gladly we schulde suffre all | maner   f. 94�v
aduersyteys, temptacyonys, and dyssesys þat mowe falle to vs in

154 ȝe muste] þe moste N   160 a clene] so clene a N   162 hem] other N   þat]
þe N   164 punyischyde] pounchede N   172 hys] our N   180 he] our Lorde N
183 In] and in N

190 þys worlde for hys loue and for oure owen profyte þat thus myche of
hys vncompreh`ens´yble charytee wythoute oure merytys mercyfully
suffryde for vs.

Aftyr thys thynkyth how Seyint Jhon takyth vp oure Lady as wel as
he maye, for he was a ful sory man and mygthte ful euyll helpe
195 hymselfe for heuynesse. And ȝytt not wythstandynge, beholdyth þat
he takyth here vp as wel as he maye and confortyth here as he canne,
and Marye Maudeleyne also, ȝe maye thynke, and oure Ladyis systryn
and othyre deuout wymmen that were there confortyde here and
halpe here as wel as they coude or mygthte. And ȝytt they were alle ful
200 heuy and sory, and so beyth ȝe wyth hem and ymagynyth also what
seruyse ȝe wolde haue doo to oure Lady yf ȝe hadde be there present
wyth hem. And `thanne´ thynkyth how they goo forth aftyr alle
togyderys softe and esyly as wel as they maye, wepynge and
sorowynge. And thys maye be the medytacyon of oure Lordys
205 Passyon att the oure of Ter`y´s.

CHAPTER 22

Of the oure of Sexte and of the werkys þat were doo in that oure.
Capitulum xxii^m

The oure `of´ Sexte ȝe maye thynke in thys wyse: Beholdyth fyrste
how the forseyde wykkyde tormentorys brynge oure Lorde amonge
f. 95^r hem wyth gret hastynesse and myche despyte to the place | þat he
6 schal be crucyfyed inne, the `whyche ys callyd´ Caluarye, but in
Ebrewe hyt ys callyd Golgata; thys `was´ a commune place þat men
were putt to deth inne, and hyt was nere the cyte of Ierusalem and
there men `were´ beheeddyd, wherfore in that place laye manye bonys
10 of deed mennys heedys, and therfore hyt ys `callyd´ Caluarye. And
whenne oure Lorde was `brought´ to þat foule place, thynkyth how
they drawe of hys clothys aȝen and þat was a passynge gret payne, for
they renuede hys woundys aȝen, as they `dede´ fyrste in the drawynge
of `of´ the purpur, and haply wors. And as they hadde `drawe´ of hys
15 clothys, ȝe maye thynke þat oure Lady comyth wyth here felawschyp,
and whenne sche seygth hym so nakyd and woundyd, thynkyth þat

195 beholdyth] he holdeth N   199 or] and N
Chapter 22   3 The] N; Tthe Gg   5 gret] myche N   6 schal] shulde N
9 wherfore] þerfore N   place] place þer N   14 drawe] drowen N   15 þat] howe N
16 so] om. N

here sorowe was encressyd, and as ofte as hys paynys were encressyd,
so ofte thynkyth wythoute eny dowte here heuynesse and sorowe were
encressyd and made more and more. And thefore hauyth inwardly
pytee and compassyon of hem bothe, for they ben in gret sorowe and 20
payne.

And thanne thynkyth þat in the forseyde stynkynge place they
crucyfye oure Lorde. How and in what wyse oure Lorde was
crucyfyed the euangelystys make no mencyon, [in specyal but in
general], wherefore I wole telle ȝow too manerys; whyche of hem 25
maye beste styre ȝow to deuocyon, that takyth. One ȝe maye thynke |
in thys wyse. Beholdyth fyrste how they take oure Lorde and leye f. 95ᵛ
hym downe vpon the crosse, and thanne haply they tye ropys to hys
armys, and so thynkyth they drawe hym tyl hys vaynys breke. And
thanne one takyth a gret nayil and smytyth hym fersly wyth an hamur 30
thorow hys hande. And that nayil, ȝe maye thynke, brekyth passynge
paynfully the skyn in and the fleyisch vndyrnede and the vaynys and
synuys, and so he na`y´lyth þat hande faste to þe crosse. And anothyr
tormentur, thynkyth, doyth the same to þat othyr hande. And thanne
they goo to the feete and drawe hem downe strayte and mygthtyly and 35
leyin þat one vpon þat othyr, and thanne thorow bothe they smyte too
naylys, þat one aboue þat othyr, and thys was a passynge gret payne,
the whyche no man maye seye wyth hys mowth as hyt was to hym þat
suffryde hyt. And `þanne´ thynkyth how they lefte hym vp wyth the
crosse, and so they lete hyt falle downe into the mortayse, and wyth 40
the fallynge downe, as some haue seyde, the`y´ braste alle þe vaynys
and synuys in hys body. And so þat shulde haue bee a passynge payne
amonge alle tho þat he suff`r´yde thys ys oo wyse as I trowe some
deuout men haue ymagynyd.

Anothyr wyse ȝe maye thynke hyt, aftyr Seyint Brygyttys `Reue- 45
lacyon´, and `þat´ I holde sykyrer to lene to and þat ȝe | maye thynke f. 96ʳ
thus. Beholdyth fyrste an hole I kytte out in þe Mount of Caluary, and
the crucyfyourys aredy, as hyt ys wryte in the *Reuelacyon* to doo
creueltee. But sche tellyth hyt in here owen persone as sche seyth hyt
doo, þe whyche I turne here into the forme of medytacyon not goynge 50

22 þat] howe N   23 crucyfye] crucyfiede N   24 euangelystys make] euangeliste
maketh N   24–5 in . . . general] *om.* N, *in marg.* Gg   25 wherefore] and therefore N
29 drawe] drowen N   hys] þe N   breke] bresten N   30 hym] it N   33 na`y´lyth]
naylede N   34 thynkyth] þan thenketh N   35 hem] *om.* N   36 leyin] leyden N
39 suffryde] feleede N   thynkyth] beholdeth N   40 so] þan N   45 Seyint] the
reuelacyon of seyint Brygitte *in marg.* Gg   46 maye] Reuelacio beate brigitte *in marg.*
Gg   48 aredy] redy N   50 doo] *om.* N   here] it N

be the grace of God fro the menynge of here wordys. Now thanne
beholdyth wyth the forseyde holy lady how the tormentorys fyiche
and make faste stron'g'ly the crosse in the forseyde hole wyth treys
mygthtyly ismyte þeraboute wyth a betyl þat hyt mygthte stande the
55 fastyr and not falle. And whenne the crosse was made so faste, they
putte tablys of tre theraboute in the maner of greys vnto the place
where the feete schulde be crucyfyed, þat bothe he and hys
crucyfyoris mygthte goo vp be hem and stande vpon hem to crucyfye
hym. Aftyr thys thynkyth how they go vp be the forseyde greys,
60 ledyngde hym wyth hem wyth stormynge and ful myche blamynge,
the whyche frely wente vp as a suete lombe iled to be sacryfyed. And
whenne he was vpon the tablys, not compellyd but anone wylfully he
strawfte out hys arme and hys 'rygth' hande openyd, he put here on
the crosse, the whyche the cruel tormentoris cruelly fastnede to the
65 crosse and holowede here wyth a nayil in that place þat the bone ys |
f. 96ᵛ   saddyst inne, and in that hyt was more payneful. And thanne
thynkyth þat they drawe strongly the lyfte hande wyth a rope and
nayle here in the same wyse.
    And thanne beholdyth how they drawe downe all the body be the
70 crosse and pote þat oo legge 'vp'on þat othyr, and thanne iune þe too
feete togyderys. And whenne they were so iunyd togyderys, they
naylyde hem to þe crosse wyth too naylys, and so myche they strawfte
oute thyke gloryus membrys strongly in the crosse þat alle the
va'y'nys and synuys tobraste. And whenne thys was doo, they putte
75 the crowne of thornys þat they hadde take fro hys heede whenne he
was crucyfyed vpon hys heed aȝen, the 'whyche' so strongly prykkyde
hys reuerent heede þat hys eyen were fylde anone wyth flowynge
blode and hys erys were stoppyd and hys face and berde were as hyt
hadde be keueryd and depte wyth that rede bloode. And anone thyke
80 crucyfyoris and knygthys meuyde aweye vyolently alle thyke tablys
þat were abowte the crosse, and thanne the crosse abode alone and
oure Lorde crucyfyed theron. Thys ys the maner how oure Lorde was
crucyfyed aftyr the *Reuelacyon* of Seyint Brygytte.
    Aftyr thys thynkyth also how oure Lady was there present and
85 seygth all thys done and therfore thynkyth inwardly how gret sorowe

51 the³] þe forseide N   56 greys] or steyrys *in marg.* Gg   59 thys] *fol. by canc.*
thynt Gg   thynkyth] yhe may thenke N   61 suete] meke N   63 here] it N
65 here] it N   þat] *om.* N   ys] is moste N   67 drawe] drewen N   68 nayle here]
naylede it N   70 iune] þei ioynede N   72 and] and in N   strawfte] streynede N
thyke] þo N   79 and] and his N   thyke¹] þo N   80 thyke¹] þo N   82 how]
þat N   84 also] *om.* N

hyt | was to here to see here suete sone and Lorde in so myche `payne´ f. 97ʳ
and despyte. And thanne thynkyth how sche wepyth and waylyth and
fallyth downe to the erthe for sorowe as half deed, for Seyint Brygytt
seyth in the *Reuelacyon* `forseyde´ þat whenne sche was fylde wyth
sorowe and behelde the crueltee of hem þat crucyfyede oure Lorde 90
sche seygth also, sche seyth, hys heuy modyr lyinge vpon the grounde
as hyt hadde be quakynge and half deed, the whyche Seyint Ihon and
here systryn confortyde þat stode thoo not fer fro the crosse att the
rygth syde therof. And therfore hauyth inwardly compassyon of ȝoure
worthy Lady, for sche ys in passynge gret sorowe and heuynesse.   95

And thanne takyth goode hede also how the goode Lorde prayith
for hys enmyis and hem þat crucyfyede hym, seyinge to hys Fadyr in
heuene thus: 'Ffadyr forȝeue hem, for they wyte not what they doo.'
And thanne takyth good hede `also´ how ther be too theuys crucyfyed
wyth hym, on`e´ att the rygth syde and anothyr on the lefte syde and 100
oure Lorde in the myddyl as thowgth he hadde be [thiefe]. And
thynkyth inwardly what despyte thys was to cowple the Lorde of all
the worlde to too theuys, and also beholdyth hys mekenesse and
pacyence þat thus lowly suffryde all thys, and also hys charytee þat so
charytably prayde for hem | þat so paynyde hym and dysspysyde f. 97ᵛ
hym.   106

And thanne ȝe maye thynke how Pylat wrote a tytyl and sette hyt
vpon the crosse for hyt was þe maner of þe Romanys, as Lyre seyth, to
wryte the cause of þe deth of hem þat were crucyfyed and sette hyt
vpon the crosse. And thys was þe tytyl þat was sette vpon oure Lordys 110
crosse: 'Ihesu Cryste Nazarenus Rex Iudeorum'; thys `ys´ in Eng-
lyische, Ihesu Cryste of Naȝareth Kynge of Iewys. And thys was
wryte in a scrowe gret hande, thynkyth, and þat scrowe was naylyd to
a tabyl and putt vpon þe crosse and hyt was `wryte´ as the euangelyste
seyth in Grewe, Ebrewe, and Latyn þat all maner men þat were come 115
to þe haly daye mygthte vndyrstande hyt. For ther were folke of
dyuerse languagys come to þe haly daye, and therfore þe tytyl was
`wryte´ in the thre princep`a´l languagys. 'Ihesu Cryste' was hys
propyr name; 'Naȝarenus' he was callyd of the contre þat he `was´
noryschyp vp inne; 'Rex Iudeorum', þat ys in Englyisch, Kynge of 120
Iewys. Thys was the cause of hys deth, as hoo seyt, therfore Ihesu

87 thynkyth] beholdeth N   89 þat] þat hadde N   91 grounde] erthe N
100 att] apon N   on] apon N   101 be] be a N   thiefe] N; chef Gg   105 paynyde
hym] pynede N   108 the] his N   þe] *om*. N   118 thre] *om*. N   121 of hys deth]
þat he was putte to deth fore N

Cryste of Naȝareth ys putt to deth for ʽheʼ wolde haue be Kynge of
Iewys. Thys tytyl manye of the Iewys redde as the euangelyste seyth
for þe place þat oure Lorde was crucyfyed att was nere the cytee, and
125 therfore they mygthte sone come thedyr to see.

And thanne thynkyth þat the byischoppys of þe Iewys cam to
f. 98ʳ Pylat | and seyde: 'Wryte not Kynge of Iewys.' For ʽsoʼ hem semyde
hyt schulde turne to here schame. 'But wryte', they seyde, 'þat he
seyde I am Kynge of Iewys.' For ʽsoʼ hem semyde hyt schulde not
130 turne to here schame and thanne Pylat seyde to hem aȝen: 'That I
haue wryte, I haue wryte.' And so be these wordys confermyde þat he
hadde doo and wolde not reuoke hyt. Aftyr thys beholdyth how the
knygtthys þat hadde crucyfyed oure Lorde departyde hys clothys in
foure partyis, eueryche knygth a parte, for ther were foure of hem þat
135 hadde crucyfyed hym, saf the cote, þe whyche hadde no seme but sche
was made a nette wyse. Wherfore they seyde: 'Lete not kytte here, but
lete vs drawe lot hoo schal haue here.' And thanne thynkeʽthʼ also how
the peple stondyth and abydyth, and some scorne hym waggynge here
heedys vpon hym and seyinge: 'Truth for the þat seydyst þat þu
140 woldyst dystroye the temple and in thre dayis arayse hyt vp aȝen, saf
thyself. Ȝyf þu be Godys sone, come downe fro the crosse.' And
beholdyth also how the pryncys of prestys, and the scrybys, and the
eldyste of the peple scornyde hym seyinge: 'Loo, he hath sauyd
othyre, but he maye not saue hymselfe. Yf he be Kynge of Isral, lete
145 hym come downe now of þe crosse, and we wole beleue in hym.' And
f. 98ᵛ in thys they seyde | false, for he hadde araysyd Lasur fro deth to lyue
and arose vp also out of the sepulcre and that was more, as Seyint
Gregory seyth, thanne to come downe fro the cros, and ȝytt wolde not
they beleue on hym. But att þys tyme he mekely fulfylde the
150 obedyence to hys ʽFadyrʼ in heuene, the whyche was þat he schulde
dye for saluacyon of mankynde. And therfore he wolde not come
downe fro the crosse and leue the obedyence to hys Fadyr in heuene
and the helthe of mankynde þat he cam fore, for here blasphemus
wordys, ne moreouyr to conforte hys modyr, the whyche he seygth

125 sone] lightly N   to] and N   126 thanne . . . þat] thenketh howe N
127 ʽsoʼ] om. N   133 hys] our lordes N   in] into N   134 eueryche] yche N
135 sche] it N   136 a] of N   Wherfore] and þerfore N   Lete] lete vs N   here¹] it N
137 here] it N   138 waggynge] waggede N   139 and] om. N   140 temple]
temple of God N   141 thyself] þiselfe nowe N   143 scornyde] scorne N   seyinge]
and seyne N   144 maye] ma fol. by canc. n Gg   147 out of] fro N   148 to]
forto N   149 on] in N   151 for] for þe N   152 to] of N   154 hys] his
blissede N

there in so myche sorowe and heuynesse for hym and the whyche he 155
louyde aboue alle othyre, ne for Seyint Ihon, ne schortly forto seye,
for no othyr frende of hys that were there present, ne forto deluere
hymselfe out of þe payne þat he was inne. But he suffryde pacyently
and abode obedyently on the crosse into hys lyuys ende.

And in thys he ʒaf vs exsample þat we schulde not leue the state of 160
good lyuynge þat we haue onys take for hys loue, be hyt neuyr so
strayte, for no temptacyonys of þe fende, ne for no schrewde wordys
of blynde worldly men, ne for none affeccyon of fadyr, modyr,
'systyr', or brothyr, ne for eny frendschype of worldly frende þat
wolde lette vs fro the loue of God and fro that þat schulde turne to 165
oure euyrlastynge profyte, ne schortly forto seye, for eny prosperyte
or aduersytee. But we schull perse|uere in þat goode weye of f. 99ʳ
penaunce wyth dyscrecyon and othyre goode werkys into oure
lyuys ende, the whyche weye of penaunce maye be callyd gostly a
crosse, in as myche as hyt ys a punyischynge to a man or a wommanys 170
senceualyte. And yf we doo so we schal haue to oure mede thys
worthy Lorde þat for oure euy'r'lastynge profyte perseueryde in the
crosse into hys lyuys ende.

Aftyr thys turnyth aʒen to the Passyon of oure Lorde and
beholdyth how one of the theuys the whyche hynge att the lyfte 175
syde of oure Lorde blasphemyde hym and seyde: 'Yf þu be Cryste, saf
thy self and vs.' And 'thanne' that othyr thef þat hynge on the rygth
syde blamyde hym, seyinge: 'Thredyst þu not God þat arte in the
same [dampnacyon]? And we be rygthfully', he seyde, 'for we haue
deseruyd hyt. But forsothe thys [man] hath doo no euyll'. And thanne 180
he seyde to oure Lorde: 'Lorde, haue mynde on me whenne 'þu'
comyste into thy kyngedom.' And thanne oure Lorde seyde to hym
aʒen: 'Fforsothe I seye to the, thys daye þu schalt be wyth me in
paradyse.' Loo, how gret charytee þys was of oure Lorde þat not only
for ʒaf hym hys synnys, but also ʒaf hym euyrlastynge lyf for he 185
knowlechyde 'hym' Godys sone whenne hys dyscyplys hadde forʒake
hym.

Aftyr 'thys', beholdyth also þat oure Lady and Seyint Ihon

---

159 into] to N   163 ne] *om.* N   164 ne . . . frendschype] frendeshipe of ony N
167 schull] shulde N   170 a man] mannes N   a] *om.* N   173 hys] our N
175 how] howe þat N   the . . . att] þat honge on N   176 Cryste] cristes N   saf]
goddes sone saue N   177 the] his N   178 blamyde] blamynge N
179 dampnacyon] dampnacioun N; dampcyon Gg   180 man] N; *om.* Gg   181 on]
of N   186 'hym' Godys sone] hym þe sone of God N   188 'thys' . . . þat] þis
thenketh howe N

euangelyste and 'the' deuout wymmen stondyn besyde the crosse of
f. 99ᵛ oure Lorde wepynge and weylynge | for they see hym in so myche
191 despyte and payne, and so doeth ȝe wyth hem. And thanne beholdyth
how oure Lorde spekyth to hys modyr as he hangyth [on] the crosse,
seyinge thus: 'Woman, loo thy sone', be Seyint Ihon þat stode besyde.
He callyede not here modyr but woman, laste, as Lyre seyth of
195 tendyrnesse of þat name modyr, yf hyt hadde 'be' openyd, the
vyrgynys soule 'schulde' haue be more greuyd, seynge here sonys
Passyon. And thanne he seyde also to the dyscypyl: 'Loo, thy modyr';
as hoo seyth, be þu to here seruysable as to thy modyr. And fro that
oure he toke here into hys kepynge as hys modyr. And thys 'was' a
200 gret tokene of specyal loue and truste þat oure Lorde 'hadde' to thys
gloryus apostyl whenne he betoke hys owen worschypful modyr to
hym and putte 'hym' in hys owen stede. And therefore, hoosoeuer
loue oure Lorde Ihesu Cryste, he muste nedys loue specyally þys holy
apostyl and euangelyste, the whyche oure Lorde so specyally 'louyde'
205 and so manye tokenys of specyal loue schewde to, as ȝe schal, be the
grace of oure Lorde here in the laste capetele of thys boke with othyr
commendacyon of the same worschypful apostyl.

But lete vs now turne aȝen to þe Passyon of oure Lorde and
'thanne' thynkyth how, as þe euangelyst seyth, þat þe scrypture
210 mygthte be fulfylde, and also what for gret payne þat he was inne and
f. 100ʳ the blo|de þat he hadde sched, he waxe ful drye and seyde: 'I
thyr[s]te.' And thanne thynkyth how an harlot rennyth forth to a
vessel þat stode there wyth aysel and fyllyth ful a sponge therof and
putt'yth' hyt vp to hys mouth wyth a rede þat he schulde drynke.
215 Now, gostly systyr, beholdyth wyth gret pytee and compassyon all
thys pouerte, despyte, and payne þat oure Lorde suffryde for the
saluacyon of mankynde and thynkyth inwardly how sore we schulde
drede to haue or to desyre eny prosperyte in thys worlde sygth oure
Lorde suffryde thus myche aduersytee.

220 For Seyint Gregory seyth in an Omelye that oure Lorde wolde not
haue prosperyte in thys worlde. He suffryde, he seyth, repreuys and
scornys, and he suffryde also spetyngys, scorgys, bu[f]fetys, and the

---

190 weylynge] sorowynge N   so] *fol. by canc.* my? N   191 beholdyth] beholdeth
also N   192 on] N; in Gg   193 besyde] þer with hir N   195 name] name of N
196 be] be þe N   197 Loo] loo here N   203 loue] loues N   205 the] *fol. by
canc.* the Gg   206 oure Lorde] God N   208 þe . . . Lorde] our purpose N
209–30 scrypture . . . fulfylde] scrypture *follows* fulfylde *with corr. marks placing it before*
mygthte Gg   210 for] for þe N   212 thy[r]ste] thyrte Gg; thruste N   how] howe
þat N   213 there] there fillede N   222 buffetys] butfetys Gg; buffette N

crowne of thorne. And for we fylle fro the inwarde ioye be delyte of
temperal thyngys, he schewde vs wyth what byttyrnesse we muste goo
thedyr aȝen. What therfore, seyth he, schulde a man suffre for   225
hymselfe yf God suffryde so myche for men? Therfore, he þat now
beleuyth in Cryste, but ȝytt he folowyth the wynnyngys of coueytyse,
he ys lefte vp in the pryde of worschype, he brennyth wyth brondys of
enuye, he dyffulyth hymselfe wyth the vnclennesse of lecherye, he
coueytyth the prosperyte of thys worlde, he despysyth to folow   230
Ihesu | that he beleuyth inne. For he goeth a diuerse weye yf he   f. 100ᵛ
desyre ioyys and delytys to whom hys duke schewde the weye of
byttyrnesse. These be Seyint Gregoryis wordys in the Omely vpon
the Gospel þat ys red in the Sondaye of Quynquageseme.

CHAPTER 23

Of the oure of None and of þe werkys þat were doo in þat oure.
Capitulum xxiiiᵐ

In the begynnynge of þys oure ȝe maye thynke fyrste how fro the oure
of Sexte into the oure of None there was made therkensse vpon all the
londe of Iurye, the whyche duryde aftyr the seyingys of doctorys thre   5
ourys. For Lyre seyth þat the mone was vnmeuable vndyr the sunne
thre ourys and that was merueylus, for he seyth þat in þe natural
clypse of the mone ys contynually meuyd vndyr the sunne. And be
thys ȝe maye vndyrstande þat oure Lorde was lyuynge on the crosse
thre ourys in al þat despyte and payne þat I haue tolde ȝow of in the   10
oure of Sexte, and þat was passyngly paynful to lyue so longe in
payne. And therfore yf ther ʽbeʼ eny compassyon in ȝoure herte,
hauyth inwardly compassyon of hym.

   And ʽþanneʼ thynkyth how hyt drawyth faste towarde the oure of
None and how he hangyth stylle in the crosse in all the payne forseyde   15
in the oure of Sexte. And beholdyth also hys modyr and othyre that
were there wyth here, weylynge and wepynge byttyrly for compass-
yon of hym, and spe|cyally hys modyr, and woot neuere what sche   f. 101ʳ
maye doo or whethyr to turne here for sorowe and heuynesse, for ȝe
maye trowe ʽforʼsothe þat here sorowe and heuynesse vndyr the crosse   20
of oure Lorde passyde eny seyintys martyrdom þat euyr was. For hyt

227 but] *om.* N   folowyth] *fol. by canc. of* Gg   228 wyth] with þe N
Chapter 23   10 in al þat] and all þe N   of] *om.* N   17 there] *om.* N   18 neuere]
not N   19 ȝe] þe N   20 and heuynesse] *om.* N

was merueyle that sche mygthte lyue in all þat sorowe saf þat the
myghte of God and the beleue þat sche hadde þat hyt was for the
saluacyon of mankynde, and also the hope þat sche hadde of hys
25 Resurreccyon, for the feyth of holy chyrche abode þat tyme in here
alone. And beholdyth also how the othyr peple stondyth and waytyth
when he schulde dye, and some of hem haply scorne hym and despyse
hym. And `þanne´ thynkyth how oure Lorde Ihesu Cryste lyftyth vp
hys heed wyth myche payne, and fyrste leyeth hyt att þat oo syde and
30 aftyr att þat othyr for ther was no place þat he mygthte reste hys
blyssyde heed vpon. For the `crosse´, ȝe maye thynke, hadde no heed
aboue, and therfore ther was no restynge place but vpon hys breste or
vpon hys armys and þat was passynge payneful.

Aftyr thys thynkyth how oure Lorde Ihesu Cryste seynge þat all
35 was fufylde þat was forseyde of hym be prophetys, he began faste to
drawe to dethwarde. And so all the tokenys of deth began to appere
vpon hym, for hys fayre face began to wexe all pale, and hys nose
f. 101ᵛ scharpe, and here to falle. | And so alle `þe´ othyre sygnys of deth
apperyde in alle the placys of hys body. And þat was a passynge
40 pytefull sygth and an heuy to oure Lady and hys louarys that were
there present, and so hyt maye be to ȝow also and to eueryche louarys
of the same worschyful Lorde þat wole deuoutly thynke thys.

And thanne thynkyth how aboute the oure of None he lyfte vp hys
heed mygthtyly and wyth an hye voyce deuotly and louly he seyde to
45 hys Fadyr in heuene: 'Ffadyr, into thy handys I be take my spryryt.'
And wyth the seyinge of thyse wordys, he ȝaf vp the goste. And
thanne hes heed fylle downe vpon hys breste, as hyt `hadde´ be
thankynge hys Fadyr that `he´ hadde fulfilde hys obedyence for the
helthe of mankynde. And so he was obedyent for vs to hys Fadyr vnto
50 `þe´ deth, as Seyint Poule seyth. And thanne the vayle of the temple
was rente into pesys, and ther was `also´ an erthequaue and the stonys
tobrake, in betokenynge, as Lyre seyth, þat hertys, be they neuyr so
harde, schulde haue compassyon of Cryste dyinge. And grauys were
openyd wyth the erthequaue, to betokene, as þe same doctur seyth,
55 that Crystys Resurreccyon was nere and othyre þat schulde aryse
wyth hym. Seyint Gregory seyth also in þe Omelye of the Tuel`f´the
Daye thus: 'In alle the sygnys, the whyche were schewde whenne oure

23 of] *fol. by canc.* þat Gg   26 And] and þan N   the] þat N   28 `þanne´] *om.* N
29 att¹] on N   30 att] on N   othyr] other syde N   36 to¹] to þe N   38 and¹]
and his N   `þe´] þat N   39 þat] þis N   40 and¹] and all N   41 eueryche] yche
deuoute N   46 ȝaf] ȝelde N   the²] þe þe N   50 as] as þe apostle N
53 schulde] þei shulde N   54 wyth] of N   56 hym] *om.* N   57 the] *om.* N

Lorde was borne and dyde, hyt ys to be con|syderyd to vs what   f. 102ʳ
hardnesse was in some Iewys hertys, the ʽwhyche´ nothyr be the ȝyfte
of prophecye ne be myraclys knewe hym. For alle the elementys bare 60
wytnesse þat here makare was come: the see knewe, for sche ȝaf
hereself able to be trode vndyr hys feete; the erthe knewe, for whenne
he dyde hyt schoke; the sonne knewe, for sche hydde the bemys of
here lyght; the stonys and wallys knewe, for in the tyme of hys deth
they tobraste; helle knewe, for he ȝeldyde hem þat ʽbe´helde deed. 65
And neuyrdeles, hym whom alle insensyble elementys felte a Lorde,
ȝytt the vntrewe Iewys knowe not God and here hertys hardyr thanne
flyntys wole ʽnot´ be broke to penaunce, for they denye to knowleche
hym whom elementys, as we haue seyde, othyr be sygnys or
brekyngys crydyn God.' 70

Aftyr thys, thynkyth how ʽa´ century, the whyche was a knygthte
þat hadde an hundryd knygthys vndyr hym, and they that were wyth
hym kepynge oure Lorde, seynge the erthequaue and the myraclys
that were doo, and that he ȝaf vp the spyryt wyth so gret a crye (the
whyche mygthte ʽnot´ bee, Lyre seyth, be þe uertu of kynde) they 75
dred sore, seyinge: 'Fforsothe, thys man was Godys sonys.' And all
the othyr peple þat were att þys spectacle and seygth þat that ʽwas´
done, smote hemselfe vpon the breste, turnynge aweywarde, | forth- f. 102ᵛ
ynkynge þat they hade pursuyd oure Lorde to the deth.

Aftyr thys ȝe maye thynke how the peple goeth home, but oure 80
Lady and here systryn and Seyint Ihon euangelyste and Marye
Maudeleyne abyden there stylle, and haply moo. And thanne maye
ȝe beholde wyth oure Lady and hem that were wyth here how oure
Lorde Ihesu Cryste hangyth vpon the crosse so nakyd þat he hadde no
cloth vpon hym, and so despysyd betuene to theuys as thowgth he 85
hadde be chef, and so ipaynyd þat fro the soole of the foot to the top of
the heed ther was no hole skyn vpon hym. And also how hys blyssyd
heed, pytefully ys pry ʽcʹkyd wyth thornys, hangyth downewarde vpon
hys breste all pale and ʽbe´ ronne wyth bloode, and hys holy handys
and feete rente wyth horryble naylys. And thys, ʽwel´ co[n]syderyd, 90
maye be to ȝow or eny deuout soule a ful pyteful sygthte.

And thanne ȝe maye thynke how oure Lady, ful of sorowe and

---

60 For] fforsoth N   69 seyde] *fol. by canc.* ort N   70 crydyn] knewe N
71 ʽa´] þat one N   72 an] a N   73 myraclys] merueylles N   75 ʽnot´] *om.* N
76 Godys sonys] þe sonne of God N   77 that] *om.* N   78 breste] breestes N
79 the] *om.* N   81 Marye] *om.* N   84 vpon] on N   86 þat] *om.* N   88 ys
pry ʽcʹkyd] yprikkede N   hangyth downewarde] hangede doun N   89 ʽbe´ ronne]
ouerronne N   91 or] or to N

heuynesse, arysyth vp and stondyth betuene the theuys crosse and
oure Lordys, and wyth myche lamentacyon sche lyftyth vp here
95 handys, seyinge sueche maner ˋwˊordys or lyke: 'Acth, suete sone, alas
that euyre I seyˋgˊth thys daye. Why ne hadde I dyde er I sawgth thys
daye and the in thys plyte? I wot wel, blyssyde sone, þat þu
f. 103ʳ deseruydest neuere thys pay|ne, for I am rygth sykyr þat þu neuyr
dedyst synne, ne eny mygthyst doo, for þu arte verry Godys Sone,
100 and in that my Lorde and my God, and in that kynde þu arte
impassyable. But þu woldyst, suete sone, for þe helthe of mankynde
be my sone, and in that þat þu haste take of me þu wolˋdyst be alsoˊ
passyble and haste suffryd ful pacyently and mekely all thys pouerte,
despyte, and payne. But I beleue þat hyt ys for the saluacyon of
105 mankynde, and also haue ful hope and truste of thy ioyeful and
gloryus Resurreccyon and ellys I shulde for sorowe dye here vndyr
thy crosse. For, louely sone, þu knowyst wel þat I hadde ˋleuyrˊ dye
wyth the thanne lyue wythoute the. And also, suete sone, þu wost wel
I mygthte not delyuere the fro thys deth the whyche þu haste chose
110 for the helthe of mankynde. But, louely sone, I wole stonde here
vndyr thy crosse and fylle my soule and herte wyth sorowe and
lamentacyon, sygth I maye no more doo. And I wolde hyt were the
wyll of thy Fadyr in heuene and thyne, suete sone, þat I mygthte dye
here wyth the.'
115   Aftyr thys ȝe maye thynke how ˋscheˊ lyftyth vp here ˋherte andˊ
handys to the Fadyr in heuene, seyinge sueche maner wordys or lyke:
'Allmygthty God, Fadyr in heuene, þat wolde ȝoure owen Sone take
fleyisch and bloode of me, ȝoure seruaunt, for the helthe of
mankynde, and so also be my Sone, and in that he hath take of
f. 103ᵛ me | to suffre deth for the saluacyon of the same kynde, now ȝoure
121 belouyd sone and myne hath fulfylde þe obedyence þat ȝe wolde he
schulde fulfylle. And now I beseke ȝow wyth ˋallˊ myne herte þat ˋȝeˊ
vowchasafe to sende me helpe to byrye hym, and that I maye hole
wythoute eny brekynge of hys bonys putt hym in hys sepulcre.'
125   And in seyinge of sueche maner wordys as beforseyde, or lyke þat
mowen mekely be conseyuyd in a deuout ˋsouleˊ aftyr the forme of
medytacyon, ȝe maye thynke sche fylle downe for heuynesse and

93 crosse] crosses N   94 lyftyth] lyftede N   95 seyinge] haply seyynge N
Acth] a N   96–7 Why . . . daye] om. N   102 be] þu ˋertˊ N   þat þu] þou N
wolˋdyst be alsoˊ] erte N   108 thanne lyue wythoute the] N; thanne wythoute the lyue
with corr. marks moving lyue after thanne Gg   also suete] so N   110 the] om. N
115 lyftyth] lyfte N   121 belouyd] welbelouyd N   122 myne] om. N   124 eny]
om. N   127 thynke] thenke þat N

sorowe, and arose vp aȝen of the affeccyon of loue, and waylyde and
sorowyde wyth abundaunce of manye terys for here only sone, the
whyche sche louyde wyth all here herte, mygthtys, and strengthys. 130
And therfore hauyth inwardly pyte and compassyon of here, fro hoo
mygthte see thys worthy Lady and blyssyd virgyne in so myche
sorowe and heuynesse and not haue compassyon of here and of here
sone and othyre deuout folke þat were 'there' also and wepe wyth
hem? And thynkyth also how in all thys tyme seyint Ihon euangelyste 135
and oure Ladyis systryn wyth Marye Maudeleyne conforte here as
they kunne and mowen, and ȝytt they were alle in gret heuynesse, as
no wondyr was. And thys maye be the medytacyon of þe oure of
None.

CHAPTER 24

Of the openynge of oure Lordys syde | aftyr None wyth othyre f. 104ʳ
edyfycatyf materys acordynge wyth the Passyon of oure Lorde.
Capitulum xxiv

Aftyr the oure of None 'ȝe maye thynk' how the Iewys cam to Pylat
aȝen and prayde 'hym' that the schene bonys of hem þat were 5
crucyfyed schulde be broke, and that they mygthte be take downe
of the crossys. The cause þat they wolde haue here schynys broke was
þat they schulde not ascape yf they hadde be take downe quyk, and
the cause þat they wolde haue hem take downe was for reuerence of
the halydaye þat was the nexste daye aftyr, and hyt beganne att the 10
euyn of the same daye that oure Lorde was crucyfyed inne. Thanne ȝe
maye thynke how they cam thedyr anoone aftyr None, and Pylatys
knygthtys wyth hem. And 'thanne' beholdyth 'how' oure Lady lokyth
to the cyteewarde, and perseyuyth how the peple comyth aȝen, and
whenne 'sche' sawgth þat thynkyth here sorowe was encressyd. And 15
thanne thynkyth how sche arysyth vp wyth myche heuynesse and
lamentacyon, merueylynge what they wole doo now to here suete sone
sygth he was deed.

And 'thanne' beholdyth how the peple comyth into the place wyth
myche noyse and haste, and thanne anoone too knygthtys brake the 20
too theuys leggys þat were crucyfyed wyth oure Lorde. And whenne

134 othyre] othe N   136 conforte] confortynge N   137 they] þe N

Chapter 24 1 of] of of N   5 schene] *in marg.* or leggys Gg   7 of] fro N   cause]
cause whi N   schynys] *in marg.* or leggys Gg   12 thedyr] þider aȝene N   17 wole]
wolde N

they cam to oure ˋLordeˊ and perseuyde þat he was deede, they brake

not | hys schynys, but one of the knygthtys openyde hys syde wyth a
spere þat they mygthte be sykyr whethyr he were deed or not. And
25 anoone ther ranne out bloode and watyr: bloode into oure redempcyon, watyr into the weyischynge aweye of oure synnys. Hyt ys to be
knowe, thowgth, Lyre seyth, þat thys watyr cam out merueylusly for
hyt was not the flˋeˊumatyke ˋhumorsˊ, as some seyin, but hyt was
clene watyr to schewe þat Crystys body was ˋmadeˊ of trewe
30 elementys aȝenst the errur of hem þat seyde that he hadde a fantastyke
body, as were the Manycheys, the whyche were perlus herytykys
sometyme aȝenste holy chyrche. The forseyde knygthtys name þat
openyde oure Lordys syde was Longyne, the whyche whenne he
sawgth þe merueylys þat were doo att oure Lordys Passyon, þat ys to
35 seye, the sonne whenne sche waxe derke and the erthe quaue, he
beleuyde in oure Lorde. And moste, as some seyin, þat whenne of
infyrmytee or for age he was almoste blynde, be happe he tuchyde hys
eyen wyth sum of the ˋblodeˊ þat cam downe be the spere and anoone
he mygthte see clerely, and so aftyrwarde he was turnyd and a martyr.

40   Aftyr thys ȝe maye thynke also þat whenne oure Lady seygth oure
Lordys syde openyd sche mygthte not bere hyt, but sche fylle downe a
snowne in Seyint Ihonys armys as thowgth | sche hadde haad the
same stroke hereselfe. And thanne thynkyth what sorowe and
heuynesse hyt was to Seyint Ihon and the deuout ˋwymenˊ þat were
45 there present whenne theˋyˊ sawgth all thys, and therfore hauyth
compassyon and pytee of hem alle for they been in gret sorowe and
heuynesse. And ȝytt not wythstandynge they conforte oure Lady as
wel as they maye.

Now thanne here ȝe maye beholde a pyteful spectacle how the
50 worschypful Sauyoure of mankynde hangyth vpon the crosse in all the
pouertee, despyte, and payne forseyde, and hys syde openyd wyth a
spere, the whyche wounde ȝe maye thynke was gret and wyde,
horryble to see. And hys blyssyd modyr, a tendyr virgyne allmoste
deed for sorowe and heuynesse, and hys othyre deuout louarys
55 wepynge and makynge myche sorowe and lamentacyon bothe for
hym and for here also. And what deuout Crystyn soule mygthte
inwardly ˋbeholdeˊ thys wythˋouteˊ abundaunce of terys?

Beholdyth also deuoutly wyth a goode avysement and a dylygent

23 schynys] *in marg.* or leggys Gg   35 sche] it N   quaue] quakede N   37 for]
of N   39 martyr] matier N   40 Aftyr thys] than maye yhe N   þat] *om.* N
43 thanne] *om.* N   50 vpon] on N   53 virgyne] mayden N

consyderacyon how the louely Lordys heed hangyth downewarde as
hyt were to kysse, hys armys spred abrode as hyt were to beclyppe,   60
hys feete faste naylyd to abyde, hys suete herte ipersyd wyth a spere in
betokenynge of the vnspekeable loue and charyte þat he hadde to
mankynde. And how mygthte he haue schewde vs more loue and |
kyndnesse thanne to dye so payneful a deth for vs wyth so myche   f. 105ᵛ
despyte and pouertee, and schede hys owen precyouse `herte´ bloode   65
for the same clene loue and excellent charytee, and soo weyische vs fro
oure synnys in hys owen precyouse bloode, for Seyint Ihon euangelyste seyth in the Apocalypse that he louyde vs and weyische vs fro
oure synnys in hys bloode.

What loue maye be lyknyd to thys loue? Sothly none, ffor   70
whatsoeuere eny martyr euyr suffryde or confessur euyr dede for
oure Lorde, hyt maye not be lyknyd to hys loue. For hyt was more
charyte, wythoute comparyson, God that owfte not to dye, frely of hys
mercy in mankynde to suffre deth for a wre`c´chyd synful man thanne
a man þat muste nedys dye to suffre deth for blyssyd and rygthful   75
God. And thowgth hyt were so þat a man mygth suffre þe same
penaunce for hys loue þat he suffryde for hym or more, ȝytt mygthte
hyt `not´ be lyknyd to hys charyte, for whatsumeuere eny man or
woman doo or suffre for oure Lorde God, he schal haue hys mede
therfore, but he hadde none. For he frely of hys imcomprehensyble   80
charyte and endles mercy sauyde mankynde, þat be hys owyne synne
schulde haue be loste foreuere but yf he so mercyfully hadde bowgthte
hyt aȝen.

Also, rygth as the persone was moste excellent and worthyest, so
was the c`h´aryte of the `same´ persone moste | excellent and wordyest   f. 106ʳ
þat euyr was or mygthte be. For ther was neuyr charyte or loue þat   86
euyr was schewde of creature to God `or´ of oo creature to anothyr þat
maye be lyknyd to `þe´ loue and charyte þat oure Lorde Ihesu Cryste
schewde to mankynde, and rygth so of hys mekenesse, of hys
pacyence, of hys obedyence, and of alle othyr vertuys þat he dede   90
here in hys blyssyde manhede. And therfore whatsumeuere be wryte
or seyde of martyr, confessur, or vyrgine, or of eny othyr trewe
seruaunt of God ther ys none exsample so worthy so prophytable, `ne´
so edyfycatyf `schulde be´ to a Crystyn soule as þat oure Lorde dede

59 hangyth] hangede N   60 as . . . beclyppe] to halsede N   64 vs] *om.* N
67 Ihon] ihon þe N   73 wythoute] withoute ony N   77 for hys loue] *om.* N
89 eny] *om.* N   79 oure Lorde] *om.* N   82 yf] *om.* N   86 For] so N
87 `or´²] *om.* N   90 of alle othyr] all N   92 of] *om.* N   93 God] our lorde ihesu
criste N

95 hymselfe. And in þe forseyde vertuys and alle othyre he perseueryde
vnto the deth, and so in obedyence and for obedyence, and in charyte
and for charyte, wyth the fulnesse of alle othyre vertuys, he dyde.
Wherefore yf we wole be hys membrys and be that come thedyr were
he ys, we muste folowe hym here aftyr oure pouere and kunnynge, in
100 mekenesse, charyte pacyence, obedyence, and othyre vertuys, and
euyr desyre whyle we lyue in thys worlde to growe and encresse in
hem wyth perseueraunce. For perseueraunce ys the vertu of a goode
worke, as Seyint Gregory seyth, and oure Lorde seyth in the gospel
þat he þat perseueryth into the ende, vndyrstondyth in goode, he
f. 106ᵛ schal be safe. And so doo we neuyr | so wel, but we perseuere
106 therinne, we maye 'not' be sauyd.

Also, gostly systyr, thre thyngys ȝe maye consydere in the Passyon of
oure Lorde: þat he suffryde aȝenste thre thyngys þat men and wymmen
settyn here louys most vpon in thys passynge worlde, þat ys to seye,
110 worschypys and dygnyteys; lustys and lykyngys; and worldly
rychessys. The fyrste longyn propyrly to the fende, the secunde to
the fleyisch, and the thyrde to the worlde. Aȝenste the fyrste, oure
Lorde suffryde myche despyte and reproue; aȝenste þe secunde, myche
payne and trylacyon; aȝenste the thyrde, myche pouertee. All thys ȝe
115 maye beholde also in all hys holy lyuynge, but moste specyally and
excellently in hys precyouse Passyon. And therfore here vndyrstondyth how sore we schulde drede to desyre or to seke eny sueche
thynkys in thys lyf, yf we wole folowe oure Lorde Ihesu Cryste and so
be partenerys of the ioye þat he hath be hys mercy bowgth vs to. For
120 'Seyint' Ihon seyth in hys pystyl þat he þat seyth hymselfe to duelle in
Cryste, þat ys to seye, be charyte he muste goo as he wente. How
folowyth he thanne oure Lorde Ihesu Cryste þat desyryth
'worschyppe', lustys, and rychessys? Namely for the loue of hem for
whom hys Lorde suffryde so myche despyte payne and pouertee. Also,
f. 107ʳ ho mygthte beleue þat God suf|fryde all the forseyde payne for hys
126 loue and not loue hym? Sothly, itrowe no man. Lete vs thanne loue
hym for he fyrste louyde vs, as 'Seyint Ihon' seyth, and lete vs schewe
þat loue in kepynge of hys commaundmentys for he seyth in the
Gospel of Seyint Ihon thus: 'Ȝyf ȝe loue me, kepyth my commaund-
130 mentys.' And so'ne' aftyr in the same gospel he seyth also thus: 'He þat
hath my commaundementys and kepyth hem, he hyt ys þat louyth me.'

99 here] om. N   and] an N   p. 104   109 þat] þe whiche N   109 vpon] on N
112–13 oure Lorde] he N   113 myche] he suffrede   114 thyrde] thirde he
suffrede   118 wole] shulde N   131 commaundementys] commaundentes N

Now thanne, oure Lorde Ihesu Cryste, louarys and aʒenbyarys of mankynde and ʒeuare of all trewe and chaste loue, ʻsooʼ ʒeue vs grace to loue hym and drede hym to serue hym and plese hym ouyrall and in all thynge, þat we maye come to þat ioye þat neuere schal haue 135 endynge. Amen.

CHAPTER 25

Of the takynge downe of oure Lordys body fro þe crosse the whyche ys callyd þe oure of Euynsonge.

Now ʒe maye thynke and mekely beleue that [cᵐxxvᵐ] oure Lady and here felawschyp wente not fro the place þat oure Lorde was crucyfyed inne tyll the holy body was take downe of the crosse, but they abode 5 stylle there in mornynge and lamentacyon, as I haue tolde ʒow afore. And oure Lady, ʒe maye thynke, ful deuoutly and hertyly prayeth to the Fadyr in heuene that he wolde vowchasafe to sende here helpe be some deuout seruaunt of hys to take downe þat blyssyd body, for sche hadde no powere ne | instrumentys to take hyt downe wyth and schʻeʼ f. 107ᵛ mygthte not goo thennys for loue tyll þat body þat sche louyde so 11 myche were take downe.

Aftyr thys ʒe maye thynke þat Ioseph of Arymathye, a nobyl courtyoure, wente in boldʻlʼy to Pylat and askyde oure Lordys body to byrye hyt worschypfully. Arymathye was a cytee of Iurye, the 15 ʻwhycheʼ was some tyme callyd also Ramatha, and there was the holy ʻprofeteʼ Samuel borne. And thanne Pylat callyde a centurye to hym. Centurye ys the name of an offyce and not propyrly of the man, for hyt was a knygth þat hadde an hundryd knygthtys vndyr hym. And sueche one ʻPylatʼ callyde to hym and askyde hym whedyr he 20 were deed or not, and ʻwhenneʼ he wyste of hym þat he was deed he ʒaf thʻeʼ body to Ioseph. And thanne Ioseph bowgthte a clene syndele to wynde hyt inne, the whyche was a lynnyn cloth, as Lyre seyth, and therfore hyt ys ordeynyd þat oure Lordys body in the autyr ys not halowyd but vpon lynnyn cloth. 25

Aftyr ʻthysʼ ʒe maye thynke þat Ioseph of Arymathye toke helpe wyth hym, and whenne hyt drewe to euynwarde he cam thedyr wyth mayne wyth hym, for ʒe maye wel trowe þat sueche a man as he was wente not to sueche a werke alone. And thanne ʒe maye thynke also

133 ʻsooʼ] so to N   134 to] and N   135 þat ioye] his blys N
Chapter 25   2 Euynsonge] Euensonge Capitulum xxvᵐ N   3 cᵐxxvᵐ] *right marg.*
Gg   5 tyll] vnto N   14 boldʻlʼy] bodily N   15 of] of þe N   23 hyt] hym N

f. 108ʳ how Nychodemus herde telle þat Ioseph hadde gette the | body of
31 Pylat and wolde goo to take hyt downe and so cam wyth hym. þe
whyche Nychodemus was a prynce amonge the Iewys and `he´ also, ȝe
maye thynke, hadde men wyth hym. And thys Nychodemus also,
afore the Passyon of oure Lorde, was a pryuy dyscypyl of hys, as wel
35 as Ioseph, but aftyr the Passyon, of feruoure he made hymselfe opyn
rygth as Ioseph dede. And he browgth wyth hym as hyt hadde be an
hundryd pounde of myrre and aloes imenglyd togyderys in the maner
of a vnement, the `whyche´ puttyth aweye wormys fro deed bodyis
and kepyth hem fro rotynge. And in thys hyt semyth þat Nycho-
40 demus, thowgth he hadde made that vnement of deuocyon, ȝytt hyt
semyth as Lyre seyth þat he hadde not ful knowynge of oure Lorde
Ihesu Cryste. For hyt ys wryte of hym in the [Fyu`e´tenthe] Psalme of
þe Sautyr thus: '[Non] dabis sanctum tuum videre corrupcionem.'
Thys ys in Englyisch: 'Thow schalt not ȝeue thy seyint to see
45 corrupcyon', thys ys to seye in more opyn Englyisch: 'Thow schalt
not suffre thy seyint, þat ys, the body of oure Lorde Ihesu Cryste, the
whyche was holy and oned to the Godhede vndepartably, to see
corrupcyon'; þat ys to seye, to rote in the erthe as synful mennys
bodyis doen, and therfore hyt nedyde not sueche an vnement to kepe
50 fro rotynge.
f. 108ᵛ   Aftyr thys ȝe maye thynke also how the forseyde deuout men
browgth wyth hem instrumentys, as laddrys and pynsorys and sueche
othyre þat longyde to take downe the body wyth. And thanne
`thynkyth´ þat oure Lady lokyde vp and sawgth afer men comynge
55 wyth sueche maner instrumentys as ben forseyde, and thanne anone
sche hopyde þat they cam to take downe that holy body and wyth that
ȝytt sche was sumwhat confortyd and haply badde Seyint Ihon goo
and mete wyth hem, for sche hopyde þat they cam to helpe hem. And
thanne beholdyth how Seyint Ihon goyth forth faste aȝenste hem, and
60 whenne `he´ sawgh hem nere he knewe hem þat they were oure
Lordys dyscyplys and cam to take downe hys body, and thanne ȝe
maye thynke that he was glad and welcomyde hem curteyisly and
thankyde hem of here charytee. And thanne thynkyth þat they aske
hym hoo they bee þat been att the crosse and he seyth þat they ben

31 to] *om.* N   35 he] þerfore `þe´ seide Nichodeme N   41 semyth] semeth
þoffe N   42 ys] was N   Fyu`e´tenthe] fyuethe Gg; ferth N; *see note*   43 Non] N;
no Gg   49 nedyde] nedeth N   52 and¹] *om.* N   54 `thynkyth´] yhe may
thenke N   57 sumwhat] *om.* N   58 hopyde] trowede N   63 aske] asked N
64 seyth] seyth haply N

oure Lady [hys modyr, Marye Maudeleyne], and hys aunte. And 65
thanne thynketh how they aske hym aȝen where Petyr ys and the
othyre apostlys, and `he´ seyth aȝen þat he seygth none of hem of all
that daye, and so beholdyth they goo forth ta`l´kynge togyderys tyll
they cam to the place.

And whenne they were come thedyr, thynkyth how they doo fyrste 70
reuerence to the body and thanne they conforte oure | Lady, the f. 109ʳ
whyche sche thankyth mekely of here charytee þat they cam to doo
þat seruyse. And thanne ȝe maye thynke þat fyrste they sette oo schort
ladyr vp to the feete, and vp by þat goyth vp Ioseph of Arymathye
wyth a fayre lynnyn cloth vpon hys schuldyr that he hadde brougth to 75
wynde the body inne. And thanne they sette a lengyr ladddyre vp to
the rygth hande, and vp by þat goyth vp Nychodemus wyth a peyre
pynsorys in hys hande to take out as esyly as he mygthte þe nayil in
the rygth hande. And `thanne´ thynkyth also þat they sette the thyrde
laddyre vp to lyfte hande, and by þat goyth vp anothyr man wyth a 80
peyre pynsorys to drawe out also the nayle in the lyfte hande.

And thanne beholdyth how they drawe hem out as softe and as
esyly as they mygth, and ȝytt they maye not doo hyt wythoute
brosynge of oure Lordys handys. And thanne thynkyth how Ioseph
supportyth the body in comynge downe, and thanne anothyr as esyly 85
as he can or maye, drawyth out the naylys þat were in the feete, and so
vndyr hem alle they brynge downe þat worschyful body. And `thanne´
thynkyth þat anone oure Lady rennyth too and kyssyth hys handys
and hys mowth and weyischyth hys face wyth watyr of here eyen, and
Seyint Ihon and the deuout wymen stode also besyde wepynge. And 90
thanne hys heuy | modyr, as hyt ys wryte in Seyint Brygyttys f. 109ᵛ
Reuelacyon, wypyde all hys body and woundys wyth a lynnyn cloth
and closyde hys eyen and kyssyde hym. And thys maye be the
medytacyon att Euynsonge tyme.

65 . . . Maudeleyne] *con. em.* marye maudeleyne hys modyr Gg   67 seyth] seith to
hem N   70 how] þat N   71 conforte] confortede N   72 charytee] charite and N
74 vp¹] *om.* N vp by] vppon N   76 lengyr] *om.* N   77 vp by] vpon N vp] *om.* N
peyre] payre of N   78 mygthte] may N   80 to] to þe N   81 peyre] peyre of N
83 mygth] *in marg.* maye Gg; maye N   84 brosynge] bursynge N   85 thanne]
om. N   88 þat] *om.* N and kyssyth] kys N   93 and] and she N hym] hem N

CHAPTER 26

Of the beryinge of oure Lordys body the whyche ys callyd þe oure of Complen. Capitulum [xxvi^m].

The beryinge of oure Lordys body ȝe maye thynke in thys wyse: whenne oure Lady hadde closyd oure Lordys, eyen as ys forseyde in
5 the chapetele nexste afore thys, thanne beholdyth how sche, wyth the forseyde deuout wymmen and Ioseph and Nychodemus, wynde the body in the clene syndele that Ioseph hadde bougth for the same cause wyth othyre lynnyn clothys and spyserye as the maner ʼofʼ Iewys was to berye. Aftyr thys thynkyth also how nere the place þat oure Lorde
10 was crʼuʼcyfyed inne was a gardyn, and in that gardyn ʼwasʼ a newe tumbe in the whyche was neuyr man putt into þat tyme, and thedyr they bare oure Lordys body. And ʼinʼ the berynge ȝe maye beholde þat oure Lady as worthyest beryth the heed, the men the body, and the othyre deuout wymmen the feete, and so vndyr hem alle they bare
15 ʼþatʼ blyssyd body to þe sepulcre.

The sepulcre of oure Lorde, ȝe maye thynke aftyr the seyinge of
f. 110^r doctorys, was made in thys wyse: ther was a rounde house ikytt out |
of the rok lyinge vndyrnede of so myche heygthe þat a man mygthte vnede tuche the rofe wyth hys hande hauynge an entrynge att the
20 northe syde to þe whyche was put a gret stone instede of a dore. And in þat house was the place þat oure Lordys body was beryed inne, imade of the same stone, the whyche was a tumbe of vii feete of leʼeʼnʼgʼthe and thre spannys hyer thanne the othyr pauyment; the coloure of the same sepulcre was a thowgh hyt hadde be rede coloure
25 and whyte menglyd togyderys, and there thynkyth they beryede oure Lordys body wyth myche wepynge and lamentacyon. And ʼwhenneʼ þys was doo, thynkyth þat oure Lady was passynge sory and looth to departe fro þat body þat sche louyde so myche, but ȝytt att þe laste, att þe conseyil and preyere of Seyint Ihon and the othyre deuout men,
30 sche graunttyde, ȝe maye thynke, to goo home.

And thanne thynkyth þat wyth myche lamentacyon sche kyssyde the body, bounde as hyt was, and aftyr þat the sepulcre commyttynge that blyssyd body wyth here owen soule to the Fadyr in heuene

---

Chapter 26   1 the²] þe N; the the Gg   2 xxvi^m] N; xxvii^m Gg   4 as] as it N
5 beholdyth] thenketh N   6 the] his N   9 oure] of our N   10 ʼwasʼ] om. N
12 the] þat N   13 þat] howe N   14 the¹] þat N   18 the] a N   vndyrnede]
vndeneth N   20 þe] om. N   gret] om. N   21 in] om. N   22 vii] eght N
23 the¹] þat N   the²] þat N   24 a] as N   29 men] wymmen N   32 þat] om. N

hauynge ful truste and hope of hys gloryus Ressurreccyon, for in here
alone abothe the feythe of holy chyrche that tyme. Aftyr 'thys' 35
beholdyth how sche goyth homewarde, and as sche goyth sche
worschypyth the holy crosse, | and the othyre deuout folke, also f. 110ᵛ
thynkyth, dede the same. And thanne beholdyth how they goo forth
vpon the weye togyderys towarde the cytee tyl they cam to a certayne
place where they schulde departe, and thanne thynkyth how the meke 40
Lady ful louly thankyth bothe Ioseph and Nychodemus of here
charyte, traueyle, and seruyse done abowte oure Lorde, and ful
mekely takyth here leue of hem and they of here and so they wente
home 'to' here placys. And oure Lady also, 3e maye thynke, wente to
that place in Ierusalem that was callyd Mello, þat ys into Mount Syon, 45
and there sche abode, for there was the place þat oure Lorde made hys
laste sopere inne afore hys Passyon. And in that same place duelde the
xi apostlys, as the Maystyr of Storyis seyth, but the othyre dyscyplys
and the wymmen duelde there aboute in dyuerse innys.

Aftyr thys thynkyth that 'þe' pryncys of prestys and the Pharyseys 50
cam togyderys to Pylat, seyinge: 'Syre, we haue mynde that þat
dysseyuare seyde whenne he lyuyde þat he wolde aryse þe thyrde daye
and therfore commaunde the sepulcre to bee kepte into the thyrde
daye, laste hys dyscyplys come and stele hym and seye to the peple þat
he ys aryse fro deth to lyue, and thanne schal the laste errur be worse 55
thanne the fyrste.' And thanne Pylat 3af hem leue to ordeyne
knygthys to kepe the sepulcre, and soo they wente and ordeynyde
knyghtys iarmyd to kepe hyt wyth stronge | hande, aselynge also the f. 111ʳ
stone wyth here seele lest eny man mygthte goo inne wythoute 'here'
wytynge, Lyre seyth. And thys maye be the medytacyon att Complen 60
tyme.

36 goyth] gothe homewarde N   37 also] *om.* N   39 towarde the cytee] to þe
cytewarde N   41 bothe] *om.* N   45 was] is N   into] to seye in N   50 of] of
þe N   51 seyinge] seyynge þus N   52 dysseyuare] deceyuer Criste N   54 hym]
his body N   59 seele] seles N   60 wytynge] knowynge as N   61 tyme] tyme
Deo gracias N

CHAPTER 27

A medytacyon the Satyrdaye of oure Lady and the othyre deuout wymmen and what they dede and also of the apostlys of oure Lorde. Capitulum xxvii^m.

What oure Lady 'dede' the Satyrdaye the euangelystys make no
5 mencyon, and therefore ȝe maye thynke þat sche was stylle in that place þat oure Lorde made hys laste sopere inne, the whyche was in that parte of Ierusalem þat ys callyd Mello in Mount Syon, as I haue tolde ȝow in the capetele nexste afore. And there sche was in myche lamentacyon for thowgh sche hadde ful truste of hys Resurreccyon,
10 ȝytt sche mygthte not be wythoute myche sorowe and gret heuynesse for the vnkyndnesse, payne, and despyte þat sche sawgh doo to here suete sone the daye afore, the whyche ȝe maye thynke wente 'not' fro here mynde, for þat a man or a woman moste louyth or thredyth moste comyth to mynde and also moste stedfastly abydyth therinne.
15 And sche louyde hym vttyrly aboue all thynge, for ther was neuyre so trewe loue be'tuene' tueyne as betuene hem too. And therfore, whedyr sche satte, laye, or stode, or eny othyr thynge dede, contynually hyt cam to here mynde how mercyfully he wolde be borne of here, and how meke and lowly he was euyrmore to here, and
f. 111^v how holy, blyssyd, and parfyth he was in all hys lyuynge. | And att þe
21 laste moste sorest wyth gret sorowe and heuynesse, the horryble Passyon þat sche seygh hym suffre so mekely the daye afore wyth myche wronge, despyte, and reprouynge. And also how he commyt-tyde here to Seyint Ihon, and att the laste how he dyde and was take
25 downe and heryed. All thys wyth manye othyre cyrcumstauncys of hys Passyon and othyr thyngys þat were doo there cam to here mynde, the whyche ful sore and more thanne maye be seyde, heuyede, and paynyde here blyssyd herte.

And therfore hauyth inwardly pytee and compassyon of here for
30 sche ys in myche sorowe and heuynesse. And the othyre deuout wymmen, thynkyth, the same Satyrdaye sesyde of all maner bodyly werkys and were in reste and pece for reuerence of the haly daye, the whyche beganne fro the oure þat oure Lorde was beryed inne into þe

---

Chapter 271 A] the N   the] *om.* N   3 euangelystys make] euangeliste maketh N
5 maye] may mekely N   7 parte] place N   8 there] þerfore N   12 ȝe maye
thynke wente 'not'] wente neuer N   1329 þat] þat that N   17 othyr] ther N
19 and³] *om.* N   20 blyssyd] how blessede N   30 the] þat N   31 maner] maner
of N   32 for] at þe N   33 inne] *om.* N

euyn of the nexste daye folowynge. In the whyche haly daye hyt was
not laweful to bye enythynge, and therfore [they] sesyde þat daye tyl 35
the sonne was goo downe of suechemaner werkys as the lawe wolde.
But in all thys tyme, thynkyth, þat they confortyde oure Lady as wel
as they mygthe, and ʒytt they were ful sory and heuy hemselfe,
purposynge whenne the haly daye were done to bye spyserye and
thereof to make vnementys, and so the nexste daye ful rathe to ʼgooʼ 40
and ʼanoyinteʼ anuyncte oure Lordys body.

The apostlys, ʒe maye thynke, were dysparblyd and abrode,
eueryche man wʻhʼere hym semyde best, for they hadde no hope
of | oure Lordys Resurreccyon, ne the wymmen, but oure Lady alone, f. 112ʳ
for in here abode the feyth of holy ʼchyrcheʼ þat tyme. And therfore as 45
hyt ys seyde ys the Satyrdaye specyally appropryed to here. Whethyr
the apostlys cam togyderys aʒen the Satyrdaye or not, I dare not
afferme, but ʒytt not wythstondynge, hyt maye be thowgthte soo, and
therfore ʒe maye thynke hyt in thys wyse. Thynkyth fyrste how
Seyint Petyr cam out of the caue þat he wente into whenne he hadde 50
denyed oure Lorde, þe whyche ys callyd in Englyisch Kockrowyinge.
And thanne beholdyth how he cam to the place where oure Lady was
and Seyint Ihon, and the othyre deuout wymmen wyth myche
heuynesse for oure Lordys deth, and specyally þat he hadde soo
denyed hym. And whenne he was come thedyr, ʒe maye thynke, þat 55
he knʻoʼckyde att the dore, and thanne Seyint Ihon herde hyt and lent
hym in. And whenne he was come in, beholdyth how he accusyth
hymselfe to oure Lady and to alle þat were there wyth gret
compunccyon þat he hadde so denyed oure Lorde. And thanne
thynkyth þat sche ful mekely [and] gracyusly, as sche was alweye 60
ful of mercy and grace confortyde hym aʒen.

Aftyr þys ʒe maye thynke þat the othyre apostlys cam thedyr also
be processe of tyme, eueryche aftyr othyr, alle sory men and heuy.
And whenne they were come alle togyderys, thynkyth the dore was
schytt, for they thurste not | be seyin in opyn ne be knowe togyderys f. 112ᵛ
for drede of Iewys. And thanne they cowde none othyr conforte but
talke togyderys of þat that hadde falle and wepte and made myche
lamentacyon þat here suete maystyr and worthy Lorde was so

35 they] þei N; the Gg   37 thys] þat N   þat] *om.* N   39 done] gone N
40 rathe] hastely N   41 anuyncte] *interlinear* anoyinte Gg   43 eueryche] yche N
semyde] semeste N   45 as] *om.* N   46 ysˀ] þat N   specyally] is N   49 hyt]
om. N   54 þat] *om.* N   57 was] *om.* N   60 andⁱ] N; as Gg   63 eueryche]
ychone N   64 come alle] all comen N   66 of] of þe N   68 here] þere N

vnrygthfully put to deth, ffor ȝe maye thynke for certayne þat
70 whereeuyr they were, they were in myche sorowe and heuynesse,
and therfore hauyth inwardly pytee and compassyon of hem alle. For
hoo mygthte thynke the Lady of all the worlde, wyth þe othyre
deuout wymmen, and the pryncys of all holy chyrche, in soo myche
sorowe and heuynesse and not haue pytee and compassyon of hem
75 and be sory wyth 6 hem?

Aftyr thys ȝe maye thynke þat whenne þe sonne was goo downe and
hyt was laweful to werke, the deuout wymmen toke leue of oure Lady
and wente to bye spyserye to make vnementys of, purposyinge in the
mornynge ful rathe to goo and annoynite oure Lordys body. And in
80 thys ȝe maye consydere the loue and the deuocyon of these blyssyde
wymmen that soo dylygently traueylyde for here Lorde, haply wyth
manye terys and syghyngys. And whenne they hadde bowgth the
forseyde spyserye, thynkyth that they made therof vnementys to
annoyinte oure Lordys body wyth, and haply oure Lady halpe to. And
85 thys maye be the medytacyon the Satyrdaye.

CHAPTER 28

f. 113ʳ Anothyr deuout medytacyon how the soule of oure Lorde | ionyd to
the Godhede wente to helle. cᵐxxviiiᵐ

[Aftyr] the forseyde medytacyon ȝe maye thynke anothyr deuout
medytacyon how the soule of oure Lorde Ihesu Cryste, ionyd to the
5 Godhede, wente to helle to fette out the holy fadrys soulys þat were
therinne. Here ȝe schal vndyrstande fyrste that þys was not helle þat
dampnyd soulys bee inne, but hyt was a place aftyr the seyinge of
doctorys, isette in the ouyr parte of helle and therfore hyt ys callyd
helle, and the same place ys callyd also lembus patrum, þat ys in
10 Englyisch, the boot of fadrys, for alle 'þe rygthful' soulys þat passyde
out of thys worlde into the Resurreccyon of oure Lorde wente to þat
place. And hyt ys callyd also Abrahamys bosum, for Abraham ys
callyd 'þe fadyr' of oure feyth. And that place þe Maystyr of 'Storyis'
seyth, hadde a maner lyght wythoute eny materyal payne, in the
15 whyche alle predestynat soulys were into the Resurreccyon of oure

72 þe] om. N   79 rathe] arly N   80 the²] om. N   84 halpe] helpeth N
95 medytacyon] meditacioun of N

Chapter 28   3 Aftyr] aftre N; aaftyr Gg   5 to²] and N   12 Abrahamys] in marg.
the bosum of abrahamys Gg   13 place] place as N   of] of þe N   14 maner] maner
of N

Lorde, as ys forseyde. And into that wente oure Lorde Ihesu Cryste, as the Apostlys Crede makyth mencyon, and there he was wyth hem into the tyme of hys gloryus Resurreccyon.

And whyle he was there wyth hem, thynkyth þat they were in perfyth ioye for the sygthte of God ys the moste ioye þat a resunnable soule maye haue, and the soulys þat were there seygh the beynge of God clerely, as a worthy doctur | Lyre seyth in a tretye þat he makyth f. 113ᵛ of the seinge of the beynge of God of holy soulys departyd fro the bodyis. And therfore the forseyde place, whyle oure Lorde was there present wyth hem, was callyd paradyse for the clere syghte þat they hadde of the beynge of God. And therof hyt was þat oure Lorde seyde, as the same doctur seyth, in the forseyde tretye to the thef þat hangyde besyde hym: 'Hodie mecum eris in paradyso.' þys ys in Englyisch: 'Thys daye þu schalt be wyth me in paradyse'; þat ys to seye in the place forseyde, the whyche was callyd paradyse, for the clere syghte þat the theuys soule hadde clerely ʽwythʼ othyre soulys þat were there of the beynge of God. For paradyse as the forseyde doctur seyth ys seyde in scrypture in thre manerys: one maner hyt ys callyd ʽþe erthlyʼ paradyse, out of the whyche Adam was putt whenne he synnyde; the secunde maner paradyse ys seyde the empyre heuene, the whyche ys the place þat blyssyde soulys bee inne; the thyrde maner paradyse ys seyde the clere syghte of God, and thys paradyse hyt was þat oure Lorde seyde of to the thef thys daye þu schalte be wyth me in paradyse, as ys forseyde.

What oure Lorde dede ther, or what wordys he hadde to hem or they to hym, or what songys of preysynge there were seyde or songe in hys presence hyt maye | not sykyrly be seyde but yf a man hadde hyt f. 114ʳ be specyal reuelacyon, but ȝytt Nychodemys euangelye makyth mencyon what he dede there. But for hyt ys not autentyke, and also for the forseyde ʽdocturʼ Lyre preuyth hyt euydently false be autoryte of Holy Wryt and seyingys of othyre doctorys, I ouyrpasse hyt and wole not pote sueche thynge here þat ys so vnsykyr and mygthte be cause of erroure to sympyl creaturys. But thys ȝe maye thynke for certayne, þat they were in perfyth ioye in hys presence, as ys forseyde, and in more ioye þat eny deedly man maye seye. And ther he was

20

25

30

35

40

45

50

---

16 as] as it N   that] that place N   17 he] he was N   20 the²] *om.* N   22 a] þe N   24 Lorde] *om.* N   27 in] and N   27–8 þat hangyde] hangynge N 28 hym] hym on þe crosse N   33 doctur] doctor Lyre N   ys] is þat is N   34 ʽþeʼ] *om.* N   of] *om.* N   36 þat] of N   bee inne] *om.* N   37 maner] *fol. by canc.* Th Gg 40 what] what what N   he hadde] *om.* N   41 of] or N   49 ys forseyde] it is afforeseide N   50 þat] þan N   man] creature N

wyth hem into the tyme of hys Resurreccyon, the whyche was the
Sondaye in the dayinge, aftyr the moste commune seyinge of
doctorys.

55   And here consyderyth inwardly the merueylus charyte of oure
suete Lorde, þat wolde so mercyfully and mekely in hys owen persone
go to helle þat mygthte haue sente thedyr an angil yf he hadde wolde
to haue fette hem 'out' and presentyd hem to hym where he hadde
wolde. But the suete 'Lorde' wolde do hyt in hys owen persone, in
betokenynge of the excellent charyte þat he hadde to mankynde, and
60   specially to the holy fadrys þat were there abydynge wyth gret desyre
hys comfortable and ioyeful comynge, and how mygthte he haue
schewde more kyndnesse?

     Here therfore conseyuyth deuoutly how myche we be bounde to
f. 114ᵛ   thanke and loue þys lo|uely Lorde þat thus myche hath doo and
65   wroughte for oure kynd, and [contynualy] doyth wythoute sesynge be
hys benfetys þat he euery daye schewyth vs in ȝeueynge mete and
drynke and cloth wyth othyr necessaryis to oure bodyis wythoute,
mercy and grace to oure soulys wythinne. And at the laste behetyth vs
euyrlastynge ioye wyth angyllys in heuene, yf we trewly serue hym
70   and loue hym whyle we lyue in thys passynge lyf. And therfore louyth
ȝoure worthy Lorde hertyly and seruyth hym trewly and kepyth 'hys'
commaundmentys contynually, and thanne at ȝoure laste ende ȝe
maye seye to hym of conscyence sykyrly þat Seyint Austyn seyth in
the ende of a sermon þat he makyth seyinge thus: 'I haue doo that þu
75   baddyst, ȝyf þat þu behettyste.' Thys maye be the medytacyon how
the soule of oure Lorde Ihesu Cryste, ionyd to the Godhede, wente to
helle and visytyde and broughte out þe holy fadrys soulys þat were
there.

CHAPTER 29

Of the Resurreccyon of oure Lorde Ihesu Cryste and how he
apperyde fyrste to oure Lady. Capitulum xxixᵐ.

Now I schal telle ȝow of þe Resurreccyon of oure Lorde Ihesu Cryste,
as he wole ȝeue me grace, þat rygth as ȝe haue beheuyed wyth oure
5   Lady and the apostlys, as I trowe, of the Passyon 'and þe deth' of oure
Lorde, so ȝe mygthte be confortyd and ioyed wyth hem of the gloryus

---

52 commune] *om.* N   5 presentyd] presente N   65 contynually] N; cytynually
Gg   68 behetyth] he hetyth N   74 seyinge] *om.* N   75 Thys] and þis N
Chapter 29   3 telle ȝow] yowe somewhate N   6 so] *om.* N

Resurreccyon, for hyt ys a medytacyon of gret ioye and conforte to a
soule þat veryly louyth oure | Lorde. Ffyrste ȝe schal vndyrstande þat   f. 115ʳ
oure Lorde arose mygthtyly, for he arose be hys owen mygthte; and
also merueylusly, for the sepulcre beynge close, rygth as aftyr hys   10
Resurreccyon he wente inne to hys dyscyplys the ȝatys beynge schytt.

The Maystyr of Storyis seyth that ther ʽwasʼ a mounke at Rome þe
ȝere of oure Lorde a thousende an hundryd and xi att Seyint
Laurencys wythoute the Walle, the whyche merueylyde gretly of
hys gerdyl þat he was gerde wyth, sodeynʽeʼly vnlosyd and caste afore   15
hym. And thanne ther was a voyce herde in the eyre seyinge: 'Goo
mygthte Cryste come out of hys sepulcre, þe sepulcre beynge close.'

Now thynkyth fyrste þat whenne the tyme of oure Lordys
Resurreccyon was icome, as he be hys mercy hadde ordeynyd afore,
the whyche was the Sondaye in the dawynge, as Seyint Austyn seyth,   20
and þat ys moste communely holde in holy chyrche. And at that oure
thynkyth how ʽþe souleʼ of oure Lorde cam out of helle and browgthte
out wyth hym all the companye of chosyn þat were there, and cam to
the blysful body þat laye in the sepulcre and araysyde hyt vp, and so
he arose vp out of þe sepulcre perfyth God and man be hys owyn   25
mygthte, the sepulcre abydynge close, as I haue tolde ȝow afore.

And att thys gloryus Resurreccyon ȝe maye thynke was a gret
multytude of angyllys, for hyt ʽysʼ conteynyd in a reuelacyon | of   f. 115ᵛ
Seyint Mawte þat here semyde sche seygh sueche a muʽlʼtytude of
angyllys aboute the sepulcre þat fro þe erthe vp to the skye they ʽwenteʼ   30
aboute oure Lorde as hyt hadde be a walle. Also the euangelyste seyth
þat ther was a gret erthequaue and the angyl of oure Lorde cam and
remeuyde awey the stone and satt downe thervpon þat the wymmen
mygthte see þat oure Lorde was aryse. And the face of hym was as hyt
hadde ʽbeʼ lyghtnynge to make the keparys agaste, and hys clothynge as   35
snowe to ȝeue conforte to the wymmen. And for drede of hym the
keparys were adrad and made as deede men, for they mygthte not bere
the syghte of hym for all here armys.]

And sone aftyr, thynkyth þat some of the keparys wente into the
cytee and tolde the prynces of the prestys all þat was done. And   40
ʽthanneʼ they gaderyde togyderys the eldyste of the peple þat were the
chef gouernorys amonge the Iewys, and toke here conseyil togyderys,

8 ȝe schal] *om.* N   10 the sepulcre] ʽitʼ N   18 Now] nowe þan N
23 chosyn] chosen soules N   24 hyt] *om.* N   25 arose] rose N   27 thynke]
thenke þer N   30 vp] *om.* N   31 Also] and also N   35 to] *twice* Gg
37 hym] þe aungell N   41 the¹] *om.* N

and ȝaf the keparys plente of monye and badde hem þat the`y´ schulde
seye þat oure Lordys dyscyplys cam be nyg`h´tte and stale hym awey
45 whyle they slepte. 'And yf the iugge heere þerof', they seyde, 'we
schul suggeste to hym and make ȝow sykyr inowf.' And thanne they
toke the moneye and dede as they were taugthe. And so hyt ys opyn
amonge the Iewys into þys daye, and so they were dysseyuyd be the
f. 116ʳ falsnesse of | here prynces and the lesynge of the knyghtys, the
50 whyche lesynge ȝytt holdyth hem stylle in here errur, as Lyre seyth.
   Now thanne lete vs turne aȝen to þe Resurreccyon of oure Lorde,
and fyrste ȝe schal vndyrstande þat oure Lorde, aftyr the seyinge of
th`e´ euangelystys, apperyde tenne tymys aftyr hys Resurreccyon, þat
ys to seye, fyue tymys in the daye of hys Resurreccyon and othyr fiue
55 tymys aftyrwarde. Othyre thre apparycyonys ther be, the whyche be
tolde to haue falle also the same daye of þe Resurreccyon, but they be
not in the texste of the gospellys; of the whyche one ys þat oure Lorde
schulde haue apperyd fyrste to hys modyr, oure Lady Seyint Marye.
And þat ys rygth resunnably seyde to my vndyrstondynge, and þat, as
60 hyt semyth, the Chyrche of Rome approuyth, þe whyche the same
daye of the Resurreccyon halowyth a stacyon att a chyrche of oure
Lady in Rome, as Ianuense seyth in the Legende þat ys callyd Aurea.
And for oure Lady ys the wordyest persone of all othyre, and also for
oure `Lorde´ apperyde fyrste to here as ȝe maye mekely beleue
65 wythoute eny dowte, thowghtys the euangelystys make no mencyon
therof, for Ianuense seyth þat the euangelistys wolde not wryte hyt,
but they lefte hyt as for stabyl and sertayne, as ho seyth, they knewe
f. 116ᵛ hyt so opyn þat hyt nedyde not to wry|te hyt. For they wyste wele
inowf that eny manor woman þat hadde resunnable wytt mygthte wel
70 wyte þat he apperyde fyrste to here, for hyt ys no doute þat sche was
moste sory for hys deth and therfore sche nedyde moste the conforte
of hys gloryus Resurreccyon. And also, sygh he byddyth hymselfe þat
we `schulde´ worschype oure fadyrs and oure modrys, hyt hadde not
be conuenyent that he schulde not haue do hyt in hys `owen´ persone.
75 And therfore I wole sette þe apparycyon þat was to here fyrste.
   Ffyrste thanne ȝe maye thynke, as ys forseyde, þat he apperyde to
oure Lady hys blyssyd modyr, as worthy was, and that thynkyth in
thys wyse. Beholdyth fyrste how the blyssyd Lady syttyth alone in the

46–7 they toke] the taken N   51 thanne] om. N   55 apparycyonys] fol. by canc.
apparycyonys Gg   56 also] om. N   57 gospellys] gospell N   60 the²] þat N
same] prec. by canc. same of the Gg   68–9 wyste wele inowf] wele inowf wyste with corr.
marks placing wyste before wele Gg; wele inowf wyste N   71 sory] soryeste N
72 byddyth] badde N   75 was] was doo N   77 that] þan N

same place þat oure Lorde made hys laste sopyr inne, the whyche was
in Mount Syon. For there ȝe maye thynke sche abode stylle aftyr sche 80
was broughtys 'dethyr' be Seyint Ihon a Goode Frydaye at euyn, tyl
oure Lorde apperyde to here there, alweye desyrynge the presence of
here blyssyd sone wyth grettyr desyre thanne maye be seyde. And as
sche was in sueche desyrynge and loongynge aftyr hym, and also
haply merueylynge þat he cam not, sygh hyt was the thyrde daye, for 85
that a man or a woman louyth and desyryth hym thynkyth loonge tyll
he haue hyt, and the more þat the desyre ys the paynefullyr hyt ys tyll
hyt be performyd. And thanne | thynkyth þat sche lokyde besyde f. 117ʳ
here and sodeynely sche seyghe here louely sone [stondynge] besyde
here. And as some seyin, he schulde haue seyde these wordys to here: 90
'Salue sancta parens'; thys 'ys' in Englyish: 'Ha'y'le holy modyr.'
    Now what herte or mynde mygthte fully thynke what ioye and
gladnesse þys worthy lady hadde whenne sche sawghe here sone aryse
fro deth to lyf, neuyr to dye more? Sothly, I trowe, none. Aftyr thys
beholdyth how the goode Lady wyth more ioye and gladnesse thanne 95
maye be seyde clyppyth and kyssyth here dere sone and makyth all the
'ioye' þat sche can or maye, askynge hym wyth all here hoole herte
how hyt ys wyth hym. And thanne beholdyth how the meke Lorde ful
gladly suffryde here to doo and seye what sche wolde, and aftyr þat ful
benyngly comfortyde here. And thanne thynkyth how they sytte 100
downe togyderys ful famylyarly, and thanne oure Lorde haply tellyth
here how he hath delyueryd the holy fadrys out of helle, and what he
dede there and also whythyr 'he' hath broughtys hem for a tyme and
seyth þat whenne he wole ascende hymselfe into heuene he wole lede
hem wyth hym to euyrlastynge ioye. For hyt ys to be leuyd þat the 105
holy soulys þat oure Lorde broughtys out of helle wyth hym cam not
in that heuene that ys callyd empyre tyll he ascendyde hymselfe, and
thanne he ledde hem wyth hym thedyr. Thys heuene ys callyd |
empyre, þat ys as myche to seye in Englyisch as fyre, for hyt ys rede f. 117ᵛ
aftyr the seyingys of doctorys, as fyre ys, [vndyrstondyth in clernesse] 110
and hyt ys the place þat seyintys schal see the beynge of 'God' clerely
inne. Where they were in the menetyme, þat ys to seye, fro the
Resurreccyon of oure Lorde into hys Ascencyon, oure Lorde wote,

81 a] on N   85 merueylynge] meueylynge N   86 that] þan N
89 stondynge] stonde N; stodynge Gg   95 beholdyth] beholdeth deuoutely N
96 clyppyth] halseth N   100 benyngly] benygly N   104 wole¹] wole N   wole²]
wolde N   105 to] to be N   leuyd] beleuede N   107 in that] into N
110 vndyrstondyth . . . clernesse] in marg. Gg   111 schal] shulde N

but certayne hyt ys as Lyre seyth, þat euery place longyth to hys
115 lordschype and therfore he myghte be wyth hem were he wolde.

Aftyr thys thynkyth þat oure Lorde prayeth hys modyr to be of
good conforte, for he schal neuer dye more. And also haply he tellyth
here þat he wole goo and appere to Marye Maudeleyne and to hys
dyscyplys, and so ful mekely takyth hys leue of here. And ʼþanneʼ
120 thynkyth that sche thankyth hym ful lowly and prayeth hym þat he
wolde not tarye loonge fro here. Fferthymore, ʒe maye mekely beleue
þat not only oure Lorde apperyde to hys modyr att þys tyme, but also
dyuerse tymys and ofte afore hys merueylus Ascencyon and haply
broughte wyth ʼhymʼ othyrwhyle to here some of the holy fadrys þat
125 he hadde delyuered out of helle that sche mygthte see hem.

CHAPTER 30

Of the fyue apperyngys þat ben conteynyd in the gospellys, the
whyche were doo þe same ʼdayeʼ of the Resurreccyon, and of ʼothyreʼ
too that be tolde to haue falle also the same daye of the Resurreccyon
þat be not conteynyd in the gospellys, and to what personys they were
5 and how. Capitulum tricesimum.

f. 118ʳ Now I wole telle ʒow fyrste, be the grace of God, schortly of the fyue
apperyngys þat were doo þe same daye of the Resurreccyon þat the
euangelystys make mencyon of, and to what personys they were and
how. And aftyr ʼhemʼ of othyre too þat be not in the texte of the
10 gospellys.

The fyrste apperynge thanne, ʒe maye thynke, was to Marye
Maudeleyne as of ʼtʼhoo, [vndyrstondyth], þat be reed in the gospellys
and that ʒe maye thynke in thys wyse. Marye Maudeleyne on Estyr
daye, ful rathe in the mornynge, thynkyth, wyth othyre too Maryis
15 ʼcamʼ to the sepulcre to anoyinte oure Lordys body as they hadde
purposyd the euyn afore. And whenne Marye Maudeleyne sawghe þe
stone iremeuyd fro the graue and oure Lordys ʼbodyʼ not therinne,
sche wende þat hyt hadde be take aweye, and therfore sche cam

118 wole] wolde N   119–20 ʼþanneʼ thynkyth] þan yhe may thenke N
120 thankyth] thonkede N   ful] om. N   121 wolde] woll N   maye] may
thenke and N

Chapter 30   1 gospellys] gospell N   2 of] om. N   3 of the Resurrecyon] om. N
4 they] om. N   8 euangelystys] eungelistes N   9 of¹] om. N   12 as] and N
vndyrtsondyth] vnderstondeth N; vndystondyth Gg   gospellys] gospell N   14 rathe]
areley N   15 ʼcamʼ] to come N

rennynge to Petyr and Ihon and tolde hem þat oure Lordys body was
take weye and sche wyste neuyr where hyt was done. And thanne 20
beholdyth how they ʽtooʼ rennyn thedyr faste to see, for they tueyne
louyde oure ʽLordeʼ more thanne othyre, but Ihon ranne afore Petyr,
for he was the ʒongyr man and therfore he mygthte bettyr renne
thanne he, and so cam fyrste to the sepulcre and Petyr cam folowynge
aftyr. And whenne they were come thedyr and foonde not þe body 25
they trowyde soth þat the woman seyde, þat ys to | seye, þat oure f. 118ᵛ
Lordys body hadde be take aweye, and so they wente home aʒen for
they thurste not abyde there loonge for drede of Iewys.

   But Marye Maudeleyne þat cam thedyr wyth hem aʒen, thynkyth,
abode stylle wythoute the place þat the sepulcre was inne, wepynge. 30
And thanne sche enclynyde hereselfe and lokyde aʒen into the
sepulcre, for the mygthte of loue multyplyeth the entent of the
sekynge, as Seyint Gregory seyth, and therfore hyt was not inowgh
to here þat sche hadde lokyd onys or oftyr, but ʒytte sche lokyde efte
sonys aʒen yf sche mygthte see ʒytt enyʽthyngeʼ of hym. And thanne 35
sche sawgh too angyllys syttynge, one att þe heed of the sepulcre and
anothyr att the feete, the whyche seyde to here: ʻWoman, why
wepyste þu?ʼ And sche seyde aʒen: ʻFfor they haue take aweye my
Lorde, and I note ʽwhereʼ they haue doo hym.ʼ And thanne sche
turnyde here abowte and sche sawgh oure Lorde Ihesu Cryste 40
standynge there, but sche wyste not though þat hyt was he. The
cause þat sche turnyde here bakwarde was, as Lyre seyth, for sche
sawgh the angyllys that spake to here aryse vp for reuerence of oure
Lorde þat apperyde there and therfore sche turnyde here so aboute to
see hoo hyt was þat they dede sueche reuerence to. And ʽþanneʼ oure 45
Lorde seyde to here: ʻWoman, why wepyste þu? Whom sekyste
thow?ʼ And ʽscheʼ wende þat he had|de ʽbeʼ the gardener, and f. 119ʳ
therfore sche seyde to hym: ʻSyre, yf þu haue take hym aweye, telle
me where þu haste putt hym, and I wole fette hym.ʼ Thys sche seyde
of passynge gret loue for sche wende þat sche mygthte haue borne all 50
ʽþatʼ blyssyd body deed.

   And thanne beholdyth how the mercyful Lorde ful suetly and
famylyarly callyth here be here name, Marye, and thanne anone sche
fylle downe att hys feete and wolde haue kyssyd hem, but the goode

22 Ihon] Seynte Iohn N   24 so] so he N   26 trowyde] trowede þat N   woman]
wymmen hadde N   28 of] of þe N   29 wyth hem] om. N   39 note] wote
neuer N   41 þat hyt was] all it were N   42 here] hir so N   44 Lorde] Lordes
presence N   54 att] to N

55 'Lorde' badde here þat sche schulde not tuche hym as for 'þat' tyme,
for here mysbeleue for sche wende þat he hadde not be aryse. But
aftyrwarde 3e maye mekely trowe þat he suffryde 'here' to 'haue' here
entent, for here deuocyon and loue to hym. And aftyrwarde thynkyth
þat he sende here to hys apostlys and made here the messangere of hys
60 gloryus Resurreccyon, and therfore sche ys callyd the apostlys
apostyllasse. And so ryght as a woman was the messangere of deth
ryght so a woman was the massagere of lyf.

The secunde apparycyon was to the wymmen comynge fro the
sepulcrewarde, and þat 3e maye thynke schortly in þys wyse. Marye
65 Maudeleyne, thynkyth, cam whenne sche hadde spoke wyth oure
Lorde to telle the dyscyplys of hys Resurreccyon as sche was bode.
But fyrste sche cam to the to Maryis þat hadde be fyrste wyth here at
f. 119ᵛ þe sepulcre and tolde hem. And thanne thynkyth þat they were |
ryght glad of thyke tydyngys, but for they hadde not seeye hym 3ytt
70 'also', they were heuy and desyre'de' ful sore to see hym. And so they
wente forth togyderys to the dyscyplys to telle hem, and ere they cam
fully to the cytee oure Lorde mette wyth hem and salutyde hem. And
thanne thynkyth þat they fylle downe and deuoutly kyssyde hys feete,
worschypynge hym as God. And thanne oure Lorde badde hem goo
75 and telle hys bredryn þat they shulde goo into Galyle for there they
schulde see hym. And in thys 3e maye vndyrstande þe gret charytee
and mekenesse of oure Lorde þat callyth hem þat hadde forsake hym
'hys' brethryn þat they schulde not despeyre and drede to come to
hym a3en.

80 The thyrde apperynge was to Symon Petyr, but where or whenne
hyt ys not wyste sykyrly. Notwythstandynge, aftyr the seyinge of
doctorys hyt mygthte haue be whenne Petyr wente be hymselfe alone,
merueylynge what was done of oure Lorde. For whenne the wymmen
cam to the apostlys and tolde hem as oure Lorde hadde bode hem,
85 they helde here wordys but as fantasyis and beleuyde hem not. But
Petyr arose vp and ranne to the sepulcre to see, and whenne he cam
dethyr he fonde but the schetys there only, and thanne he wente
thennys merueylynge be hymselfe of that þat was done. And thanne
f. 120ʳ hyt mygthte be þat oure Lorde apperyde | to hym.

56 aryse] rysen N   57 aftyrwarde] afterwarde þoffe N   58 And] om. N   59 and]
and so N   60 callyd] callede of N   63 secunde] in marg. ii Gg   fro] to N   66 hys]
þe N   67–8 at þe sepulcre] om. N   69 thyke] þo N   70 'also'] om. N   72 and
salutyde hem] om. N   75 for] and N   77 hadde] hadde firste N   80 despeyre]
dispeyre of hym N   80 thyrde] in marg. iii Gg   apperynge] apparicyoun N   84 hadde]
om. N   85 but] om. N   86 ranne] wente rynnynge N   88 be] om. N

The fourthe apparycyon was to too dyscyplys goynge into Emaus, 90
and `þat´ ȝe maye thynke in thys wyse. Tueyne of `þe´ dyscyplys of
oure Lorde wente the same daye of the Resurreccyon to a castel sexty
forow loongys fro Ierusalem whas name was Emaus, and they spake
togyderys of alle tho thyngys þat hadde falle. And as they wente
talkynge togyderys, so thynkyth how oure Lorde ouyrtoke hem and 95
wente wyth hem in the lyknesse of a pylgryme and therfore they
knewe hym not. And so att the askynge of oure Lorde they tolde hym
whereof they spake, for they spake of hym and of hys deth and how
they hopyde þat he schulde haue bowghte aȝen the peple of Israel, and
`thanne´ he reprouyde here mysbeleue and tolde hem also þat Cryste 100
muste `suffre´ that and so entre into hys ioye. And thanne he began att
Moyses and alle the prophetys and exponyde to hem in all the
scrypturys þat were of hym.

And so in sueche maner communycacyon they nyghede to the
castel þat they wente to and he faynyde hymselfe to goo ferthyr and 105
thanne they compellyde hym, seyinge: 'Syre, abyde wyth vs, for hyt
drawyth to nyghte.' And so he wente in wyth hem, and whenne they
were come in, theynkyth, þat they sate downe to sopere. And thanne
oure Lorde toke the brede and blyssyd hyt and putte hyt forth to hem
as he was wonde to doo afore hys Passyon, and hyt semyde as though | 110
hyt hadde be kytte wyth a knyfe, for Lyre seyth that he brake so brede f. 120ᵛ
as though hyt hadde kytt wyth a knyfe. And anone here eyin were
openyd and they knewe hym, for wylfully he schewde hymselfe to
hem in sueche lyknesse as he mygthte be knowe inne. Neuyrdeles,
they knewe þat fyrste be the maner brekynge of the brede. And anone 115
he vanyischede fro here eyen and thanne they arose vp the same oure
and wente aȝen into Ierusalem, and whenne they cam thedyr they
foonde the xi apostlys igaderyd togyderys and the othyre that were
wyth hem, seyinge forsothe þat oure Lorde was aryse and apperyde to
Symon Petyr. And thanne they tolde tho thyngys þat were doo in the 120
weye and how they knewe hym in the brekynge of the brede. But
Seyint Thomas the apost`y´l nothyr beleuyde hem, thynkyth, ne the
othyre, but for a tyme he wente fro hem.

The fy`ue´the apperynge was to the dyscyplys igaderyd togyderys,
Seyint Thomas `þe apostyl´ beynge absent, and þat ȝe maye thynke 125
thus. Whenne Seyint Thomas was goo fro hem, as ys forseyde, the

90 fourthe] *in marg.* iiii Gg   into] to N   92 a] þe N   94 wente] walked N
96 the] *om.* N   99 hopyde] trowede N   108 þat] *om.* N   111 hadde] had be N
117 into] to N   124 fy`ue´the] *in marg.* v Gg   126 as] as it N   the] þat N

othyre dyscyplys abode stylle, thynkyth talkynge togyderys of oure
Lorde. And sodeynely oure Lorde apperyde amoonge hem, for he
cam in, the gatys beynge schyt and seyde to hem: 'Pees be to ʒow. I am
130 he, dredyth not.' And thanne they `were´ sore adrad and dystroblyd
f. 121ʳ and wende that they sawgh a spryryt. And thanne oure Lorde | seyde
to hem: 'Why be ʒe dystroblyd and thowgthtys come vp into ʒoure
hertys? Seeth my handys and my feete, for I am he. Ffelyth and seeth,
for a spyryt hath no fleysch and bonys as ʒe `see´ me haue.' And
135 whenne he hadde seyde thys, he schewde hem hys handys and hys
feete.

Also, to more opyn preuynge of hys gloryus Resurreccyon and to
more stabyllynge of hem in the feyth and vs be hem, he askyde hem yf
they hadde eny thynke þat mygthte be ete, and they toke hym parte of
140 a feyisch rostyd and an honycombe. And `þanne´ the goode Lorde, þat
hadde `no´ nede to ete, ate afore hem alle to schewe therby þat he
`was´ trewly aryse verry God and man in the same body þat he dyde
inne for the helthe of mankynde igloryfyed. Though also he openyde
here wyttys þat they mygthte vndyrstande scrypturys, and in þat he
145 schewde þat he was God, for Lyre seyth, to lyghtte þe myndys of hem
that kunne not `to´ the vndyrstondynge of holy wryt and sodeynely
hyt longyth propyrly to God.

These fyue apperyngys were idoo the same daye of the Resurreccyon, and these the preste presentyth in þe masse as hyt ys seyde in
150 the *Legende Aurea* in turnynge hymselfe fyue tymys to þe peple. But
the thyrde tyme ys wyth sylence, the whyche betokenyth the thyrde
apperynge þat was to Petyr, of the whyche hyt ys not wyste sykyrly
f. 121ᵛ where or whenne hyt was done. Othyre | to apperyngys ther ben, the
whyche be tolde also to haue falle þe daye of þe Resurreccyon, besyde
155 þat that I haue tolde ʒow afore of oure Lady. Of the whyche one
schulde haue be to Iamys the lasse, þe whyche was Alpheyis sone and
the fyrste byschoppe of Ierusalem, and that ʒe maye `thynke´ in thys
wyse. Seyint Ierom seyth þat thys Iamys on Good Frydaye, whenne
oure Lorde was deed, made a vowe þat he wolde neuyr ete brede tyll
160 he sawgh oure Lorde aryse fro deth to lyue. Thanne þe same `daye´ of
þe Resurreccyon, whenne Seyint Iamys into þat tyme hadde not ete,
oure Lorde apperyde to hym and to hem þat were wyth hym he seyde:

131 sawgh] *below sawgh* seyin Gg   137 gloryus] *om.* N   138 the] her N
140 a] *om.* N   141 ate] *om.* N   143 igloryfyed] in hym and N   148 These]
the N   150 in] *om.* N   hymselfe] hym N   151 tyme] turnynge N   154 þe] þe
same N

'Leyith a cloth.' And aftyr `that´ oure Lorde toke the brede and
blyssyde hyt and ȝaf hyt to Seyin`t´ Iamys, sayinge to hym: 'Aryse vp
my brothyr and ete, for the maydenys sone ys aryse fro deth.'   165
    That othyr ys þat oure Lorde schulde haue apperyd also þe same
daye to Ioseph of Arymathye, as hyt ys red in the Gospel of
Nychodeme, and that ȝe maye thynke þus. Whenne the Iewys
herde telle þat Ioseph hadde askyd oure Lordys body of `Pylat and´
beryed hyt in hys owen towmbe, they toke indygnacyon aȝenste hym.   170
And therfore they toke hym and closyde hym vp in a close place,
purposynge aftyr the haly daye to putt hym to deth. And so the same
nyghtte of oure Lordys Resurreccyon the | house þat Ioseph was inne   f. 122ʳ
was drawe vp be the iiii cornerys. And so oure `Lorde´ cam into hym
and wypyde hys face and kyssyde hym and toke hym out þerof, the   175
selys beynge safe, and broughte hym into hys house at Arymathye.
Thys apperynge ys red in the Gospel of Nychodeme, as ys forseyde.
But `for´ hyt ys not autentyke as I haue tolde ȝow afore in the xxviii
chapetele, I commytte hyt to the dome of the `redur´ whedyr he wole
admytte hyt or none.   180

CHAPTER 31

Anothyr deuout medytacyon of the othyre fyue apperyngys þat ben
conteynyd also in the gospellys þat were doo aftyr the daye of þe
Resurreccyon, and to what personys they were, and also anothyr þat
Seyint Poule tellyth of in one of hys pystyllys. Capitulum xxxiᵐ.

Anothyr deuout medytacyon ȝe maye thynke of the othyre fyue   5
apperyngys þat be red also in the gospellys, but they were doo aftyr
þe daye of þe Resurreccyon. Of the whyche þe fyrste was the viii daye
fro the Resurreccyon to þe dyscyplys igadryd togyderys, Seyint
Thomas beynge present wyth hem, and þat ȝe maye thynke in thys
wyse. Aftyr oure Lorde hadde apperyde to hys dyscyplys, Thomas   10
beynge absent, as ȝe maye here afore and was goo fro hem, Seyint
Thomas cam to hys felawys aȝen. And thanne they tolde to hym þat
they hadde seyin oure Lorde and he seyde aȝen: 'But yf I see in hys

163 Leyith] lyeth N   cloth] clothe and brede N   164 vp] *om.* N   171 they]
þe N   175 the] and the N   177 as] as it N   178 xxviii] eghtenthe N
180 none] nono N

Chapter 31 1 deuout] *om.* N   apperyngys] apparicions N   2 also] *om.* N
5 othyre] *om.* N   6 gospellys] gospell N   9 Thomas] seynte thomas N   12 to²]
om. N

f. 122ᵛ handys | the stykyngys of the naylys, and putt my fyngyr in the placys
15 were the [naylys] stode, and pote also myne hande into hys syde, I
schal not beleue.'
   Thanne aftyr viii dayes, thynkyth þat the dyscyplys were togyderys
aȝen and Thomas wyth hem. And as they were togyderys oure Lorde
cam into hem, the gatys beynge schytt, and stode in the myddyl of
20 hem and seyde: 'Pees be to ȝow.' And aftyr þat he seyde to Thomas:
'Putt in thy fyngyr here and see myne handys and take thyne hande
and putt hyt into myne syde. And be not vnbeleuefull but trewe'; þat
ys, in the feyth of myne Resurreccyon. And thanne Seyint Thomas
ansueryde and seyde to hym: 'My Lorde and my God.' And thanne
25 oure Lorde seyde to hym aȝen: 'Ffor þu haste seyin me, Thomas, þu
beleuyst. Blyssyd be they þat see not and beleuyn.' These be wordys
of gret conforte to vs þat neuer seygh oure Lorde bodyly and ȝytt be
hys grace trewly beleue in hym.
   Here mygthte somme man or woman apartye merueyle why oure
30 Lorde suffryde hys specyally chosyn dyscyplys, and specyally thys
dyscypyl Thomas, to dowte so loonge of hys Resurrecyon. Fforsothe,
aftyr þe seyinge of doctorys hyt was a gret and a mercyful
dyspensacyon of the goodnesse of God for the profyte of vs þat
schulde come aftyrwarde. For yf they hadde beleuyd anone, oure
f. 123ʳ Lorde | schulde neuer haue nedyd to haue schewde so manye opyn
36 prouys of hys gloryus Resurreccyon, the whyche whenne we here,
what ys hyt to vs but cause of more stabylnesse in oure feyith? And
therfore seyth Seyint Leo the Pope in a sermon þat he makyth of the
Ascencyon of oure Lorde thus: 'Lete vs ȝeue thankyngys to the
40 dyspensacyon of God and to the holy fadrys necessarye taryinge. Hyt
was dowtyd of hem that hyt schulde not be dowtyd of vs.' And
'Seyint' Gregory seyth also in the Omelye of the Ascencyon: 'Seyint
Thomas ȝaf me more þat loonge dowtyde thanne Marye Maudeley
þat sone beleuyde, for he be hys dowtynge tuchyde the placys of oure
45 Lordys woundys and so put for oure hertys the wounde of dowtynge.'
   The secunde apperynge aftyr the daye of the Resurreccyon was to
vii dyscyplys fyischynge, and þat ȝe maye thynke in thys wyse. Ther
were todygerys Symon Petyr and Thomas and Nathanael and
ȝebedyis tueyne sonys, þat ys to 'seye', Iamys the more and Ihon

15 naylys] nayles N; naþyly corr. to naylys in marg. Gg   17 þat] om. N
18 Thomas] seynte thomas N   And as they were togyderys] om. N   19 myddyl of]
myddes N   25 to hym] om. N   36 prouys] priue thynges N   38 seyth] om. N
40 the] om. N   44 sone beleuyde] so belouede and more N   45 for] fro N
46 apperynge] aparicyon N

hys brothyr and othyre too of oure Lordys dyscyplys, to the whyche 50
alle Petyr seyde þat he wolde goo fyische, and they seyde aȝen to hym
þat they wolde goo wyth hym. And so thynkyth they wente forth
togyderys and thanne they wente into a boot, but þat nyghtte they
toke nothynge and in the mornynge oure Lorde stode in the brynke |
of the see, but they wyste not, thowgh, þat hyt was oure Lorde. And   f. 123ᵛ
thanne oure Lorde seyde to hem: 'Chyldryn, haue ȝe eny ȝowle?'; þat   56
ys to seye, enythynge þat maye be sode or ete. And they seyde, 'Naye',
and thanne he badde hem þat they schulde leye the nette in the rygh
syde of the schyppe and they schulde fynde, and so they dede as he
badde hem and thanne they mygthte vnnede drawe the nette for   60
myltytude of fyische.

And thanne seyde Seyint Ihon to Petyr: 'Hyt ys oure Lorde.' And
`whenne´ Petyr herde that hyt was oure Lorde, he dede on a cote and
sterte into the see of gret fe`r´uoure, þat he mygthte the sonnyr come
to oure Lorde. And tho, as hyt semyth be Lyre, he wente vp`on þe   65
watyr´ as he dede anothyr tyme to oure Lorde. But the othyre
dyscyplys cam be boote, for they were not, as the euangelsyte seyth,
fer fro the londe. And whenne they were come to the londe they
sawgh brennynge colys putt and fyische thervpon, and also they
sawgh brede there aredy. The`se´ thyngys were made of newe `be´ the   70
vertu of God to the more confermynge of the dyscyplys in the feyth of
the Resurreccyon, as Lyre seyth. And thanne oure Lorde seyde to
hem: 'Bryngyth of the fyischys þat ȝe haue cawfte now.' And `thanne´
Symon Petyr drewe the nette into þe londe ful of grete fyischys, in
numbyr an hundryd | fyfty and thre. And thanne oure Lorde ful   f. 124ʳ
suetly seyde to hem: 'Comyth and ethyth.' But none of hem that sate   76
`there´ att dynere dursthe aske hym: 'Hoo art thow?' Not for drede,
but for sykyrnesse of knowynge that they hadde of hym, as Lyre
seyth. As hoo seyth, thys apperynge was so opyn þat hyt nedyde not
to aske þat questyon, for the euangelyst seyth folowynge: 'Wytynge   80
wel þat hyt was oure Lorde, and therfore hyt hadde be but folye to
haue askyd that questyon.' And thanne thynkyth that oure Lorde toke
brede and ȝaf hem and fyische also.

The thyrde apperynge aftyr the daye of the Resurreccyon was to

50 hys brothyr] *om.* N   52 thynkyth] thenketh þat N   54 nothynge] noght N
54–5 in . . . see] apon þe seeside N   57 or] and N   60 the] *fol. by canc.* þe N
65 tho] þat N   vp`on´] on N   66 the] þat N   74 into] vnto N   75 an] a N
76 But] and N   77 att] at þe N   78 of¹] *om.* N   hym] *om.* N   80 aske] aske
hym N   81 folye] in veyne N   82 askyd] askede hym N   that] howe N   toke] toke
þe N

85 the dyscyplys in an hylle þat ys callyd Tabor, the whyche ys in Galyle
the contre, and hyt 'ys' foure myle fro Naȝareth, the cytee þat the
angyl salutyde oure Lady inne. And in the same hylle was oure Lorde
transffyguryd, as I haue forseyde in the xv chapetele of thys boke. And
in that hylle oure Lorde apperyde to hys dyscyplys, as ys seyde afore,
90 and to manye moo as Lyre seyth. And that he prouyth be þat that the
euangelyst seyth thus: 'Some of hem worschyppyde hym and some
doutyde.' Be the whyche wordys hyt ys opyn, he seyth that there were

f. 124ᵛ othyre thanne the apostlys the whyche were certyfyed of | hys
Resurreccyon, and also Thomas þat amonge othyre was moste
95 harde to beleue.

Aftyr thys ȝe maye thynke þat oure Lorde Ihesu cam 'to hem' þat
dowtyde, to certyfye hem also of hys Resurreccyon, and seyde to hem:
'All the powere in heuene and erthe ys ȝeue to me.' And thanne he
seyde to hem alle: 'Goyth and techyth alle folkys, baptysynge hem in
100 the name of the Fadyr and the Sone and the Holy Goste, techynge
hem to kepe all that euere I haue bode ȝow. And loo I am wyth ȝow
into the worldys ende'; the whyche maye specyally be vndyrstande of
þe precyouse sacrament, in the whyche he ys veryly and bodyly
present, and also of hys Godhede be the whyche he ys ouyrall present.
105 The ix apparycyon was to the dyscyplys syttynge in the sopynge
place where he repreuyde here vnbeleue and the hardenesse of here
hertys. The x and the laste of thyke þat ben conteynyd in the gospellys
was to 'hys dyscyplys' in the Mounte of Olyu'e'te. These to laste
apperyngys were ido in the daye of the Ascencyon, and therfore I wole
110 telle ȝow more opynly of hem in the medytacyon of the same
worschypful feste.

Anothyr apperynge ther ys ȝytt þat Seyint 'Poule' tellyth of in one
of hys pystyllys, but where or whenne he makyth no mencyon. And
that, he seyth, was to fyue hundryd brethryn togyderys, vndyrston-
115 dyth in feyth, rygth as 'alle' Crystyn peple be brethryn in feyth. |

f. 125ʳ Thys wyth that þat ys seyde in the othyre to chapetelys afore, I trowe
be inowgh of the Resurreccyon of oure Lorde. But in all thys ȝe
muste 'kepe' ȝowselfe in ȝoure ymagy'n'acyon as though ȝe were
present and seygh all thys doo afore ȝow, and beholdynge inwardly

89 as] as it N   96 ȝe maye thynke þat] thenketh howe N   101 ȝow] yow all
deyes N   104 hys] þe N   105 to] twice Gg   dyscyplys] elleuen disciples N
106 vnbeleue] vnkyndenes and mysbeleue N   107 thyke] þo N   gospellys] gospell N
109 the] his N   112 apperynge] om. N   115 feyth] in marg. ad corintheos xv hyt ys
trowyd and lykly inowf hyt ys the same appearinge þat ys seyde afore in the hylle of Tabor
Gg   116 the] þat N

oure Lordys gret mekenesse and charytee and how homely `he´ 120
spekyth wyth hys dyscyplys and schewyth hem so manye opyn
prouys of hys Resurreccyon, `as ben forseyde´ bothe for here profyte
and for ourys þat schulde come aftyrwarde. And so be hys grace schul
ȝe conseyue ioye and gladnesse wyth oure Lady and the apostlys of
hys Resurreccyon, ryght as ȝe haue hadde cause afore wyth hem of 125
heuynesse, pytee, and compassyon in the beholdynge of hys precyus
Passyon. Ffor sueche maner affeccyonys ben ful profytable to a
deuout seruaunt of God, specyally in hys begynnynge.

CHAPTER 32

Of the Ascencyon of oure Lorde and of the werkys þat maye be
consyderyd therabowte. Capitulum xxxii^m.

The Ascencyon of oure Lorde Ihesu Cryste was the fourythyeth daye
fro hys Resurreccyon, and that daye he apperyde too tymys; of the
whyche the fyrste was to the dyscyplys syttynge att mete in the cytee 5
of Ierusalem; the secunde was in the Mounte of Olyuete `in´ the oure
of hys Ascencyon.

The fyrste thanne was to the dyscyplys syttynge att mete in the
sopynge place, that | ys `to´ seye, in that place in Ierusalem þat oure f. 125^v
Lorde made hys laste sopere inne, where `he´ reprouyde here 10
vnbeleue and the hardnesse of here hertys, for they `be´leuyde not
hem þat hadde seye hym aryse. Thys maye `be´ vndyrstande too
manerys, as Lyre seyth. One maner not of the apostlys but of some
othyre þat were there wyth hem, the whyche not fully beleuyde the
apostlys of the Resurreccyon of oure Lorde. Anothyr manyr hyt maye 15
be vndyrstande of the apostlys, not of that vnbeleue þat `was´ in hem
þat tyme, but of þat that `was´ in hem aforetyme, as hyt ys opyn of
Seyint Thomas, þe whyche beleuyde not the othyre dyscyplys. And
also the othyre beleuyde not Marye Maudeleyne, the whyche `hadde´
seye hym, ne the othyr þat hadde seye hym also. And `att´ thys tyme 20
he ate wyth hem and whenne he hadde ete wyth hem he badde hem
goo to the Mounte of Olyuete for the`re he´ wolde appere to hem aȝen,

122 Resurreccyon] gloriouse resurreccioun N   123 schul] schulde N   125 wyth
hem] *om*. N   126 heuynesse] heuynes with N   127 maner] maner of N

Chapter 32   4 Resurreccyon] *fol. by canc.* of oure lorde Gg   6 the³] his N
8 thanne] *om*. N   11 vnbeleue] mysbeleue N   12 aryse] to haue rysen N
vndyrstande] vnderstonde in N   13 maner] mane N   14 there] *om*. N   16 that
vnbeleue] þe mysbeleue N   17 as] and N   18 not] not þat N   dyscyplys] disciples
dede N   19 the¹] þat N   20 the othyr] þat other wymmen N   22 to] into N

the whyche ys a myle fro Ierusalem. And hyt ys callyd the Mounte of
Olyuete for the plente of olyuys þat growyn there.

25 And thanne thynkyth þat he vanyischyde fro hem, and anone 'as'
they hadde ete, beholdyth how oure Lady and the xi apostlys and the
othyre dyscyplys and wymmen also wente togyderys to the forseyde
Mount of Olyuete, as oure Lorde hadde bode hem. And whenne they
were icome thedyr there oure Lorde apperyde to hem aȝen, and thys
f. 126ʳ 'was' the | secunde apperynge in the daye of the Ascencyon. And
31 thanne thynkyth þat some of hem þat were come togyderys there
askyde hym yf he schulde restore aȝen the Kyngedom of Israel that
tyme. Thys some doctorys expone gostly of the kyngedom þat ys to
come in the ioye of heuene, the 'whyche' schal be fully in alle chosyn,
35 bothe in body and soule, aftyr the general daye of dome. And some
vndyrstonde hyt of the temporal kyngedom of the pepyl of Israel, and
so ex'po'nyth hyt Lyre as to lettureall vndyrstondynge, for hyt maye
be vndyrstande bothe manerys. The Romaynys, ȝe schal vndyrstande,
hadde itake the temporal kyngedom fro the Iewys and ordeynyd an
40 alyon kynge amonge hem. And therfore the dyscyplys askyde oure
Lorde yf he schulde restore aȝen the kyngedom to the peple of Israel
þat tyme.

And thanne he seyde to hem: 'Hyt longyth not to ȝow to knowe the
tymys and the momentys þat the 'Fadyr' hath putt in hys powere', as
45 hoo seyth, hyt nedyth 'not' to ȝow to know that, ne to aske that
questyon. 'But', he seyde, 'ȝe schal take the vertu of the Holy Gooste
comynge into ȝow'; as hoo seyth, þat ys more necessarye to ȝow. 'And
ȝe schal be wytnessys to me in Ierusalem and in all Samarye and into
the laste ende of the erthe.' And also, as 'a'nothyr enaungelyste seyth,
f. 126ᵛ he badde hem goo forth into all | the world and preche the euangelye
51 to euery creature, that ys to seye, to mankynde. For by euery creature,
as doctorys seyin, here in thys texste ys vndyrstonde only man, for as
myche as he hath sumwhat wyth euery creature. For Seyint Gregory
seyth that 'he' hath to bee wyth stonys, to lyue wyth herbys, not be
55 soule but be grenesse, to fele wyth bestys, and to vndyrstonde wyth
angyllys.

Also oure 'Lorde seyde' to hys dyscyplys: 'That hooso wolde
beleue and 'be' baptysyd, he schulde be sauyd'; vndyrstondyth, yf

23 a myle] two myles N; see note 26 the²] þat N 27 to] into N; twice Gg
29 there] om. N 32 Israel] Israell in N 33 Thys] ȝitt N 34 ioye] blysse N
35 And] om. N 37 to] to þe N 38 vndyrstande] vnderstonde in N The] Ffor
the N 39 an] om. N 43 the] om. N 45 that] om. N 50 euangelye]
gospell N 53 wyth] of N Seyint] om. N 57 That] om. N

he leue theraftyr. 'And hoo wolde not, he schulde be dampnyd.' All
thys vndyrstondyth oure Lorde badde they schulde doo aftyr they 60
hadde resceyuyd the Holy Goste in a vysyble sygne. For they were not
bolde to do that þat tyme, and therfore hyt was necessarye that they
schulde be confermyd be the Holy Goste fyrste to doo so excellent a
werke. And whenne he hadde seyde þe forseyde wordys, thynkyth
how he lyfte ʻvpʻ hys handys and blyssyd hem, and so hem seynge, he 65
was lyfte vp be hys owyn mygthte and a clowde toke hym fro here
syghtte. Not þat he nedyde helpe of clowde, but to schewe therby þat
euery creature ys redy to doo seruyse to hys makare. And as they stode
lokynge vp into the skyewarde merueylynge of þat merueylus
ascencyon, too angyllys stode besyde hem in whyte clothys in the 70
lyknesse of men seyinge to hem: | 'Menne of Galylye', for manye of f. 127ʳ
hem were of the contre of Galyle, ʻwʻhʻereto stonde ʒe lokynge vp into
heuene? Thys Ihesu Cryste þat ys assumpte fro ʒow into heuene,
ryght so he schal come aʒen as ʒe haue seyin hym goynge into heuene';
þys ys to seye, in the same lyknessse þat ʒe haue seyin hym styinge 75
into heuene, in the same lyknesse schal he come aʒen to the general
dome. And ʻwhenneʻ they hadde seyde the forseyde wordys, they
vanyischyde aweye fro here syghtte.

Now thynkyth wyth a goode avysement wyth how myche ioye and
gladnesse the dyscyplys were fylde whenne ʻtheyʻ seygh oure 80
worschypful Lorde, the whyche they hadde seyin so holy, so suete,
and parfyth in all hys lyuynge, and att the laste was putt to so
despytʻeʻful deth, and aftyr that so gloryusly arose, and thanne so
opynly apperyde to hem, and also so famylyarly spake and ate wyth
hem at thys tym so merueylusly hem alle seyinge, stye into heuene. 85
And yf they were fylde wyth myche ioye and gladnesse, wyth how
myche ʻmoreʻ trowe ʒe was that blyssyd Lady, hys worthy modyr,
fylde, that louyde moste of alle othyre? And how gret desyre also
trowe ʒe hadde sche to haue goo wyth hym? God wote alone.
Notwythstandynge, hyt was ful necessarye þat sche schulde abyde 90
ʒytt in erthe for the conforte of the dyscyplys and also ʻtoʻ the
infor|mynge of the euangelystys of the incarnacyon and the ʒougthe f. 127ᵛ
of oure Lorde, for sche knewe þat best of alle othyre.

59 hoo] whoso N   he�²] om. N   60 vndyrstondyth] vnderstondeth þat N   badde]
badde þat N   aftyr] aftre þat N   62 that] om. N   63 confermyd] conformede N
6 nedyde] nedede þe N   of] of þe N   69 þat] þe N   73 heuene] heuenwarde N
75 þys] þat N   styinge] styynge vpp N   76 to] into N   79–80 wyth . . . gladnesse]
howe grete ioy N   80 fylde] fillede wyth N   83 deth] a deth N   85 hem²] to
hem N   88–9 also trowe ʒe] trowe yhe also trowe yhe N   89 sche] om. N

Thanne aftyr thys maye ȝe beholde how deuoutly wyth manye terys
95 the blyssyd Lady wyth the apostlys and alle the othyre þat were there
kyssyde the stappys that oure Lorde stode laste inne. The Maystyr of
Storyis seyth þat Suplycy, that was Byischoppe of Ierusalem, seyth
þat whenne a chyrche schulde haue be bylde`d´ in the place where
oure Lorde stode laste, the place þat oure Lordys feete stode laste inne
100 mygthte neuer be pauyd, but alweye the stonys wente aweye aȝen as
they were leyde and mygthte not abyde there. And also the stappys of
oure Lorde ben pryinte in the same place in the erthe, the whyche
lyknesse the same erthe kepyth stylle. And whenne they hadde
worschypyd that place, thynkyth how they wente aȝen fro the
105 Mount of Olyuete into Ierusalem, wyth gret ioye abydynge there
the comynge of the Holy Goste. And alle the apostlys and wymmen
were perseuerynge togyderys wyth oure Lady in prayere that they
mygthte be made the more abyl to the resceyuynge of the Holy
Gooste, þat oure Lorde hadde behette hem. And thys ys a gret
110 exsample to alle deuout men and wymmen how they schulde deuoutly
f. 128ʳ ȝeue hem to prayere, and specyally fro the Ascencyon | of oure Lorde
into Wytt Sondaye, that they mygthte be the ablyr to resceyuynge of
more specyal grace of the Holy Goste.

Here ȝe maye also deuoutly consydere the excellent benfeet of oure
115 Lorde Ihesu Cryste, how in hys gloryus Ascencyon he exaltyth oure
kynde aboue all angyllys. And to þat kynde, to the whyche was seyde
in Adam: 'Erthe þu arte, and into erthe þu schalte torne aȝen', ys now
seyde in oure Lorde Ihesu Cryste of hys Fadyr of heuene: 'Sytt on my
ryght syde.' And in that þat oure kynde ys onyd to God we be
120 worthyer thanne angyllys, as Seyint Austyn seyth in hys Solyloquyis
thus: 'God ys man, and man God, and not angyl. And therfore', seyth
he, 'I schal seye man wordyest of creaturys.' Also hyt schal be one of
þe specyal ioyes þat the chosyn of mankynde schal haue in the blysse
of heuene þat they schal see here kynde in God. How `myche´ thanne
125 be we bounde to loue, preyse, and thanke thys mercyful Lorde þat
thus myche worschype hath doo to oure kynde.

Thanne in the consyderacyon of thys gret benefeet of oure Lorde,
wyth othyre frely and mercyfully schewed and done to mankynde, ȝe

95 the othyre] *om.* N   96 The] Ffor the N   of] of þe N   97 that was] þe N
98 whenne] when þer schulde N   schulde haue be bylde`d´] be beildede N
98–9 where . . . place] *om.* N   99 þat] where N   101 the] *fol. by canc.* spa N
105 of] *om.* N   106 wymmen] wymmen þer N   109 þat] þe whiche N
111 and] *om.* N   112 to] to þe N   118 Lorde] *om.* N   122 seye] see N; *see note*
125 mercyful] worthieste N

maye falle to prayere and deuoutly wyth herte and mouth seye to hym
thus: 'Oracio, Lorde Ihesu Cryste, verry God and man, Kynge of 130
Kyngys and Lorde of Lordys, suettnesse, blyssydnesse, and prey-
synge of angyllys, floure, ioye, | and gladnesse of mankynde, f. 128ᵛ
worschype, ioye and preysynge be to the wyth the Fadyr and the
Holy Goste wythoute endynge. Amen.'

'Fferthyrmore, suete Lorde, blyssyd mote þu be þat of the wyll of 135
the Fadyr, wyrkynge wyth ȝow the Holy Goste, wolde frely and
mercyfully take mankynde of the blyssyde and clene virgyne Marye
and lyue in the same kynde xxxiiiᵗʸ wyntyr in myche pouerte and
penaunce, and att the laste for the saluacyon of the same kynde mekely
and pacyently suffre deth wyth myche pouerte, despyte, and payne; 140
and thanne goo to helle to fette out the holy fadrys soulys þat were
therinne; and the thyrde daye gloryusly aryse and appere to thy
blyssyd modyr and othyre deuout wymmen, and also to thyne
dyscyplys; and at þe laste, hem alle seynge, merueylusly ascende
'be' thyne owen mygthte and now syttyste on the ryght hande of thy 145
Fadyr, and schalt come aȝen in the same kynde to deme bothe quyke
and deede.'

'Lorde, these benfeetys to me and to all mankynde mercyfully
schewde and done, I knowleche 'to' the and blysse and thanke the
wyth alle myne herte of hem and alle othyre, mekely askynge of þat 150
vnspekeable charyte þat þu woldyste doo all thys for mankynge, and
be the same holy werkys forȝeuenesse of alle my synnys, grace of
dylygent amendement of hem and of all my lyuynge. And goode |
Lorde, þat 'þu woldyste' vowchasafe mercyfully to sende the Holy f. 129ʳ
Goste þat þu behettyste thy dyscyplys into my soule and make me thy 155
trewe seruaunt and meke louarys. And for trewe loue and clene
charytee so to be dylygent in the amendement of my lyuynge and
stabyll in the wyrkynge of thy wyll, bothe inwarde and outwarde
whyle hyt plesyth the, þat I lyue in thys valeye of wrecchydnesse be
grace, that whenne I schal be the partyd hennys I maye haue the to 160
myne euyrlastynge herytage and glad'nesse' in the meke companye of
thyne sayintys to loue and preyse the in ioye wythoute endynge.
Amen.

130 Oracio] *om.* N   131 and¹] *om.* N   suettnesse] suetnes and N   135 mote]
myghte N   142 thy] *fol. by canc.* to thy N   145 on] at N   hande] side N
148 Lorde] *fol. by canc.* of N   149 blysse] blysse the N   162 loue] loue þe N   in]
by N

CHAPTER 33

Of the comynge of the Holy Goste and sumwhat what the apostlys
dede aftyr they hadde rescyuyd the Holy Goste in a vysyble sygne,
and also a specyal commendacyon of the worschypful apostyl Seyint
Ihon euangelyste. Capitulum xxxiii^m and vltimatum^m.

5   Relygyus systyr, I haue tolde ȝow in the chapetele nexste afore of the
Ascencyon of oure Lorde. Now hyt were conuenyent to telle ȝow in
thys folowynge, also vndyr the forme of medytacyon, of the comynge
of the Holy Goste and a`l´so sumwhat what the apostlys dede aftyr
they hadde resceyuyd hym in a vysyble sygne. Ffyrste ȝe schal
10 vndyrstande þat `þe´ comynge of the Holy Goste `was´ the
f. 129ᵛ fyfthyeth | daye fro the Resurreccyon of oure Lorde and the tenthe
fro hys Ascencyon, in the whyche dayis, þat ys to seye, betuene the
Ascencyon and the comynge of the Holy Goste, Seyint Mathy the
apostyl was chose.

15   Thanne maye ȝe thynke fyrste þat whenne the dyscyplys were all
togyderys in the same place þat Seyint Mathy was chose inne into the
dygnyte of apostyl, the fyfthyeth daye, as ys forseyde, fro the
Resurreccyon of oure Lorde ther was sodeynely made a noyse fro
the eyre, a`s´ hyt hadde be a gret wynde or a dundyr, and in þat maner
20 noyse cam the Holy Goste and fylde alle þe house where they were
syttynge wyth a merueylus clerenesse. And there apperyde to hem
vysybly to here bodyly eyen, as hyt hadde be tungys of fyre isparblyd
abrode and satte vpon eueryche of hem to betokene, as Lyre seyth, be
þat vysyble sygne wythoute, the vnuysyble grace of þe Holy Goste
25 iresceyuyd wythinne, be the whyche they schulde be feruent in loue of
God and speke in alle langagys to þe openynge of the gospel. And so
they were fulfylde alle wyth the Holy Goste and beganne to speke in
dyuerse langagys as the Holy Gost ȝaf hem.
        And in that tyme thynkyth also þat there were duellynge in
30 Ierusalem Iewys, relygyus men, þat ys to seye, men ȝeuyn to the
f. 130ʳ worschypynge of God as the | maner of Iewys was that tyme of euery
nacyon þat ys vndyr heuene. And whenne they herde the forseyde
noyse fro the eyre, a multytude of hem cam thedyr to the dyscyplys of
oure Lorde merueylynge bothe of the noyse þat they hadde herde and
35 myche more for, whenne they cam to hem they herde hem speke the

---

Chapter 33   6 were conuenyent to] is conuenyente þat N   21 syttynge] duellynge N
23 eueryche] yche N   25 in] in þe N   26 openynge] publicacioun N   29 in
that] þat same N   also] *om.* N   34 they] and N

langagys þat they were borne inne. And thanne they wondryde alle
and merueylyde, seyinge togyderys: 'Be not alle these þat spekyn thus
men of Galyle?' 'And how haue we herde eueryche of vs the langage
þat he was borne inne?' And rekenyde manyr ʼof þe langagys and
contreyis thatʼ they were borne inne and some of hem scornyde hem   40
and seyde þat they were dronke of muste.

    And thanne maye ȝe beholde how Seyint Petyr stode vp wyth the xi
apostlys and schewde þat they were not dronke but fylde wyth the Holy
Gooste aftyr the prophecye of the prophete Ioel. And the same daye be
the prechynge of Petyr were iturnyd to the feythe abowte thre   45
thowsende soulys, and so Petyr þat fyrste was so ledye and ferful þat
he denyede oure Lorde att the voyce of a woman, att thys tyme, be the
grace of the Holy Goste was made so stronge þat he dredʼdeʼ no deth
and to preche the worde of God opynyly. And also bothe he and the
othyre dyscyplys þat fyrste kepte hemselfe close in an | howse for   f. 130ᵛ
drede ʼofʼ Iewys, and thurste not preche the worde of God in here owen 51
langage, att thys tyme be the mygthte of God and specyal grace of the
Holy Goste were made so stronge þat they dredde not to knowleche
God and preche hys worde in all langagys. For Seyint Gregory seyth
þat they began to preche oure Lorde Ihesu Cryste in an othyr langage   55
þat fyrste dredde to speke of hym in here owen. And also whenne the
pryncys of prestys forbede Petyr and Ihon þat they schulde no more
preche in the name of oure Lorde Ihesu Cryste, wyth gret constaunce
they seyde: 'Yf hyt be ryght in the syght of God to here ȝow rathyr
thanne God, deme ȝe. For þat we haue herde and seye, we maye not but   60
speke.' And thanne they dretyde hem and lett hem goo for a tyme, for
they thurste ʼnotʼ punyische hem opynly for drede of the peple.

    Anothyr tyme the prynce of prestys and the Saduceys caste hande
vpon the apostlys and putte hem in opyn prysone. The Saduceys were
men of a secte þat tyme in Ierusalem þat denyde that ther schulde be   65
eny Resurreccyon or angyl or spyryt; these consentyde to þe pryncys
of prestys in the persecucyon of the apostlys, for they prechyde the
resurreccyon þat they denyede. But aftyr the apostlys were putte in
prysone, the angyl of oure Lorde ledde hem out and badde hem goo
and teche in the tem|ple the weye of Crystyn lyf. And so in the   f. 131ʳ
mornynge theʼyʼ wente into the temple and tawgthe.   71

    38 eueryche] yche N   39 he was] we were N   42 how] *om.* N   45 were]
was N   46 ledye] weyke N   48 the] þat N   50 ʼofʼ] of þe N   51 langage]
langages N   63–4 hande vpon] to take N   65 a] on N   þat tyme] *om.* N
71 into] in N

Aftyr thys ȝe maye thynke how the prynce of prestys and they þat
were wyth hym, wenynge þat they hadde be ȝytt stylle in prysone,
callyde togydere here conseyil þat they mygthte take avysement what
75 they mygthte do wyth hem, for therfore they were putt in prysone þat
they schulde be browghte to dome, and so they sente to the prysone
aftyr hem. And ʻwhenneʼ the seruauntys cam thedyr and openyde the
prysone and fonde hem not therinne, they wente aȝen to hem and
seyde: ʻWe fonde the prysone schytt wyth all maner dylygence and the
80 keparys stondynge afore the gatys. And thanne we openyde hyt, but
we fonde no man therinne.ʼ And ʻwhenneʼ the maystyr of the temple
and the pryncys of the prestys herde these wordys, they dowtyde
gretly what was doo of hem. And ʻthanneʼ ther cam one and seyde:
ʻThe men þat ȝe putte in prysone stonde in the temple techynge the
85 peple.ʼ And ʻthanneʼ the maystyr of the temple wente wyth seruauntys and browgthte hem wythoute vyolence. And whenne they
hadde browgthte hem, they browgthte hem also into the conseyil, and
thanne the prynce of prestys seyde to hem: ʻIn commaundynge we
forbede ȝow þat ȝe schulde no more teche in thys nameʼ; þat ys to
90 seye, in the name of oure Lorde Ihesu Cryste. ʻAnd ȝytt ȝe haue fylde
Ierusalem wyth ʻȝoureʼ doctryne.ʼ

f. 131ᵛ And than|ne Petyr and the apostlys ansueryde and seyde: ʻWe
muste obeye to God more thanne to men.ʼ And whenne they herde
thys, they were made blynde in here hertys for angyr and vnpacyence
95 and thowgthte to scle hem. And ʻthanneʼ ther arose vp one in the
conseyil whas name was Gamalyel, a doctur of the lawe and ʻaʼ
worschypful man to all the peple, and be hys goode conseyil he
suagyde here malyce aȝenste hem. Thys Gamalyel, as Seyint Clement
seyth in a pystyl, was a dyscypyl of the apostlys and be conseyil of the
100 apostlys he was amonge the Iewys þat he schulde suage here malyce
aȝenste hem, as he dede. And ȝytt at the laste thynkyth þat they
callyde the apostlys and made hem to be scorgyd and so lett hem goo,
forbedynge hem as the Maystyr of Storyis seʻyʼth, vndyr the dretynge
of deth þat they ʻschuldeʼ no ʻmoreʼ preche in the name of oure Lorde
105 Ihesu Cryste. For thowgh they were suagyd of here malyce be
Gamalyelys conseyil as for to scle hem, ȝytt they were not so clerely

75 were putt] hadde putt hem N   76 schulde] shulde haue N   82 of the prestys]
om. N   83 was] was to N   85 wyth] with his N   86 hem] hem oute N
87 also] om. N   89 thys] his N   90 oure Lorde] om. N   93 more] corr. mark
with rathyr in the marg. Gg   99 be] by the N   106 Gamalyelys] in marg. be the
conseyil of gamalyel

suagyd but that they made hem be scorgyd er they lefte hem, for hyt
was fayre þat he mygthte suage hem so myche. And ʼthanneʼ
beholdyth dylygently how they wente fro the conseyil ioyinge þat
they were made wordy to suffre wronge for the name of oure Lorde   110
Ihesu Cryste.

Thys, gostly systyr, I haue schortly seyde to ʒow of the werkys | f. 132ʳ
the apostlys aftyr the comynge of the Holy Goste þat ʒe or enye othyr
deuout seruaunt of God maye [vndyrstonde] hereby how stronge they
were made be the specyal grace of the Holy Goste þat they hadde   115
resceyuyd, þat for no wordys ne strokys ne dretynge of deth sesyde to
preche Crystyn feyth. And also wyth so gret ioye and gladnesse toke
despyte and wronge for oure Lordys loue, as ys forseyde, that afore
hys Passyon were to ledye and dredful þat they forsoke hym
euerychone and aftyrwarde kepte hemselfe close in an howse for   120
drede of Iewys. And ʼþysʼ maye be ʼþeʼ medytacyon of the comynge of
the Holy Goste, and sumwhat what the apostlys dede aftyr they
ʼhaddeʼ resceyuyd hym. And thus I ende these symple medytacyonys.
Deo gracias.

Gostly syster, now here comyth to mynde the beheste þat I behette   125
ʒow in xxiiᵉᵗʰ chapetele of thys boke, þat ys, þat I wolde telle ʒow
more of þe commendacyon of the worthy apostyl Seyint Ihon
euangelyste to the worschype of God and to the encressynge of
ʒoure decuocyon ʼorʼ of eny othyr deuout seruaunt of God, to God
and to the same holy apostyl. For I mygthte not tarye conuenyently to   130
longe in the forseyde chapetele, for the matere þat I hadde there in
hande of the Passyon of oure Lorde, and therfore here in the laste
cʼhʼapetele of thys boke be the grace of | God, I purpose to parforme   f. 132ᵛ
my promysse as I haue behette ʒow in the chapetele forseyde.

Iohn ys exponyed the grace of oure Lorde or in whom grace ys, [or   135
to whom grace was ʒeue], or to whom aʒenste was ʒeue of God. Be
these ʼiiiiʼ exposysyonys of hys name be vndyrstonde foure pryuylegys
þat were in Seyint Iohn. The fyrste ys the specyal loue of oure Lorde
Ihesu Cryste, for he louyde hym afore othyre and grettyr tokenys of
loue and famylyaryte schewde to hym, and therfore he ys seyde the   140
grace of oure Lorde as ho seyth gracyus to oure Lorde. The secunde

107 be] *om.* N   lefte hym] lette hem go N   110 the] *om.* N   114 vndyrstonde]
vnderstonde N; vndystode Gg   119 ledye] weyke N   126 in] in þe N   133 to]
to fulfyl and N   134 haue] *om.* N   135 oure Lorde or] God N   135–6 or . . .
ʒeue] *om.* N; *in marg.* Gg   137 ʼiiiiʼ exposysyonys] exposicouns N   hys] þis N
138 specyal] *fol. by canc.* the specyal Gg   loue] louynge N   139 afore] aboue al N
grettyr] getter N

ys the incorrupcyon of fleyisch, for he was chose a mayde of oure
Lorde, and therfore he ys seyde in whom grace ys, for in hym was þe
grace of [vyrgynytee]. The thyrde ys the schewynge of pryuyteys, for
145 hyt was ȝeue to hym to knowe manye pry`uy´teys and depe thyngys,
as of the Godhede of oure Lorde and of the worldlys ende, and
therfore he ys seyde, to whom grace was ȝeue. The fourethe pryuylege
ys the recommendynge of Godys modyr, and of that he ys seyde, to
whom a ȝyfte was ȝeue of God, for tho a gret ȝyfte was ȝeue to hym of
150 God whenne Godys modyr was commyttyd to hym. And thys
suffysyth of the expocysyon of the name, and þys maner expocysyon
as to the menynge ys conteynyd in the Legende þat ys callyd Aurea,
afore hys lyf.

As to the commendacyon of the worsc`h´ypful apostyl Seyint Ihon
155 euangelyste, ȝe schal vndyrstande fyrste þat he was oure Lo`r´deys
cosyn, as in the kynde of man, for he was `oure Ladyis´ syst`r´ys sone,
as I haue forseyde in the xiiii chapetele of thys boke. And whenne he
schulde haue be weddyd, as Seyint Ierom seyth in the Prologe vpon
hys Gospel, oure Lorde callyde hym therfro, and so made hym one of
160 hys dyscyplys and kepte `hym´ stylle a clene virgyne. And for the
clennesse of vyrgynytee, as doctorys seyin, oure Lorde louyde hym
afore othyre, and therfore he schewde hym moste of hys pryuyteys
and moste famylyaryte and sygins of specyall loue. For Adam
Cartusyens seyth in a worthy `sermon´ þat he makyth of `t´hys
165 worschypful apostyl þat oure Lorde Ihesu Cryste worschypyde hym
in hys lyf thre wysys, þat ys to seye, in ȝeuynge hym vyrgynytee,
clennesse, and famylyarytee: vyrgynyte in body, clennesse in soule,
ffamylyaryte in suete and clene loue to hym. Of these thre lett vs see
now be rowe.

170 The fyrste ys vygynytee in body, for oure Lorde chese hym a
virgyne, as Seyint Ierom seyth in the Prologe vpon hys Gospel, as ys
forseyde, and also vpon the Apocalypse. And `he´ that `was´ chose a
mayde of God, be ȝe sykyr, be the grace of God abode stylle a mayde
foreuere. Dubbyl wytnesse of hys vyrgynytee ys in hys euangelye, as
Seyint Ie|rom seyth in the forseyde Prologe. One ys þat oure `Lorde´
176 louyde hym afore othyre. Anothyr ys that he commyttyde hys modyr

142 the] *om.* N   was] *fol. by canc.* he was Gg   144 vyrgynytee] virgynyte N;
vyrgytee Gg   148 of that] þerof N   149 tho] why N   150 Godys modyr] þe
moder of God N   155 ȝe] þe N   156 as] *om.* N   157 I haue] it is N
158 schulde] wolde N   vpon] of N   166 lyf] lyfe in N   172 that] that so N
174 hys] þe N   as] of N   175 seyth] *om.* N

to hym, the whyche ys an euyrlastynge virgyne, whenne he hynge
vpon the crosse, þat a virgyne mygthte kepe a virgyne.

The secunde ys clennesse in soule, as to thys Adam Cartusyens seyth
in hys sermon thus: 'Whyche of vs maye comprehende how myche 180
clennesse in herte and how myche clerenesse in mynde he hadde?
Fforsothe, he was a man of myche clennesse the whyche ouyrpassyde
alle vysyble thyngys and also hymselfe, and sawgh be the clerenesse of
the inner eye, Godys 'sone' to be in the begynnynge and to be att God
and to be God, and all thynge to be made be hym and wythoute hym no 185
thynke be made, and that þat ys made to be lyf in hym. Art þu not
compellyd', seyth the forseyde doctur, 'to merueyle gretly and to
wondre whenne þu heryste hys gospel red, herynge 'hym' so propyrly
and be rowe, aftyr so loonge tyme, telle the wordys of oure Lorde to
othyre and of othyre to hym, as thowgh he hadde herde hem the same 190
oure? And therfore wher othyre euangelystys be lyknyd to goynge
bestys, he, for the synglere perrogatyf of clennesse þe whyche oure
Lorde ȝaf hym, ys lyknyd to an egle, and not symply to an egle, but to
an egle fleynge.' For an egle | fleynge ys Seyint Ihon, vndyrstondyth in f. 134ʳ
lyknesse, afore othyre comprehendynge be the clennesse of soule the 195
hye pryuyteys of eurylastynge mysteryis. Thys wytnesseth the merueylus depnesse of hys gospel, and þat also cryeth the Apocalypse, þat
ys to seye, the Reuelacyon of oure Lorde Ihesu Cryste. In the 'whyche'
Apocalypse, as doctorys seyin, he wrote the notable thyngys þat
schulde falle in holy chyrche fro hys tyme into 'þe' worldys ende. 200
And the'r'fore wel and conuenyently we synge and seye of hym þat
oure Lorde fedde hym wyth the brede of lyfe and vndyrstondynge, and
ȝaf hym drynke the watyr of heleful wysedom.

Also, worschypful Bede seyth in a sermon þat he makyth of hym of
hys doctryne thus: 'All Seyint Ihonnys doctryne semyth so bespronge 205
wyth the salte of wysedom of God þat he maye be seyde in meryte the
mowth of God, þe tunge of the Holy Goste, a cedyr tre of paradyse,
þe worschype of the worlde, the bedyll of heuene, the lyght of þe
erthe, the sterre of men, the fayrenesse of angyllys, a quyke stone, a
myrrowre of lyf, the spekynge place of the Godhede, the forme of 210
God, a pylowre of þe temple, a makare of the verry tabernacle þat
God hath sette and not man.'

179 as to] and as N   184 inner eye] euerlastynge N   186 thynke] thynge to N
187 seyth] seyth he N   195 soule] soule in N   205 Seyint . . . doctryne] þe
doctryne of seynte Iohn N   206 of] of þe N   211 a²] þe N   makare] *in marg.*
makare Gg

Now of the thyrde poyint, þat ys to seye, of the famylyaryte þat
f. 134ᵛ oure Lorde vowschedesaf to haue wyth hym | afore othyre, sumwhat
215 lete vs seye. Wyth how myche glad suettenesse and suete gladnesse
maye we be clyppe hym in oure affeccyonys, amonge othyre moste
belouyd of oure Lorde and also be clyppyd in a maner synglere
famylyaryte afore othyre, thys dyscypyl seyth of hymselfe as hyt were
of anothyr in diuerse placys of hys gospel thus: 'The dyscypyll þat
220 Ihesu Cryste louyde'. What ys betokenyd therby, trowe ȝe? Louyde
not oure Lorde othyre? Ȝys, for'so'the dede he. But he wolde to be
vndyrstonde therby þat oure `Lorde' louyde hym afore othyre, as
Seyint Austyn seyth vpon hys gospel.

'O hye and ful blyssydnesse', seyth Adam Cartusyens, 'to loue
225 Cryste and to be louyd of Cryste and to haue famylyaryte wyth hym.
But how', seyth he, 'was Seyint Ihon belouyd of hym and famylyar
wyth hym? Whenne was eny of the apostylys att the pryuyteys of oure
Lorde Ihesu Cryste that Seyint Ihon was fro? Where hyt fylle hym to
be sente out, to whom was hytt ȝeue to be resceyuyd?' As ho seyth, to
230 none. 'Seygh hym Petyr and Iamys transfyguryd in the hylle, and not
Ihon? The nyghtte afore the daye of hys Passyon, whenne he wente to
p`r'aye, toke he wyth hym Petyr and `Iamys and' not Ihon? Wolde he
haue Petyr and Iamys att the araysynge of the thowghtyr of the chefe
man of the synagoge, and putt aweye Iohn? Ȝe schal nowre fynde eny
235 pryuyte icommunyd to eny dyscypyl ihydde fro Seyint `Ihon'.'

f. 135ʳ Neuyrdeles he was admit|tyd to some thyngys, and `þat' ryght
famylyarly and so myche more famyllyarly þat hyt was vttyrly
synglerely, that same thynge opynly and stedfastly berynge wytnesse
none to be pere to hym, þat I seye not hyer in the loue of charyte
240 whyle none deseruyde to be pere wyth hym in the resceyuynge of
famylyaryte. Herefore hyt ys þat I maye brynge sumwhat in opyn that
he restyde vpon oure Lordys breste in hys laste sopere, makynge hym
a pylow of oure Lordys holy breste. Fful louely was þat hede to oure
Lorde þat he wolde suffre to reste vpon hys breste, and thys `was' a
245 gret famylyaryte. Neuy`r'deles, hyt was wythoute, but wythinne was
myche more, for hyt was inwardly. Fforsothe, wythoute, Seyint
Iohnnys heede restyde vpon oure Lordys breste; but wythinne hys
heede, þat ys to seye, hys soule sette and restyde hytselfe in the

216 affeccyonys] affeccioun N   othyre moste] all other beste N   217 clyppyd]
belouede N   228 fylle] befelle N   230 transfyguryd] trasfigurede N   231 Ihon]
seynte Ihon N   232 `and'²] and toke N   233 the¹] om. N   236 ryght] full N
239 none] no N   247 oure] his N   wythinne] in N   2248 sette] in marg. sat N

tresourys of wysedom and kunnynge, the whyche alle be hydde in
oure Lordys breste.   250
   Now what schal we seye to that þat in the daye aftyr hys laste
sopere 'whenne' he wolde dye for all mankynde and hyt was nere the
tyme þat he wolde ȝelde the spyryt in the handys of hys Fadyr, he
wolde vowchesafe to commende hys belouyd modyr to hys belouyd
dyscypyl, that a virgyne mygthte kepe a virgyne? What tellyth thys 255
Ihon in hys gospell whenne he seyth oure 'Lorde' seygh hys modyr
and the dyscypyl standynge þat he louyde? He seyde to hys modyr:
'Womman, loo thy sone.' And aftyr he seyde to the dyscypyl: 'Loo,
thy modyr.' O | worschype aboue all worschype that maye be hadde f. 135ᵛ
in þys lyfe, to be oure Lorde Ihesu Crystys brothyr and in a maner 260
oure Ladyis sone, and 'to' thys hy worschype alone was Seyint Ihon
specyally chose. To what man euer seyde oure Lorde Ihesu Cryste of
hys modyr, 'Loo, thy sone', but to Seyint Ihon euangelyste? Or of
whom to hys modyr: 'Womman, lo thy sone', but of Seyint Ihon. Ath,
how myche belouyd was to the o innocent lombe, meke and suete 265
Ihesu how myche was he belouyd of the to whom þu woldyste
commytte to be kepte þat precyouse tresoure of heuene and erthe,
thy modyr? Thow seydyste to thy modyr, 'Loo thy sone', and to the
dyscypyll, 'Loo, thy modyr'. I beseke, what menyth thys? Why
byddyste þu not thy dyscypyll seyinge: 'Serue and mynystyr and do 270
seruyse to here as to thy lady and my modyr?' And why seydyste not
also to thy modyr: 'Vse the seruyse of my dsycypyll as thy seruaunt?'
But hyt semyth to soune myche hyer and worschyfullyer þat þu
seydyste of thy dyscypyll to thy modyr, 'Lo thy sone', and of thy
modyr to thy dyscypyll, 'Loo thy modyr'. Ys not thys to seye, in a 275
maner: 'Into thys tyme whyle I was wyth the, not only I was to the a
sone in trewthe, but also I was to the a deuout 'sone' in obeynge. Now
forsothe, for here, as þu seyste, I dye vpon thys 'crosse' and 'so' be þat
goo fro the bodyly, I am not wyth the. I wole not thowgh, thowgh þu
mayest not haue 'me' att þys tyme, þat þu be wythoute a sone. Haue 280
thys 'for a sone' in my stede and | þu, in stede of me, take here as f. 136ʳ
thyne modyr. Modyr, amonge wymmen in þys worlde þu haste no
pere. None amonge hem þat ben of thyne kynde, dyscypyll, in þe
worlde ys aboue the. Wherfore, hyt ys semely that sygh sche in the

251 to that] þerto N   251 all] *om.* N   253 in] into N   254 belouyd]
welbelouyd N   259 O] One N   264 Ath] a N   267 of] to N   268 the] þi N
269 beseke] beseche þe N   270 thy²] þe N   271 seydyste] seydeste þou N
273 worschyfullyer] more worshipfull N   275 Loo] loue N   279 bodyly] *om.* N
thowgh] *om.* N

285 kynde of wymmen in bodyly incorrupcyon hath no pere, thow
forsothe in mankynde, outtake me, haste no souerayne þat ȝe be
iunyd togyderys. Lete a virgyne take hede to a virgyne, Ihon to
Marye, Marye to Ihon, sche be modyrly affeccyon, þu be seruyse and
sonely bysynesse.

290   Loo, gostly systyr, how gret a sygne of specyall loue and truste thys
was of oure Lorde þat he wolde commytte thus louely hys worschypful modyr to thys blyssyd apostyl. And thys ys a worschype aboue all
the worschype þat maye be hadde in thys worlde, for be thys
cowplynge togyderys of oure Lady and Seyint John he maye in a
295 maner be callyd oure Ladyis sone and oure Lordys brothyr, and so
callyth hym worschypful Bede in a sermon þat he makyth of hym, and
Adam Cartusyens also in hys sermon, as ȝe haue herde afore. And
therfore lete vs loue and worschype hym þat oure Lorde so specyally
louyde and worschypyde, for the forseyde Adam seyth also of hym in
300 hys sermon thus: 'Oure Lorde Ihesu Cryste worschypyde hym.
Wherfore hyt ys wordy þat hosoeuere be oure Lorde Ihesu Crystys
f. 136ᵛ seruaunt worschype hym. | For amonge men, whom the kynge
worschypyth, alle the kyngys seruauntys be wonde to worschype.'
Also, worschypful Bede seyth, almoste in the begynnynge of hys
305 sermon þat he also makyth of hym thus: 'Fforsothe hyt ys worthy þat
he that was specyally belouyd of Cryste afore all deedly men, also
moste belouyd of Crystys trewe peple.'

Thus ȝe haue herde sumwhat be the grace of oure Lorde how he
worschypyde hys specyally belouyd dyscypyll, Seyint Ihon euange-
310 lyste, in hys lyfe thre manerys, þat ys to seye, in ȝeuynge hym amonge
othyre ȝyftys of hys grace the whyche he made hym ryche wyth
vyrgynyte in body, clennesse in soule, and loue in clene famylyaryte,
or yf hyt be bettyr 'seyde' so, famylyaryte in clene loue, aftyr the
seyinge of a worthy clerke þat ys callyd Adam Cartusyens (or in more
315 opyn Englyisch, Adam of the Charturhowse).

Gostly systyr, for ȝe haue herde afore how oure Lorde worschypyde hys specyally belouyd dyscypyll, Seyint Ihon euangelyste, in hys
lyfe, now hyt were goode to here how he worschypyde hym also in hys
deth. And 'as' to thys, ȝe schal vndyrstande þat ryght as he
320 worschypyde hym thre wysys in hys lyfe, ryght so he worschypyde
'hym othyre' thre wysys in hys deth, as the forseyde Adam seyth. The

---

287 hede] tente N   288 Marye¹] Mary and N   297 Adam] Adam Cartusiense N
also] *om.* N hys] a N   310 lyfe] lyfe in N   313–15 aftyr . . . Charterhowse] *this*
phrase is placed after wyth *two lines earlier in* N   319 a] *om.* N   319 þat] *om.* N

fyrste ys that oure Lorde hymselfe cam to hym afore hys deth. The
secunde ys þat, as hyt ys leefful to be beleuyd, he ledde hys hooly |
soule to euyrlastynge ioye. The thyrde ys that aftyr hys deth ther was   f. 137ʳ
founde nothynge in hys sepulcre but angyllys brede. All thys maye be   325
seye be rowe in hys *Legende* almoste abowte the ende.

As to the fyrste, we rede in hys *Legende* that oure Lorde apperyde
to hys derelynge wyth hys dyscyplys and seyde: 'Come to me, my
derelynge, for hyt ys tyme þat þu ete wyth thy bredryn in my feste.'
As to the secunde, we rede there also that whenne oure Lorde hadde   330
seyde the forseyde wordys to hym, he arose vp and began to goo. And
thanne oure Lorde seyde to hym: 'A Sondaye þu schalt come `to me'.'
And whenne the Sondaye was come, alle the peple cam togyderys in
the chyrche þat was foundyd in hys name, to the whyche he prechyde
fro the fyrste koc crowynge, byddynge hem þat they schulde be   335
stedfaste in the feythe and feruent in the kepynge of the commaundmentys of God. And aftyr that he dede make a foure corneryd
sepulcre besyde the autyr and the erthe to be caste out of the chyrche.
And thanne he wente downe thereinnne and lefte vp hys handys to
God and seyde: 'Lorde Ihesu, I `y'bode to thy feste. Loo, I come. Loo,   340
I come thankynge the þat þu vouchestsafe to calle me to thy feste,
wytynge þat wyth all myne herte I desyryde the.' And whenne he
hadde prayde, so gret a lyght schone vp on hym þat ther myghte no
man loke on hym and wyth that lyght, vndyrstondyth, hys | holy   f. 137ᵛ
soule wente to euyrlastynge ioye. As to the thyrde poyint, þat ys to   345
seye, þat aftyr hys deth ther was nothynge founde in hys sepulcre but
angyllys brede, we rede also in hys *Legende* that whenne the forseyde
lyght was goo, the graue founde ful of angyllys brede, the whyche in
the same place into thys daye, as hyt `ys' seyde, ys brought forth there
so þat hyt semyth in the bottome of the sepulcre to quelle vp as hyt   350
were small grauel, as hyt `ys' wonde to doo in wellys, and thys ys a
gret and `an' vnherde myracle.

Loo, gostly systyr, how fayre an ende thys worschypful apostyl and
euangelyste hadde. Forsothe iredde neuer a fayrer, ne I trowe ȝe herde
neuer a fayrer of eny sayint. And here vndyrstondyth how myche oure   355
Lorde louyde hym that vouchedsaf to vysyte hym and calle hym in

323 beleuyd] belouede N   324 to] to his N   325 All] all `al' N   As] and
as N   330 there] *om.* N   332 A] on N   333 in] into N   337 make] to be
made N   340 I¹] I am N   344 on] apoun N   346 founde] *om.* N
347 *Legende*] legende founde N   350 hyt semyth] *om.* N   sepulcre] sepulcre it
semeth N   quelle] welle N   351 were small] *om.* N   352 and . . . myracle]
merueyle and an vnherde N   355 here] herby N

hys owen persone, and ȝaue hym so fayre an ende and worschypyde
hys sepulcre wyth so synglere a myracle þat ther was founde nothynge
þerinne but manna, þat ys callyd in Englyisch angyllys brede, for hyt
360 was worthy as Adam Cartusyens seyth in hys sermon, þat angyllys
brede schulde make fayre the place þat the vyrgynys body wente inne.

Also, worschypfull Bede seyth, in the sermon þat he makyth of
hym of hys passynge ʽfro þe worldeʼ thus: 'So hyt ʽwasʼ worthy þe
dyscypyll belouyd to the auctur of lyfe to passe oute of thys worlde,
f. 138ʳ þat so he mygthte be stroonge fro the | sorowe of deth as he was
366 alyene fro the corrupcyon of fleyisch. Of how myche reuerence', seyth
he, 'ys þys blyssyd Ihon to be hadde amonge men, whom the makare
of lyfe worschypyde lyuynge in flesche and also passynge out of thys
worlde.'

370 Thus ȝe haue schortly herde, belouyd systyr in God, how oure
Lorde Ihesu Cryste worschypyde hys derelynge, Seyint ʽIhonʼ apostyl
and euangelyste, in hys deth also thre wysys, þat ys to seye in
visytynge hym in hys deth, in ledynge hys soule to euyrlastynge
ioye, and in makynge fayre hys sepulcre be a newe and an ʽvnʼherde
375 myracle.

Now hyt ʽwereʼ also conuenyent and comfortable to knowe, hoso
mygthte, how oure Lorde that thus worschypyde hys worschypful
apostyl in ʽhysʼ lyfe and in hys deth be grace, how myche he hath
worschypyd hym now in euyrlastynge ioye. But þat maye no man seye
380 ne telle lyuynge in deedly flesche, for Seyint Poule seyth þat neythyr
eye hath seye, ne eere herde, ne ʽhytʼ hath come into mannys herte þat
oure Lorde hath ordeynyd to hem þat loue hym. Notwythstandynge,
thowgh hyt maye not be seyde as hyt ys, ȝytt sumwhat maye be
conseyuyd ʽtherʼof be þe grace of God and in partye be seyde. And so
385 sumwhat be þat oure Lorde ȝaue hys belouyd dyscypyl in thys ʽlyfeʼ
be grace, maye ʽbeʼ conseyuyd in partye what he hath ȝeue hym in
euyrlastynge lyfe be ioye. Wherfore sumwhat of the mercy of ʽGodʼ
f. 138ᵛ trustynge, I wole seye ther | to þat I hope maye be trewly conseyuyd
aftyr goode conscyence and seyinge of holy doctorys.

390 Aftyr the seyingys of doctorys, ther bee too medys in the blysse of
heuene þat oure Lorde ȝeuyth to chosyn soulys. That one ys callyd
essencyal and þat ys souerayne and pryncepal, as ys loue and

359 manna] manna and N   364 auctur] auter N   366 alyene] alyue N
367 amonge] to N   370 belouyd] welbelouede N   371 hys] his blyssede N
374 an] *om.* N   378 in ʽhysʼ] and euangeliste in þis N   380 Seyint] þe apostell N
381 eye] he N   384 conseyuyd] conseruede N   386 conseyuyd] conseruede N
388 conseyuyd] conseruede N   391 That] *om.* N

knowynge of oure Lorde aftyr þe mesure of charytee iȝeue of God to a
soule lyuynge in deedly flesche; thys mede ys best and souerayne, for
hyt ys God hymselfe, and hyt ys commune to alle chosyn soulys þat 395
schal be sauyd, in what state or degre they bee inne lyuynge in holy
chyrche, more and lasse aftyr þe quantyte and mychylnesse of here
charytee. As to thys mede, I wote neuer ho mygthte be seyde hyer in
the blysse of heuene thanne Seyint Ihon euangelyste of a clene man
but oure Lady alone, for the synglere `grace´ þat was ȝeue to here 400
afore alle othyre. And that maye trewly be seyde of Seyint Ihon
euangelyste, for the gret clennesse þat was ȝeue to hym bothe in body
and soule, and the hynesse of knowynge of the Godhede and the
pryuyteys of God, as wytnessyn hys gospel and the Apocalypse and
also hys pystyllys. And hyt `ys´ no dowte þat he that was so specyally 405
belouyd of oure Lorde and hadde of hys grace so hy knowynge þat he
louyde hym synglerely. Wherfore, as in þat mede þat ys callyd
essencyal, I wote neuer ho mygthte þat ys only of mankynde be
preferryd | afore Seyint Ihon euangelyste but oure Lady, alone as ys f. 139ʳ
forseyde. 410

Anothyr mede ther ys þat ys callyd accydental, and þat ys
secundarye, þe whyche oure Lorde ȝeuyth for specyal goode dedys
þat a man doyth wylfully, ouer þat he ys bounde to. Of thre dedys
specyally doctorys of holy chyrche make mencyon, as of martyrdom,
prechynge, and maydynhode. These thre haue an excellence or 415
wordynesse afore othyre, and in as myche as they passe othyre
the`y´ schul haue a specyal mede þe whyche `ys´ callyd an auryole.
And þat `ys´ nowght ellys but a synglere worschype and a specyal toke
iordeynyd of God in rewarde of that specyal dede by fore othyre men
and wymmen þat dede not so, ouyr þat souereyne `mede´ of loue of 420
God, the `whyche ys´ commune to hem and to alle othyre. These thre
auryolys hath Seyint Ihon euangelyste, þat ys to seye, the auryole of
martyrdom, the auryole of prechynge, and the auriole of maydynhode, for he ys a martyr, a doctor, and a virgyne.

A martyr he ys, for he was putt in `a´ tunne ful of brennynge oyle 425
afore a gate of Rome þat ys callyd Latyne. And therfore he hath the
crowne of martydom, þe whyche ys an auryole, as ys forseyde, for the
redynesse of soule þat was in hym to suffre martyrdom whenne `he´

397 mychylnesse] mekenes N   398 As] and as N   409 as] as it N   411 ys³] is
þe N   412 for] for a N   dedys] dede N   414 make] makynge N   420 and
wymmen] *om.* N   þat²] þe N   of] of þe N   421 commune] comen N   425 in]
into N

was caste into the forseyde tunne. And therfore seyth Seyint Austyn
430 that hyt ys not vnpere meryte of pacyence in Seyint Ihon þat suffryde
f. 139ᵛ not | and in Petyr þat suffryde passyon, for thowgh be the mygthte of
God hyt mygthte no`t´ greue hym, ȝytt he dede that in hym was, and
therfore hyt ys approuyd and worschypyd of holy [chyrche] as for a
martyrdom. And the daye `ys´ þe vi daye of Maye and hyt ys wryte in
435 the kalendere in Latyn: 'Sancti Iohannis ante Portam Latinam'. And
Englyisch peple callyd hyt comunely in Englyisch, Seyint Ihon
Portelatyneys Daye. And so he hath the crowne of matyrdom, the
whyche ys an auryole, as ys forseyde.

A doctur also he ys, for he ys one of þe apostlys, the whyche `bee´
440 the chefe doctorys of holy chyrche. And also he ys `a´ doctur in hys
wrytynge, as wytnessyn hys gospel, hys pystyllys, and the Apocalypse.
And so he hath the auryole of prechynge. Also a virgyne he ys, for he
ys a virgyne chose of oure Lorde, as Seyint Ierom seyth in the
Prefacyon afore hys gospel and also afore the Apocalypse. And othyre
445 doctorys also seyin the same. And so he hath also the auryole of
vygynytee. And thus ȝe maye opynly vndyrstande be þat that ys
forseyde þat he hath `þe´ thre auroyolys. And so ryght as oure Lorde
worschypyde hym thre manerys in `hys´ lyfe and thre manerys in hys
deth, ryght so he hath worschypyd hym othyre thre manerys
450 euyrlastyngly in heuene, in the accedental mede besyde the souereyne
f. 140ʳ and pryncypal mede þat he hath | ȝeue hym in the essencyal mede,
and also in othyre statys and dygnyteys in the blysse of heuene þat
byth in þe dome of holy chyrche wordyest amonge othyre, as
patryarkys and prophetys, apostlys, and euangelystys and confessorys.
455   In euyryche of these seint Ihon euangelyste maye be seyde to haue a
meryte, and be þat the ioye and the mede of the same meryte. Amonge
patryarkys he hath a meryte, for ryght as the xii patryarkys, Iacobys
sonys, be patryarkys of the olde laue, ryght so be the xii apostlys gostly
patryarkys of the newe lawe. Of the whyche Seyint Ihon euangelyste
460 ys one, and therfore he maye be seyde a patryarke. A prophete he ys,
as wytnessyth the Apocalypse, whereinne hyt ys seyde thus: 'Blyssyd
be he þat redyth and heryth the wordys of þys prophecye and kepyth
þat that ys wryte therinne.'

    429 therfore] *fol. by canc.* seyth Gg   432 that] þat that N   433 chyrche] chirche
N; chyche Gg   as] *om.* N   435 And] and in N   436 callyd] calle N
437 Portelatyneys] *in marg.* the daye of Seyint Ihon portelatyne Gg   444 Prefacyon
afore] prologe vpon N   afore] vppon N   448 `þe´] *om.* N   450–1 besyde . . . mede]
om. N; *see note*   453 as] as bene N   454 and¹] *om.* N   455 to] and N
458 be] were N

Amonge apostlys he ys one of the worthyeste, as ys opynly knowe. Wherfore worschypful Bede seyth in hys sermon of hym thus: 'What ys in vertuys, what in merytys, in the whyche blyssyd Ihon incomperably ouyrpassyth not? Fforsothe, he ys apostyl in hys pystyllys, a euangelyste in the gospel, a prophete in the Apocalypse. I seye a prophete, and not whatsumeuere', as ho seyth, a sympyl or of lytyl reputacyon, 'but a merueylus, and to the lyknesse of þat othyr Ihon (þat ys Seyint Ihon Ba`bty'ste), more thanne a prophete. In the beholdynge', he | seyth, 'of the beynge of the hy Godhede, he goyth afore prophetys, he ouyrpassyth patryarkys, he ouyrcomyth apostlys. Therfore be the meryte þat oure Lorde louyde hym afore othyre, he lefte hym vp hyer thanne othyre. And we, dere brethryn, be oure lytyl maner lete vs', seyth he, 'studye to lefte hym vp be worthy prey-syngys, lete vs worschype hym alweye be worthy seruysys.'

Amonge euangelystys he ys the worthyeste, aftyr the seyinge of doctorys. A confessur also he ys, for he knowlechyde oure Lorde in feythe, in wordys and in werkys. Of matyrys, doctorys, and vyrgynys ȝe haue herde afore. Thus, belouyd systyr in God, ȝe haue herde how oure Lorde worschypyde hys derelynge Seyint Ihon, apostyl and euangelyste in hys lyfe, in hys deth, and also sumwhat in partye ȝe maye conseyue be þat that ys forseyde how he hath worschypyd hym euyrlastyngly aftyr hys precyouse deth in heuene, bothe in the essencyal mede and also in the accydental mede. Wherfore, lete vs loue and worschype hym þat oure Lorde so myche louyde and louyth, worschypyde and hath [euyrlastyngly] worschypyd, þat we maye be oure Lordys mercy and hys merytys and prayerys fynde in thys lyfe mercy and grace, and in that othyr reste and ioye wythoute ende. Amen.

Gostly syster, for Seyint Gregory seyth þat othyrwhyle the ensamplys of werkys more edyfye þe | myndys of herarys thanne the wordys of doctorys, therfore I wole telle ȝow here be the grace of oure Lorde some exsamplys þat mowen, be the mercy of God, stere ȝow or eny othyr deuout seruaunt of God to the more loue and deuocyon to thys worschyful apostyl and euangelyste. Hyt ys red in hys *Legende* þat Seyint Ewarde, þe kynge of Yngelonde, wolde denye nothynge to eny man þat askyde in the name of Seyint Ihon

464 Amonge] amonge þe N   opynly] open ynogh N   469 of] a N   471 þat . . . Ba`bty'ste] *om.* N   474 the] *om.* N   476 studye] studyede N   478 Amonge] amonge þe N   481 belouyd] welbelouede N   487 so] as N   488 euyrlastyngly] euerlastyngly N; euyrlastynly Gg   489 oure Lordys] hys N   493 of¹] of here N   494 wole] wolde N   497 thys] his N   499 þat askyde] askynge N

500 euangelyste. And so hyt hapyde in a tyme þat a pylgryme, whyle the
chambyrleyne was absent, importunely in the name of Seyint Ihon
euangelyste askyde almasse. To whom the kynge, whenne he hadde
none 'othyr thynge' a redy, ȝafe a precyouse rynge. But manye dayis
aftyrwarde, a knygthte of Yngelonde þat was be ȝende the see toke þe
505 same rynge of the same pylgryme to be borne aȝen to the kynge in
suechemaner wordys: 'He to whom and also for whos loue þu ȝauyste
thys rynge sendyth hym aȝen to the.' Wherfore hyt ys opyn þat Seyint
Ihon apperyde to hym in a pylgrymys lyknesse.

Also, hyt ys redde in Seyint Elyȝabethys lyfe, þe kyngys dowghttyr
510 of Hungry, þat sche chese oure Lady, Godys modyr, into here patrone
and mene, and Seyint Ihon euangelyste into the kepare of here
chastytee. And so in a tyme whenne ther were scrowys wryte wyth
f. 141ᵛ eueryche | of the apostlys namys and were put vpon an autere and
eueryche damsele þat was wyth here be happe toke the scrowe þat
515 fylle to here, sche, fyrste prayinge thre tymys as sche desyryde, toke
þe scrowe þat Seyint Ihon euangelyste'ys name' was wryte inne, to
whom sche hadde so gret deuocyon þat 'sche' wolde denye nothynge
to hem þat askyde in hys name.

Also, hyt ys wryte in Seyint Edmundeys lyfe the Byischop, and hyt
520 ys put also in þe *Myraclys of Oure Lady*, þat whenne in daye he was
occupyed in scole, he forȝate to seye an oryson þat he was wonde to
seye dylygently and deuoutly to oure Lady and Seyint Ihon euangelyste, þe whyche begynnyth thus: 'O intemerata'. And in the nyghtte
folowynge, Seyint Ihon apperyde to hym, seyinge: 'Stretche out thyne
525 hande.' And whenne 'he' hadde do so, Seyint Ihon dretyde to smyte
hym wyth a pamyr þat he bare in hys hande, þe whyche yf he hadde
doo hym semyde be the gretnesse of the dretynge þat he schulde haue
dyde of þe stroke. Bot the blyssyd euangelyste was sone made mekyr
and helde hym be þe hande þat he hadde strawte out, and badde hym
530 famylyarly þat he schulde no more leue þe 'for'seyde 'oryson'
vnseyde.

Fferdyrmore hyt ys founde in the *Myraclys of Oure Lady* þat ther
'was' a monke þat steryde a ȝonge clerke to be a monke in the
monasterye þat 'he' duellyde inne. But whenne he wolde not

---

503 ȝafe] ȝaffe hym N   507 hym] it N   508 a . . . lyknesse] þe lykenes of a
pylgryme N   509 Elyȝabethys] *in marg.* in the lyfe of Seyint Elyȝabeth Gg
511 the] a N   513 eueryche] yche N   514 eueryche] yche N
516 euangelysteys] *om.* N   517 so] a N   520 in¹] in a N   529 he
hadde strawte] had bydyn hym streche N   530 leue] 'forȝete' N   531 vnseyde]
om. N

consente, he styryde hym to seye euyry daye | an oryson to oure Lady f. 142ʳ
and Seyint Ihon euangelyste, and he toke hym the oryson. And fyrste 536
the chylde forsoke to seye hyt, seyinge þat 'he' durste not seye þat
oryson for drede of hys maystyr, for 'he' compellyde 'hym' to take
hede to anothyr lessun. Neuyrdeles, att the laste bestyrynge of the
forseyde monke, he consentyde and behette to seye hyt. And so the xv 540
daye aftyr he hadde begunne to seye hyt he dyde, the whyche not
manye dayis aftyr apperyde to a preste, hys brothyr and a relygyus
man. And whenne he was askyd of hym how hyt stode wyth hym, the
same childe seyde to hym þat whenne hys soule was goo out of the
body, euylle spyrytys toke hyt and drew hyt to the placys of paynys, 545
wyth the whyche sodeynely Seyint Ihon euangelyste mette, seyinge
þat he was sente fro oure Lordys modyr, þe whyche badde hem þat
they schulde lete here seruauntys soule goo fre. And 'whenne' they
wolde not lete þe soule goo, Seyint Iohn ranne aȝen to oure Lady, and
cam aȝen and seyde to þe euyl spyrytys þat oure Lordys modyr sente 550
hem worde but 'yf' they wolde lete 'þe soule' goo sche wolde come
hereselfe to deliuere hyt. And thanne anone they thurste no lengyr
wythholde hyt, but lete hyt goo fre. And so be 'þe' oryson þat the
monke ȝaf hym, the whyche he hadde seyde xv dayis, he was
delyueryd fro the fendys. And thanne the preste askyde hym were 555
þat oryson was, and he seyde þat he schulde fynde hyt | att hys f. 142ᵛ
beddys hede. And thanne the 'preste' softe hyt there and fonde hyt,
þe whyche he toke and cam to the chapetur of Systersiense Ordyr,
were manye abbottys of þat ordyr were come togyderys. And to hem
þat were there present þat tyme, he tolde what he hadde herde of hys 560
brothyr and 'schewde hem' the oryson, the whyche was *O Intemerata*.
And thanne the abbottys wrote hyt aȝen and bare hyt to be red into
manye placys.

Also, hyt ys red in the same *Myraclys of Oure Lady* þat ther was a
monke the whyche wente out of hys monasterye wythoute leue and 565
lyuyde an euyl lyfe in the worlde. But hys abbot, er he wente out,
seyde to hym: 'Sone, abyde in the monasterye and seye thyne ourys
and othyre prayerys.' And he ansueryde: 'Not only orysonys, ne 'I'
wole seye the Pater Noster.' And thanne the abbot seyde aȝen: 'Take
thys oryson thanne and seye hyt euery daye.' And thanne the monke 570

535 to] of N   543 the] *om.* N   546 wyth] *om.* N   547 fro] of N
551 wolde] wolde sone N   552 to] and N   564 red] writen N   565 the whyche]
þat N   568 orysonys] *in marg.* that ys iwole seye vndyrstondyth that thys monke was
but a nouyce fo'r' ellys he mygth not go awey so Gg

wente out of the abbye and toke the oryson wyth hym, and as God
wolde he seyde hyt euery daye þat ʒere. And whenne the ʒere was
endyd þat vagabunde monke dyde. And whenne the abbot herde
therof, he wente to anothyr monke of goode lyuynge and seyde to
575   hym: 'Whenne tomorowe in the mornynge þu schalt synge masse,
take sueche a `man in´ mynde', and tolde hys name, 'the whyche ys
now deed, but seye not hys name.' And so in the mornynge whenne
f. 143ʳ   `þe´ monke seyde hys masse, he | toke þat deed man to mynde, but he
namyde not hys name. And as he lokyde to þe oo syde of the autere he
580   sawgh `there´ þe blyssyde virgyne, oure Lady, and att þat othy`r´ syde
Seyint Ihon euangelyste, seyinge to hym: 'Why namyste þu `not´
sueche a man? Wyte þu for certayne þat `be´ oure prayerys for hym he
hath ascapyd the euyrlastyngys paynys of helle.' And therfore hyt ys
to be beleuyd and stedfastly to beholde, as hyt ys seyde there, þat that
585   man ys sauyd be þe prayerys of oure Lady and Seyint Ihon
euangelyste. The oryson þat the abbot toke hym, as hyt ys `wryte´
in th`e´ tytyll of thys same myracle, was *O Intemerata*. Wherfore,
hoosoeuere haue specyal `deuocyon´ to oure Lady and thys worthy
apostyl, hyt ys goode þat he vse to seye þat oryson to hem, for hyt ys a
590   goode oryson and a deuout, and an acceptable to hem as ʒe maye
vndyrstande be the forseyde myraclys. And therfore I wole wryte þat
oryson after these medytacyonys þat hoso lykyth to seye hyt maye
fynde hyt hole aftyr thys boke.

   Hyt ys also red in the *Boke of Beys, and hyt ys also wryte in the*
595   *Myraclys of Oure Lady*, that ther was a chanon, þe whyche feruently
louyde in hys lyfe Seyint Ihon euangelyste. And so aftyr hys deth
anothyr chanon þat was hys felawe in a vysyon semyde that he sawgh
sueche a maner apperynge. The same apostil wente to the gloryus
f. 143ᵛ   virgyne, oure Lordys modyr, | pray`i´nge here mekely and thus
600   seyinge: 'Loo, oure frendys soule ys tormentyd in paynys, and
therfore I beseke the come and delyuere hyt. For thowgh in hys
lyfe he lyuyde not parfythly, for a gret parte thowgh he mendyde hys
lyuynge.' And anone the virgyne, wythoute taryinge, grauntyde the
virgyne, and so they wente bothe to purgatorye and fette out þat soule
605   wyth hem. And hyt `ys´ seyde there þat he bare wytn`e´sse hereof, of
the whyche hyt ys knowe þat hys wytnesse ys soth.

572 daye] day in N   575 mornynge] mornynge þat N   576 `in´] to N
mynde] mynge N   578 seyde] songe N   579 oo syde] tone ende N   580 `there´]
om. N   othy`r´ syde] tother ende of þe auter N   582 a] a dede N   588 haue] haue
a N   and] and to N   590 an] one N   594 *Beys*] worshipful bede N; *see note*
598 maner] maner of N   602 thowgh] *om.* N   603 lyuynge] lyfe N

Also in Seyint Gregoryys lyfe, of Seyint Ihon euangelystys relyquyis ys wryte sueche a fayre myracle. Ther were some pryncys þat askyde of Seyint Gregory some precyouse reliquyis. And he ʒaf hem sumwhat of Seyint Ihon euangelysteys turnycle, the whyche 610 fyrste they resceyuyde, but aftyrwarde as vyle relyquyis they ʒaf hem hym aʒen wyth gret indynacyon. And thanne Seyint Gregory prayde, and whenne he hadde prayde he askyde a knyfe and therwyth he prykkyde þat cloth, of þe whyche anone blode wente oute. And so hyt was schewde therby, be the dome of God, how precyouse thyke 615 relyquyis were.

And thus I ende thys symple boke, prayinge ʒow here or eny othyr 'deuout' seruaunt of God þat ys be hys grace to rede þys boke or eny parte þerof, for charytee to seye the same prayere that | I askyde in the f. 144ʳ fyrste chapetele of þys boke, and also aboute the myddyl, to the 620 worschype of the Holy Trynytee, oo euerlastynge, verry, and almyghtty God, to whom be all worschype, ioye, and preysynge, now and wythoute endynge. Amen. Deo gracias.

Ffinito libro sit laus et gloria Christo.

De uita Christi 'libro' finis datur isti,   625
Paruos lactabit solidos quasi pane cibabit.
De Bethlem pratum dedit hos Ihesu tibi flores,
post hunc ergo statum reddas sibi semper honores.

O INTEMERATA

Oracio bona et deuota ad Sanctam Mariam, matrem Dei et beatum Iohannem apostolum et Euangelistam.

O Intemerata et in eternum benedicta, singularis atque incompar-abilis uirgo, Dei genitrix Maria, gratissimum Dei templum, Spiritus Sancti sacrarium, ianua regni celorum, per quam post Deum totus 5 uiuit orbis terrarum, inclina aures tue pietatis indignis supplicacioni-bus meis, et esto michi peccatori pia in omnibus auxiliatrix. O beate Iohannes, Christi familiaris amice, qui ab eodem Domino nostro

608 some] sometyme N   611 resceyuyde] resceyuede hem N   hem] hem to N
613 whenne . . . prayde] aftre N   614 þat] þe N   615 thyke] þose N
623 wythoute] ony N   Deo gracias] *om.* N   624 Christo] Christo soluite nunc mentem
pro W. H. ad omnipotentem N

O Intemerata 1 Sanctam] beatam N   Dei] domini nostri ihesu cristi N
2 Iohannem] iohannem apostolum et N   6 orbis] orbi N   7 peccatori] *in
marg.* peccatorici Gg

Ihesu Christo uirgo es electus et inter ceteros magis dilectus atque
10 misterijs celestibus ultra omnes imbutus, apostolus eius et euangelista
factus ʼesʼ preclarissimus. Te eciam inuoco cum Maria matre eiusdem
Domini nostri Ihesu Christi, ut michi opem tuam cum ipsa ferre
digneris.

O due gemme celestes, Maria et Iohannes, O duo luminaria
f. 144ᵛ diuinitus ante Deum | lucencia, uestris radijs scelerum meorum
16 effugate nebula. Vos estis illi duo, in quibus Deus Pater per Filium
suum specialiter edificauit sibi domum et in quibus ipse Filius Patris
vnigenitus, ob sincerissime uirginitatis uestre meritum, dilectionis sue
confirmauit priuilegium. In cruce pendens vni uestrum ita dixit:
20 Mulier, ecce filius tuus. Deinde ad alium: Ecce mater tua. In huius
ergo sacratissimi amoris dulcedine, qua ita tunc ore Dominico uelud
mater et filius inuicem coniuncti estis, uobis duobus ego miser
peccator in hac die et semper animam ʼmeamʼ et corpus meum
commendo, ut omnibus horis atque momentis intus et exterius
25 firmi custodes et pij apud Deum intercessores pro me existere
dignemini.

Credo enim firmiter et fateor indubitanter quod velle uestrum,
velle Dei est, et nolle uestrum nolle Dei est. Vnde quicquid ab eo
pecieritis, sine mora optinebitis. Per hanc ʼegoʼ tam potentissimam
30 uestre dignitatis uirtutem, poscite michi corporis et anime salutem.
Agite, queso, agite vestris gloriosis precibus ut cor meum inuisere et
inhabitare dignetur Spiritus Sanctus, qui me a cunctorum viciorum
sordibus expurget, virtutibus sacris exornet, in dileccione Dei et
proximi perfecte stare et perseuerare faciat, et post huius uite
35 cursum ad gaudia ducat electorum suorum benignissimus Paraclitus,
graciarum largitor optimus, qui Patri et Filio consubstancialis et
f. 145ʳ coeternus, cum eis et in eis viuit et regnat | omnipotens Deus, per
omnia secula seculorum. Amen.

Nos tibi, uirgo pia semper commendo, Maria.
40   Nos, rogo, conserues Christi dilecte Iohannes.
Virgo Maria, Dei genitrix, quam scriptor honorat,
Sis pia semper ei per hic te sperat et orat.
Ex alia uice Iohannes Cristi dulcis amice,
Da sibi solamen cum sanctis omnibus. Amen.

---

19 priuilegium] *fol. by canc.* vos estis illi duo Gg   23 peccator] *in marg.* vel peccatorix
Gg   29 ʼegoʼ] igitur N   32 Sanctus] almus N   me] *om.* N   cunctorum] cuntis N
42 per] prout N   43 alia] aliaque N

In omni tribulacione, temptacione, necessitate, et   45
angustia, succurre nobis, piissima uirgo Maria. Amen.

O vndefulyd and wythoute ende, blyssyd synglere and incomper-
able vyrgyne, the mothyr of God, Marye, moste kynddest temple of
God, the halowynge place of the Holy Gooste, the ȝate of the
kyngedom of heuene be whom aftyr God all the worlde lyuyth. 50
Inclyne the eerys of thy pytee to myne vnworthy supplycacyonys and
be ʽto meʼ a synnare or a synful womman in all thyngys a meke lady
and helpare.

    O þu blyssyd Ihonn, [the] famyliar frend of Cryste, the whyche ʽof
þeʼ same oure Ihesu Cryste arte a vyrgyne chose anʽdʼ amonge othyre 55
moste belouyd, and also above alle othyre in heuenely thyngys tawgth,
thow arte made hys apostyl and euangelyst most clerest. The also I
calle in wyth Marye the mothyr of oure Lord Ihesu Cryste that thow
fowchesaff wyth here to ȝeve me thy help.

    O ȝe tueyne heuenely stonys, Marye and Ihon, | tueyne lygthtys f. 145ᵛ
brenynge afore God, dryuyth aweye wyth ȝoure brygth ʽschynyngysʼ 61
the clowthys of my therke synnys. Ȝe be ther tueyne in the whyche
God the fathyr be hys sone specyally hath byldyd hym an howse, and
in the whyche oure Lorde Ihesu Cryste, the onebegotyn sone of the
fathyr, for ʽtheʼ meryte of ȝowre moste clenyste vyrgynyte hath 65
confyrmyd the pryuylege of hys loue. He hangynge vpon the crosse
to one of ȝow he seyde thus: 'Womman, loo they sone.' Aftyr that he
seyde to that othyr: 'Loo, thy mothyr.' In thys, therfore, moste holy
suetenesse of loue be ʽþeʼ whychʽeʼ tho be ʽtheʼ mowth of oure Lorde
as mothyr and sone ȝe were iunyd togydere, to ȝow tueyne I synful 70
wrecche or synful womman thys daye and alwey commende my body
and soule that in alle ourys and momentys wythinne and wythoute ȝe
fowchesaff to be fyrme and stabyl keparys, and for me att God meke
besekarys. I stedsafly beleue and knowleche vndowtfully that ȝowre
wyllynge ys the wyllynge of God and ȝowre not wyllynge yt the not 75
wyllynge of God.

    Wherefore, what euere ȝe aske of hym wythʽouteʼ taryinge ȝe schal
gete. Be thys therfore the so mygthty vertu of ȝowre dyngnytee askyth
for me the helthe bothe of my bothy and soule. Doeth, I praye ȝow, 79
doeth be ȝowre gloryus prayerys thaʽtʼ the Holy Goost fowche|saff to f. 145ᵛ

46 Amen] amen in omni tribulacione temptacione necesseitate [sic] et angustia succurre
nobis piissima uirgo Maria amen N   47 [first word] *The English translation of O
Intemerata does not appear in* N   52 womman] *in marg.* to me Gg   54 the] te Gg
61 brenynge] *in top marg.* godly schynynge Gg ʽschynyngysʼ] *in marg. with corr. marks* Gg

vysyte and inhabyte my herte, the whyche maye clense me fro the
felthe `of´ alle vycys. Make me fayre wyth holy vyrtuys in the loue of
God and my neygthbore make stande parfythly and `to´ preserue
contynually. And aftyr the cowrst of thys lyf the Holy Goost, moste
85 benynge confortowre and beste ȝeuare of gracys, brynge me to the
ioyis of hys chosyn, the whyche to the fathyr and the sone comsub-
stancyll and wyth hem euyrlastynge wyth hem and in hem lyuyth in
regnyt all mygthty God wythoute ende. Amen.

82 felthe] *fol. by canc.* of synn Gg

EXPLANATORY NOTES

PREFACE

3/2 **Gostly syster**. The author addresses the reader as 'gostly syster' throughout the *Mirror*, implying that his intended audience is a female religious, probably a nun. If the work did indeed originate at the Charterhouse of Sheen, then the 'gostly syster' is, in all likelihood, a sister of the Birgittine Syon Abbey.

3/3 **we spake laste togyderys**. The Carthusian author is likely referring to a textual exchange, rather than suggesting he spoke directly with a Syon nun. Most communication between the two houses probably occurred between the Prior of Sheen and the Abbess of Syon.

3/7 **or to eny othyr deuot seruant of God**. The author is likely aware that many devotional texts made their way to lay readers through Syon Abbey. Vincent Gillespie also argues ('Haunted Text', 146–7) that the author may be addressing the work both to a female religious reader and to the male priests and laymen working at Syon Abbey.

3/12–14 **thre and thyrty . . . lyuyde in erthe**. According to this passage, the division of the *Mirror* into thirty-three chapters is meant to represent each of the years Christ lived on earth. Of the seven Middle English pseudo-Bonaventuran lives of Christ, the *Mirror* is the only one with thirty-three chapters and the only one to explicitly relate that number to the years of Christ's life.

3/23 **Bonauenture**. Saint Bonaventure (1218–74) joined the Franciscan Order in 1243, was made a cardinal in 1273, canonized in 1482, and declared a Doctor of the Church in 1588. He was often mistakenly credited with writing the *MVC* and the *Stimulus Amoris*.

3/25 *Vita Cristi*. This is a reference to *MVC*. Often attributed to Saint Bonaventure, it was probably written in the fourteenth century by Iohannis de Caulibus, a Franciscan friar of San Gemigniano in Tuscany (CCCM 153, pp. ix–xi). *MVC* consists of a series of devotions that relate the life of Christ according to the gospel narrative, including a few apocryphal episodes.

3/25–6 **a man of oure ordyr of charturhowse**. A reference to Nicholas Love, Prior of Mount Grace Charterhouse in Yorkshire during the first quarter of the fifteenth century and author of *The Mirror of the Blessed Life of Jesus Christ* (Love, Introduction, p. 31). N omits 'of charturhowse', which might indicate its intended lay audience.

5/77 *Orlege of Wysedome*. *Horologium Sapientiae* by Henry Suso.

5/77–83 **Be . . . ende.** Henry Suso, *Horol. Sap.*, Liber I, Cap. iii.

5/84–9 **The ofte thynkynge . . . helthe.** Henry Suso, *Horol. Sap.*, Liber I, Cap. xiv. An error exists in both Gg and N at line 64, where both manuscripts read 'to profyte into'. The correct reading, 'into perfyte', is supported by the passage from Suso's *Horologium Sapientiae*: 'Frequens passionis huius memoria indoctum quemque reddit doctissimum, et imperitos ac idiotas facit proficere in magistros.'

5/89–92 **Blyssyd . . . gracys.** Henry Suso, *Horol. Sap.*, Liber I, Cap. xiv. The *Mirror* author's translation of this passage implies that the comma should follow 'uirtutum', making it dependent on 'amore'. In Künzle's edition, 'cunctarumque uirtutum' depends on 'incrementum': 'Felix, qui eius studio seriose intenderit; quia proficiet in contemptu mundi et in amore Dei, cunctarumque uirtutum et gratiarum sumet incrementum.'

6/103–6 **He . . . hym.** John 12: 26.

6/119–20 **Maystyr of Storyis . . . *Scole Storye*.** Peter Comester, *Historia scholastica*.

6/127 **approuyd wymmen.** The women to whom the *Mirror* author refers are Catherine of Siena, Mechtild of Hackeborn, and Birgitta of Sweden. See the discussion in the Introduction for more on the approved women.

TABLE OF CONTENTS

7/3 **Capitulum primum.** Both N and Gg have numbers (N has Arabic, Gg has Roman) along the outer margins that correspond to the chapter descriptions in the Table of Contents.

7/15 **Kateryne of Sene.** Saint Catherine of Siena.

8/35 **Seynt Brygytte.** Saint Birgitta of Sweden.

CHAPTER I

10/5 **Capitulum primum.** In the outer margins of N and Gg there appear 'Capitulum primum' and 'c^m i^m' respectively. In addition, N places an Arabic numeral in the inner margin to correspond with the opening of each chapter. These numbering pratices are consistent throughout both manuscripts.

11/19 **Formauit . . . terre.** Genesis 2: 7.

11/25–6 **of mynde . . . perfyth God.** Walter Hilton, *The Scale of Perfection*, Book I, ch. 43.

11/27–8 **Et creauit . . . suam.** Genesis 1: 27.

11/31–2 **paradyse . . . lykynge.** Genesis 2: 8.

11/34–5 **he sente . . . rybbys.** Genesis 2: 21.

11/38–9 **Lete vs . . . to hym.** Genesis 2: 18.

11/42–3 **Dominamini . . . terram.** Genesis 1: 28.

12/73–4 **De omni . . . comedas.** Genesis 2: 16–17.

13/85–6 **Inuidia . . . terrarum.** Wisdom 2: 24.

13/106–7 **Homo . . . illis.** Psalm 48: 13. This same verse is used by Hilton to make a similar point in ch. 43 of the *Scale of Perfection* (p. 78).

14/116–21 **We . . . aȝen.** Walter Hilton, *Scale of Perfection*, Book I, ch. 43.

CHAPTER 2

15/39–40 **Sicut . . . viuificabuntur.** 1 Corinthians 15: 22.

15/46 **God.** The margin of N has 'ffigura ante legem'. These marginal comments are marked with two red dots that correspond to the word or words in the main text. The use of red abbreviation marks is consistent throughout N.

15/46–58 **God bad . . . vpon.** Genesis 22: 1–6.

16/62 **For the gospel.** Margin of N has 'Veritas'.

16/62–4 **For the gospel . . . mankynde.** John 24: 17.

16/68–9 **God badde Moyses.** Margin of N has 'ffigura sub lege'.

16/68–79 **the rood of Aaron . . . confermyd.** Numbers 27: 1–11.

16/77 **And so Aaronys rood.** Margin of Gg has 'the rood of aaron'.

16/79–82 **And in that rood . . . froyte.** Saint John Chrysostom, *Orationes VIII Adversus Judaeos*, Homily VI (*PG* 48.912).

16/81 **Marye.** Margin of N has 'Veritas'.

16/91–2 **Ecce virgo . . . emanuel.** Isaiah 7: 14.

16/94 **Euangelyst seyt . . . vs.** Matthew 1: 23.

CHAPTER 3

17/11–15 **angyl Gabryel . . . Marye.** Luke 1: 26–7.

18/24–19/68 **schulde be . . . creaturys were.** These lines comprise ff. 13ᵛ– 14ʳ of Gg, which is a single leaf of parchment in a second hand inserted into the manuscript to repair a lacuna caused by a paper leaf that has fallen out.

18/32–3 **And fyrste . . . here.** While attributed to Saint Jerome, this passage actually derives from Paschasius Radbertus, *De Assumptione Sanctae Mariae Virginis* (CCCM 56C, p. 123, ll. 251–3).

18/35–19/70 **Hayle Marye . . . mercy.** This account is taken from the narrative of the Annunciation in Luke 1: 28–38. The *Mirror* author follows verses 28, 30–1, and 38 closely through both translation and paraphrase.

19/68 **so meke, how meke.** At the opening of f. 14^r, the ten lines preceding these words have been crossed out, since they had already been copied on to the replacement leaf that is the present f. 13 (see note to 17/24–19/69). The lines read: 'to make an ende therof & so att the laste our lorde of hys mercy ȝaf me I hope to performe hyt of the blyssyd virgyne & also howe mekely sche callyth herself but a seruaunt whenne sche wyste herself be hym that sche shulde be werkynge of the holy `goste´ brynge forth to be quene of heuene lady of worlde & empresse of helle & takyth example of her mekenesse for yf sche that was so excellently chose afore all othyr creaturys wer' (f. 14^r).

19/78 **Now vn[der]stondyth here.** Margin of N has 'Nota'.

19/78–20/95 **Now vn[der]stondyth here . . . we haue take.** Although Saint Augustine is mentioned as the source, the quotation actually derives from Saint Quodvultdeus, Bishop of Carthage, *Sermo* 10: *Aduersus Quinque Haereses* (CCSL 60, p. 279, ll. 65–70).

19/84–5 **For Seyint Austyn seyt.** Right margin of N has 'Augustinus'.

20/99–104 **oure Lady . . . hymself.** The *Mirror* author primarily follows Nicholas of Lyre, *Postilla* on Luke 1: 29 in his reasons for Mary's unease at being adored by Gabriel. Iohannis de Caulibus, *MVC*, CCCM 153, Cap. iv, p. 21, ll. 52–5 contains a similar passage.

20/107–21/142 **Doctorys . . . materys.** This long quotation incorporated details of the life of Catherine of Siena as found in the *Legenda Maiora* by Raymond of Capua. It is often misidentified as Catherine of Siena's *Dialogues*. See Brown, 'The Many Misattributions of Catherine of Siena'.

20/116 **fforsothe the weye of penaunce.** Margin of N has 'Nota bene'.

20/122 **But I wole.** Margin of N has 'Nota'.

21/125 **the knowynge of trewthe.** Left margin in Gg has 'the knowynge of ys trewthe'. This is used to confirm a correction in the text, which has 'trewthe the knowynge of' with '*d, a, b,* and *c*' placed interlineally over each word respectively. This directs the reader to rearrange the order of the words, and the marginal comment affirms the corrected order.

CHAPTER 4

21/4–5 **Marye . . . prayere.** Luke 1: 39.

21/6 **as Lyre seyt.** Nicholas of Lyre, *Postilla* on Luke 1: 39.

22/23–7 **For Seyint Ambrose . . . placys.** Saint Ambrose, *Expositio Evangelii secundum Lucam*, Liber II, pp. 39–40, ll. 293–9. Mary's desire not to be seen in public is mentioned by Nicholas of Lyre, with Ambrose named as the source, in his comment on John 2: 1.

22/36–47 **Ely3abeth . . . generaciones.** Luke 1: 41–8.

23/65 **Fyrste.** Margin of N has 'of þe mekenes of spirite 1'. The next three degrees of meekness of spirit are similarly enumerated in the margins.

23/77 **Aftyr.** Margin of N has '2'.

24/90 **profytarys.** This word does not appear in the *MED* in this form, but it appears to be a variant spelling of the word 'profiter', which the *MED* glosses as 'one who is making progress'.

24/91 **Aftyr.** Margin of N has '3'.

24/111 **Beati . . . celorum.** Matthew 5: 3.

24/115–18 **My soule . . . sauyour.** This is the opening of the *Magnificat*, Mary's song of praise to the Lord found in Luke 1: 46–55. It echoes Hannah's prayer in 1 Samuel 2: 1–10.

24/114–15 **For Seyint Austyn . . . God.** This passage remains unidentified. It could be taken from Augustine's *Confessions*, Book 7, ch. 9; however, there are numerous passages from Augustine that are similar in nature.

24/119 **The iiii degre . . . spyryt.** Margin of N has '4'.

25/122–4 **Noo man . . . come.** Ecclesiastes 9: 1–2.

25/125 **thare.** N's scribe misreads 'thar', a variation of 'dare', for 'þere' or 'there'. The misreading suggests that despite N's different dialect, the N scribe was copying his text from an exemplar with the same dialect as Gg.

25/131–2 **Whenne . . . place.** Luke 14: 10.

25/148 **For whatsumeuer.** Margin of N has 'Nota'.

26/159–60 **He that . . . exaltyd.** Luke 14: 11.

26/166 **Also, 3e schal vndyrstande.** Margin of N has 'Nota of mekyng and mekenes'.

26/178–81 **Goo sytt . . . place.** Luke 14: 11.

26/189–90 **Iuxta est . . . saluabit.** Psalm 33: 19.

27/194 **mekenesse of herte.** Margin of N has 'mekenes of herte'.

27/207 **in meke wordys.** Margin of N has 'mekenes in wordes'.

27/212 **also in werkys.** Margin of N has 'mekenes in werkes'.

28/231–2 *Boke of Rygthful Men* **. . . erthe.** This reference is most likely taken from Peter Comestor, *Historia Scholastica*: 'Et legitur in libro Iustorum, quod beata Virgo eum primo levavit a terra' (*PL* 198: 1538).

28/235–6 **as Seyint Ambrose seyt . . . opyn.** *Expositio Evangelii secundum Lucam*, Liber II, pp. 39–40, ll. 293–9.

28/245–7 **For Crys[o]steme seyt . . . so.** This quotation is from the *Opus imperfectum in Mathaeum*, often mistakenly attributed to Chrysostom in the Middle Ages (*PG* 54.632–3).

28/247–59 **for he dowtede . . . synnys.** Matthew 1: 19–25.

28/260 **doctorys . . . [virgynytee].** There is little written on the virginity of Joseph and no general tradition exists among the Latin Fathers. Comments on Joseph's virginity are confined to Jerome, Augustine, and Ambrose. The Middle Ages saw a number of theologians expand on the comments of the Latin Fathers; among them were Bede and Peter Comestor. The *Mirror* author does not name a source for his assertion that Joseph made a vow of virginity along with Mary. However, the *Mirror* author relies on a small group of authors for his arguments and the idea of Joseph's pledge of virginity likely derives from these sources. Saint Jerome, in his *De perpetua uirginitate Beatae Mariae aduersus Heluidium*, writes: 'Tu dicis Mariam virginem non permansisse: ego mihi plus vindico, etiam ipsum Joseph virginem fuisse per Mariam, ut ex virginali conjugio virgo filius nasceretur' (*PL* 23: 203). Saint Augustine writes in *De opere monachorum*: 'homo ille iustus et ad testimonium coniugalis semper mansurae uirginitatis electus, cui desponsata erat uirgo Maria, quae peperit Christum, faber fuit' (ed. Zycha, CSEL 41, p. 555, ll. 15–21). Similarly, Bede writes in Liber II, *Homily* I of his *Opera homiletica*: 'Nec defuere heretici qui Ioseph uirum beatae uirginis Maria putarunt ex alia uxore genuisse eos quos fratres domini scriptura appellat' (p. 184, ll. 4–6). Finally, Peter Comestor writes in the *Historia Scholastica*: 'Cum virgine virgo permansit' (*PL* 198: 1539).

CHAPTER 5

29/3–21 **The byrthe . . . to hym.** The *Mirror* author follows Jacobus de Voragine's account of Octavian's census of the people of Syria (*Legenda Aurea*, ed. Maggioni, i. 63–4).

29/23–31/71 **Thre Kynges of Coleyne . . . seyt.** John of Hildesheim, *Historia Trium Regum*, cap. iv, which was translated into Middle English as the *Three Kings of Cologne*. The *Mirror* author omits a number of details. For the Latin and English texts, see Horstmann's edition.

29/26 **too smale myle of that contre.** Gg reads 'too' and N 'eghte'. The English and Latin texts of the *Historia Trium Regum* also indicate two miles. See Horstmann's edition, pp. 62, 234 n. 16. While the *Mirror* author follows cap. iv of the *Historia Trium Regum* for the narrative, he takes the distance between Jerusalem and Bethlehem from cap. xviii.

29/29–30 **in the whyche . . . prophete.** 1 Kings 14: 12–13.

30/45 **treyn.** In his edition, Horstmann points out that one of the Middle English manuscripts of the *Historia Trium Regum* (Cambridge, University Library, MS Ee. 4.32) has 'tymber' (p. 24) and the Latin MS Horstmann takes as his base text reads: 'Et postquam Dauid fuit rex effectus, extunc domus patris eius mansit ad vsus regios, et postmodum, propter destructionem terre, de ipsa domo nemo curauit, et sic fuit destructa; sed in tugurio et spelunca ligna et huiusmodi communia, que ad forum uenerant et uendi non poterant, quousque uendi poterant, obseruabantur, et asini et animalia uillanorum que ad forum peruenerant, intus et circum tugurium ligabantur' (pp. 221–2). However, I take 'treyn' as an adjective in the *Mirror* meaning 'wooden' and modifying 'vessellys'.

30/60–1 **sche wrappede hym . . . seyt.** Luke 2: 7.

31/68–71 **And in . . . Euangelyste seyt.** Luke 2.7.

31/73 **the *Boke of þe Ʒougthe of Oure Lorde*.** *Gospel of Pseudo-Matthew* (*Pseudo-Matthaei Evangelium*), cap. xiv: 'et ingressa est in stabulum et posuit puerum in praesepio, et bos et asinus genua flectentes adorauerunt eum' (CCSA 9, p. 431, ll. 2–3). It used to be known as the *Liber de Infantia* or *Historia de Nativitate Mariae et de Infantia Salvatoris* (see *The Apocryphal New Testament*, ed. Elliott, 84–99). A similar passage occurs in the chapter on Christ's Nativity in Jacobus de Voragine's *Legenda Aurea*: 'Bos igitur et asinus miraculose dominum cognoscentes flexis genibus ipsum adorauerunt' (ed. Maggioni, i. 71).

31/76–33/147 **Seyint Brygytt . . . ioye and gladnesse.** Saint Birgitta, *Revelaciones*, Book VII, ch. 21.

31/85 **a candyl lygth.** Medieval art often depicts Joseph with a candle at the Nativity. See Silver, 'Nature and Nature's God', for examples of this theme in fifteenth-century German art and Panofsky, *Early Netherlandish Painting*, for examples of Joseph's transition in fourteenth- and fifteenth-century art from an object of condescension to an adored *Gemma mundi* (Panofsky, i. 70, 164).

33/155–65 **as the gospel . . . wyl.** Luke 2: 8–14.

33/157–8 **a myle fro Bethl`e´em . . . seyt.** The *Historia Scholastica* reads 'Et pastores erant secundo millario a Bethlehem . . .' (*PL* 198: 1540) and the *MVC*, Cap. vi: 'prope forte per miliare' (CCCM 153, p. 34, line 117).

33/172–34/179 **And whenne . . . angyl.** Luke 2: 15–16.

34/202–4 **Aftyr thys . . . hem.** Luke 2: 20.

CHAPTER 6

35/5–7 **Aftyrwarde . . . wombe.** Luke 2: 21.

35/11 **And hyt was aȝenste . . . synne.** Margin of N has 'Nota'.

35/15 **wyth a knyfe of stone.** Iohannis de Caulibus, *MVC*, Cap. viii reads 'cum cultello lapideo' (CCCM 153, p. 38, l. 24).

36/40–7 **For in too . . . rygth.** Jacobus de Voragine, *Legenda Aurea*, cap. xiii (ed. Maggioni, i. 125).

36/48–37/67 **Also . . . bounde too.** *Legenda Aurea*, cap. xiii (ed. Maggioni, i. 124–5).

36/60–1 **'for' he cam not . . . hyt.** Matthew 5: 17.

37/69–81 **Thys name . . . gret vertu.** Both passages that are attributed to Saint Bernard are from *Legenda Aurea*, cap. xiii: 'Nomen quod secundum Bernardum est in ore mel, in aure melos et in corde iubilus; nomen quod, sicut dicit idem Bernardus, instar olei lucet praedicatum, pascit recogitatum, lenit et ungit inuocatum' (ed. Maggioni, i. 121).

37/81–4 **Wherefore anothyr worthy clerke . . . fende.** Both Gg and N have marginal notes that read 'Ricardus de sancto victore' and 'Petrus rauennas'. The *Legenda Aurea* reads: 'Item Richardus de Sancto Victore: "Ihesus nomen dulce, nomen delectabile, nomen confortans peccatorem et beatae spei. Ergo Iesu esto mihi Iesus." Secundo est multe uirtuositatis unde Petrus Rauennas: Vocabis nomen eius Ihesum. Hoc est nomen quod dedit cecis uisum, surdis auditum, claudis cursum, sermonem mutis, uitam mortuis totamque dyaboli potestatem de obsessis corporibus uirtus huius nominis effugauit' (ed. Maggioni, i. 123).

37/84–7 **And in the name . . . apostyl seyt.** Philippians 2: 10 with the last two lines taken from Acts 4: 12.

CHAPTER 7

38/17–23 **And thys daye . . . hym.** Matthew 2: 1–2.

38/24–5 **a boke that ys drawe of hem.** The *Mirror* author is referring to the *Three Kings of Cologne*, on which much of chapter 7 is based.

38/32–3 **vpon . . . Vaus.** Chapter 3 of the Middle English *Three Kings of Cologne* connects Vaus to India: 'þe grettest of berthe þat were of þis progenye of Vaws com oute of ynde in to Acon' (ed. Horstmann, p. 8). The same chapter in the *Historia Trium Regum* states: 'extunc quidam mons nomine Vaus, qui ibidem uictorialis dicitur, in Oriente fuit' (p. 213).

38/33 **tuelue astronomerys.** *Historia Trium Regum*, cap. v, p. 218.

38/34–44/233 **And that sterre . . . into thys daye.** Almost all of this passage is taken directly from the *Historia Trium Regum*, including the description of the star that leads the kings to Bethlehem (cap. v, ix), the account of their trip to Jerusalem (cap. x), the meeting that took place near the city (cap. xiv), and their return trip (cap. xxiii).

39/54–6 **And in alle cyteys . . . daye.** The three kings were able to move safely during day and night because at this time Rome was experiencing a period of relative peace that began in 27 BCE when Augustus Caesar declared an end to the great civil wars of the first century. The reference to the gates echoes Apocalypse 21: 25.

41/108–10 **Kynge Herowde herde thys . . . with hym.** Matthew 2: 3.

41/118–23 **Herowde callede togydere . . . prophecye.** Matthew 2: 4–5.

41/126–7 **as Seyint Gregory seyt . . . beleue:** This is from Pope Gregory I's *Homily* 10: 'ut ipsa eorum scientia et illis fieret ad testimonium damnationis, et nobis ad adiutorium credulitatis'; *Homiliae in Evangelia* (CCSL 141, p. 67, ll. 40–2).

41/137–9 **Goeth . . . hym.** Matthew 2: 8.

41/139–42/144 **Thys he seyde . . . chapetele.** Nicholas of Lyre, *Postilla* on Matthew 2: 8.

42/157–61 **Golde . . . wormys:** Jacobus de Voragine, *Legenda Aurea*, cap. xiv (ed. Maggioni, p. 139.

42/162–43/182 **Also Seyint Gregory . . . to oure Lorde.** Pope Gregory I, *Homily* 10, *Homiliae in Evangelia* (CCSL 141, pp. 69–71, ll. 97–133). This passage is also part of the Lessons for the Fourth Day in the Octave of Epiphany.

42/165 **that beleue hym God.** After these words in N, 'bot þei beleuen hym god' is cancelled with red ink.

44/234–5 **Seyint Gregory seyth . . . daye.** Pope Gregory I, *Homily* 10, *Homiliae in Evangelia* (CCSL 141, pp. 71–2, ll. 134–66).

44/235–6 **Per aliam . . . suam.** Matthew 2: 12.

CHAPTER 8

45/8–23 **And there sche abode . . . temple.** Luke 2: 21–4 indicates that Jesus was circumcised on the eighth day following his birth. Verses 23 and 24 of this passage show that Mary followed the Old Testament law by going to the temple after the fortieth day (seven plus thirty-three) to offer a sacrifice for her son. This entire passage is taken from Luke 2: 21–4 and Leviticus 12: 1–8 by way of the *Legenda Aurea* (ed. Maggioni, i. 238–9).

45/20 **xxxiii**^{ty}. N incorrectly states 'one and thirty daye'. Gg reads 'xxxiii^{ty}' and the source, Leviticus 12: 4, reads 'triginta tribus dies'.

46/37–51 **Here . . . worlde.** In this passage the *Mirror* author follows the general theme of humility found in cap. xxxvii of the *Legenda Aurea* (ed. Maggioni, i. 238–51).

46/53–60 **dayis of the purgacion of our Lady . . . lombe.** Luke 2: 22–4.

46/59 **Thys was the offerynge of poure pepyl.** The idea that Mary and Joseph gave an offering associated with the poor derives from Jacobus de Voragine's *Legenda Aurea* (ed. Maggioni, i. 243).

46/63–8 **And in the same . . . Cryste.** Luke 2: 25–6.

46/69–47/77 **Seyint Austyn seyth . . . Cryste.** Pseudo-Augustine, *Sermo* 370, *De Nativitate Domini*, cap. iii (*PL* 39: 1658).

47/78–88 **be reuelacyon . . . mankynde.** Luke 2: 26–32.

47/88–9 **Seiynte Austyn seyth . . . Criste.** Pseudo-Augustinian *Sermo* 370, *De Nativitate Domini*: 'Salutare Dei, Dominus Ihesus Christus' (*PL* 39: 1659).

47/96–48/108 **holy prophetesse . . . Naȝareth.** Luke 2: 36–9.

48/114–49/71 **Legende that ys callyd Aurea . . . delyuered.** This lengthy passage is taken from the chapter concerning Mary's Purification in the *Legenda Aurea* (ed. Maggioni, i. 249–51). The passage deviates from the *Legenda Aurea* only in that the *Mirror* author omits two sentences concerning the noble lady's selling of all her possessions for her love of Mary: 'uel, ut alibi legitur, omnia que habere poterat et uestimenta pro amore uirginis dabat. Vnde cum clamidem dedisset et ad ecclesiam ire non posset, sine missa illa ea die manere oportebat' (i. 249).

48/115 **Hyt ys seyde there.** Left margin of N has 'Narracio'.

CHAPTER 9

50/7–16 **Whenne þe Kynge Herowde . . . not.** *Legenda Aurea* (ed. Maggioni, i. 98). The *Legenda Aurea* cites from the *Historia Scholastica* and much of this passage appears in Peter Comestor's work. At times it is difficult to tell on which work the *Mirror* author relies, but it seems likely most of this is taken from the *Legenda Aurea*.

50/17–23 **angyl of oure Lorde . . . angyl.** Matthew 2: 13–14.

50/26–7 **And in . . . schewed.** Margin of N has 'Nota Nota'.

50/38–51/48 **a lytyl boke . . . iorneye.** Pseudo-Matthew, *Libri de Natiuitate Mariae* (CCSA 9).

51/43–7 **att the byddynge . . . bestes also.** Pseudo-Matthew, *Libri de Natiuitate Mariae*, (CCSA 9, cap. xx, pp. 463, 465, ll. 1–2, 12–16).

51/53–8 **alle þe ydolys . . . false god.** *Legenda Aurea* (ed. Maggioni, i. 99).

51/60 **they duellyde vii ȝere.** N reads 'eght yhere'. However, the *Legenda Aurea* affirms Gg's reading: 'Ad monitionem autem angeli Ioseph cum puero et matre in Aegyptum, in ciuitatem Hermopolis fugit ibique septem annis usque ad obitum Herodis mansit' (ed. Maggioni, i. 98–9). The *MVC* also states seven years (CCCM 153, p. 51, ll. 85–8).

51/62–52/86 **the story of Kynge Herowde . . . elthyr.** At line 1258 the *Mirror* author attributes this passage to Peter Comestor's *Historia Scholastica*, *PL* 198: 1543. Much of the same material is contained in chapter 10 of the *Legenda Aurea* (ed. Maggioni, i. 97–102).

52/86–8 **But all . . . Wyse Man seyth.** Wisdom 21: 30.

52/97–9 **Kynge Herowde . . . Seyint Remygye seyth.** *Legenda Aurea* (ed. Maggioni, i. 102).

52/102–4 **Aryse . . . lyf.** Matthew 2: 19–21.

52/107–53/116 **the *Thre Kynges of Coleyne* . . . ellys.** This passage appears to draw on chapter 26 of the Middle English *Three Kings of Cologne*: 'And in þis wey þat oure lady seynt Marie ȝede in to Egipt, and in þe weye þat sche come aȝene, growe drye roses þe wich be cleped þe roses of Ierico, and þes roses growe in no place of all þe contrey but onlich in þe same weye' (ed. Horstmann, p. 90). The *Mirror* author omits the *Three Kings of Cologne*'s anti-Semitic passage, which describes how the jealous Jews made the place where the roses appeared a cursed place, and replaces it with the details relating to the Saracen women's use of the roses. This passage also appears in cap. xvii of the *Historia Trium Regum* (p. 249).

52/110 **Rosys of Ierico.** 'Mira res' is in margin N.

52/117–19 **hyt ys seyde in that same boke . . . iorneye.** *Three Kings of Cologne* (ed. Horstmann, p. 90).

53/124–32 **whenne Ioseph . . . Naȝareth.** Matthew 2: 22–3.

CHAPTER 10

53/8–10 **Marye . . . Estyr.** Luke 2: 41.

54/16–23 **And so in a tyme . . . falawschyp.** Luke 2: 42–4.

54/24–36 **Lyre seyth . . . Ierusalem².** Nicholas of Lyre, *Postilla* on Luke 2: 44.

54/46–55/47 **Be thys ensample maye ȝe lerne.** Right margin of N has 'Nota bene'.

55/53 **not in the market as Lyre seyth.** Nicholas of Lyre, *Postilla* on Luke 2: 46.

55/71–2 **Sone . . . isofte the.** Luke 2: 46–8.

55/72–6 **Lyre seyth . . . lorde.** Nicholas of Lyre, *Postilla* on Luke 2: 48.

55/73 **vndyrneme.** N has 'displese', which seems to miss the point of the passage. Gg's 'vndyrneme' ('to rebuke, chastise') better fits the context of Joseph's inability to admonish Christ after his remaining in the temple, despite being in the role of Christ's father.

55/75–6 **for ouyrpassynge . . . lorde.** The Gg reading, 'for ouerpassynge loue canne no lorde', is supported by Nicholas of Lyre's text, which reads: 'quia amor excellens dominum nescit.' N's 'kan no man shewe our Lorde' appears to be scribal rewriting.

55/79–56/91 **Vp῾on῾ thys texte . . . prowde.** This passage is taken from Saint Augustine's *Sermo* 51. The only change is that the *Mirror* author omits 'fratres': 'Primo non est praetermittenda, fratres, maxime propter disciplinam feminarum, sororum nostrarum, tam sancta modestia uirginis Mariae' (*RB* 91, p. 34, ll. 431–3).

56/91–3 **How myche lasse . . . prowde.** 'Quanto minus debent superbire caeterae feminae!' (Saint Augustine, *Sermo* 51, *RB* 91, p. 34, l. 441).

56/103–5 **Why . . . Fadyr.** Luke 2: 49.

56/105–7 **Seyint Austyn . . . sone also.** Saint Augustine, *Sermo* 51, *RB* 91, p. 34, ll. 425–6.

56/107–12 **And Lyre seythe . . . of hym.** Nicholas of Lyre, *Postilla* on Luke 2: 49.

56/109–10 **But they vndyrstonde . . . Cryste.** Luke 2: 50.

56/111–12 **as the forseyde doctur seyth . . . hym.** Nicholas of Lyre, *Postilla* on Luke 2: 50.

56/113–14 **as the euangelyste seyth . . . hem.** Luke 2: 51.

56/114–17 **as þe forseyde doctur Lyre . . . pryde.** Nicholas of Lyre, *Postilla* on Luke 2: 51.

CHAPTER 11

57/6–9 **And that tyme . . . Lyre seyth.** Nicholas of Lyre, *Postilla* on Luke 3: 23.

57/22–59/62 **aftyr þe *Reuelacyon* of Seyint Brygytte . . . ȝougthe.** When the *Mirror* author claims in line 1441 that he translated Saint Birgitta's *Revelaciones* 'in Englyische tonge almoste worde for worde', he is being accurate. The entirety of Book VI, ch. 58 (ed. Bergh, pp. 200–2) of the *Revelaciones* is translated almost verbatim.

58/24 Forsothe. Right margin of N has 'verba beate marie semper virginis'.

CHAPTER 12

59/6–7 as I haue tolde yow in þe chapetele nexte. The *Mirror* author is referring to chapter 11, ll. 58/24–40.

59/7–10 And att þys tyme . . . hym. Matthew 3: 13.

59/10–60/12 Iordan, as Seinte Ierom seythe . . . Dan. Saint Jerome, *Commentarii in euangelium Matthaei*: 'et habet duos fontes, unum nomine Ior et alterum Dan, qui simul mixti Iordanis nomen efficiunt' (*Opera*, CCSL 77, p. 139, ll. 9–11).

60/13 and hyt ys . . . xviii myle. Iohannis de Caulibus, *MVC*: 'ad Iordanem, ubi erat Ioannes baptizans, qui locus distat a Hierusalem per septuaginta quattuor miliaria' (CCCM 153, cap. xvi, p. 73, ll. 11–3).

60/18–21 barefoot . . . faste. The *Mirror* author's discussion of Jesus' footwear derives from the *MVC*: 'pedibus nudis' (CCCM 153, cap. xvi, p. 73, l. 15).

60/27–9 Seyint Berna[r]de seyth . . . mygthty God. Saint Bernard, *Sermo* 15 (*Sancti Bernardi Opera*, i. 87, ll. 6–9).

60/29–32 in the *Legende of Symon and Iude* . . . sadnesse. The Legend of Simon and Jude in Jacobus de Voragine's *Legenda Aurea* relates the story of Abgar, who wished to have a portrait of Jesus. When he called a painter to make the portrait, the radiance of Christ's face was so intense that the painter could not make out the details of the Savior's face. So Jesus took a linen cloth and pressed his face to it, thus making an imprint of his features. The *Mirror* author may have based his description of the humility of Christ's features on the *Legenda Aurea*: 'Fuit enim, ut ibidem dicitur, bene oculatus, bene superciliatus, longum uultum habuit et accliuis, quod est signum maturitatis' (ed. Maggioni, ii. 1081).

60/35 Speciosus . . . hominum. Psalm 44: 3.

60/37 Also, oure Lady tolde Seyint Brygrytte. Left margin of N has 'Nota bene'.

60/37–8 fyrste chapetele . . . *Reuelacyonys*. Saint Birgitta of Sweden, *Revelaciones*, Book VI, ch. 1, ll. 3–4 (ed. Bergh, p. 59).

61/55–8 Lorde . . . rygtwysenesse. Matthew 3: 14–15.

61/59 thre degreys of mekenesse. Cap. xvi of Iohannis de Caulibus's

MVC deals with the three degrees of humility at great length. It quotes Saint Bernard extensively. See also Peter Comestor's *Historia Scholastica* in *PL* 198: 1555: 'Est enim debita humilitas, subdere se maiori propter Deum; abundans, subdere se pari; superabundans, subdere se minori.' The left margin of N has a 'Nota bene' at the opening of this passage, then '1, 2, 3' in the margin at each of the three degrees.

61/76–62/86 **Also for thre causys . . . herytage**. 'Tres fuerunt causae praecipuae cur baptizatus est Iesus a Ioanne: ut baptismum Ioannis approbaret; ut omnem humilitatem impleret, et implendam doceret; ut tactu sui corporis vim regeneratiuam conferret aquis, etsi forte non statim' (Peter Comestor, *Historia Scholastica*, *PL* 198: 1554). The word 'tactu' supports Gg's 'tuchynge' over N's 'techynge'.

62/91–7 **Aftyr thys thynkyth . . . plesyd**. Matthew 3: 16–17.

62/97–8 **as Lyre seyth . . . mankynde**. Nicholas of Lyre, *Postilla* on Matthew 3: 17.

CHAPTER 13

62/6–7 **he was ledde . . . fende**. Matthew 4: 1–2.

62/9–11 **Here . . . Maister of þe Storyis seyth**. Peter Comestor, *Historia Scholastica*, *PL* 198: 1556.

63/13–15 **as Lyre seyth . . . seruauntys**. Nicholas of Lyre, *Postilla* on Matthew 4: 2.

63/25–6 **For hyt ys wryte . . . teche**. Acts 1: 1.

63/27–9 **For Lyre seyth . . . voyce**. Nicholas of Lyre, *Postilla* on Acts 1: 1. Left margin of N has 'Nota bene'.

63/35–7 **Thanne beholdyth . . . seyth**. Peter Comestor, *Historia Scholastica*, *PL* 198: 1556.

63/37–42 **Ȝyf þu be . . . glotenye**. Matthew 4: 3–4.

63/42–64/50 **But oure Lorde ansueryth . . . glorye**. Nicholas of Lyre, *Postilla* on Matthew 4: 3–5.

64/52–7 **And 'thanne' . . . Lorde God**. Matthew 4: 6–7.

64/57–9 **Vpon thys texte . . . synne**. Nicholas of Lyre, *Postilla* on Matthew 4: 7.

64/58 **Forsothe to tempte**. Right margin of N has 'Nota bene'.

64/63–4 **For whenne . . . be þe grecys**. No source has been found for Christ descending the temple stairs.

64/69–75 **After þys . . . seruyd hym**. Matthew 4: 8–11.

64/75 **hym.** At this point N reads: 'hym. Thies bene þe wordes of þe eungeliste. Apon thies wordes Lyre seyth þus.' In the left margin of Gg, a hand with an extended index finger points to where these lines would have appeared. However, this could simply be a indicator of importance, similar to the 'Nota bene' in N (see next note below).

64/75 **Here.** Right margin of N has 'Nota bene'.

64/75–80 **Here oure . . . feende¹.** Nicholas of Lyre, *Postilla* on Matthew 4: 10.

65/100–3 **For Seyint Iamys . . . hym.** James 1: 12.

65/104–66/120 **Seyint Gregory seyth . . . hys deth.** This passage is taken from Pope Gregory I's *Homily* 16, *Homiliae in Evangelia* (CCSL 141, p. 110, ll. 7–19). The source confirms the correctness of Gg's reading at ll. 66/126–7; N's omission is due to eyeskip. Further, Gg's 'vnbeleuable' conforms to the Latin better than N's 'beleuable' (65/109). This homily, as the *Mirror* author states, is typically read during Lent.

66/121 **But hyt ys to be knowe.** Right margin of N has 'Nota bene'.

66/132–67/157 **the same doctur seyth . . . sufferynge.** Like the preceding passage (see note to 65/104–66/120), this is taken from Pope Gregory I's *Homily* 16, *Homiliae in Evangelia* (CCSL 141, p. 112, ll. 51–69).

66/137–68/64 **[þe seconde . . . gostely systre, yhe].** At this point in Gg (f. 54ᵛ), two leaves containing this long passage are missing.

66/141 **[helde].** N has 'helede'. The Latin in Pope Gregory I's *Homily* 16 reads, 'quo nos aditu intromissus tenebat'. *Homiliae in Evangelia* (CCSL 141, p. 112, l. 54). 'Tenebat' (held) indicates that the passage in the *Mirror* should read 'helde' rather than 'helede'.

CHAPTER 14

67/10–11 **And yhe shal vnderstonde . . . as Lyre seyth.** Nicholas of Lyre, *Postilla* on Matthew 4: 18–21.

67/14–21 **His twelfe chefe disciples . . . laste.** The names of the disciples are listed in the Gospels of Matthew, Mark, and Luke. Since the *Mirror* relies on Matthew 10: 1–4 for the majority of this chapter, the list is probably taken from Matthew.

67/21–3 **This fals man betrayede our Lorde . . . as Lyre seyth.** Nicholas of Lyre, *Postilla* on Matthew 10: 4.

67/24–68/63 **Nowe `þan´ . . . Archebisshope of Ierusalem.** Jacobus de Voragine, *Legenda Aurea* (ed. Maggioni, ii. 901–3) and Peter Comestor's *Historia Scholastica*, PL 198: 1563.

68/41–4 **Bot þis Ioseph . . . hangede hymselfe.** Acts 1: 23–6. Saint Joseph Barrabas was one of the two persons nominated to replace Judas as the twelfth Apostle. The disciples drew lots and the lot fell on Saint Matthias.

68/45 **Ioseph is callede also Barsabas and ryghtfull.** Acts 1: 23.

68/45–6 **for þe euydence of his holynes, as Lyre saythe.** Nicholas of Lyre, *Postilla* on Acts 1: 23.

68/55–61 **Also, þat other Iames . . . Iames þe lesse.** Peter Comestor's *Historia Scholastica*, *PL* 198: 1563.

69/74–6 **Petyr and Andrewe, Iamys and Iohn were ycallede fro fyishynge.** This line is taken directly from Mark 1: 16.

69/74–80 **Also, þe chefe of the apostlys . . . stronge.** 1 Corinthians 1:27.

69/82–4 **Also, Lyre seyth . . . Nychodeme.** Nicholas of Lyre, *Postilla* on Matthew 4: 18.

69/89–90 **For haply.** Left margin of N has 'Nota optime'.

69/95–104 **[And þis is ayeyns . . . withoute heresye.]** These eight lines are missing from Gg. Vincent Gillespie suggests that these lines may be referring to the brethren of Syon. If so, they seem to reveal that the monks of Sheen found them to be intellectually intimidating because of the advanced degrees held by many of the Syon brethren and their public mission of preaching to the laity ('The Haunted Text', 146–8).

70/108–10 **For Seyint Bernarde seyth . . . poure.** Saint Bernard of Clairvaux, 'Sermo 3: De lepra Naaman', *Opera*, v. 104, ll. 9–10.

70/113–14 **And aftyrwarde . . . folke.** Since Saint Bernard often asserts that the poor will receive the Kingdom of Heaven, this passage could be taken from any number of his writings.

70/114–20 **Also Seyint Gregory seyth . . . worlde.** From Pope Gregory I's *Moralia in Iob* (CCSL 143A, Liber 13, cap. 10, ll. 31–6, p. 676).

70/117 **contrarye.** N has 'contrey', which probably derives from 'contrare' (a variant spelling of 'contrarie'), with 'ar' represented by an abbreviation mark which was omitted in the exemplar or not seen by the N scribe, so that the word was misinterpreted as 'contre' ('country').

70/126–9 **To these tuelue . . . hyt.** Matthew 10: 8.

70/135–71/143 **Ferthyrmore, besyde these tuelue . . . hys corne.** Luke 10: 1–2.

71/149–50 **a devout man seyth in metre thus . . . mortalium.** These lines derive from some rhythmic verses (incipit 'Si vis esse coenobita') edited as *Rhythmi Veteres de Vita Monastica*, *PL* 184: 1327–30 at 1327:

Multos habemus doctores / Paucissimos factores / In vita mortalium. According to Walther's *Initia* (18079) these lines were widespread.

CHAPTER 15

71/13 **Fyrste thanne, ȝe maye thynke.** Right margin of N has 'De nuptiis in Chana Galilee'.

71/13–15 **þer was made a weddynge . . . fro Naȝareth.** John 2: 1.

71/15–16 **hyt ys comynly seyde . . . Seyinte Ihon Euangeliste.** The idea that this was Saint John's wedding is recorded in a number of medieval treatises used in the *Mirror*, such as Iohannis de Caulibus's *MVC* (CCCM 153, cap. xx, pp. 96–100) and Peter Comestor's *Historia Scholastica*, *PL* 198: 1559.

71/18–20 **For Lyre seyth . . . loongyd to here.** Nicholas of Lyre, *Postilla* on John 2: 1.

72/24–9 **Also oure Lorde . . . godhede.** John 2: 2–11.

72/29 **and thys he doeth gostly.** Right margin of N has 'Nota nota'.

72/36 **fro castel to castel.** N has 'fro castell to castell to castell' with the second 'to castell' crossed out with red ink.

72/39–41 **in makynge blynde men . . . herde afore that tyme.** John 9: 32. N has 'heled' instead of 'herde'; however, based on the source, Gg's reading is correct.

72/44–6 **Also, he wente . . . makare.** Matthew 14: 24–33.

72/46–8 **Also, he fedde fyue thowsende men . . . leuelys.** Matthew 14: 15–21. Left margin of N has 'Nota'.

72/47–50 **with u louys . . . chyldryn.** A mechanical scribal error has caused the omission of these lines in Gg. The scribe's eye skipped from 'with fyfe lofes' to 'with seuen lofes'. The lines have been inserted within a shield in the left margin of Gg (f. 57ᵛ).

72/48–51 **Anothyr tyme he fedde . . . baskettys.** Matthew 15: 32–8.

73/60 **In a tyme ȝe maye thynke.** Outer margin of N has 'Transffiguracio domini', Gg has 'Transfiguracio domini' in its outer margin.

73/60–86 **Mathew makyth mencyon . . . deth to lyue.** The author follows Matthew 17: 1–9 closely for this account of the Transfiguration, while also including passages from the *Postilla* of Nicholas of Lyre and a phrase from Luke 9: 31: 'spekynge wyth oure Lorde of hys Passyon and deth þat he schulde suffre withoute Ierusalem' (73/66–7).

73/63–5 **And he was . . . of hys face.** Nicholas of Lyre, *Postilla* on Matthew 17: 2.

73/71–5 **He spake not of . . . tabernacle.** Nicholas of Lyre, *Postilla* on Matthew 17: 4.

73/87 **he helyde a lunatyke chylde.** Matthew 17: 14–20.

73/88 **Here ȝe schal vndyrstande.** Right margin of N has 'Nota bene'.

73/94–74/97 **For hyt ys seyde . . . wythoute cause.** Matthew 17: 17.

74/110 **The scribys.** Left margin of N has 'Quales fuerunt scribe et pharisei'.

74/118–20 **And for they . . . as the Maystyr of Storyis seyth.** Peter Comestor's *Historia Scholastica* (*PL* 198: 1553).

74/127 **for he seyde þat he was Goddys sone.** Matthew 26: 63–5; 27: 43; John 19: 7.

74/127 `he´ **brake þe haly daye.** Mark 3: 1–6; Luke 6: 6–11.

74/128–9 **he turnyde the peple fro þe lawe.** Luke 23: 14; John 7: 12.

75/134 **In a tyme the Pharyseys.** N's outer margin has 'Quomodo pharisei miserunt discipulos ad capiendum Ihesum in sermone' while Gg's margin has 'Quo modo pharisei miserunt discipulos suos vt caperent ihesum in sermone'.

75/134–76/165 **In a tyme the Pharyseys . . . God to God.** Matthew 22: 15–21, with commentary from Nicholas of Lyra's *Postilla* intermixed throughout.

75/136–7 **for a man . . . as Lyre seyth.** Nicholas of Lyre, *Postilla* on Matthew 22: 15.

75/138 **Kynge Herowdeys knygthtys.** Matthew 22:16 has 'Herodians', a political party that supported the Herod dynasty. They are also mentioned at Mark 3: 6 and 12: 13. In each case they are coupled with the Pharisees.

75/148–9 **For Lyre se`y´th . . . malycyusly.** Nicholas of Lyre, *Postilla* on Matthew 22: 18.

76/170–77/207 **Anothyr tyme . . . no more to synne.** John 8: 3–11. At line 76/170, the outer margin of Gg has 'De muliere comprehensa in adulterio' marked off by four crosses. N's margin has 'De muliere deprehensa in adulterio'.

76/183–6 **And therfore . . . the lawe.** Nicholas of Lyre, *Postilla* on John 8: 6.

77/230 **For foure `causys´·** Left margin of N has 'Nota quatuor causas diuinae incarnacionis' followed immediately by a '1'. Each of the next three causes is marked by a number in the margin.

77/234–78/236 **Venit . . . pro multis.** Matthew 20: 28.

78/238 **The secunde cause.** Right margin of N has '2'.

78/242–3 **Qui . . . me sequatur.** John 12: 26.

78/247–8 **Et vbi . . . meus erit.** John 12: 26.

78/249 **The thyrde cause.** Right margin of N has '3 Nota bene'.

78/254–5 **Si mundus . . . odio habuit.** John 25: 18.

78/256–7 **The foureth cause.** Right margin of N has '4'.

78/261–7 **for Seyint Austyn . . . gett aȝen.** Pseudo-Augustine, *Liber Soliloquiorum Animae ad Deum*, cap. XVIII (*PL* 40: 879).

CHAPTER 16

79/7–18 **Amoo[n]ge othyr myraclys . . . be hem gostly.** The opening of Chapter 16 recounts three resurrections performed by Christ. It relies on the gospels and two works by Saint Augustine: *Sermo* 98 on the raising of Lazarus (*PL* 38: 591–5) and Tractatus XLIX (on John 11: 1–54) from Saint Augustine, *In Iohannis Euangelium* (CCSL 36, pp. 419–33).

79/11–14 **For Seyint Austyn seyth . . . lyf gostly.** *Sermo* 98 (*PL* 38: 591).

79/18–21 **For Seyint [Austyn] seyth . . . to be vndyrstonde gostly.** *Sermo* 98 (*PL* 38: 592).

79/22 **The fyrste of hem.** Right margin of N has '1'.

79/23–4 **And she was . . . Iayre.** Luke 8: 41–56.

79/29–80/34 **as Seyint Austyn seyth . . . pryuy.** From Saint Augustine, Tractatus CXXIV, *In Iohannis Euangelium* (CCSL 36, p. 421, ll. 11–15).

80/35 **The secunde was a wydowes sone.** Right margin of N has '2'.

80/35–46 **The secunde was a wydowes sone . . . and magnyfyede God.** Luke 7: 11–16.

80/36–7 **thys was in the contre . . . Maystyr of Storyis seyth.** Peter Comestor, *Historia Scholastica, PL* 198: 1566.

80/50–7 **For Seyinte Austyn seyth . . . Modyr holy chyrche.** Saint Augustine's Tractatus CXXIV, *In Iohannis Euangelium* (CCSL 141, p. 421, ll. 15–20).

80/59 **The thyrde deede was Lasur.** Left margin of N has '3'.

80/59–62 **The thyrde deede was Lasur . . . leyde vpon hym.** John 11: 1–45.

80/59–81/75 The ideas developed in this paragraph, as well as many of the expressions, are taken from Saint Augustine's Tractatus XLIX, *In Iohannis Euangelium* (CCSL 141, p. 421, ll. 20–41).

81/76–8 **Aftyr thys . . . Lorde Ihesu Cryste.** John 11: 45.

81/78–80 **For the same euangelyste . . . deth.** John 11: 19.

81/85 **Fo'r' Lyre seyth.** Right margin of N has 'Nota bene'.

81/85–7 **Fo'r' Lyre seyth . . . harde in euyl.** Nicholas of Lyre, *Postilla* on John 11: 46.

81/93–9 **they gaderyde . . . oure peple also.** John 11: 47–8.

82/104–9 **Aftyr þys ȝe maye thynke . . . for the pepyl.** John 11: 49–51.

82/109 **Here we be taugwth.** Left margin of N has 'Nota bene'.

82/109–11 **Here we be taugwth . . . be euyl men.** Saint Augustine's Tractatus XLIX, *In Iohannis Euangelium Tractatus* (CCSL 31, p. 432, ll. 6–7).

82/118–21 **Domine . . . operamini iniquitatem.** Matthew 7: 22–3.

83/138–43 **fro that daye . . . as they mygthte.** John 11: 53.

CHAPTER 17

83/1 **Of the sopere.** In Iohannis de Caulibus's *MVC*, the account of the supper at Bethany (CCCM 153, cap. xlv, pp. 171–3, ll. 1–56) contains a discussion of the active and contemplative lives. The thirteen chapters following this account in the *MVC* (caps. xlvi–lviii, pp. 173–216) discuss the positive and negative aspects of both active and contemplative worship in great detail. These chapters rely on St Bernard and the Gospels as principal sources. The *Mirror* author does not address active and contemplative worship in his account of the supper.

83/11–13 **as the euangelyste Seyint Ihon . . . Betanye.** John 12: 1.

84/16–25 **Thys feste . . . Passynge of oure Lorde.** Exodus 12: 1–51.

84/29–34 **And so vi dayis . . . wyth oure Lorde.** John 12: 1–2.

84/34–7 **Thys sopere . . . myracle.** See, for example, Peter Comestor's *Historia Scholastica*, PL 198: 1597. In Nicholas of Lyre's *Postilla*, he comments on this when discussing John 12: 2.

84/37–9 **And the same man . . . in hys house.** Nicholas of Lyre, *Postilla* on John 12: 2.

84/40–6 **Marye Maudeleyne . . . of gret pryse.** John 12: 3. In the Middle Ages Mary Magdalene, who had seven devils cast out of her by Christ (Luke 8: 2), is often identified with Mary of Bethany (Luke 10: 38–42), sister of Martha and Lazarus, and the woman who anointed Christ's feet (Luke 7: 37–50). The proximity of the verses in which the three women appear caused many theologians to identify all three passages with Mary Magdalene. Pope Gregory I added authority to the misidentification in 591 when he said: 'Hanc uero quam Lucas peccatricem mulierem, Iohannes Mariam nominat, illam esse Mariam credimus de qua Marcus septem daemonia eiecta fuisse testatur'; *Homily* 33, *Homiliae in Evangelia* (CCSL 141, p. 288, ll. 7–9).

85/48–54 **Aftyr thys . . . in othyr vsys.** John 12: 4–6.

85/54–5 **For he bare . . . hys dyscyplys.** Nicholas of Lyre, *Postilla* on John 12: 6.

85/57–8 **Seyint Gregory seyth . . . euylle.** *Homiliae in Evangelia* (CCSL 141, p. 366, ll. 167–8).

85/60–3 **Why be ʒe heuy . . . me.** Matthew 26: 10–11.

85/65–7 **Neuyrdeles, Lyre seyth . . . couetyse.** Nicholas of Lyre, *Postilla* on Matthew 26: 8. See also Peter Comestor's *Historia Scholastica*, PL 198: 1598.

85/68–75 **Thanne aftyr thys . . . in oure Lorde Ihes Cryste.** John 12: 9–11.

85/75–9 **Aftyr þys thynkyth . . . cam aʒenste hym.** John 12: 12–13.

85/79–80 **And some . . . in the weye.** Luke 19: 36.

85/82–86/87 **Thanne aftyr thys . . . sytte vpon.** Matthew 21: 1–2.

86/87–91 **Thys asse . . . nede.** The source of this information regarding the colt and ass being available for the poor derives from Iohannis de Caulibus's *MVC* (CCCM 153, cap. lxxi, p. 238, ll. 20–3).

86/95–87/121 **Thanne ʒe maye thynke . . . he cam ofte thedyr.** This section concerning Christ's entry into Jerusalem contains a mixture of verses taken from Mark 11: 7–11 and John 12: 12–19.

86/105–7 **For they wende . . . as Lyre seyth.** Nicholas of Lyre, *Postilla* on John 12: 13.

86/111–14 **Thanne thynkyth also . . . goyth aftyr hym.** John 12: 19.

87/121–4 **And there he abode . . . hys deth.** Nicholas of Lyre, *Postilla* on Matthew 21: 1–2.

87/124–33 **And thanne thynkyth . . . for hym.** Matthew 26: 3–5.

87/134–43 **Thanne ʒe maye thynke . . . of the peple.** Matthew 26: 14–16.

87/143–5 **for there . . . myraclys þat he wrowthe.** Matthew 21: 46 and Luke 20: 19.

87/147 **Holy.** At this point in N is an erasure. It is not clear what is cancelled.

CHAPTER 18

88/1 **Of þe soper.** Throughout this chapter's account of the Last Supper, the *Mirror* author chiefly relies on Matthew 26: 17–35, Luke 22: 8–34, and John 13: 2–38.

88/13–26 **And thanne thynkyth . . . downe to sopere.** Luke 22: 8–14.

89/26–89/64 **and whenne they . . . othyrys be rowe.** John 13: 2–12.

89/68–90/76 **Aftyr thys thynkyth . . . doo \so/ also.** John 13: 12–15.

90/81 **For hyt ys . . . some louarys.** Left margin of N has 'Nota'.

90/92 **I am wyth . . . worldlys ende.** Matthew 28: 20.

90/96 **Sykyrly.** Left margin of N has 'Nota nota bene'. The 'bene' is written at an angle and may be by a different hand. Gg's right margin also has 'Nota bene'.

90/96–100 **Sykyrly, trewly . . . of my Fadyr.** Henry Suso, *Horologium Sapientia*, Liber II, (ed. Künzle, p. 549, ll. 6–10).

90/97–92/159 **I am conteynyd . . . to hem.** This lengthy passage on the communion, beginning with the quotation from Henry Suso's *Horologium Sapientiae*, appears to be original to the *Mirror to Devout People*.

91/119 **Here, as me semyth.** Right margin of N has 'Nota'.

91/136 **Why.** Left margin of N has 'Nota nota'.

92/153–9 **[Also, hyt ys wryte . . . so as to hem.]** This paragraph is inserted in the right margin of Gg and runs into the lower margin of the page. It is inserted into the text here because it is a natural extension of the argument, and, while it may be scribal, it shows an important addition to the transmission of this text and a natural conclusion to the discussion of the sacrament.

92/175 **Also.** Right margin of N has 'Nota'.

93/191–2 **And þat oure Lorde.** Left margin of N has 'Nota'.

93/201–3 **Fforsothe one . . . haue be borne.** Matthew 26: 21, 24.

93/203–94/223 **Thanne thynkyth þat . . . but pryuyly.** John 13: 22–6.

94/224–5 **but Lyre seyth . . . oure Lorde seyde.** Nicholas of Lyre, *Postilla* on John 13: 28.

94/248 **And also.** Left margin of N has 'Nota bene'.

95/251–7 **Thanne aftyr þys . . . as the [euangelyste] seyth.** John 13: 28–30.

95/260–4 **oure Lorde tolde . . . neuyr forsake the.** Matthew 26: 31–3.

95/264–5 **For I am aredy . . . deth also.** Luke 22: 33.

95/270–2 **oure Lorde ansueryde . . . denye hym threys.** Christ's prophesying Peter's denial occurs in each of the gospels: Matthew 26: 34; Mark 14: 30; Luke 22: 34; John 13: 38.

95/273 **a fayre sermone.** The *Mirror* author presumably had in mind the lengthy account of Christ's words found in John 14–16.

95/279 **and aftyrwarde.** Right margin of N has 'Nota bene'.

95/282 **And so in thys.** Right margin of N has 'Nota bene'.

CHAPTER 19

96/11–14 **as Lyre seyth . . . Estyr lombe.** Nicholas of Lyre, *Postilla* on John 14: 31.

96/16 **Arysyth vp and goo we hennys.** John 14: 31.

96/21–2 **Lyre seyth þat Cedron . . . Mounte of Oly`ue´te.** Nicholas of Lyre, *Postilla* on John 17: 1.

96/26 **Gessemany.** The place where Jesus suffered his Agony. It appears in Matthew 26: 36 and from this point in the *Mirror* to the end of the chapter, the author follows Matthew 26: 36–66 for the story of Christ's Passion. He does, however, integrate details from Mark 14, Luke 22, and John 18.

97/40–1 **Thanne beholdyth . . . a stonys caste.** This detail is found in Luke 22: 41.

97/49–53 **how he comyth . . . one oure wyth me.** Matthew 26: 40.

97/53–4 **Why sclepe ȝe . . . not into temptacyon.** Luke 22: 46.

97/55–6 **The spyryt ys rethy, but the fleyisch ys feble.** Matthew 26: 41.

97/67 **and thys stryfe.** Right margin in N has 'Nota bene'.

97/67–98/70 **and thys stryfe . . . propyr to hym.** Nicholas of Lyre, *Postilla* on Luke 22: 43.

98/73, 75 **dropys of blode; angyl fro heuene.** these details are taken from Luke 22: 44 and 43 respectively. The authenticity of these two verses from Luke has been called into question because of their absence from other synoptists as well as from several ancient codices of Luke. See Tuckett, 'Luke 22, 43–44', and Ehrman and Plunkett, 'The Angel and the Agony'.

98/88 **wypyth hys face.** This detail also appears in Iohannis de Caulibus's *MVC* (CCCM 153, cap. lxxv, pp. 255–63, ll. 111–15). The *MVC* describes Christ wiping his body and washing himself in the river before returning to his disciples.

98/96–102 **Arysyth vp . . . knowe oure Lorde.** Matthew 26: 46–8.

98/100 **lanternys.** This detail is taken from John 18: 3.

98/102–3 **for ther was one of hys dyscypllys . . . one fro þat othyr.** Matthew 26: 47–8. The details of this passage are recounted in Jacobus de Voragine's *Legenda Aurea* (ed. Maggioni, i. 447).

99/106–20 **Thanne thynkyth . . . eny harme.** This paragraph closely follows John 18: 4–8.

99/121–100/148 **And `thanne´ beholdyth how Iudas . . . tolde hem afore.** Matthew 26: 49–56.

99/129–30 **Malchys, as the euangelyste seyth.** John 18: 10.

99/130 **And thanne beholdyth.** Right margin of N has 'Nota bene'.

99/132–5 **Put vp they suerde . . . legyonys of angyllys.** Matthew 26: 52–4.

99/135–6 **A legyon ys vi thowsende.** Left margin of N has 'Nota'.

99/138–9 **How schulde scripturys . . . hyt muste bee.** Matthew 26: 54.

99/140–100/143 **3e come to me . . . the pouere of derkenesse.** Luke 22: 52–3.

100/154–69 **For to hym . . . lete come in.** John 18: 13, 15–16.

100/175–101/194 **And thanne he wente . . . koc crewe a3en.** John 18: 17–27.

101/186–7 **And þu were wyth Ihesu of Na3areth.** Mark 14: 67.

101/178–9 **Seygth I not the in the gardyn wyth hym.** John 18: 26.

101/187–92 **And `thanne´ Petyr . . . crowe tueys.** Matthew 26: 74–5. Peter's cursing also appears in Mark 14: 71 and Christ's looking on Peter is found in Luke 22: 61.

101/192–4 **And thanne Petyr . . . callyd koc crowynge.** Peter Comestor, *Historia Scholastica*, PL 198: 1624.

101/206–102/221 **And he askede oure Lorde . . . byischop that 3ere.** John 18: 19–24.

102/225–9 **And there they softe . . . browgth forth.** Matthew 26: 59–60.

102/230–1 **Thys man seyde . . . handys of men.** Matthew 26: 61 and Mark 14: 58.

102/231–3 **and withinne . . . handys of men.** The biblical sources, Matthew 26: 61 and Mark 14: 58, suggests that N's scribe committed an eyeskip and left out this phrase, which appears in Gg.

102/233–41 **And thanne thynkyth þat Cayphas . . . þat he blasphemyde.** Matthew 26: 62–5.

102/245–7 **Loo, 3e haue herde . . . to be deed.** Matthew 26: 65–6 and Mark 14: 64.

102/248–103/252 **Aftyr thys . . . hym laste.** Matthew 26: 67–8 and Mark 14: 65.

103/254 **Here dylygently.** Left margin of N has 'Nota ista subsequencis'.

103/267 **anone.** After the letter 'o' in 'anone' (at the bottom of f. 83ᵛ in Gg) the Gg scribe has left out twelve lines: f. 84ʳ begins 'And therfore ȝe maye thynke' (103/277–8). In the bottom margin of f. 83ᵛ is a pointing manicule in red ink with the message 'Turne to þe iiii lef to sueche a syne', followed by a small marker, which is the sign for which the reader is to look. The matching sign appears at the top of f. 87ᵛ, where the missing paragraph is copied. See note to 108/140.

103/273–4 **þat they schulde kepe hym in faste holde into the mornynge.** There is no biblical account of Christ being held overnight in prison. However, each of the four gospels ends the account of the evening in question with Peter's betrayal and begins again the next morning with Christ facing his accusers. One could assume, as the *Mirror* author has, that Christ was imprisoned throughout the night.

CHAPTER 20

104/3–7 **Now beholdyth . . . pote hym to deth.** Matthew 27: 1.

104/20–1 **Sicut ouis . . . aperiet os suum.** This passage is from Isaiah 53: 7 and it is applied to Christ at Acts 8: 32–5.

105/46–60 **Aftyr thys beholde῾th' . . . berye pylgrimys inne.** Matthew 27: 3–7.

105/52–54 **And in that . . . he betrayede hym.** The attribution of this passage to Saint Jerome is found in Peter Comestor, *Historia Scholastica* (*PL* 198: 1625).

105/62–106/67 **and how Pylat . . . to scle eny man.** John 18: 29–31.

106/68–72 **And ῾thanne' they accusyde hym . . . Godys sone.** Left margin of N has 'Nota bene' with '1, 2, 3' immediately below it in the margin corresponding to each of the three accusations.

106/80–96 **Thow arte Kynge of Iewys . . . heryth my wordys.** Luke 18: 33–8.

107/100–6 **And anone they cryde aȝen . . . thyke dayis.** Luke 23: 5–7.

107/108–22 **And whenne he sawgth hym . . . enmyis eueryche to othyr.** Luke 23: 8–12.

108/135–6 **and therfore he wolde . . . goo hys weye.** Luke 23: 16.

108/137–40 **Hyt ys a custum . . . was a thef.** John 18: 39–40.

108/139–41 **And that Barraban . . . in prysone.** Luke 23: 19.

108/140 **sclaugthyr idoo in the.** At the top of f. 87ᵛ in Gg is a small symbol signalling the beginning of the paragraph missing between the bottom of f. 83ᵛ and the top of f. 84ʳ. The paragraph is inserted here and runs to 'cytee' (108/140). At this point in Gg (f. 87ᵛ) is a small symbol preceding 'cytee'. In the left margin is a direction with a red hand pointing towards it: 'turne aȝen were þu leftyst & rede at sueche a syne'. This directs the reader back to f. 83^v (see note to 103/267).

108/141 **As to the vndyrstondynge.** Left margin of N has 'Nota bene'.

108/156–60 **he made his knygthtys . . . to scorge hym.** Matthew 27: 26–31; Mark 15: 15–20; Luke 19: 1–3.

109/178–9 **Ffro the sole . . . helthe on hym.** Isaiah 1: 6.

109/186–7 **And therfore the ewangelystys . . . in scharpenesse and hardnesse.** Matthew 27: 29; Mark 15: 17; John 19: 2.

109/188–90 **for the Maystyr of Storyis seyth . . . ryischyssys of the see.** Peter Comestor, *Historia Scholastica* (*PL* 198: 1628).

109/190 **and Lyre also seyth the same.** Nicholas of Lyre, *Postilla* on Matthew 27: 29.

109/192 **Seyint Lodewyke, the Kynge of Fraunce.** This story about Saint Louis IX, King of France, an unidentified man, and the crown of thorns is quoted verbatim from Nicholas of Lyre's *Postilla* on Matthew 27: 29.

109/195–7 **Also Maundeuelde . . . iun'c'kys of þe see.** This is taken from chapter 2 of *Mandeville's Travels* (ed. P. Hamelius, i. 8).

109/202–3 **they take a purpur clothe . . . aboute hym.** Mark 15: 17 and John 19: 2.

109/203–110/210 **And they 'toke' also . . . passyngly paynful.** Matthew 27: 29–30.

110/216–22 **And thanne Pylat seyde to hem . . . Loo, man.** John 19: 4–5.

CHAPTER 21

110/3–113/91 **Now thanne takyth . . . deth as they desyryde.** This section of Chapter 21 relates the last trial of Jesus before Pilate by closely following the narrative in John 19: 6–15.

110/8–111/11 **Crucyfye hym . . . no cause in hym.** John 19: 6.

111/16–17 **We haue a lawe . . . Goddys sone.** John 19: 7.

111/26–7 **he askyth hym . . . mekely helde hys pece.** John 19: 9.

111/30–112/50 **And thanne Pylat seyde . . . and there he satt to deme.** John 19: 9–13.

111/36 **In thys worde betokenynge.** Right margin of N has 'Nota bene'.

112/53–8 **Anone he brought . . . vysyon for hym.** Matthew 27: 19.

112/59–62 **Haply the 'feende' perseyuyde . . . delyuere oure Lorde.** The idea that Satan came to Pilate's wife in a dream was widespread in the medieval period. Many of the Passion plays, including the York and N. Town plays, contained a scene with Satan influencing Pilate's wife. In his *Postilla* on Matthew 27: 19, Nicholas of Lyre relates this story. Paschasius Radbertus also relates this story in his *Expositio in Matheo*, CCCM 56B, Book 12, l. 2931.

112/65–70 **And thanne 'Pylat' . . . vpon oure chyldryn.** Matthew 27: 24–5.

112/69 **Hys blode.** Left margin of N has 'Nota bene'.

112/71–6 **And so aftyrwarde . . . for thyrty pense.** This derives from Jacobus de Voragine's *Legenda Aurea*, ch. 67: 'sicut Iudei Christum XXX denariis emerant, sic et ipse uno denario triginta Iudeos uendidit' (ed. Maggioni, i. 457). Following four years of conflict, the Romans, led by Titus, ransacked the city and burned the temple in 70 CE. Josephus provides the only eyewitness account of the city's destruction (see Josephus, *The Jewish War*).

112/81–113/88 **Schal I crucyfye . . . but the Emperoure.** John 19: 15.

112/114 **xv feete longe.** This detail is also found in Iohannis de Caulibus's *MVC*, CCCM 153, cap. lxxvii, p. 268, ll. 36–7.

114/120–2 **they take too theues . . . Trewthe icouplyd to tueyne theuys.** Matthew 27: 38; Mark 15: 27; Luke 23: 33; John 19: 18.

114/135–52 **And thanne thynkyth also . . . sorwe and heuynesse.** This passage closely resembles Iohannis de Caulibus's *MVC*, CCCM 153, cap. lxxvii, p. 269, ll. 52–9.

115/175–7 **Aftyr þys thynkyth . . . aftyr oure Lorde.** Matthew 27: 32; Mark 15: 21; John 23: 26.

<h3 style="text-align:center">CHAPTER 22</h3>

116/6–7 **the 'whyche ys callyd' Caluarye . . . Golgata.** Matthew 27: 33; Mark 15: 22; John 19: 17.

117/23–44 **How and in what wyse . . . men haue ymagynyd.** Both the supine and upright methods of crucifixion are also mentioned in Iohannis de Caulibus's *MVC*. However, the upright method is given preference in the *MVC* (CCCM 153) and described at cap. lxxviii, p. 271, ll. 20–4. The supine method is described at cap. lxxviii, pp. 271–2, ll. 44–7.

117/45–118/83 **Anothyr wyse . . . *Reuelacyon* of Seyint Brygytte.** Saint Birgitta, *Revelaciones*, Book I, ch. 10.

117/47 **Beholdyth fyrste an hole.** Right margin of N has 'Reuelacio beate Britte'.

118/65–6 **the bone ys saddyst inne.** Saint Birgitta, *Revelaciones*, Book I, ch. 10.

119/88–92 **for Seyint Brygytt . . . and half deed.** Saint Birgitta, *Revelaciones*, Book I, ch. 10.

119/98 **Ffadyr forȝeue hem . . . what they doo.** Luke 23: 34.

119/99–101 **And thanne takyth good hede . . . he hadde be [thiefe].** Matthew 27: 38; Mark 15: 28; Luke 23: 33.

119/107–8 **Pylat wrote . . . vpon the crosse.** John 19: 20.

119/108–10 **for hyt was þe maner . . . sette hyt vpon the crosse.** Nicholas of Lyre, *Postilla* on John 19: 19.

119/111 **Ihesu Cryste Nazarenus Rex Iudeorum.** Matthew 27: 37; Mark 15: 26; Luke 23: 38; John 19: 19.

119/114–15 **as the euangelyste . . . and Latyn.** John 19: 20.

120/123–4 **Thys tytyl manye . . . nere the cytee.** John 19: 20.

120/126–37 **And thanne thynkyth . . . hoo schal haue here.** John 19: 21–4.

120/137–45 **And thanne thynketh . . . beleue in hym.** Matthew 27: 39–42.

120/145–9 **And in thys they . . . beleue on hym.** This is from Pope Gregory I, *Homily* 21, *Homiliae in Evangelia* (CCSL 141, p. 178, ll. 128–9).

121/160 **And in thys.** Right margin of N has 'Nota bene'.

121/174–84 **Aftyr thys turnyth aȝen . . . wyth me in paradyse.** Luke 23: 39–43.

121/188–122/192 **Aftyr ˈthysˈ . . . hys modyr.** John 19: 25–7.

122/194 **He callyede not here modyr but woman.** Left margin of N has 'Nota'.

122/194–7 **He callyede not here modyr . . . here sonys Passyon.** Nicholas of Lyre, *Postilla* on John 19: 26.

122/212–14 **And thanne thynkyth . . . þat he schulde drynke.** John 19: 28–9.

122/220 **For Seyint Gregory seyth.** Right margin of N has 'Nota ista subsequencis'.

122/220–123/234 **For Seyint Gregory seyth . . . Sondaye of Quynquageseme.** The homily is Saint Gregory's *Homily* 2 on the Gospel for the Sunday before Lent, or Quinquagesima, *Homiliae in Evangelia* (CCSL 141, pp. 12–19).

CHAPTER 23

123/3–6 **In the begynnynge . . . thre ourys.** Matthew 27: 45; Mark 15: 33; Luke 23: 44.

123/6–8 **For Lyre seyth . . . vndyr the sunne.** Nicholas of Lyre, *Postilla* on Matthew 27: 45.

124/43–6 **seynge þat all was fufylde . . . drawe to dethwarde.** John 19: 28.

124/34–6 **And thanne thynkyth . . . he ȝaf vp the goste.** Luke 23: 46.

124/49–50 **And so he was obedyent . . . Seyint Poule seyth.** Philippians 2: 8.

124/50–3 **And thanne the vayle . . . of Cryste dyinge.** Matthew 27: 51 and Nicholas of Lyre, *Postilla* on Matthew 27: 51.

124/53–6 **And grauys were openyd . . . aryse wyth hym.** Matthew 27.52 and Nicholas of Lyre, *Postilla* on Matthew 27.52.

124/56–125/70 **Seyint Gregory seyth . . . crydyn God.** Pope Gregory I's *Homily* 10, *Homiliae in Evangelia* (CCSL 141, pp. 66–7, ll. 20–35). This passage is used in the Third Nocturn of Matins for the Feast of the Epiphany.

124/71–6 **Aftyr thys, thynkyth . . . Godys sonys.** Matthew 27: 54.

124/74–5 **the whyche mygthte . . . uertu of kynde.** Nicholas of Lyre, *Postilla* on Matthew 27: 46.

124/76–9 **And all the othyr peple . . . Lorde to the dethe.** Luke 23: 48.

124/92–126/124 **And thanne ȝe maye thynke . . . putt hym in hys sepulcre.** This passage is an example of the popular *planctus Mariae*. Iohannis de Caulibus's *MVC* (CCCM 153, cap. lxxix, pp. 276–7, ll. 1–19) contains a similar, but briefer, account of Mary's suffering. See Sticca, *The Planctus Mariae*, 122–5.

CHAPTER 24

127/4–13 **Aftyr the oure of None . . . knygthtys wyth hem.** John 19: 31.

127/13–128/25 **And 'thanne' beholdyth . . . and watyr.** John 19: 32–4.

128/26–9 **Hyt ys to be knowe . . . clene watyr.** Nicholas of Lyre, *Postilla* on John 19: 34.

128/28 **as some seyin.** A similar account can be found in the legend of Saint Longinus in Jacobus de Voragine's *Legenda Aurea* (ed. Maggioni, i. 307–8).

128/31 **Manycheys.** The Manichaeans were a religious sect founded by the Persian Mani. They purportedly believed that Christ never existed in a physical body, but only in spirit. As a result, they denied Christ's resurrection and the principles of transubstantiation.

129/67–9 **for Seyint Ihon . . . in hys bloode.** Apocalypse 1: 5. In the Middle Ages, Saint John the Evangelist was commonly believed to be the same person as Saint John the Divine, author of the Apocalypse.

130/102 **For perseueraunce.** Left margin of N has 'Nota nota'.

130/102–6 **For perseueraunce . . . not be sauyd.** Pope Gregory I, *Homily* 25, *Homiliae in Evangelia* (CCSL 141, p. 205, ll. 15–8).

130/107 **Also, gostly systyr.** Left margin of N has 'Nota optime'.

130/116–17 **And therfore here vndyrstondyth.** Right margin of N has 'Nota ex causa'.

130/119–21 **For Seyint Iohn seyth . . . as he wente.** 1 John 2: 6.

130/126–7 **Lete vs thanne . . . as `Seyint Ihon´ seyth.** 1 John 4: 19.

130/129–30 **Ʒyf ʒe loue me, kepyth my commaundmentys.** John 14: 15.

130/130–1 **He þat hath . . . louyth me.** John 14: 21.

CHAPTER 25

131/13–23 **Aftyr thys ʒe maye thynke . . . wynde hyt inne.** Mark 15: 43–6.

131/15–17 **Arymathye was . . . Samuel borne.** The information on Ramatha comes from Bede, *In primam partem Samuhelis libri iiii* (CCSL 119, Book 1, p. 11, ll. 11–14). For the birthplace of Samuel, see also 1 Samuel 1: 1.

131/23 **the whyche was a lynnyn cloth, as Lyre seyth.** Nicholas of Lyre, *Postilla* on Matthew 27: 59.

131/29–132/38 **And thanne ʒe maye thynke . . . a vnement.** John 19: 39.

132/39–42 **And in thys . . . oure Lorde Ihesu Cryste.** Nicholas of Lyre, *Postilla* on John 19: 39.

132/42 **[Fyu`e´tenthe] Psalme.** Gg reads 'Fyuethe'; N reads 'ferth', but the correct reference is Psalm 15: 10.

132/51–133/90 **Aftyr thys ʒe maye thynke . . . besyde wepynge.** Iohannis de Caulibus's *MVC* (CCCM 153, cap. lxxix, p. 279, ll. 71–123) contains a similar description of the removal of Christ's body from the cross.

133/91–4 **as hyt ys wryte in Seyint Brygyttys** *Reuelacyon* . . .
Euynsonge tyme. Saint Birgitta of Sweden, *Revelaciones*, Book I, ch. 10.

CHAPTER 26

134/6–9 **Ioseph and Nychodemus . . . was to berye.** Matthew 27: 55,
61; Mark 15: 40, 47; Luke 23: 55.

134/9–12 **Aftyr thys thynkyth . . . oure Lordys body.** John 19: 41–2.

134/16–25 **The sepulcre of oure Lorde . . . menglyd togyderys.** The
description of the sepulcre in which Christ is buried is recounted in Peter
Comestor's *Historia Scholastica* (*PL* 198: 1634). He uses a passage from
Bede's *In Marci Euangelium Expositio* (CCSL 120, Liber 4, cap. 15, p. 638,
ll. 1680–8) to describe the tomb. The details do not always correspond with
the *Mirror*'s account, but they contain numerous similiarities.

135/44–9 **And oure Lady . . . in dyuerse innys.** Peter Comestor, *Historia
Scholastica* (*PL* 198: 1645).

135/50–60 **Aftyr thys thynkyth . . . Lyre seyth.** Matthew 27: 62–6;
Nicholas of Lyre, *Postilla* on Matthew 27: 66.

CHAPTER 27

136/13 **for þat a man or a woman.** Right margin in N has 'Nota'.

138/76–9 **Aftyr þys ȝe maye thynke . . . annoynite oure Lordys body.**
Mark 16: 1.

CHAPTER 28

138/6–11 **Here ȝe schal vndyrstande . . . Resurreccyon of oure Lorde.**
Peter Comestor, *Historia Scholastica* (*PL* 198: 1589).

138/12–13 **And hyt ys callyd . . . of oure feyth.** Christ refers to
Abraham's bosom in Luke 16: 22.

139/20–4 **for the sygthte of God . . . fro þe bodyis.** Nicholas of Lyre,
De visione divinae essentiae. The only edition of the *De visione* is a working
edition with translation found in Michael Scott Woodward's unpublished
University of Notre Dame dissertation, 'Nicholas of Lyra on Beatific
Vision'.

139/24–39 **And therfore the forseyde place . . . be wyth me in
paradyse.** Nicholas of Lyre, *De visione divinae essentiae*. He gives a similar

explanation of paradise in the *Postilla* on Luke 23: 43. The *Historia Scholastica* (*PL* 198: 1631) also provides three similar meanings of paradise.

139/28 **Hodie mecum eris in paradyso.** Luke 23: 43.

139/33–7 **one maner . . . the secunde maner . . . the thyrde maner.** In N's right margin, each of these manners is highlighted with a number '1', '2', and '3' respectively.

139/43 **but ʒytt Nychodemys.** Right margin in N has 'Nota'. See *Nichodemus his gospel*, ed. John Warrin.

139/43–8 **but ʒytt Nychodemys . . . sympyl creaturys.** The opinion that the *Gospel of Nicodemus* is false comes from Nicholas of Lyra's *De visione divinae essentiae* (ed. Woodward, 231). Jacobus de Voragine's *Legenda Aurea*, however, does rely on the *Gospel of Nicodemus* for its account of Christ's Passion (ed. Maggioni, i. 336).

140/73–5 **Seyint Austyn seyth . . . ʒyf þat þu behettyste.** Saint Augustine, *Sermo* CVIII, Cap. vii (*PL* 38.636).

CHAPTER 29

141/12 **The Maystyr of Storyis seyth.** Right margin in N has 'Narracio.'

141/12–17 **The Maystyr of Storyis seyth . . . sepulcre beynge close.** Peter Comestor, *Historia Scholastica* (*PL* 198: 1636). Jacobus de Voragine's *Legenda Aurea* gives the same version and refers to the *Historia Scholastica* as its source (ed. Maggioni, i. 358).

141/20 **the whyche was the Sondaye . . . as Seyint Austyn seyth.** This detail actually comes from Peter Comestor's *Historia Scholastica* (*PL* 198: 1637).

141/27–31 **And att thys gloryus Resurreccyon . . . hadde be a walle.** This is taken from Mechtild of Hackeborn, *The Booke of Gostlye Grace* (ed. Halligan), a Middle English translation of her *Liber specialis gratiae*. See also Voaden, 'The Company She Keeps'.

141/31–7 **Also the euangelyste seyth . . . deede men.** Matthew 28: 2–4.

141/39–142/48 **And sone aftyr . . . into þys daye.** Matthew 28: 11–15.

142/48–50 **and so they were dysseyuyd . . . as Lyre seyth.** Nicholas of Lyre, *Postilla* on Matthew 28: 15.

142/52–5 **and fyrste ʒe schal . . . fiue tymys aftyrwarde.** Jacobus de Voragine, *Legenda Aurea* (ed. Maggioni, i. 360–1).

142/57–62 **of the whyche one . . . Legende þat ys callyd Aurea.** Jacobus de Voragine, *Legenda Aurea* (ed. Maggioni, i. 364).

142/76–144/125 **Ffyrste thanne ʒe maye thynke . . . sche mygthte see** hem. This apparition is similarly described in Iohannis de Caulibus, *MVC* (CCCM 153, cap. lxxii, pp. 240–2).

143/91 **'Salue sancta parens'** . . . **Ha`y´le holy modyr.** These are the opening words of the *officium* to the Mass of the Commemoration of the Blessed Virgin in the Sarum missal (*Sarum Missal*, ed. Wickham Legg, p. 389). These words also appear in Iohannis de Caulibus, *MVC* (CCCM 153, cap. lxxxii, p. 301, ll. 28–9).

143/108–12 **Thys heuene ys callyd** . . . **clerely inne.** Peter Comestor, *Sententiae in iv libris distinctae* (*PL* 192: 80).

144/114–15 **Lyre seyth** . . . **were he wolde.** Nicholas of Lyre, *De visione divinae essentiae* (ed. Woodward, 231).

CHAPTER 30

144/13–145/27 **Marye Maudeleyne on Estyr** . . . **they wente home aȝen.** John 20: 1–10.

145/29–146/55 **But Marye Maudeleyne** . . . **for þat tyme.** John 20: 11–17.

145/32–3 **for the mygthte** . . . **as Seynte Gregorye seyth.** Pope Gregory I's *Homily* 25, *Homiliae in Evangelia* (CCSL 141, p. 205, ll. 27–8).

145/41–2 **The cause þat.** N has 'Nota bene' in right margin.

145/41–5 **The cause þat** . . . **sueche reuerence to.** Nicholas of Lyre, *Postilla* on John 20: 14.

146/58–149/166 **And aftyrwarde thynkyth** . . . **That othyr.** N has a marginal comment to 'aftyrwarde' that reads 'Nota optime'. Each of the following apparitions is numbered in the margin with '2, 3, 4, 5, et al.' Similarly, Gg uses 'i, ii, iii, et al.' to number the apparitions.

146/58–61 **And aftyrwarde thynkyth** . . . **apostlys apostyllasse.** This passage may be based on Saint Augustine's *Sermo* 51 (ed. Verbraken, *RB* 91, pp. 25–6, ll. 104–7).

146/70–6 **And so they wente** . . . **schulde see hym.** Matthew 28: 8–10.

146/81–9 **aftyr the seyinge of doctorys** . . . **to hym.** For example, the *Historia Scholastica*, comments on Luke 24: 34, the basis for this information: 'Petrus autem surgens cucurrit ad monumentum, ut Lucas dicit. Et tunc verisimile est, quod Dominus apparuit ei in via, et si non legatur in Euangelio' (*PL* 198: 1639).

146/83–8 **For whenne** . . . **þat was done:** Luke 24: 10–12.

147/90–115 **The fourthe apparycyon** . . . **brekynge of the brede.** Luke 24: 13–35.

147/111–12 **for Lyre seyth . . . wyth a knyfe.** Nicholas of Lyre, *Postilla* on Luke 24: 30.

147/95–148/143 **talkynge togyderys . . . igloryfyed.** Luke 24: 36–43.

148/144–7 **and in þat he schewde . . . propyrly to God.** Nicholas of Lyre, *Postilla* on Luke 24: 45.

148/148–50 **These fyue apperyngys were idoo . . . to þe peple.** Jacobus de Voragine, *Legenda Aurea* (ed. Maggioni, i. 363).

148/158–60 **Seyint Ierom seyth . . . aryse fro deth.** Jacobus de Voragine, *Legenda Aurea* (ed. Maggioni, i. 449).

149/166–76 **That othyr ys þat oure Lorde . . . Arymathye.** Jacobus de Voragine, *Legenda Aurea*: 'Alia est qua ipsa die dicitur apparuisse Ioseph, sicut legitur in euangelio Nychodemi. Nam cum audissent Iudei quod Ioseph corpus Ihesu a Pilato petisset et ipsum in monumento suo posuisset, indignati aduersus ipsum eum ceperunt et in quodam cubiculo diligenter clauso et sigillato recluserunt, post sabbatum eum occidere uolentes. Et ecce, Ihesus in ipsa nocte resurrectionis suspensa domo a quatuor angelis ad eum intrauit et faciem eius extersit et osculum ei dedit et inde saluis sigillis eum educens in domum suam in Arimathiam ipsum adduxit' (ed. Maggioni, i. 363–4). Note that 'quatuor angelis' has become 'foure correneres' in the *Mirror*. It is possible that the *Mirror* author may have misread 'angelis' as 'angulis'.

CHAPTER 31

149/12–150/26 **And thanne they tolde . . . and beleuyn.** John 20: 25–9.

150/37–41 **And therfore seyth Seyint Leo the Pope . . . dowtyd of vs.** Jacobus de Voragine, *Legenda Aurea* (ed. Maggioni, i. 481).

150/41–5 **And 'Seyint' Gregory seyth . . . wounde of dowtynge.** Pope Gregory I, *Homily* 29, *Homiliae in Evangelia* (CCSL 141, p. 245, ll. 5–9).

150/47–151/83 **Ther were todygerys . . . fyische also.** John 21: 2–13.

151/65–6 **And tho . . . to oure Lorde.** Nicholas of Lyre, *Postilla* on John 21: 7.

151/70–2 **The'se' thyngys were made . . . as Lyre seyth.** Nicholas of Lyre, *Postilla* on John 21: 9.

151/77–9 **Hoo art thow . . . as Lyre seyth.** Nicholas of Lyre, *Postilla* on John 21: 12.

151/84–152/102 **The thyrde apperynge . . . the worldys ende.** Matthew 28: 16–20.

152/85 **Tabor.** Mount Thabor is often named as the location of Christ's transfiguration, and the *Mirror* author refers the reader to his own account of the transfiguration in Chapter 15 (73/60–66). In this account he cites Nicholas of Lyre's *Postilla* as a source but calls the mountain a 'hye hylle' (73/63). The *Postilla* never names the location of the transfiguration. When the *Mirror* author names Thabor as the mountain where Christ makes his third appearance, it seems more likely that the information derives from Iohannis de Caulibus's discussion of the transfiguration in the *MVC* (CCCM 153, cap. xli, p. 154, ll. 1–5), where he locates the event on Mount Thabor.

152/88–95 **And in that hylle . . . harde to beleue.** Nicholas of Lyre, *Postilla* on Matthew 28: 16–7.

152/100–1 **techynge hem.** Right margin of N has 'Nota'.

152/105–7 **The ix apparycyon . . . of here hertys.** Luke 24: 30–5; Acts 1: 4–5.

152/107–8 **The x and the laste . . . Mounte of Olyu'e'te.** Acts 1: 9–12. Mount Olivet is not specifically identified as the place of the ascension; however, the passage in Acts implies that this is where it occurred. Jacobus de Voragine's *Legenda Aurea* also places Christ's ascension at Mount Olivet (ed. Maggioni, i. 481).

152/112–15 **Anothyr apperynge . . . brethryn in feyth.** 1 Corinthians 15: 6.

CHAPTER 32

153/8–12 **The fyrste thanne was . . . seye hym aryse.** Mark 16: 14.

153/12–20 **Thys maye 'be' vndyrstande . . . seye hym also.** Nicholas of Lyre, *Postilla* on Mark 16: 14.

153/21–2 **he ate wyth hem . . . goo to the Mounte of Olyuete. Luke 24: 30–5, Acts 1: 4–5. For Mount Olivet, see note to 152/107–8.

154/25–33 **And thanne thynkyth . . . that tyme.** Acts 1: 6.

154/33–42 **Thys some doctorys . . . þat tyme.** Nicholas of Lyre, *Postilla* on Acts 1: 6.

154/38 **The Romaynys.** Left margin of N has 'Nota'.

154/43–9 **And thanne he seyde to hem . . . of the erthe.** Acts 1: 7–8.

154/49–51 **And also . . . to mankynde.** Mark 16: 15.

154/51 **For by euery creature.** Left margin of N has 'Nota bene'.

154/53–6 **For Seyint Gregory . . . angyllys.** Pope Gregory I, *Homily* 29, *Homiliae in Evangelia* (CCSL 141, p. 246, ll. 34–6).

154/57–155/59 **Also our Lorde seyde . . . schulde be dampnyd.** Mark 16: 16.

155/64–74 **And whenne he hadde seyde . . . goynge into heuen.** Acts 1: 9–11 with the exception of the detail concerning the hands uplifted in blessing, which is found in Luke 24: 50.

156/96–103 **The Maystyr of Storyis seyth . . . erthe kepyth stylle.** Peter Comestor, *Historia Scholastica* (*PL* 198: 1647). Jacobus de Voragine's *Legenda Aurea* also mentions Sulpicius's comments on Christ's ascension (ed. Maggioni, i. 481). In N, the left margin corresponding to line 156/96 has 'Nota ex causa'.

156/106–9 **And alle the apostlys . . . behette hem.** Acts 1: 14.

156/109–10 **And thys ys a gret exsample.** Left margin in N has 'Nota optime'.

156/116–19 **And to þat kynde . . . Sytt on my ryght syde.** Genesis 3: 19, Psalm 109: 1, Acts 2: 34, Hebrews 1: 13.

156/119–21 **And in that þat oure kynde . . . and not angyl.** Pseudo-Augustine, *Liber Soliloquiorum Animae ad Deum* (*PL* 40: 871). The source text suggests that Gg's 'seye' is a better reading than N's 'see'. In N a marginal comment corresponding to 'And in that' reads 'Nota deus homo'.

157/130–4 **Oracio, Lorde Ihesu Cryste . . . wythoute endynge. Amen.** At the beginning of this long prayer, the word 'Oracio' appears in the right margin of N. Gg begins the prayer with 'Oracio'. It is one of the few times in the *Mirror* that a prayer is directly addressed to Christ in a manner similar to that of prayers written by Saint Anselm and Saint Bernard.

CHAPTER 33

158/12–14 **in the whyche dayis . . . was chose.** Acts 1: 26.

158/15–159/41 **Thanne maye 3e thynke . . . dronke of muste.** Acts 2: 1–13.

158/22–4 **as hyt hadde be tungys of fyre . . . sygne wythoute.** Nicholas of Lyre, *Postilla* on Acts 2: 3.

159/42–4 **And thanne maye 3e beholde . . . prophete Ioel.** Acts 2: 14–21.

159/44–6 **And the same daye . . . thre thowsende soulys.** Acts 2: 41.

159/46 **and so Petyr.** Left margin in N has 'Nota bene'.

159/54–6 **For Seyint Gregory seyth . . . in here owen.** Pope Gregory I, *Homily* 30, *Homiliae in Evangelia* (CCSL 141, p. 266, ll. 255–8).

159/56–62 **And also whenne the pryncys . . . of the peple.** Acts 4: 18–21.

159/63–160/90 **Anothyr tyme the prynce . . . of oure Lorde Ihesu Cryste.** This lengthy passage closely follows Acts 5: 17–41, with the usual insertion of comments from other sources.

160/98–101 **Thys Gamalyel, as Seyint Clement seyth . . . as he dede.** Peter Comestor, *Historia Scholastica* (*PL* 198: 1661).

160/101–5 **And 3ytt . . . Lorde Ihesu Cryste.** Peter Comestor, *Historia Scholastica* (*PL* 198: 1662).

162/150–3 **And thys suffysyth . . . afore hys lyfe.** Jacobus de Voragine, *Legenda Aurea* (ed. Maggioni, i. 87–8).

162/157–63 **And whenne he . . . of specyall loue.** The *Prologues* of Saint Jerome were often included in copies of Nicholas of Lyre's *Postilla*, together with his own commentary on the *Prologues*. It seems likely that the *Mirror* author is quoting Jerome's *Prologues* through Nicholas of Lyre's *Postilla*. This quotation comes from the *Prologue to St. John's Gospel*. See Oxford, Bodleian Library, MS Rawlinson G.164, a late fourteenth-century manuscript containing Nicholas of Lyre's *Postilla* and Saint Jerome's *Prologues*. The text of Jerome's *Prologues* is included in the edition of the Vulgate by B. Fischer et al., *Biblia Sacra*.

162/163–8 **For Adam Cartusyens seyth . . . loue to hym.** All quotations from Adam the Carthusian originate in his *Sermo* 33, entitled *In Die S. Ioannis apostoli et euangelistae* (*PL* 198: 301).

162/170–2 **The fyrste ys . . . vpon þe Apocalypse.** The *Prologues of Jerome* to the Gospel and to the Apocalypse of Saint John, as found in Nicholas of Lyre's *Postilla*.

163/179–96 **as to thys Adam Cartusyens seyth . . . eurylastynge mysteryis.** Adam the Carthusian, *Sermo* 33 (*PL* 198: 301).

163/204–12 **Also, worschypful Bede seyth . . . not man.** While attributed to Bede, this passage and all subsequent quotations from Bede actually are from Peter Damian's *Sermo* 64: 'Hoc autem diuinae sapientiae sale ita omnis beati Iohannis uidetur doctrina respersa, ut merito dicatur os Dei, lingua Spiritus Sancti, cedrus paradise, lux ecclesiae, decus orbis, praeco caeli, lumen mundi, sidus hominum, specimen angelorum, lapis uiuus, speculum lucis, logotheta diuinitatis, fundator fidei, columpna templi, architectus ueri tabernaculi, quod fixit Deus et non homo' (CCCM 57, pp. 385–6, ll. 375–82). The CCCM edition notes that a variant for 'fundator' is 'forma'. The *Mirror* author's phrase 'þe fourme of God' at line 4150 suggests that his text read 'forma dei'.

164/218–20 **thys dyscypyl seyth . . . þat Ihesu Cryste louyde.** John 13: 23; 21: 20.

164/220–3 **What is betokenyd therby . . . vpon hys gospel.** Saint Augustine, *In Iohannis Euangelium Tractatus* (CCSL 36, Tractatus 124, p. 682, ll. 7–8).

164/224–35 **O hye and full . . . fro Seyint `Iohn'.** Adam the Carthusian, *Sermo* 33 (*PL* 198: 303).

165/255–9 **What tellyth thys Ihon . . . Loo, thy modyr.** John 19: 26–7.

165/259 **O worschype.** Right margin of N has 'Nota bene'.

166/295–7 **so callyth hym worschypful Bede . . . herde afore.** Peter Damian, *Sermo* 64 (CCCM 57, p. 378, ll. 108–9).

166/299–303 **for the forseyde Adam . . . wonde to worschype.** Adam the Carthusian, *Sermo* 33 (*PL* 198: 300–1).

166/304–7 **Also, worschypful Bede seyth . . . trewe peple.** Peter Damian, *Sermo* 64 (CCCM 57, p. 375, ll. 7–9).

166/319–167/325 **And `as' to thys . . . but angyllys brede.** Adam the Carthusian, *Sermo* 33 (*PL* 198: 306).

167/328–52 **As to the fyrste . . . and `an' vnherde myracle.** This passage relating the three ways in which John was honoured in his death follows Jabobus de Voragine, *Legenda Aurea* (ed. Maggioni, i. 95–6).

168/359 **manna, þat ys callyd in Englyisch angyllys brede.** Psalm 77: 24–5.

168/359–61 **for hyt was worthy as Adam Cartusyens seyth . . . body wente inne.** Adam the Carthusian, *Sermo* 33 (*PL* 198: 309).

168/362–9 **Also, worschypfull Bede seyth . . . thys worlde.** Peter Damian, *Sermo* 64 (CCCM 57, pp. 378–9, ll. 138–40; p. 383, ll. 281–3).

168/379–82 **But þat maye no man . . . þat loue hym.** 1 Corinthians 2: 9 reads: 'sed sicut scriptum est quod oculus non uidit nec auris audiuit nec in cor hominis ascendit quae praeparauit Deus his qui diligunt illum'. The use of 'uidit' shows that Gg's reading of 'eye' is superior to N's 'he'.

168/390–169/424 **Aftyr the seyingys of doctorys . . . martyr, a doctor, and a virgyne.** This is a summary of Saint Thomas Aquinas's *Summa Theologica*, Quaestio XCVI, Articulus I. A number of other Church Fathers discuss essential and accidental rewards, but this passage adheres closely to Aquinas.

170/429–31 **And therfore seyth Seyint Austyn . . . Petyr þat suffryde passyon.** Saint Augustine, *De bono coniugali* (CSEL 41, cap. xxi, p. 221, ll. 17–18).

170/430 **vnpere.** This word is not in the *MED* but Saint Augustine's *De*

Bono Coniugali has 'inpar'at this point. The *MED* lists 'per' *adj*, meaning 'equal'. The *Mirror* author has most likely formed a Middle English equivalent to the Latin 'inpar' by adding the negative prefix 'vn-' to the positive form 'per'.

170/437 **Portelatyneys.** The Porta Latina was the gate at which the via Latina began in Rome. It was part of the Aurelian Walls, which were built between 270 and 273 CE. The walls and the gate still exist today. According to tradition, the church was built in the fifth century by Pope St Gelasius I (492–6). Maker's stamps on roof tiles have been dated to the end of the fifth century, so it seems likely that it was built during St Gelasius's time. It was rebuilt *c.*720, and restored in 1191.

170/442–4 **Also a virgyne . . . afore the Apocalypse.** *The Prologues of Jerome* to the Gospel and to the Apocalypse of Saint John, as found in Nicholas of Lyre's *Postilla*.

170/450–1 **besyde the souereyne and pryncypal mede.** N's scribe deletes this line by apparently committing an eyeskip.

170/460–3 **A prophete he ys . . . that ys wryte therinne.** Apocalypse 1: 3.

171/465–77 **Wherfore worschypful Bede . . . worthy seruysys.** Peter Damian's *Sermo* 64 (CCCM 57, p. 375, ll. 27–32; p. 376, ll. 54–6; p. 383, ll. 306–9).

171/465–6 **What ys in vertuys.** Right margin in N has 'Nota'.

171/492–7 **Gostly syster, for Seyint Gregory seyth . . . apostyl and euangelyste.** Pope Gregory I's *Homily* 38, *Homiliae in Evangelia* (CCSL 141, pp. 373–4, ll. 361–4).

171/497–172/508 **Hyt ys red in hys *Legende* . . . pylgrymys lyknesse.** Jacobus de Voragine, *Legenda Aurea*. However, the saint in the *Legenda Aurea* is Edmund, king of England, not Edward the Confessor (ed. Maggioni, i. 96).

172/509–18 **Also, hyt ys redde in Seyint Elyȝabethys lyfe . . . in hys name.** Jacobus de Voragine, *Legenda Aurea* (ed. Maggioni, ii. 1157). For more on the identity of Saint Elizabeth, see Riehle, *The Middle English Mystics*; Barratt, 'The Revelation of Saint Elizabeth of Hungary', and *The Two Middle English Translations*, ed. McNamer.

172/519–31 **Also, hyt ys wryte in Seyint Edmundeys lyfe . . . `oryson´ vnseyde.** The Life of Saint Edmund of Abingdon, archbishop of Canterbury (*c.*1175–1240), does not appear in Jacobus de Voragine's *Legenda Aurea*, but it was widespread in England. A Middle English version can be found in *Yorkshire Writers: Richard Rolle and his Followers*, ed. Horstmann, 219–61. For another version, see Matthew Paris, *The Life of St. Edmund*, ed. Lawrence.

172/532 *Myraclys of Oure Lady*. Unidentified passage. The *Mirror* author relates seven miracles associated with Saint John. Of these miracles, he attributes two solely to the *Miracles of Our Lady*, and cites it as an alternate source for two others. Only the miracle found at 4365–87 has been identified; appears in Wilmart, *Auteurs spirituels*, 485–6. The other three do not appear to be contained in any of the larger collections of miracles attributed to Mary.

172/532–173/563 **Fferdyrmore hyt ys founde in the** *Myraclys of Oure Lady* . . . **manye placys.** For a text of this miracle, edited from two thirteenth-century Paris manuscripts, see Wilmart, *Auteurs spirituels*, 485–6. See note to 4365.

173/564–174/593 **Also, hyt ys red . . . thys boke.** Unidentified passage. See note to 4365.

174/594–606 **in the** *Boke of Beys* . . . **wytnesse ys soth.** Thomas de Cantimpré, *Bonum uniuersale de apibus* (Liber II, cap. liii, p. 498).

174/595 *Myraclys of Oure Lady*. Unidentified passage. See note to 172/532.

175/607–16 **Also in Seyint Gregoryys lyfe . . . relyquyis were.** Jacobus de Voragine, *Legenda Aurea* (ed. Maggioni, i. 299).

O INTEMERATA

175/1–176/44 **O intemerata.** For an edition of this prayer, see Wilmart, *Auteurs spirituels*, 488–90. See also de Hamel, *Syon Abbey*, 168–99. The *O intemerata* appeared in nearly every book of hours and plays a prominent role in three of the miracles described in Chapter 33 of the *Mirror*. Gg has a translation, written in a different hand, following its version of the *O intemerata*.

177/47–178/88. This Middle English translation of the *O intemerata* does not appear in N.

GLOSSARY

This glossary does not contain words that are easily recognizable to readers of modern English and whose meaning is unchanged. When a word appears in the text under different parts of speech, it contains a separate entry for each part. Words spelled in more than one way are contained in a single entry with variant spellings following the headword in parentheses. Where the variant spelling is so divergent that it might be difficult to locate the main entry, cross-references are provided. If possible, variant spellings have been conflated into a single form, with the variation indicated by brackets (e.g. **affeccio(u)n**). A tilde ($\sim$) represents the headword in phrases quoted within entries. Within the phrase, alternative versions are separated by a solidus, optional words provided for clarification of the phrase are in parentheses, and a comma separates alternative phrases with the same meaning. Glosses are arranged with the most important meaning of the word listed first, and following each gloss is a reference to one to three examples of the word in the *Mirror*. As a rule, regular verb inflections are not included, but forms that are likely to cause the reader difficulty are recorded separately. Verbs are entered in the infinitive form (without the final -n), unless the infinitive does not appear in the *Mirror*, in which case an inflected form is given as the head word. Words beginning with *þ* are placed after those beginning with *t*; those beginning with *ȝ* after *g*. Medial vocalic *y* is treated as *i*. Words in which *u* is substituted for *v* are treated as *v*; those where *i* is substituted for *j* are treated as *i*. The references are to page and line numbers.

Abbreviations

adj. adjective	*perf.* perfect tense
adv. adverb	*pl.* plural
comp. comparative	*pr.* present tense
conj. conjunction	*pr. p.* present participle
dem. demonstrative	*prep.* preposition
esp. especially	*pron.* pronoun
fem. feminine	*refl.* reflexive
fut. future tense	*rel.* relative
imp. imperative	*sg.* singular
inf. infinitive	*subj.* subjunctive
interj. interjection	*superl.* superlative
n. noun	*v.* verb
pa. p. past participle	*vbl. n.* verbal noun
pa. past tense	

A

abaschyd (abayischyd) *pa. p.* upset, taken aback 20/100, 89/39

abyde *inf.* live, dwell 26/180, 49/178, 73/70; **abydeth, abydyth** *imp. pl.* 97/36; *3 pr. sg.* remain, stay 15/54; 16/182; $\sim$ *in* persist in 27/222; $\sim$ *vpon* persist in 26/175, 26/176; **abode** *3 pa. sg.* 28/229, 30/42, 30/62, 40/80; in possession of 30/39; *3 pa. pl.* 39/63, 40/92, 41/116, 77/199; **abothe** *3 pa.*

sg. 28/259, 96/32 $\sim$ *to* belonged (by right) to 30/44

abydynge *vbl. n.* 31/89, 39/40, 46/65

abiecte *adj.* humble, menial 27/213

abyl(l) *adj.* of a person: capable of doing something 23/60, 156/108; of an action: agreeable 29/12

abrode *adv.* so as to cover a wide space 137/42; $\sim$ *spreden* to spread out, stretch out, extend 31/90, 129/60, 158/23

abundaunce *n.* a great quantity, plenty 127/129, 128/57

abusyon *n.* wicked act or practice 70/109

accydental *adj.* incidental, secondary 169/411, 171/486

acloyede *pa. p.* beset, harassed 14/15

acordyde *pa. p.* came to an agreement 40/103

acordynge *adv.* in agreement with, similar to 8/40, 9/81, 48/113

acth *interj.* an exclamation of concern or surprise 126/95

acursyd *pa. p.* accursed 19/87

admytte *subj. sg.* allow 149/180; **admittyd** *p. pa.* ~ *to* permitted to 164/236

adrad *adj.* afraid 28/244, 50/13, 50/22, etc.

afer *adv.* far off 15/54, 100/162; at a distance 100/163, 132/54

afore *prep.* preceding, before 3/15, 7/142, 7/10, etc.

afore-goynge *n.* predecessor, preliminary 21/6

agaste *adj.* terrified, frightened 100/174, 111/22, 141/35

agreuyd *pa. p.* afflicted 97/62

aȝene (aȝeyn(e), ayeyne) *adv.* again 3/19, 7/141; back 41/134; *seye* ~ reply 133/67; *answere* ~ reply 27/211, 61/57; *come/go* ~ return 45/4; *gete* ~ recover 78/266; ~ *write aȝeyne* copy 172/507

aȝenste *prep.* against 12/70, 17/21, 79/4; towards 85/79, 86/99, 88/14; in anticipation of 97/35; in contrast to 130/114

aȝenbyare, aȝenbyere *n.* redeemer 47/105, 65/116, 131/132

algatys *adv.* nevertheless 89/44

alyon *adj.* alien, foreign 154/40

almasse *n.* alms 172/502

alwey(e) *adv.* all the way, in every way 18/32, 20/110, 20/113, etc.; continually 85/61, 101/209, 137/60, 143/82; for all time, forever 20/123, 171/477

aparty(e) *adv.* partly, to some extent 94/223, 150/29

apparycyon *n.* appearance or showing 44/247, 142/55, 142/75, etc.

appreuynge *vbl. n.* put to the proof 72/39

approue *3 pr. sg.* sanction 61/78

approuyd *pa. p.* sanctioned 6/127, 170/433

apropryed, appropryde *pa. p.* attributed, assigned 37/93, 137/46

araye *n.* clothing, equipment 39/46

arayde *3 pa. sg.* saddled 15/51

arayse *inf.* resurrect 70/127; *1 fut. sg.* raise 102/232; **araysyde (araysyd, araysede)** *3 pa. sg.* 8/53, 79/2, 79/8, etc.

araysynge *vbl. n.* resurrecting 164/233

aredy *adv.* ready, already 31/81, 31/96, 88/13, etc.

armys *pl. n.* limbs, arms 32/134, 33/145, 43/188, etc.

as *adv.* as 3/6, 20/93; ~. . .~, as . . . so 18/45, 20/93; ~ *myche to seye* as if to say 37/80, 84/16, 143/109; *for* ~ *myche as* forasmuch as 23/57, 29/17; *in* ~ *myche as* inasmuch as 21/132, 24/104, 26/185

ascape *3 pr. pl.* escape 127/8; **ascapyd** *pr. p.* 174/583

ascencyon *n.* the ascension of Christ into Heaven 10/104, 17/98, 44/223, etc.

aschamyd *pa. p.* filled with shame 50/10, 76/195

aselynge *vbl. n.* setting seal to a contract 135/58

as(s)ent(e) *n.* be one ~, *comune* ~ mutual agreement 44/222, 105/59

aspyde *pa. p.* spied upon, saw 50/25, 55/65

assercyon *n.* declaration, assertion 40/71

astonyed *pa. p.* stunned, stupified 93/204, 94/224

auctur *n.* instigator, originator 13/83, 168/364

auryole, auriole *n.* crown or halo of a saint 169/417, 169/421, 169/423, etc.

autentyke *adj.* authentic, canonical 139/44, 149/178

auter(e) *n.* altar 48/122, 172/513, etc.

autor *n.* writer, author 13/83

autoryte *n.* authority, official sanction 81/91, 105/38, etc.; written authority 139/45

avyse *imp. sg.* deliberate, reflect 105/51, 112/68

avysement(e) *n.* consideration, reflection 6/111, 103/254, 128/58, etc.

aysel *n.* vinegar 122/213

B

barayne *adj.* sterile 19/54
be *prep.* by 3/5, 3/8, etc.
beclyppe *inf.* embrace 129/60
bedyll *n.* messenger, herald 163/208
begeten, begetyn, begotyn *pa. p.*
  begotten, born 5/47, 16/60, 51/55, etc.
beheste *n.* promise 36/64, 161/125
behet(t)(e) *inf.* promise 97/56, *1 & 3 pa.*
  sg. 3/2, 65/103; *3 pa. pl.* 87/140; *pa. p.*
  161/134; **behettyste** *2 pa. sg.* 140/75
bere *n.* bier 80/38, 80/42
bere *inf.* bear, carry 65/90; to give birth
  to 19/82; *3 pa. pl.* thrust 52/92; *3 pr.*
  sg. endure 73/80; *3 fut. sg.* 64/77; ∼
  witnes, witnes(se) of{s}to testify (to)
  106/95; give evidence of 102/217, 106/
  95; **bare** *3 pa. sg.* gave birth to 45/22;
  carried 15/58; sent, paid (tribute) 75/
  143; yielded (fruit) 16/78; *3 pa. pl.* ∼
  apoun hande to accuse (someone) 74/
  126; **bore** *pa. p.* 53/115, 80/33; ∼
  vp(p) lifted up 4/36, 24/107; **beryth** *3*
  pr. sg. 18/26, 46/65, 69/76, etc.
berye *inf.* to bury, entomb 80/65, 105/60
beryinge *vbl. n.* burying 9/86, 44/222,
  134/1, etc.
beschone *3 pa. sg.* shone 73/77
besee *v. refl.* look to oneself 105/50
beseke *1 pr. sg.* beg, entreat 83/146,
  126/122, 165/269, etc.
bespronge *pa. p.* sprinkled 163/205
beste *n.* beast 12/50, 24/92, etc.
bestly *adj.* bestial 12/60, 13/110
bete *inf.* beat, whip 108/167; **beete,**
  ibeete *pa. p.* beaten 113/115, 114/124
bethowgth *pa. p.* thought upon,
  remembered (*refl.*) 49/4
betyl *n.* hammer 118/54
betynge *vbl. n.* beat (air) 39/37
betoke *3 pa. sg.* committed, entrusted
  122/201; *3 pa. pl.* handed over 103/273
betokene *inf.* indicate, signify 124/54,
  158/23; *3 pa. pl.* 42/164, 44/238;
  betokenyd *pa. p.* pointed out, made
  evident 7/10, 8/54, 14/4, etc.
betokenynge *vbl. n. in* ∼ *of* as a sign (of)
  86/101, 95/258; *in* ∼ *pat* as a sign
  (that) 7/143, 26/182
betue(y)ne *prep.* between 19/61, 22/20,
  etc.
bydde *3 pa. sg.* ordered, commanded 88/

20; *3 pa. pl.* 57/121, 103/252; **bad(de)**
  3 pa. sg. 12/71, 15/46, 15/54, etc.;
  baddyst *2 pa. sg.* 140/75; **byddyste** *2*
  pr. sg. 165/270; **byddyth** *3 pr. sg.* 6/
  103, 50/29, etc.; **bode** *pa. p.*
  summoned 25/131, 25/133; **ibode** *pa.*
  p. ordered, commanded 106/75
biddynges *vbl. n.* requesting 66/143
bydynge *vbl. n.* staying, dwelling 46/43,
  58/36
bye *inf.* buy, purchase 30/178, 95/254,
  137/35, etc.; **bye** *3 pa. sg.* 77/231;
  bowgth(te) *3 pa. sg.* 130/119, 131/22;
  pl. 105/59; *pa. p.* 77/233, 129/82, etc.
bylddyd *pa. p.* built 48/117, 156/98,
  177/63
bynde *inf.* to bind 31/94; *3 pa. pl.* 100/
  146, 103/275, etc.; **bo(u)nde** *3 sg &*
  pa. pl. 32/134, 45/24, etc.; **bo(o)unde**
  pa. p. obliged 37/67, 45/26, etc.;
  ibounde *pa. p.* 100/150, 102/219, etc.
bysyly *adv.* busily 94/230
bysynesse *n.* business 3/22; attention
  166/289
blameable *adj.* guilty, with fault 69/102
blamyde, blamyth *pa. p.* accused, found
  fault 64/76, 121/178
blamynge *vbl. n.* act of criticizing,
  reprimanding 118/60
blysful *adj.* joyful, happy 19/72, 33/150,
  35/178, etc.
blysse *n.* joy 24/100, 92/172, 156/123,
  etc.
blysse *1 pr. sg.* bless 157/149; **blyssyth**
  3 pr. sg. 36/35, 47/84; **blyssyd(e)** *pr.*
  p. blessed 5/89, 18/37, etc.; *ppl. adj.*
  7/14, 13/98, 17/4, etc.; **iblyssyd** *pr. p.*
  86/104
blyssydnesse *n.* blessedness 13/84, 157/
  131, 164/224
bodyly (bothyly) *adj. & adv.* physical,
  physically 8/34, 12/79, 26/188, etc.
boke *n.* book 5/84, 5/88, 6/117, etc.
boot *n.* salvation 138/10
boot(e) *n.* boat 151/53, 151/67
borde *n.* table 88/28
borgene *3 fut. sg.* burgeon, sprout leaves
  16/73; **borgenyde** *pa. p.* 16/68, 16/78
boste *n.* boast 111/33
bothy *n.* body 32/117, 177/79
boustously (boystuly, bustusly) *adv.*
  roughly 27/210, 100/150, 108/161

bowed *adj.* sloping, tilted forward 33/
146, 37/85, 60/31

breke *inf.* break 36/60; **brake** *3 pa. sg.*
12/68, 12/80, 74/127; infringe, violate
1845; **brake** *3 pa. pl.* 127/20, 128/22;
braste *3 pa. pl.* burst, broke 117/41;
broke *pa. p.* 109/172, 125/68, etc.

brennynge *vbl. n.* 39/36, 78/264, 151/
69, etc.

brennyth *3 pr. sg.* burn 123/228

brymmys *pl. n.*pools 109/193

broke *n.* brook, stream 96/20, 96/22,
109/172, etc.

brondys *n.* torch for illumination 39/36,
123/228

brosynge *vbl. n.* bruising, a bruise 133/
84

buffetys *pl. n.*blows delivered with the
fist 122/222

bundel *n.* bundle 48/130

C

candyl *n.* candle 31/85, 32/105, 32/108

can(ne) *3 pr. sg.* be able, know 5/75, 22/
178, 55/76, etc.; **kunne** *2 pr. sg.* 92/
164; *3 pl. pr.* 79/13, 127/137, 148/146;
coude *3 pa. pl.* could 102/226, 102/
227, 116/199

capacytee *n.* capacity 24/97

capetele *see* **chapetele**

cardynal *n.* an eminent churchman 3/23

care *n.* sorrow 115/158

carnal *adj.* worldly, sinful 6/131, 6/133,
12/60, etc.; ~ *medlynge* sexual
intercourse 18/50

caste *n. stonys* ~ throw 97/41

caste *inf.* to throw 59/78; *1 pa. pl.* cast
out, exorcized 82/123; *3 pa. sg.* 105/
51, 4223, 4289; *3 pa. pl.* placed forcibly
159/63; planned 75/132; turned the
eyes 96/15; *3 pr. imp.* throw 76/190;
castyth *3 pa. sg.* intended, planned
26/180

castel *n.* town 72/37, 147/92, 147/105

cawften *2 pl. pr.* caught; *haue* ~ 151/73

century *n.* centurion 125/71, 131/17,
131/18

ceptur *n.* sceptre 109/204

certayne, certeyne *adj.* certain 20/123,
18/53, 40/70, etc.

certaynely *adv.* certainly 25/135, 33/150

cesse *inf.* to cease 72/46; **cesyde** *pa. p.*
ceased 94/241

cessynge *vbl. n.* ceasing 94/241

chambyrleyne *n.* chamberlain; a servant
to a lord in his bedchamber 172/501

chanon *n.* clergyman living under canon
rule 174/595, 174/597

chapetele *n.* chapter 6/113, 6/134, etc.;
capetele 122/206, 136/8

charytably *adv.* charitably 4/33, 119/105

charyte(e) *n.* loving kindness, affection
5/87, 13/98, 13/103, etc.

charturhowse *n.* Carthusian monastery
3/26, 166/315

chastytee *n.* chastity 172/512

chause *n.* cause 74/125

chef(e) *adj.* chief, best 13/83, 29/9, 41/
108, etc.

cheke *n.* cheek 32/127

chekenenys *pl. n.* young bird, chickens
46/58

chese *inf.* to choose 70/119; *3 fut. sg.* 16/
72; *3 pa.* 12/69, 44/222, 46/61;
chesyth *3 pa. sg.* 98/84; **chosyn** *pa.*
pl. 6/107, 6/108, 23/76, etc.; **chose** *3*
pr. sg. 70/111; *2 pa. sg.* 126/109; *3 pa.*
sg. 19/67, 68/62, etc.

cheuolry *n.* host (of angels) 33/163

chongede, chongyd *pa. p.* changed 73/
63, 33/140

circumsydyd *pa. p.* circumcised 45/28

circumsysyon *n.* circumcision 35/1,
35/3

clene *adj.* clean, unsoiled 31/92, 32/112;
morally pure 36/46, 57/10, etc.;
ceremonially clean 45/18; chaste, pure,
esp. virgin 15/36, 18/51, etc; free from
disease 60/44; splendid, elegant 131/
22, 134/7; **clenyste** *comp. adj.* chaste,
pure 177/65

clen(e)ly *adv.* wholeheartedly 12/63, 59/
61

clennesse *n.* moral purity, sinlessness
46/50, 60/28, etc.

clense *inf.* to heal (leprosy) 70/127; *subj.*
sg. may purify 178/81

clensynge *vbl. n.* purifying 45/11, 72/40

clere *adj.* of eyes, vision: clear, keen 139/
25, 139/30; **clerest** *superl.* 177/57

cler(e)ly *adv.* with purity, blameless 12/
60; clearly, plainly, 31/79, 93/190,
128/39, etc.; entirely 76/167, 160/106

cler(e)nesse *n.* clarity 13/97, 13/101,
etc.; brightness 73/65, 158/21

clerke *n.* member of the clergy 3/24, 4/
60, 37/77, etc.

clodyd *pa. p.* clothed, dressed 107/119;
iclodyd *pa. p.* 31/78, 48/136

close *pa. p.* closed, shut 141/10, 141/17;
enclosed, shut up 149/171, 159/50,
etc.

closyd(e) *pa. p.* closed 43/192, 133/93,
134/4, etc.

clothys, clowthys *n.* clothes 30/34, 30/
61, 31/92, etc.

clowde *n.* cloud 73/76, 73/77, etc.

clowtes, clowt(h)ys *pl. n.* cloths 31/94,
32/133, 32/137, etc.

clyppe *3 pl. pr.* embrace 164/216;
clyppyth *3 pa. sg.* 143/96; clyppyd
pa. p. 164/217

clypse *n.* eclipse 123/8

colys *pl. n.* coals 151/69

collectes *pl. n.* acolytes 48/137

colloquyis *pl. n.* discourses, meetings
22/27

commendacyon *n.* praise,
commendation 10/108, 37/88, 122/
207, etc.

com(m)ende *inf.* entrust 165/254; *1 pr.
sg.* 177/71; *3 pa. pl.* 69/102;
comenden *3 pa. pl.* praised 69/97

commytte *1 pr. sg..* submit 149/179;
commyttyd(e) entrusted *p. pa.* 29/21,
136/23, etc.

commyttynge *vbl. n.* entrusting 134/32

commune, comyn *adj.* of a low rank
91/121, 91/141, 112/63, etc.; public
2920; ~ *profyte* the common good 108/
152; of frequent occurrence, ordinary
140/52, etc.; ~ *speche* popular (as
opposed to learned) 86/115; shared by,
or serving, the members of a
community or organization 169/395,
etc.

communely *adv.* jointly, in one body
141/20, 170/178

co(m)munyd *pa. p.* administered Holy
Communion 90/79; *pr. p.* 91/122;
icommunyd *pa. p.* revealed,
communicated 164/235

compendyus *adj.* brief, succinct 59/72

compendyusly *adv.* concisely, succinctly
17/100

compunccyon *n.* remorse, contrition
137/59

condempne *1 pr. sg.* pass judgement on,
condemn 77/178; *2 pr. sg.* 112/57;
condempnyd(e) *pa. p.* 77/205, 102/
220, 113/90

confermyd(e) *pa. p.* secured,
strengthened 16/85, etc.; sanctioned
16/79, etc.; approved 92/176

confermynge *vbl. n.* strengthening 98/
76, 151/71

conforme *v. refl.* to model, make like
45/34, 46/45

coniure *1 pr. sg.* charge, urge 102/237

conscyence *n.* the faculty of knowing
what is right 4/39, 4/53; *good* ~ clear
conscience 168/389; *after* ~; *of* ~ fairly
6/131, 140/73; *have, make* ~ *to* have
scruples about 105/43

consecracyon *n.* consecration 91/128,
91/133

consey(i)l(e) *n.* counsel 3/8, 3/27, 3/31,
etc.

conseyle *1 pr. sg.* advice 71/144, 92/160

conseyue *3 pr. sg.* comprehend,
understand 4/63; *2 pr. sg.* 115/166; feel
153/124; imagine 171/484; give rise to
37; *subj. sg.* conceive (a child) 4/50,
etc.; conseyuy(e)d *pr. p.* 6/128, 126/
125,etc.; *pa. p.* 19/72, 19/76, etc.; ~ *of
man* conceive a child with a man 45/
25; conseyuyth *2 pr. sg. imp.* 140/63

constaunce *n.* steadfastness 159/58

conteynyd *pa. p.* contained 10/95, 10/
98, 10/101, etc.

contynuant *adv.* assiduously, persistently
58/25; continually 81/66

contynu(w)ally *adv.* without ceasing,
continually 12/63, 20/114, 59/61, etc.

contradyccyon *n.* contradiction 104/26

contrarye *n.* opposite 4/47, 21/131,
112/66

contrarye *adj.* hostile, disobedient 75/
150; contrary 20/111, 57/122, 75/147,
etc.

contraryus *adj.* rebellious, refractory 66/
129

contraryustee *n.* animosity,
rebelliousness 12/62

contre (contr(e)y(e)) *n.* country, region
17/15, 17/16, 29/12, etc.; contrey(i)s
*pl. n.*43/202, 159/40

conuenyent *adj.* convenient 18/46, 59/ 68, 87/139, etc.

conuenyentely *adv.* suitably, appropriately 53/7, 63/20, 161/130; effectively 75/156; fittingly 163/201

copherys *pl. n.* basket, trunk 72/48

costes, costys *pl. n.* region 51/77; borders 39/57

cote *n.* , hovel, shed 30/35, 30/45, 30/ 57, etc.; robe 120/135, 151/63

coueytyse *n.* covetous, greed 12/64, 13/ 103, etc.

coueytyth *3 pa. sg.* coveted 123/230

courte *n.* heavenly host 83/148

courtyoure *n.* courtier 131/14

cracche *n.* manger 30/62, 31/68, 31/77, etc.

craftyly *adv.* dexterously 32/130

creature *n.* created thing 24/96, 24/109, 59/70, etc.; **creaturys, creaturis** *pl. n.* 11/41, 12/45, 12/52, etc.

crewe *see* **crowe**

cristyndon (crystyndon) *n.* Christianity, Christians collectively 35/12, 35/13, 62/84

crowe *3 pa. sg.* crowed or cawed 101/ 192; **icrowe** *pa. p.* 95/271

cune *n.* coin 75/157

cunyd *pa. p.* minted, stamped coin 75/ 162

curyosytee, curyustee *n.* curiosity 74/ 101, 107/114

curse *inf.* to damn, condemn 101/188; **cursyd** *pa. p.* 70/112

curteyisly *adv.* courteously 132/62

D

dam(e)sele *n.* girl, unmarried woman 8/ 54, 79/3, 79/23, etc.; **dameselys** *pl. n.* 101/183

dampnablyr *comp. adj.* reprehensible, blameworthy 20/121

dampnacyon *n.* condemnation 41/127, 179/121, etc.

dampne *inf.* to condemn 63/29; *3 pa. sg.* 107/106; **dampnyd** *pa. p.* damned 70/ 117, 138/7, 155/59

dawynge, dayinge *n.* dawn 140/52, 141/20

debate, thebate *n.* resistance 87/130; fighting, brawling 108/140

deed(e) *adj.* dead 8/53,51/56, 70/127, etc.

de(e)dly *adj.* mortal 42/170, 43/178, 85/ 63, etc.; deadly 14/117, 42/163, 43/ 204, etc.

de(e)th *n.* death 12/77, 13/86, 14/20, etc.

def *adj.* deaf 37/82

defaute *n.* fault 13/89, 13/92

defulyd(e) *pa. p.* polluted 12/67, 14/15, 58/47, etc.

degre *n.* state of advancement 23/67, 23/ 67, 23/75, etc.; condition 169/396; **degreis, degreys** *pl. n.*7/17, 21/1, 23/ 66, etc.

degreede *pa. p.* graded, awarded a degree 69/99

deynte *n.* esteem, regard 69/97, 69/100

dekene *n.* deacon 48/135, 48/138

dele *n.* part, portion 33/172, 49/163

delectable *adj.* pleasing to the senses 6/ 131, 20/120, 37/77

delyberacyon *n.* consideration 6/113

delycate *adj.* delicate 32/118

delyte *n.* delight 66/130, 80/51, 123/ 223; **delytys** *pl. n.* 123/232

delytede *pa. p.* delighted 28/234

delytynge *vbl. n.* delighting 66/122, 66/ 123

delyueraunce *n.* freeing of a prisoner 108/149, 108/152

delyuere (deliuere, delyuyre) *inf.* rescue, save 108/143, 111/43, 112/61, etc.; *1 pr. sg.* 108/137, 108/138; *2 pr. sg.* 112/57, 174/601; *3 pr. sg.* 15/37; *1 fut. sg.* 126/109; *3 fut. sg.* 98/81, 107/ 105, etc.; **delyueryd(e)**; *pa. p.* delivered 14/121, 14/17, 77/209, etc.

deme *v. inf.* to judge, give judgement 45/29; 112/ 50, 112/54, etc.; *3 fut. sg.* 99/114; **demyd(e)** *pa. p.* judged 76/ 184, 99/115, 105/40; **demyth** *imp. sg.* 106/66

demynge *vbl. n.* opinion, belief 46/35

departe *inf.* ~ *fro* to separate 134/28; *3 pl. fut.* part company 135/40; **depart(t)yd** *pa. p.* departed 35/13, 58/ 33, 89/57, etc.

depte *pa. p.* dyed 118/79

despeyre *3 pl. fut.* despair, lose hope 146/78

despyse (dispise) *inf.* despise, scorn 24/ 86, 70/108; *3 pl. pr.* 69/100, 124/27;

despysyd, dyspysyde *3 pl. pa* 24/87, 103/253, 103/276, etc.
despyseable *adj.* contemptible 36/45
despyte (dyspyte) *n.* vilification, humiliation 9/70, 61/74, 96/3, etc.; despytes *pl. n.*27/202
dyffynyde *3 pa. sg.* determined, decided 8/56, 51/68, 79/5, etc.
dylygent *adj.* diligent 5/72, 128/58, 157/153, etc.
dylygently *adv.* diligently 5/75, 5/93, 5/101, etc.
dylygentlokyr *comp adv.* more diligently 5/97
dyscorden *3 pa. pl.* differed 20/115
dyscrecyon *n.* discretion 121/168
dyscrypcyon, dyscripcyon *n.* description 29/10, 29/13
dysparblyd *pa. p.* dispersed, scattered 137/42
dyspytfully *adv.* resentfully, angrily 114/144
dysplesaunte *adj.* displeasing 78/261
dysplesyth *3 pr. sg.* displeases 78/263
disposicioun *n.* disposition 68/58
dysposyd *pr. p.* resolved 72/57
dyspowsyd *pa. p.* espoused, betrothed 17/13, 17/17
dysputyd *pa. p.* disputed 58/43
dysseyte *n.* deceit 5/73
dysseyuyd *pa. p.* tricked, deceived 19/80, 25/137, 50/8, etc.
dyssernyd *pa. p.* discerned 35/12
dyssese *n.* tribulation, suffering 9/70, 61/73, 65/94, etc.; illness 73/90; dyssesys *pl. n.*infirmities ; sufferings 76/183, 77/214, 78/252, etc.
dyssesyde *pa. p.* afflicted 65/96, distressed 112/60
dystroblyd *pa. p.* frightened, alarmed 18/40, 41/109, 148/130, etc.
dystroye *inf.* to destroy 36/53, 50/21; *fut. sg.* 78/257, 102/230, 120/140; dystroyed *pa. p.* 30/41, 81/100, 112/73
dome *n.* judgement 25/147, 25/153, 99/128, etc.; court 160/76
dorewarde *adv. to the* ∼ toward the door 96/15, 101/181
dowme *n.* dumb, unable to speak 37/83
dowte *v. inf.* doubt 150/31; doutyde, dowtyd(e), dowtede *pa. p.* doubted 28/247, 150/41, 150/43, etc.

dowtynge *vbl. n.* doubting 93/205, 150/44, 150/45
drafe, throfe *3 pa. sg.* drove, compelled, forced 13/112, 37/83
drawe *inf.* to move, gather, pull 101/181, 101/183, 124/36, etc.; *1 pl. pr.* ∼ *lot* draw lots 120/137; *1 pa. sg.* translated 59/67; *3 pr. sg.* ∼ *of* write, compose 29/22, 38/24; *3 pa. sg.* pull 49/161; ∼ *vp* lift up 149/174; *3 pl. pr.* pull 117/29, 117/35, 118/67, etc.; ∼ *of* take off (clothes) 116/12, 116/13, etc.; ∼ *of* strip off (skin) 113/96; *3 pl. fut.* go 55/58; *subj. sg.* ∼ *ful loonge* promote, advance 59/73; drew(e) *3 pa. sg.* pulled 151/74; ∼ *to* approach, come near to 131/27; *3 pa. sg.* ∼ *oute* unsheathe (a sword) 99/126; ∼ *on* put on (clothes) 113/112; *3 pa. pl.* take, pull 173/545; idrawe *pa. p.* attracted 5/79
dredyngely *adv.* fearfully 100/171
duble *adj.* false, deceitful 70/120
dublettys *pl. n.*doublets 108/164
duelle *inf.* to remain 130/120; duellyde (duellede) *pa. p.* lived, dwelt 17/16, 18/30, 21/10, etc.
duellynge *ppl. adj.* dwelling 51/59; *vbl. n.* 158/29

E

edyfycacyon *n.* spiritual benefit 48/113, 59/69
edyfycatyf (edificatyf) *adj.* edifying, beneficial 4/45, 5/100, 8/40, etc.
edyfye *3 pl. pr.* to strengthen spiritually 171/493; edyfyeth *3 pr. sg.* 5/87
eftesonys *adv.* immediately, afterwards 64/53; again 77/203; a second time 104/14
eyen *pl. n. of* eye eyes 31/99, 47/74, 47/87, etc.
eyre *n.* sky, air 12/45, 39/27, 141/16, etc.
eyrys *pl. n.* heirs 38/17, 62/85, 115/187
eleccyon *n.* election, act of choosing 38/13
elle *n.* unit of measurement 30/62
empyre *n.* Empyrean 139/35, 143/107, 143/109
encense *n.* incense 42/157, 42/159, 42/163, etc.

encresse *inf.* to increase 130/101; encresyn *3 pl. pr.* 24/90; encressyd *pa. p.* 117/17, 117/19, 127/15
encres(s)ynge *vbl. n.* increasing 3/9, 27/208, 58/29, etc.
enformyd *pa. p.* informed 38/30, 39/42
en(ne)my *n.* devil 20/99, 20/111, 21/132, etc.; enemy 67/157; enmyis *pl. n.*enemies 95/284, 96/14, 100/147, etc.
ensample, ensampyl *n.* example 36/65, 46/37, 46/42, etc.; ensamplys *pl. n.*43/189, 75/131, 171/493
entent *n.* purpose, intention 4/64, 4/65, 4/67, etc.
esyly *adv.* gently 65/90, 91/140, 113/110, etc.
esylokyr *adv.* more easily 65/93, 65/94, 78/252, etc.
essencyal *adj.* absolute, supreme 168/392, 169/408, 170/451, etc.
euyn *n.* evening 9/60, 9/65, 83/2, etc.
euyn *adj.* equal 35/24; ~ *Cristyn* fellow Christians 27/208, 89/67
euyryche *n.* each 39/65
eueryche *adj.* every, each 12/75, 16/71, 24/116, etc.
excersysys *pl. n.* activities 4/40, 21/63
execuscyon *n.* lifting, releasing 76/193
expocysyon *n.* explanation, interpretation 162/151; exposysyonys *pl. n.*161/137
expone *inf.* to explain 44/215; *3 pl. pr.* explain 154/33; exponen *3 pa. pl.* 4/56; exponed(e), exponyd(e) *pr. p.* 16/94, 161/135; *pa. p.* 43/206, 40/102, 147/102
expresse *inf.* to describe, explain 74/106; expressyd *pr. p.* 18/36

F

faylede *pa. p.* lacked 33/141, 72/26, 72/27
fantasyis *pl. n.* falsehoods 146/85
fantastyke *adj.* illusory, phantasmal 36/53, 36/55, 128/30
fende *n.* devil, fiend 8/39, 13/81, 18/28, etc.
fer *adv.* far 38/28, 43/202, 47/98, etc.
ferthyr *comp. adv.* further 26/157, 110//209, 147/105
feste *n.* feast 25/132, 25/133, 38/15, etc.
fest(e)ful *adj.* ~ *day* feast day 54/17, 84/15

fette *inf.* to fetch 95/252, 138/5, 157/141; *1 fut. sg.* 145/49; *3 pa. pl.* 140/57; fette *pa. p.* fetched 174/604
fyfthyeth *ord. num.* fiftieth 157/11, 158/17
fygure *n.* prefiguration 16/66, 93/179; fygurys *pl. n.*7/10, 14/4, 15/42, etc.
flatlynge *adv.* prostrate 73/79
fleynge *vbl. n.* flying 39/37, 163/194; fleeing 49/5
fleumatyke *adj.* phlegmatic 128/28
flode *n.* river 59/9, 60/14, 61/52
flok *n.* flock of sheep 33/157
forbede, forbadde *2 pl. pr.* forbid 160/89; *3 pa. sg.* prohibited 12/72, 106/70, 159/57; forbode *pa. p.* 44/242
forbedynge *vbl. n.* forbidding 160/103
forsclewde *pa. p.* neglected through laziness 5/81
f(f)orsothe *adv.* for truth or fact 5/82, 15/40, 18/42, etc.
forthynke *2 sg. imp.* repent 80/56; forthowgthe *3 pa. sg.* 105/47
forthynkynge *vbl. n.* repenting 125/78
forthwyth *adv.* immediately 103/267
formyd *pa. p.* created 11/24
foundmet *n.* foundation 19/24
fourythyeth *ord. num.* fortieth 153/3
fre *adj.* unconstrained, bountiful 14/8, 19/70; ~ *wyll* free will, freedom of the will 61/67
fre *adv.* without hindrance 108/155, 110/6, 173/548, etc.
fuche(a)saf *inf.* vouchesafe 34/189, 38/12

G

gadre *3 pl. pr.* gather 52/111; gaderyde *pa. p.* 81/93, 141/41; igaderyd *pa. p.* 105/57, 147/117, 147/124
gerde, gyrdyth *pa. p.* dressed 89/63, 141/15, 89/34
gerdyl *n.* belt 141/15
getynge *vbl. n.* ~ *a3en* recovery, re-creation 61/81
glosyde *pa. p.* commented on, interpreted 6/121
gostly *adj.* devout, spiritual 3/2, 5/74, 6/116, etc.
gostly *adv.* in spirit 8/54, 12/59, 22/28, etc.
gouerenaunce *n.* control, custody 34/186

gouernoure *n.* ruler 34/186; steward, director (of marriage-feast) 71/17;
gouernorys *pl. n.* 85/73, 141/42
greys *pl. n.* steps 18/56, 118/59
grenesse *n.* vitality, vigour 154/55
gret hande *n.* in large letters 119/113
greue *3 pr. sg.* harm 170/432; **greuyd** *pa. p.* hurt, wounded 122/196
grounde *n.* basis, foundation 5/70, 6/116
grucchede, grucchyde *pa. p.* murmured, grumbled 85/49, 85/65
grucchynge *vbl. n.* grumbling, complaining 27/202, 46/47, 50/29, etc.

3

3ate *n.* gate 80/36, 80/53, 114/136, etc.; **3atys** *pl. n.* 141/11
3e *pron.* you 137/62, 138/69, 138/76, etc.
3elde *inf.* to yield 76/163; *3 fut. sg.* 80/57, 165/253; **3eldyde** *pa. p.* 80/55, 125/65
3ere *n.* year 57/8, 57/19, 57/21, etc.; **3eres** *pl. n.* 3/13
3eue (3eve) *inf.* to give 63/35, 77/217, 83/148, etc.; *pr. sg.* 21/133, 61/81, 64/79, etc.; *pl. pr.* 46/46, 150/39; *1 pa. sg.* 90/75; *3 pa. sg.* 30/52, 38/10, etc.; *3 pa. pl.* 82/114; *1 fut. sg.* 20/122; *2 imp. sg.* 132/44; *3 fut. sg.* 6/109, etc.; *3 pl. fut.* 46/57; **3af(e)** *pa. sg.* 124/46, 125/61, 125/74, etc.; *pa. pl.* 142/43, 174/611; **3euyth** *pa. sg.* 20/111, 23/78, 79/270, etc.; **3eue(n)** *pa. p.* 16/66; allow, grant 5/78; **i3eue** *pa. p.* 35/9, 169/393
3if *conj.* if 67/156, 69/98
3yfte *n.* gift 19/69, 82/127, etc.; **3yftes** *pl. n.* gifts 38/23, 43/184, etc.
3ys *interj.* yes 101/187
3it (3ytt) *adv.* yet 3/2, 3/28, etc.
3oke *n.* yoke 27/219
3onge *adj.* young 15/51, 30/54, 33/160, etc.
3ongethe *sup. adj.* youngest 50/38
3ongyr *comp. adj.* younger 22/17, 52/86, 145/23
3ougthe *n.* youth 59/62, 59/64, 155/92
3owle *n.* soul 151/56

H

habyte *n.* outward form, appearance 36/43, 74/119
halowe *inf.* to consecrate 61/82;

halowyth *3 pr. sg.* 142/61; **halowyd** *pr. p.* prepared for burial 131/25
halowynge *vbl. n.* consecrating 177/49
haluyndele *n.* half portion 49/162
handmayde *n.* female servant 23/49, 27/198
happe *n. by* ~ on occasion 58/53; *be* ~ by chance 128/37, 172/514
hap(p)ly *adv.* perhaps, probably; more or less 6/130, 6/133, 34/197, etc.
hard(e)nesse *n.* hardship 32/123; physical hardness 109/187; callousness 125/59, 153/11, etc.
hardy *adv.* bold 55/73
hardyr *comp. adj.* harder 125/67
hardyste *superl. adj.* hardest 26/157
harlot *n.* ruffian 122/212
heerys *pl. n.* hairs 31/90, 84/42
helyn *3 pa. pl.* covered, blindfolded 103/251
helthe *n.* salvation 5/89, 16/62, 16/84, etc.
herborowe *n.* lodging 30/53
herborowe *3 sg. pr.* give shelter 41/116
heuenewarde *n.* toward heaven 19/57, 31/99
heuly *adv.* angrily 46/47; with weight 81/69; with grief 100/171
heuynesse *n.* sadness 35/28, 54/44, 54/45, etc.
hye *inf.* to go, to act quickly, to hasten 22/25; *3 subj. sg.* 50/23
hye *adj.* high 27/225, 48/141, 73/63, etc.; **hyer** *comp.* higher 5/80, 25/156, 39/49, etc.; **hyeste** *superl.* highest 56/85, 56/86
hyndre *3 pl. pr.* to hinder 63/24
hospytal *n.* hospice, guesthouse 31/71

I

ibrowed *pa. p.* having eyebrows of a certain kind 60/31
icouplyd *pa. p.* joined, united 114/122, 114/147
idublyd *pa. p.* ~ *dayys were* double the number of days 45/22
ikytt *see* **kytte**
innys *pl. n.* lodgings, inns 30/51, 39/62, etc.
inspyryd *3 pa. sg.* breathed life into 11/22
ioyed(e) *pa. p.* rejoiced 22/31, 22/41, 23/48, etc.

ioyinge *vbl. n.* joyful words, praise 22/
36, 161/109
ioynede, iunede, iunyd *pa. p.* joined
68/39, 32/120, 2966, etc.
ipaynyd *pa. p.* caused pain 125/86
iugge *n.* judge 105/36, 112/48, 142/45;
iuggys *pl. n.* judges 74/111
iugge *inf.* to judge 112/54
iunckys *pl. n.* rush, reed 109/197, 110/209

K

kepare *n.* protector 172/511; **keparys** *pl.
n.* keepers, managers of household
affairs 141/35, 141/37, 141/39, etc.
kepe *inf.* to retain 25/137; to preserve
132/49; maintain 135/57; guard 135/
58; to obey 152/101; *3 fut. sg.* retain 3/
18; *3 pr. sg.* maintain 25/137; *2 fut. sg.*
preserve 152/118; *3 pa. sg.* protect
163/178, 165/255; *3 pa. sg.* 49/153;
kepte *3 pa. sg.* guarded 34/200;
retained 49/169; maintained, 100/168;
3 pa. pl. 159/50, 161/120; *pa. p.*
protected, guarded 20/21; maintained
25/123, 135/53; **kepyth** *2 imp. sg.* 34/
204, 130/129; *3 pr. sg.* retains 25/128,
25/137, etc.
kepynge *vbl. n.* guarding, protecting 33/
156, 37/66; prison 103/275;
maintaining 130/128, 167/336
keuere *inf.* to cover 31/94; **keuerede
(keuyred)** *pa. p.* covered 39/66, 42/
152
kyrtyl *n.* garment, tunic 31/79, 31/89
kytte *2 pr. pl.* cut 120/135; *1 pa. sg.* 117/
47; *3 pa. sg.* 15/52, 32/131, etc.; **ikytt**
pa. p. 134/17
kyttynge *vbl. n.* cutting 35/22
knaue *n.* servant 99/123; ~ *chylde* male
infant 45/16
knowynge *vbl. n.* knowledge 5/73, 12/
76, 13/97, etc.
knowleche *n.* knowledge 54/39
knowleche *inf.* to acknowledge 125/68,
159/53; *1 pr. sg.* 157/149; *1 pr. pl.* 42/
174; **knowlechede, knowlechyde** *pa.
p.* acknowledged 22/35, 47/103, 121/
184, etc.
koc *n.* rooster 95/271, 100/173, 101/188,
etc.
kow *n.* cow 12/50

kunnynge *vbl. n.* knowledge, ability 23/
58, 59/79, 69/81, etc.

L

laysyr, leysur *n.* opportunity 3/20, 87/
140
lecherye *n.* lechery 123/229
lepyr *n.* a person with leprosy 84/37;
leprys *pl. n.* lepers 70/127, 72/40
lesyng(e) *vbl. n.* losing 12/78, 13/95,
etc.; falsehood, deceit 142/49, 142/50
lette *3 fut. pl.* hinder, impede 10/8; *3 pa.
sg.* 111/30, 121/165; **lettyd** *pa. p.*
hindered 108/165
lett(e)ryd, letterde *ppl. adj.* literate,
educated 69/84, 69/87, 69/98
lettynge *vbl. n.* preventing, stopping 4/
39, 39/60; **lettyngys** *pl. n.* 4/40
lettyrature *n.* learning, education 74/110
lettural, lettureall *adj.* literal 6/122, 6/
123, 154/37
leuyr *comp. adj.* rather 89/55, 89/58, 95/
262, etc.
lyf(e), lyue *n.* life 64, 1125, 3403, 3742,
etc.
ligthly *adv.* likely 109/187
lygthlokyr *comp. adj.* with ease 41/140
lygth(t) *n.* light 31/85, 32/106, 32/107,
etc.
lyflode *n.* food 30/66
lykyng(e) *vbl. n.* pleasure 11/31, 11/33,
12/69; **lykyngys** 130/110
lykned *pr. p.* compared 5/99; *pa. p.* 32/
105
lykur *n.* fluid 32/131; wine 91/142; drink
94/220
lynnyn *adj.* of linen 31/91, 31/94, 32/
132, etc.
lyste *3 pr. sg.* likes, pleases 3/19, 59/65;
3 pa. sg. liked 51/43
lystynge *vbl. n.* lifting 19/57
lokynge *vbl. n.* looking 31/99, 155/69,
155/72
londe *n.* land 8/30, 30/40, 39/67, etc.;
londys *pl. n.* lands 39/57
longen (longyn) *3 pr. sg.* belong 76/164,
76/165, 130/111; ~ *to* be fitting for
36/32, 56/105; ~ *therto* be relevant 8/
51; *3 pl. pr.* ~ *therto* 71/4; **longyde**
pa. p. belonged 85/51, 132/53;
longyth *3 pr. sg.* ~ *to* it is the function
of, duty of 61/70, 69/72, 144/114, etc.

looth *adv.* loath 2708, 3383
lose *3 pl. pr.* loose, free, untie 108/156, 134/27
lothe *1 pr. pl.* despise, dislike 91/112; *3 pr. sg.* 91/111
louely *adj.* gracious beloved 35/20, 90/83, 97/38, etc.
louly *adv.* graciously 113/107, 124/44, 135/41
lowe *adj.* humble, meek 19/58, 27/213, 28/137; **lower** *comp. adj.* more humble 5/81; **lowest(e)** *superl. adj.* most humble 25/125, 25/130, 25/132, etc.
lowly *adv.* kindly 22/29, 34/196, 46/42, etc.
lownesse *n.* lowness, humility 27/206, 28/233, 35/16, etc.
luste *n.* pleasure 11/31, 11/32, 12/69; **lustys** *pl. n.* pleasures 130/110, 130/123

M

mayde(n) *n.* virgin 16/65, 16/92, 28/244, etc.; **maydenys** *pl. n.* virgins 48/126, 149/165
maydenhode *n.* virginity 47/100
maye (mowe) *2 pr. sg.* can 3/11, 11/13, 12/47, etc.; **may** *1 pr. sg.* 41/138, 48/113, 102/230, etc.; **mayest** *2 pr. sg.* 165/280; **mowen** *3 pr. pl.* 4/46, 126/126, etc.; **mygth(te), myght** could, was able to *subj. sg.* 7/13, etc.; *1 pa. sg.* 3/6, 4/39, etc.; *2 pa. sg.* 140/6; *3 pa. sg.* 3/17, etc.; *3 pa. pl.* 3/20, etc.; **mygtheste, mygthyst** *2 pr. sg.* 97/52, 126/99
mayne *n.* house, lineage 17/14, 29/18; followers, retainers 51/76, 52/91; household servants 107/118
maystyr (maistre) *n.* scholar 6/120; teacher 89/51; official in charge 160/81, 160/85; **maystrys** teachers 5/86, 58/44
maystrye *n.* miracle 79/15
maner *n.* kind, form, custom 5/88, 12/45, 15/24, etc.
many(e) (mayne) *adj.* a large number, many 16/86, 16/94, 17/96, etc.
manly *adv.* bravely, courageously 49/159, 90/89
mede *n.* reward 91/113, 91/114, 91/116, etc.; **medys** *pl. n.* rewards 168/390

medeful *adj.* meritorius 61/67, 61/70
medytacyon *n.* religious discourse 3/3, 9/88, 10/91, etc.; **medytacyonys** *pl. n.* 4/59, 4/61, 6/110, etc.
medlyd *pr. p.* mixed 60/12
medlynge *vbl. n.* sexual intercourse 18/50
meke *adj.* gentle, quiet, meek 4/63, 5/79, 19/57, etc.
meke *3 pr. sg.* ~ *himself* humble oneself 25/238, 35/16
mekely *adv.* meekly, humbly 19/63, 22/29, 23/73, etc.
mekenesse *n.* benevolence, meekness 9/94, 7/17, 8/35, etc.
membyr (menbyr) *n.* part of the body 32/110; ~ *of* collaborator with 65/112; **membrys (menbrys)** *pl. n.* limbs 42/160, 65/113, 65/116, etc.; ~ *of* collaborators with 65/111
mene *n.* mediator 172/511
mete *n.* food, dinner 39/63, 43/203, 44/242, etc.
myght(e) *n.* spiritual strength 66/145, 124/23; **mygthtys** 11/25, 12/55, 26/187, etc.
mysly *adv.* sinfully, wickedly 4/63, 115/167
mysbeleue *n.* scepticism, disbelief 41/130, 146/56, 147/100, etc.
mysdoare *n.* guilty person 100/146, 106/64, 108/161, etc.
mysgouernyd *ppl. adj.* misguided 28/248
myste *n.* fog, mist 39/66, 39/67, 40/79, etc.
mysterye *n.* spiritual knowledge 18/27; **mysteryis** *pl. n.* 163/196
mone *n.* moon 73/90, 73/92, 73/94, etc.
monethys *pl. n.* months 28/230, 28/234
mortayse *n.* hole, cavity 117/40
mote halle *n.* assembly hall 105/39

N

nedeful *adj.* necessary 91/117
nethys *adv.* of necessity 12/79, 27/195, etc.
nette *n.* net for fishing 151/58, 151/60, etc.; woven material 120/136
nygth *adv.* near 26/190
nygthbore *n.* neighbour 84/38
nygthhe *1 pr. sg.* draw near, approach

83/144; **nygeth** *3 pr. sg.* 98/96;
nyg(t)hede *pa. p.* 40/75, 85/83, etc.
nygthynge *vbl. n.* drawing near 48/119
nygth(te) *n.* night 9/69, 9/71, 26/190,
etc.; **nygthtys** *pl. n.* nights 62/8, 63/
13, etc.
nobyl *adj.* noble 48/115, 131/13;
nobyllokyr *comp. adj.* nobler 39/49;
nobylereste *superl. adj.* noblest 39/47
not forthann *adv.* nevertheless 93/200
notwythstandynge *adv.* nevertheless 6/
125, 97/44, 109/174, etc.
nowgth(te) *inf.* to despise, to insult, to
set at naught 24/106, 32/107
nowre *adv.* nowhere 53/116, 164/234

O

obedyence *n.* obedience 19/83, 27/219,
37/66, etc.
obedyent *adj.* obedient 19/86, 46/41,
57/126, etc.
obedyently *adv.* obediently 58/26, 121/
159
oblyuyon *n.* state of being forgotten 12/
59
obseruaunce *n.* act of following
prescribed rules 35/9, 35/17, etc.
ofte *adj.* frequent 70/127
ofte *adv.* often 3/22, 5/84, 58/56, etc.
oftyr *comp. adv.* more often 5/96, 145/34
onehede *n.* unity 91/129, 91/135
opyn, open *adj.* evident, plain 6/128,
11/23, etc.; bare, uncovered 52/95, 91/
109; obvious 70/107, 108/152; clear
45/11, 132/45, 166/315; *in* ~ publicly
22/25, 22/27, 28/236, etc.
opynyon *n.* opinion 28/245; **opynyons**
pl. n. 73/94
opyn(y)ly *adv.* clearly, plainly 16/90, 25/
135, 31/75, etc.
ordeyne *inf.* to appoint 135/56; *3 pr. sg.*
prescribe 15/30; prepare 88/20;
ordeynyd(e) *pa. p.* prepared 47/88,
47/90, 69/85, etc.; **iordeynyd** *pa. p.*
38/34, 55/54, 58/26, etc.
ordenaunce *n.* rule, law 23/74, 90/85,
91/131; **ordenaunces** *pl. n.* 46/43
ordynatly *adv.* in order 38/5, 62/5
ordyr *n.* rank, status 48/128, 48/129,
56/88, etc.; religious order 3/26, 92/
150, etc.; ~ *of charytee* rule enjoining
charity 69/71

oryson *n.* prayer 172/521, 172/530, 173/
535, etc.
othyrwhyle *adv.* sometimes 58/31, 58/
37, 82/110, etc.
othyrwyse *adv.* differently 77/223
ouer *adv.* more 169/413
ouerall (ouyral(l)) *adv.* everywhere 152/
104; above all 27/220, 65/88, etc.; ~
regnynge omnipotent 42/165/ 42/174
ouyr parte *n.* upper part 138/8
ouyrpasse *1 pr. sg.* pass over, disregard
139/46; **ouyrpassyd(e)** *pr. p.*
disregarded 55/80; surpassed 163/182;
ouyrpassyth *3 pr. sg.* rises above 171/
467; surpasses 171/473
ouyrpassynge *vbl. n.* excelling,
transcendence 55/76
out take *prep.* with the exception of 12/
71, 16/74, etc.

P

pacyence (pacience) *n.* patience 53/121,
58/36, 59/77, etc.
pacyently *adv.* patiently 27/211, 53/122,
61/74, etc.
payne *n.* punishment, penalty 14/19, 19/
85, 35/14, etc.; **paynys** *pl. n.*
punishments 117/17, 173/545, etc.
paynyde *pa. p.* made to suffer 119/105,
136/28
paynym *n.* pagan 105/42, 105/43, 106/
73, etc.; **paynemys, paynymys** *pl. n.*
pagans 38/11, 114/130, 115/164
pamyr *n.* stick, rod 172/526
partenerys *pl. n.* partners 78/241, 82/
134, 130/119
passyinge *vbl. n.* passing of the soul
(reference to Passynge of the Lord) 84/
23, 84/28
passynge *ppl. adj.* fleeting, momentary
31/67, 84/16, 114/151, etc.
passyngly *adv.* exceedingly 55/68, 110/
210, 123/11
patryarke *n.* one of the Old Testament
fathers 15/50, 170/460, ; **patriarkys**
pl. n. 170/454, 170/459, etc.; *xii* ~
twelve sons of Jacob 170/457
patrone *n.* patron 172/510
pauyment (panyment) *n.* paved surface
32/124, 134/23
pere *n.* peer, equal 61/66, 165/283, 166/
285

pere *3 pr. sg.* compare, match, make
equal 25/126, 164/239, 164/240
perel (pereel) *n.* peril, danger 64/55,
64/61, 65/100, etc.
perfyte (perfyth, perfygth) *adj.* perfect,
flawless 5/86, 5/96, 11/26, etc.;
perfyther *comp. adj.* more perfect 25/
145; perfythlokyr *superl adj.* most
perfect 61/73
perfythly *adv.* perfectly 27/224
pese *n.* peace 33/164, 39/55, 47/86, etc.
pesys *pl. n.* pieces 124/51
pynnacle *n.* spire, pointed turret 63/46,
64/63
pynsorys *pl. n.* tongs, pincers 132/51,
133/78, 133/81
pystyl *n.* epistle 65/101, 130/120, letter
51/64; pystyllys *pl. n.* letters 10/103,
149/4, 152/113; epistles 169/405, 170/
441, 171/468
plente *n.* abundance 142/43, 154/24
plyte *n.* condition 126/97
prefacyon *n.* preface 3/1, 3/11, 3/15,
etc.
preferre *inf.* to advance, to place before,
to give precedence 56/194; *subj. sg.* 25/
150; *2 pr. sg.* 25/151; preferryd(e) *pa.
p.* preferred 56/87, 169/409;
preferryth *2 pr. sg.* 25/143, 55/77
prese *n.* crowd, throng 114/138
presently *adv.* in person 50/34, 90/91,
91/138
presumptuouseness *n.* arrogance 95/268
presumptuus *adj.* arrogant 2371
preuynge *vbl. n.* proving 148/137
preuyth *3 pr. sg.* tests, tries, proves 139/
45
pryoure *n.* Prior 3/28, 3/31
pryuy *adj.* private; secret 80/34, 96/19,
101/210; trusted 73/62, 132/34;
pryuyer *comp. adj.* more private 96/16
pryuyly (priuyly) *adv.* secretly, privately
41/133, 87/130, 87/137, etc.
pryuyte *n.* secret 18/25; pryuyteys *pl.
n.* secrets 93/210, 94/226, 162/144,
etc.
procuratur *n.* agent 95/255
profytarys *pl. n.* those who are making
progress 24/90
puncte *n.* point 106/72, 106/77
purpose *n.* plan, design 18/51, 63/31,
94/241, etc.
purpose *inf.* aim, resolve 161/133;

purposyde intended *pa. p.* 18/50, 39/
50, 51/63, etc.; purposyth *imp.* intend
23/57
purposynge *vbl. n.* purposing, intending
99/126, 137/39, 149/172

Q

quere *n.* choir 48/134, 48/141, 48/142,
etc.
quyk *adv.* quickly, fast 127/8
quyke *adj.* alive 157/146, 163/ 209
quyked *3 fut. pl.* restore to life 15/41

R

raueyischyd *pa. p.* transported 94/227
reboundyth *3 pr. pl.* to be abundant,
flow abundantly 21/124, 21/134
recomendynge *vbl. n.* committing for
care or protection 162/148
recusyth *3 sg. pr.* refuses 85/58
redylokyr *comp adj.* more prepared 3/18
redressyd, redressed *pa. p.* directed a
wrong 4/45, 4/47, 69/89, etc.
refraynynge *vbl. n.* restraining 44/245
refreyne *inf.* refrain 111/32
refugye (refute) *n.* refuge 93/187, 32/
125
rekenyde *vbl. n.* computing, naming
159/39
rekke *3 pr. pl.* care 105/51; rekkyste *2
pa. sg.* cared 75/140; rofte *3 pa. sg.* ~
of cared for 30/41, 106/73; cared 30/
58, 106/73
relygyon *n.* religious order 27/218
relygyus *adj.* person belonging to a
religious order 46/37, 81/92, 158/30,
etc.; devout 173/542; ~ *syster* nun 10/
6, 14/6, 71/6, etc.
relygyusly *adv.* piously, devoutly 54/27
relyke *n.* relic 49/169; relyquyis *pl. n.*
relics 175/608, 175/611, 175/616
renne *3 pr. sg.* run 145/23; *3 pr. pl.* 109/
200; pierce 113/97; rennyn *3 pr. pl.*
run 52/94, 145/21; rennyth *3 pr. sg.*
runs 108/167, 109/183, 109/201, etc.
rennynge *vbl. n.* running 98/73, 145/19
reparacyon *n.* repair 105/57
repreue *n.* reproach 100/153; repreuys
pl. n. reproaches 122/221
repreuyd(e) *ppl. adj.* damned, accursed
94/234; *pa. p.* reproached 152/106
restore *3 sg. fut.* heal, return to power

154/32, 154/41; **restory(e)d** *pa. p.* 7/
8, 14/121, etc.

resun *n.* intellectual faculty or power 6/
128, 11/25, 12/56, etc.

resunnable (resunyable) *adj.* intelligent,
capable of reason 12/53, 17/101, 89/
49, etc.

resunnably *adv.* rationally 92/145, 142/
59

reuelacyon *n.* visionary experience 57/
17, 82/112, 139/43, etc.;
reuelacyonys *pl. n.* 6/125, 20/98, 82/
112

rygthwyse *n.* rightful 25/120, 25/147,
25/153

rygt(h)wysenesse *n.* righteousness, moral
rectitude 12/78, 13/95, 14/119

ryischys (ryischyssys) *pl. n.* rushes 109/
185, 109/190, 109/194

rote *n.* root 23/63, 51/44, 132/48

rowe *n. be, by* ~ in turn, in order 23/66,
89/64, 93/206, etc.

S

saddyst *superl. adj.* densest, most solid
118/66

sadly *adv.* earnestly 5/90

sadlynge *vbl. n.* swaddling 42/160

sadnesse *n.* sobriety, maturity 42/160

sayinge *vbl. n.* saying 149/164

scharpe *adj.* intense, severe 20/117, 39/
61, 108/166, etc.

scharp(e)ly *adv.* harshly 27/210, 95/270,
108/167, etc.

scharpenesse *n.* sharpness, keeness 109/
187

schetys *pl. n.* sheets 146/87

schewe *inf.* to show 22/26, 27/206, 63/
34, etc.; *1 fut. sg.* 23/62, 75/131; *3 fut.
sg.* 15/49, 36/60, 76/193; *3 pa. sg.* 75/
157, **schewyth** *3 pr. sg.* 75/146, 140/
66, 153/121; **schewest** *2 pr.* 97/51;
schewed *pa. p.* 16/68, 36/36, 50/27,
etc.; **ischewde** *pa. p.* 16/86

schewynge *vbl. n.* showing 519, 1760,
2435, 4082

schyne *3 pa. sg.* shone 58/57; **schynyth**
pr. p. 37/75

schynynge *vbl. n.* shining 32/114;
shynyngys shinings 177/61

schynys *pl. n.* shins 127/7, 128/23

schyt(te) *pa. p.* shut 39/55, 137/65, 141/
11, etc.

schrewe *n.* wicked peron 87/145;
schrewys, screwys *pl. n.* 94/249, 85/
57

schrewde *adj.* wicked 114/117, 121/162

sclaundyr *n.* slander, misrepresentation
18/23, 46/35

scle(e) *inf.* to slay, murder 8/56, 50/14,
51/63, etc.; *3 pr. sg.* 979, 1200; *3 pa.
sg.* 41/136, 50/15, etc.; *3 pa. pl.* 51/76,
52/91, etc.; **sclewe** *3 pa. sg.* slew 84/
21; ~ *hymselfe* committed suicide 59/
98, **sclayne, scleyne** slain *pa. p.* 42/
142, 65/117, 94/216, etc.

sclyde *1 pa. pl.* slid 66/123

sclyme *n.* slime 11/17, 11/20

scorge *inf.* to beat, whip 108/160;
scorgyd *pa. p.* 160/102, 161/107;
iscorgyd *pa. p.* 110/4

scorgys *n.* whips, lashes 108/166, 113/
115, 122/222

scrowe *n.* scroll 119/113, 172/514, 172/
516; **scrowys** *pl. n.* 172/512

seynge *vbl. n.* seeing 125/73

seke *n.* sick 70/127

seke (syke) *adj.* sick 72/39, 74/128

seke *inf.* seek 39/41, 39/47, 39/50; *1 pr.
sg.* 106/91 *2 pr. sg.* 99/119; *3 fut. sg.*
64/61; **sekyth** *3 pr. sg.* 97/48; **sekyste**
2 pr. sg. 145/46; **softe** sought *2 pa. sg.*
56/104; *3 pa. sg.* 87/141, 111/43; *1 pa.
pl.* 58/40; *3 pa. pl.* 44/219, 52/103,
54/34, etc.; **isofte** *pa. p.* 55/72, 55/79

sekenesse *n.* sickness 33/140, 72/43;
sekenessys *pl. n.* 74/103, 76/182

sekynge *vbl. n.* seeking 32/125, 50/10,
55/69, etc.

seler *n.* storeroom 30/36

selys *pl. n.* seals 149/176

semely *adj.* fitting 30/60; 58/31, etc.

senseualyte(e) *n.* natural ability to
receive physical senses 97/68, 98/79

sermon(e) *n.* speech, discourse 46/69,
95/273, 96/10, etc.

sesyde *3 pa. sg.* cease, leave off 50/10,
161/116; *3 pa. pl.* 136/31, 137/35

sesynge *n.* ceasing 140/65

sygth *conj.* since 4/51, 18/49, etc.

sygth *adv.* afterwards 17/8, 69/92

sygth(te) *n.* sight 24/107, 25/126, 25/
134, etc.

syker, sykyr *adj.* certain, safe 27/219,

28/245, 51/73, etc.; **sykyrer** *comp. adj.*
    more certain 117/46; **sykyrest(e)**
    superl. adj. 6/129, 25/136, 25/154
sykyrly *adv.* certainly 65/110, 90/96,
    111/24, etc.
sykyrnesse *n.* certainty 151/78, 25/155,
    26/162, etc.
syndele *n.* thin silken material 131/22,
    134/7
synglere *adj.* special, exceptional 45/28,
    46/45, 57/9, etc.
syngleretee *n.* uniqueness of behavior
    46/46
syngler(e)ly *adv.* exclusively 18/38, 60/
    28, 164/238, etc.
sodeyne *adv.* sudden 32/108
sodeynely *adv.* suddenly 33/162, 41/113,
    48/123, etc.
sodekene *n.* subdeacon 48/135, 48/138
softe *adv.* gently 113/109, 113/111, 115/
    178
softyr *comp adj.* softer 108/168, 109/171
soget(t) *adj.* subject 15/33, 56/114, etc.
sonde *n.* dispensation, ordinance 44/224
sore *adv.* grievously, painfully 50/13, 50/
    22, 50/32, etc.
sorest *superl adj.* saddest 136/21
sorynesse *n.* sorrow 97/61
soth *n.* truth 20/108, 91/119, 91/124,
    etc.
sothly *adv.* truly, honestly 24/108, 129/
    70, 130/126, etc.
sotyl *adj.* delicate, thin 31/79; subtle 63/
    23, 69/81
sotylly *adv.* cunningly 75/132
spedeful *adj.* profitable, beneficial 82/
    106, 83/149, 91/117
spyracle *n.* breath of life, vitality 11/22
spyserye *n.* spices (for embalming) 134/
    8, 137/39, etc.
spouse breche *n.* adultery 76/171, 76/
    173
stabyl *n.* building for keeping animals
    42/160
stabyl(l) *adj.* constant, steadfast 142/67,
    157/157, etc.
stabylnesse *n.* constancy, steadfastness
    13/97, 13/100, 150/37
stere, styre *3 pr. pl.* guide, direct 2933;
    imp. pl. 1691, 4339; **styryde** *pa. p.*
    110/7, 112/63, 173/534; **sterede** *be* ∼
    proposed to; moved to *pr. p.* 66/152;
    imp. pl. 66/148

sterre *n.* star 38/22, 38/30, 38/32, etc.;
    sterrys *pl. n.* 52/85
sterte *adj.* stark 108/162
sterte *3 pa. sg.* leapt 113/111, 151/64
stye *3 pa. sg.* ascended 155/85; *3 fut. sg.*
    90/86
stykyngys *pl. n.* wound 150/14
styrynge *vbl. n.* impulse 112/66
strayte *adj.* close, strict 103/275, 121/
    162
strayte *adv.* strictly 117/35
suade *inf.* to swaddle an infant 32/132
suadynge bonde *n.* swaddling band 32/
    134
suage *3 pa. sg.* assuaged 161/108; *imp. sg.*
    160/100; **suagyd(e)** *pa. p.* 160/98,
    160/105, 161/107
suerde *n.* sword 99/126, 99/132, 99/133,
    etc.; **suerdys** *pl. n.* 98/99, 99/141
suete *adj.* sweet 7/22, 16/82, 33/166,
    etc.; **suettyr** *comp. adj.* sweeter 20/111
suetly *adv.* sweetly, dearly 12/63, 73/82,
    77/210, etc.
suet(e)nesse *n.* sweetness 5/74, 5/79,
    20/113, etc.
suffraun(s)ce *n.* allowing, leave 13/91,
    52/98
suggestyon *n.* prompting, urging 12/80,
    13/81, 19/80, etc.
suolle *pa. p.* swollen 32/117, 33/143;
    isuolle *pa. p.* 21/135
suolowe *3 pa. sg.* swallowed 91/110
suowynge *vbl. n.* swooning 31/101, 48/
    124

T

tabyl *n.* list of contents 3/11, 3/14;
    plank, board of wood 119/114; **tablys**
    pl. n. plank, post 118/56, 118/62, 118/
    80
take *inf.* to take, 15/47, 49/161, etc.; to
    arrest, apprehend 87/139, 99/123, etc.;
    to appropriate 15/35; to accept 28/253;
    ∼ *oure kynde* to become incarnate 34/
    190; ∼ *downe* to take down from a
    cross 131/9, 131/10, etc.; *1 pr. sg.*
    select, choose 6/122; *2 pr. sg.* 21/140,
    etc.; ∼ *to mynde* considers 79/8; *3 pr.*
    sg. 74/103, etc.; *3 pr. pl.* 86/90, 95/
    275, etc.; *3 fut. sg.* receive 5/92; take
    34/183, etc.; *subj. sg.* 16/69, etc.; *subj.*
    pl. 75/150, etc.; *imp.* 52/102, etc.;

takyth takes *2 pr. sg.* 96/6; *3 pr. sg.*
brings 50/31; receives 54/104; adopts
59/11; chooses 89/34; brings 90/69; *3
pr. pl.* receives 5/90; *imp.* notice 19/66,
50/27, etc.; **toke** *3 pa.* chose 8/50, 15/
56, etc.; adopted 11/35; offered 19/73;
received 30/49; brought 131/27; ∼
oute removed 31/91; ∼ *vp* carried 746;
itake *pa. p.* 37/84, 65/107, etc.
takynge *vbl. n.* taking 9/83, 15/51, etc.
tale *n.* story 48/113
tarye *1 pr. sg.* tarry, delay 161/130; *3 pr.
sg.* 144/121; *subj. sg.* 22/26; **taryed** *1
pa. sg.* 27/226
taryinge *vbl. n.* lingering 50/28, 150/40,
etc.
temporal *adj.* earthly, pertaining to the
world 154/36, 154/39
temporally *adv.* on earth, in the world
86/106, 106/91
tempte *inf.* tempt 63/35, 64/58, etc.; *2
imp.* 64/57; **temptyth** *3 pr. sg.* 63/42,
64/67; **temptyd(e), temptede** *pa. p.*
tempted 8/39, 62/2, 62/7, etc.
tende *3 pr. sg.* pay attention to 94/233
tendyr, tendry *adj.* young 22/22, 35/20,
etc.; gentle 32/128, 71/22; soft 35/14,
62/88; **tendyrer** *comp. adj.* 108/168,
109/171
tendyrnesse *n.* tenderness 109/173, 122/
195
terys *pl. n.* tears 35/31, 100/154, etc.
thare *3 pr. sg.* dare 25/125; **thurste,
thruste** *3 pa. sg.* 110/214, 112/ 51,
137/65, etc.
therabowte, theraboute *adv.* regarding
a matter or activity 8/46, 10/105;
regarding a specific time 153/2;
regarding a specific place or location
40/90, 51/77, 118/56
theraftyr *adv.* regarding a specific time
155/59
thraldom *n.* slavery 112/78
tobrake *3 pa. sg.* broke in pieces 49/162;
3 pa. pl. 124/52; **tobraste** *3 pa. pl.*
118/74; 125/65; **tobroke** *pa. p.* broken
in pieces 30/42, 49/166
tokene *n.* sign 20/122, 27/214, 33/160,
etc.
toterynge *vbl. n.* tearing, rending 52/96
traueyle, traveyle *n.* toil, labor 4/38;
hardship 4/39, 13/113, 22/21, etc.
treyn *adj.* wooden 30/45

trespassare *n.* wrongdoer 76/186
trespasse *n.* sin 12/87
tretye *n.* treaty 139/22, 139/27
trewe *adj.* honest, accurate 63/15, 65/94,
etc.
trewly *adv.* truly, honestly, accurately 4/
55, 6/128, etc.
trewthe *n.* truth 17/11, 20/123, 21/124,
etc.
trowe *1 pr. sg.* suppose, reckon 3/2, 14/
10; dare say 3/32, 20/96; believe 17/
101, 23/53; *2 pr. pl.* know 155/87,
155/89, etc.; **trowest** *2 pr. sg.* 1115,
2481; **trowed(e)** *pa. p.* believed 41/
107, 52/81, etc.; reckoned 53/9;
understood 50/8, 50/9; **itrowe** *pa. p.*
130/126
trowynge *vbl. n.* belief 56/100, 56/101
tunne *n.* container, barrel 169/425, 170/
429
þat *pron.* what, that which 4/46, 4/56,
4/67, etc.

V

vagabunde *adj.* renegade 174/573
vayle *n.* veil 31/88, 124/50; **valeyis** *pl.
n.* 39/59
vayne glorye (vanyne glorye) *n.*
meaningless praise 64/50, 64/67
vaynely *adv.* with vanity 12/64, 24/101
vaynys *pl. n.* veins, blood vessels 117/29,
117/32, 117/41
vanyischyde, vanyischede *3 pa. sg.*
3710, 3874; *3 pa. pl.* 3912
veryly *adv.* truly 23/71, 23/79, 24/101,
etc.
verry *adj.* true 7/138, 16/84, 20/103,
etc.
vertu *n.* power 36/65, 37/81, etc.;
vertuys *pl. n.* 3/10, 5/73, etc.
vertuouse (vertuus) *adj.* virtuous 5/95,
78/246, 82/133
vertuousely *adv.* virtuously 69/103
vycys *pl. n.* vices 20/119, 23/70, etc.
vycyusly *adv.* sinfully 12/69, 13/111
vyle *adj.* vile, evil 12/51, 70/109, 175/
611
vylytee *n.* spiritual offensiveness 21/130a
vylytee *n.* vileness 21/130
vnable *adj.* unable 76/193
vnabylnesse *n.* incompetence, inability
4/47

vnbeleue *n.* disbelief 150/22,
vnbeleueable *adj.* unbelieveable 65/109
vnbeleuefull *adj.* disbelieving 150/22
vnclene *adj.* 45/16, 45/17, etc.
vnclennesse *n.* uncleanness 32/112, 60/
47, etc.
vndefulyd *ppl. adj.* undefiled 15/36,
177/47
vndepartably *adv.* indivisibly 91/133,
132/47
vndeseyuable *adj.* not false, valid 20/122
vndeuout *adj.* not devout 110/230
vndyrnede *adv.* underside 2938, 3376
vndyrneme *inf.* rebuke 55/73
vnfleable *adj.* unavoidable 64/59
vnyuersyte(e) *n.* world, entire collection
34/182, 103/281
vnkynde *adj.* unkind 24/87, 54/41, 77/
216, etc.
vnkyndly *adv.* against nature 27/210
vnkunnynge *n.* ignorance 4/36, 4/48,
69/79
vnlernyde *adj.* unlearned 5/85
vnlosyd *pa. p.* untied 141/15
vnnede (vnnedys, vnnethe) *adv.* hardly,
with difficulty 44/214, 81/69, 151/60
vnpacyence *adj.* impatience 27/204,
160/94
vnpassyble *adj.* incapable of suffering
35/26, 43/177
vnpere *adj.* unequal, dissimilar 170/430
see Explanatory Notes
vnpossyble *adj.* impossible 4/35, 28/247,
45/33
vnscryptyble *adj.* limitless 15/30

vnsykyr *adj.* unsure 139/47
vnsykernesse *n.* uncertainty 25/120
vnvsyd *ppl. adj.* unaccustomed 5/79
vouchestsafe, vouchedsaf 2 *pr. sg.*
grant, bestow 168/341; *pa. p.*167/356
vttyrly *adv.* utterly 3/30, 49/152, 57/10,
etc.

W

waytynges *vbl. n.* ambush, trap 77/214
waytyth 3 *pl. pr.* watches for 124/26;
iwaytyd *pa. p.* 38/33
warelokyr *adv.* prudently, circumspectly
75/159
weye goynge *n.* journeying 92/171
welle *n.* spring, source (of river) 51/46,
78/265; wellys *pl. n.* rivers 59/11,
167/351
wende 3 *pa. sg.* thought, believed 54/31,
54/33, etc.; 3 *pa. pl.* 86/105, 95/253,
etc.; *pa. p.* 64/49, 95/269
wenge 1 *pr. pl.* avenge 66/153
wexe *inf.* grow 56/91, 56/93, etc.; 3 *pr.
pl.* 20/110, 56/93; 1 *pa. pl.* 46/49;
wexyth 3 *pr. sg.* 20/117
wylful *adj.* obstinate 7/5, 10/4, 14/9,
etc.
wylfully *adv.* voluntarily 13/89, 115/163,
115/185, etc.
wyrkemen *pl. n.* workmen 71/143, 71/
145
wyrkynge *vbl. n.* working 13/94, 18/53,
82/112, etc.

SUMMARY TABLE OF SOURCES

Sections	Gg folios	N folios	Biblical sources	Non–biblical sources
Preface	1ʳ–4ᵛ	1ʳ–3ʳ	John 12: 26	Henry Suso, *Horologium Sapientiae*
Table of Contents	4ᵛ–6ᵛ	3ʳ–5ʳ		
Chapter 1: Creation and Fall	6ᵛ–9ᵛ	5ʳ–7ʳ	Gen. 1: 27–8; 2: 7–8, 16–18, 21 Ps. 48: 13 Wisd. 2: 24	Walter Hilton, *The Scale of Perfection*
Chapter 2: God's plan for the world	9ᵛ–12ʳ	7ʳ–8ᵛ	Gen. 22: 1–6 Num. 27: 1–11 Isa. 7: 14 Matt. 1: 23 John 24: 17 1 Cor. 15: 22	John Chrysostom, *Orationes VIII Adversus Judaeos*, Homily VI
Chapter 3: Annunciation	12ʳ–16ʳ	8ᵛ–11ʳ	Luke 1: 26–38	Paschasius Radbertus, *De Assumptione Sanctae Mariae Virginis* (attributed to Jerome) St Quodvultdeus, *Sermo 10: Aduersus Quinque Haereses* (attributed to Augustine) Nicholas of Lyre, *Postilla* Catherine of Siena (Raymond of Capua, *Legenda Maior*, ch. 9)

Chapter			Biblical references	Sources
Chapter 4: Visitation	11r–15v	16r–22v	Ps. 33: 19 Eccles. 9: 1–2 Matt. 1: 19–25; 5: 3 Luke 1: 39, 41–8, 46–55; 14: 10–11	Nicholas of Lyre, *Postilla* St Ambrose, *Expositio Evangelii secundum Lucam* Peter Comestor, *Historia Scholastica* (as *Book of Rygthful Men*) St Ambrose, *Expositio Evangelii secundum Lucam*
Chapter 5: Nativity	15v–19v	22v–28r	1 Kgs. 14: 12–13 Luke 2: 7–16, 20	Jacobus de Voragine, *Legenda Aurea* John of Hildesheim, *Historia Trium Regum* Ps.-Matthew, *Pseudo-Matthaei Evangelium* (*Boke of þe {Y}oughte of Oure Lorde*) St Birgitta of Sweden, *Revelaciones*
Chapter 6: Circumcision	19v–21r	28r–30v	Matt. 5: 17 Luke 2: 21 Acts 4: 12 Phil. 2: 10	Jacobus de Voragine, *Legenda Aurea* St Bernard (via *Legenda Aurea*)
Chapter 7: Coming of the Magi	21r–25v	30v–36v	Matt. 2: 1–5, 8, 12	John of Hildesheim, *Historia Trium Regum* Gregory, *Homily* 10 Nicholas of Lyre, *Postilla* Jacobus de Voragine, *Legenda Aurea*
Chapter 8: Purification	25v–28v	36v–40v	Lev. 12: 1–8 Luke 2: 21–32, 36–9	Jacobus de Voragine, *Legenda Aurea* Ps.-Augustine, *Sermo* 370, *De Nativitate Domini*

Sections	Gg folios	N folios	Biblical sources	Non-biblical sources
Chapter 9: Flight into Egypt	40ᵛ–44ʳ	28ᵛ–31ʳ	Wisd. 21: 30 Matt. 2: 13–14, 19–23	Jacobus de Voragine, *Legenda Aurea* Ps.-Matthew, *Libri de Natiuitate Mariae* Peter Comestor, *Historia Scholastica* John of Hildesheim, *Historia Trium Regum*
Chapter 10: Finding the young Christ in the Temple	44ʳ–47ᵛ	31ʳ–33ᵛ	Luke 2: 41–4, 46–51	Nicholas of Lyre, *Postilla* St Augustine, *Sermo* 51
Chapter 11: Life of Christ from age 12 until baptism in Jordan River	47ᵛ–49ᵛ	33ᵛ–35ʳ		Nicholas of Lyre, *Postilla* St Birgitta of Sweden, *Revelaciones*
Chapter 12: Baptism	49ᵛ–52ʳ	35ʳ–37ʳ	Ps. 44: 3 Matt. 3: 13–17	St Jerome, *Commentarii in euangelium Matthaei* St Bernard, *Sermo* 15 Jacobus de Voragine, *Legenda Aurea* (as *Legende of Symon and Iude*) Peter Comestor, *Historia Scholastica* Nicholas of Lyre, *Postilla*
Chapter 13: Temptations in the desert	52ʳ–[ND 39ᵛ] *See Explanatory Notes*	37ʳ–39ᵛ	Matt. 4: 1–11 Acts 1: 1 Jas. 1: 12	Peter Comestor, *Historia Scholastica* Nicholas of Lyre, *Postilla* Gregory, *Homily* 16

Chapter	Folio	Folio	Biblical references	Sources
Chapter 14: Calling of the Apostles	[ND 39ᵛ]–56ᵛ See Explanatory Notes	39ᵛ–42ᵛ	Matt. 4: 18–21; 10: 1–4, 8 Mark 1: 16–9 Luke 10: 1–2 Acts 1: 23–6 1 Cor. 1: 27	Nicholas of Lyre, Postilla St Bernard, Opera, Vol. 5 Gregory, Moralia in Iob Rhythmi Veteres de Vita Monastica
Chapter 15: The miracles	56ᵛ–63ʳ	42ᵛ–47ʳ	Matt. 14: 15–21, 24–33; 15: 32–8; 17: 1–9, 14–20; 22: 15–21; 20: 28; 26: 63–5; 27: 43 Luke 9: 31; 6: 6–11; 23: 14 John 2: 1–11; 7: 12; 8: 3–11; 12: 26; 19: 7; 25: 18 Mark 3: 1–6	Nicholas of Lyre, Postilla Peter Comestor, Historia Scholastica Ps.-Augustine, Liber Soliloquiorum Animae ad Deum
Chapter 16: Raising the dead	63ʳ–66ᵛ	47ʳ–50ʳ	Matt. 7: 22–3 Luke 7: 11–16 John 11: 1–45, 47–51, 53	St Augustine, In Iohannis Euangelium; Sermo 98 Peter Comestor, Historia Scholastica Nicholas of Lyre, Postilla
Chapter 17: Palm Sunday	67ʳ–70ᵛ	50ʳ–53ʳ	Exod. 12: 1–51 Matt. 21: 1–2, 26: 3–5, 14–16, 46 Mark 11: 7–11 Luke 19: 36; 20: 19 John 12: 1–6, 9–19	Nicholas of Lyre, Postilla Gregory, Homiliae in Evangelia
Chapter 18: Schir Thursday; Last Supper; Garden of Gethsemane	70ᵛ–77ʳ	53ʳ–58ʳ	Matt. 26: 17–35 Luke 22: 8–34 John 13: 2–38	Henry Suso, Horologium Sapientiae Nicholas of Lyre, Postilla

Sections	Gg folios	N folios	Biblical sources	Non-biblical sources
Chapter 19: Capture and scourging	77ʳ–84ʳ	58ʳ–63ʳ	Matt. 26: 36–66, 74–5; Mark 14: 58, 64–5, 67; Luke 22: 41, 43–44, 46, 52–3; John 14: 31; 18: 3–8, 13, 15–27	Nicholas of Lyre, *Postilla*; Peter Comestor, *Historia Scholastica*
Chapter 20: Prime; Christ before Annas and Caiphas	84ʳ–89ᵛ (ll. 2595–2762)	63ʳ–67ᵛ	Isa. 1: 6; 53: 7; Matt. 27: 1, 3–7, 29–30; Mark 15: 17; Luke 18: 33–40; 23: 5–12, 16, 19; John 18: 29–31; 19: 2, 4–5	Peter Comestor, *Historia Scholastica*; Nicholas of Lyre, *Postilla*; John Mandeville, *Mandeville's Travels*
Chapter 21: Terce; Christ before Pilate	89ᵛ–94ᵛ	67ᵛ–71ʳ	Matt. 27: 19, 24–5; John 19: 6–15	Jacobus de Voragine, *Legenda Aurea*
Chapter 22: Sext; Crucifixion	94ᵛ–100ᵛ	71ʳ–75ᵛ	Matt. 27: 39–42; Luke 23: 34, 39–43; John 19: 20–9	St Birgitta of Sweden, *Revelaciones*; Nicholas of Lyre, *Postilla*; Gregory, *Homilies* 2, 21
Chapter 23: None; the death of Christ; Laments of the Virgin	100ᵛ–103ᵛ	75ᵛ–77ᵛ	Matt. 27: 45, 52, 54; Luke 23: 46, 48; John 19: 28; Phil. 2: 8	Nicholas of Lyre, *Postilla*; Gregory, *Homily* 10
Chapter 24: 'Aftir none'; The opening of the side; Washing clean from sin	104ʳ–107ʳ	77ᵛ–80ʳ	John 14: 15, 21; 19: 32–4; 1 John 2: 6; 4: 19; Apoc. 1: 5	Nicholas of Lyre, *Postilla*; Gregory, *Homily* 25

Chapter 25: Evensong; Deposition	107^r–109^v	Ps. 15: 10 Mark 15: 43–6 John 19: 39	Bede, *In primam partem Samuhelis libri iiii* Nicholas of Lyre, *Postilla* St Birgitta of Sweden, *Revelaciones*
Chapter 26: Compline; Burial	109^v–111^r	Matt. 27: 62–6 John 19: 41–2	Peter Comestor, *Historia Scholastica* Nicholas of Lyre, *Postilla*
Chapter 27: Saturday	111^r–112^v	Mark 16: 1	
Chapter 28: The Harrowing of Hell	112^v–114^v	Luke 16: 22; 23: 43	Peter Comestor, *Historia Scholastica* Nicholas of Lyre, *De visione divinae essentiae* St Augustine, *Sermo CVIII*
Chapter 29: Resurrection and first (apocraphyal) appearance to BVM	114^v–117^v	Matt. 28: 2–4, 11–15	Peter Comestor, *Historia Scholastica*; *Sententiae in iv libris distinctae* Mechtild of Hackeborn, *The Booke of Gostlye Grace* Nicholas of Lyre, *Postilla*; *De visione divinae essentiae* Jacobus de Voragine, *Legenda Aurea* Mass of the Commemoration of the Blessed Virgin (Sarum)
Chapter 30: First five authentic appearances	117^v–122^r	Matt. 28: 8–10 Luke 24: 10–43 John 20: 1–17	Gregory, *Homily* 25 Nicholas of Lyre, *Postilla* Jacobus de Voragine, *Legenda Aurea*

Sections	Gg folios	N folios	Biblical sources	Non-biblical sources
Chapter 31: Second five authentic appearances	122ʳ–125ʳ	91ᵛ–93ᵛ	Matt. 28: 16–20 John 20: 25–9; 21: 2–13 Acts 1: 9–12 1 Cor. 15: 6	Jacobus de Voragine, *Legenda Aurea* Gregory, *Homily 29* Nicholas of Lyre, *Postilla*
Chapter 32: Ascension	125ʳ–129ʳ	93ᵛ–96ᵛ	Mark 16: 14–16 Acts 1: 6–11, 14	Nicholas of Lyre, *Postilla* Gregory, *Homily 29* Peter Comestor, *Historia Scholastica* Ps.-Augustine, *Liber Soliloquiorum Animae ad Deum*
Chapter 33: Pentecost and Special com mendation of John the Evangelist	129ʳ–144ʳ	96ᵛ–108ʳ	Ps. 77: 24–5 John 13: 23; 19: 26–27; 21: 20 Acts 1: 26; 2: 1–21, 41; 4: 18–21; 5: 17–41 1 Cor. 2: 9 Apoc. 1: 3	Nicholas of Lyre, *Postilla* Gregory, *Homilies 30, 38* St Clement (via *Historia Scholastica*) Peter Comestor, *Historia Scholastica* Jacobus de Voragine, *Legenda Aurea* Jerome, *Prologues*

O intemerata	144^r–145^r	108^r–109^v	Adam the Carthusian, *Sermo 33* Peter Damian, *Sermo 64* (attributed to Bede) St Augustine, *In Iohannis Euangelium Tractatus*; *De Bono Coniugali* Jacobus de Voragine, *Legenda Aurea* St Thomas Aquinas, *Summa Theologica* *The Life of Saint Edmund of Abingdon*
O intemerata (Middle English Translation)	145^r		

INDEX OF QUOTATIONS AND ALLUSIONS

A. BIBLICAL QUOTATIONS AND ALLUSIONS

B. NON-BIBLICAL QUOTATIONS AND ALLUSIONS

INDEX OF PROPER NAMES